Female Subjects in Bl

Female Subjects
in Black and White

Race, Psychoanalysis, Feminism

EDITED BY

Elizabeth Abel
Barbara Christian
Helene Moglen

UNIVERSITY OF CALIFORNIA PRESS

Berkeley   Los Angeles   London

University of California Press
Berkeley and Los Angeles, California

University of California Press, Ltd.
London, England

© 1997 by
The Regents of the University of California

Library of Congress Cataloging-in-Publication Data

Female subjects in black and white : race, psychoanalysis, feminism / [edited by] Elizabeth Abel, Barbara Christian, Helene Moglen.
    p. cm.
    Includes bibliographical references.
    ISBN 0–520–20629–0 (alk. paper). — ISBN 0–520–20630–4 (pbk. : alk. paper)
    1. American Literature—Afro-American authors—History and criticism.   2. American Literature—Women authors—History and criticism.   3. Psychoanalysis and literature—United States.   4. Feminism and literature—United States.   5. Women and literature—United States.   6. Afro-American women in literature.   7. Afro-Americans in literature.   8. Race relations in literature.   9. Psychology in literature.   10. Race in literature.
    I. Abel, Elizabeth.   II. Christian, Barbara.   III. Moglen, Helene.
PS153.N5F45   1997
810.9'9287'08996073—DC20   96-23683
                                                         CIP

Printed in the United States of America
9 8 7 6 5 4 3 2 1

The paper used in this publication meets the minimum requirements of American National Standards for Information Sciences—Permanence of Paper for Printed Library Materials, ANSI Z39.48–1984.

The photographs in "Seeing Sentiment: Photography, Race, and the Innocent Eye" are reprinted courtesy of the Cook Collection, Valentine Museum, Richmond, Virginia.

CONTENTS

ACKNOWLEDGMENTS

This collection of essays originated with a conference, Psychoanalysis in African American Contexts: Feminist Reconfigurations, which was held in October 1992 at the University of California at Santa Cruz. We wish particularly to thank for his generous support James Clifford, then the director of the UCSC Center for Cultural Studies. We are also grateful for funds granted to us by the Humanities Research Institute at UC Irvine and—at Santa Cruz— the Division of Humanities, the feminist studies research group, Oakes College, and Kresge College. Our thanks as well to Saidiya V. Hartman, Harreyette Mullen, Carla Freccero, Susan Gilman, and Sylvia Winter for their active participation, which helped make the conference a success.

We have had superb help with the production of this book. Cheryl Van De Veer, the supervisor of the UCSC Word Processing Center, did an extraordinary job in preparing the original manuscript for us. We have been especially fortunate in the editorial staff of UC Press. The skill and dedication of William Murphy, Dore Brown, and Carolyn Hill were invaluable at all stages of the book's production. We are indebted to them for their thoroughness and professionalism.

Finally, Barbara Christian and Helene Moglen particularly wish to thank Elizabeth Abel for her unflagging commitment to this project. Without her persistence and intelligence, this volume would never have been completed.

INTRODUCTION

The Dream of a Common Language

Elizabeth Abel, Barbara Christian, and Helene Moglen

The narrative into which life seems to cast itself surfaces most forcefully
in certain kinds of psychoanalysis.

TONI MORRISON, *PLAYING IN THE DARK*

Psychoanalysis can . . . be seen as a quite elaborate form of ethnography—
as a writing of the ethnicity of the white western psyche.

MARY ANN DOANE, *FEMMES FATALES*

This anthology has been a site of challenge, frustration, and revelation. So-
liciting, editing, and organizing these essays has made us painfully aware that
the encounter between a predominantly white psychoanalytic feminism and
African American cultural formations reveals as many stubborn incompati-
bilities as it does transformative possibilities. Although two of us had originally hoped that a revised psychoanalytic discourse could provide a common
set of terms for coordinating race, gender, and subjectivity, the three of us
came to envisage this collection as a series of dialogues, rather than recon-
ciliations, between feminist psychoanalysis and African American representations of female subjectivity.

Of course, even to invoke female subjectivity is already to inhabit a certain discursive terrain; dialogue does not ensure discursive parity. Concern
about unequally authoritative discourses has been an issue throughout the
organization of this volume. Although some of the contributors have consistently endorsed this project, others have consistently resisted it, and still
others have endorsed it in principle and resisted it in practice, testimony to
the unarticulatable nature of the anxieties it triggers. Rather than trying to
synthesize our contributors' perspectives, we have represented the disjunc-
tions, as well as the intersections, among their disparate critical agendas. Although we insisted on approximately equal numbers of black and white contributors, we did not contrive a racial balance within each section, but allowed
the racial fault lines, where they did occur, to indicate a current discursive
geography.

What has made this endeavor difficult is also what gives it value—for it is
the first of its kind. There has never to our knowledge been a collaborative
effort between black and white feminists to generate a text on race and female subjectivity. Our point of departure here is perhaps best defined by the

conclusion of our first essay: Ann duCille's rather wistful call for a practice of black and white "complementary theorizing," in which black and white feminists think with, rather than across, one another about the intersections of racial and gender differences.

As an interrogation of the racial boundaries of psychoanalysis, our project had multiple points of origin. One was involvement with a text. Two of the editors—Barbara Christian and Helene Moglen—were invited to speak on *Beloved* at the Humanities Institute at Irvine in 1991. For both of them, writing and presenting their papers were more emotionally charged than such activities tend to be. Having taught *Beloved* in a graduate seminar the previous spring, Helene, a white psychoanalytic feminist critic, had come to feel about the novel as she imagined confirmed believers feel about their sacred texts. The novel seemed to her not only to address the American experience as no other American fiction had before, but also to speak about the formation of female subjectivities with a power that she urgently wished to understand. But because her work has been on the tradition of the English novel, she had not written previously about an African American text, and because she was scheduled to speak publicly about Morrison's novel with Barbara Christian—an African American feminist critic who had interrogated the use of theory—she felt enormous anxiety about the nature and extent of her authority to speak.

For Barbara, the presentation was also fraught with emotion. It seemed to her that in *Beloved* Morrison not only had recuperated the subjectivity of black female slaves, but had done so by creating a healing ritual, a "fixing" ceremony drawn from West African cosmologies that were radically different from Western epistemologies. Why then did the majority of pieces that Barbara was reading in literary and feminist journals approach the novel primarily from a psychoanalytic (and sometimes a Marxist) perspective? Though not opposed to these approaches, Barbara wondered whether the academy acknowledged only methodologies that fell within the Western intellectual tradition. Having previously spoken at Irvine about her essay, "The Race for Theory," which questioned the Western philosophical appropriation of "theory" and upset many theoretically oriented students and faculty, she was not looking forward to presenting a paper that advocated reading *Beloved* from an African cosmological perspective.

Ironically, despite (or maybe because of) the fact that Helene's orientation was psychoanalytic and Barbara's was concerned with African spiritual systems, their pieces spoke in extremely interesting ways to one another. Clearly, it was not accidental that *Beloved* was the text that enabled their conversation. Having inspired both critics, *Beloved* provided the ground of their connection by bringing into dialogue different cultural ways of knowing and healing: West African practices of ancestor worship, for example, with the psychodynamics of the mother-daughter bond. Through its narrative evocation of spirituality, history, and social relations, and through its presentation of communal and personal memory and desire as overlapping and complementary structures of experience, the novel challenges its readers to create similar conversations among less allusive and accommodating theoretical perspectives. Vaguely aware of this challenge, although certainly not able then to have stated it explicitly, Helene and Barbara agreed to continue their discussion, perhaps by presenting their papers together at Santa Cruz.

At the same time, Elizabeth, another white psychoanalytic feminist, was engaged in her own struggle with *Beloved*. For her too it was a kind of ultimate text. Yet precisely because it was the African American text that white feminists had embraced most eagerly, the text catalyzed for her a concern about the current white feminist investment in representations of African American women's subjectivity. Which novels are privileged, through their solicitation of recognizable psychoanalytic models, by white feminist critics' obsession with African American women's texts? Does reading this obsession psychoanalytically unmask or reentrench racial stereotypes and hierarchies? Does the conceptual apparatus of projection, identification, and mirroring that works so well to theorize the cross-racial operations of white women's subjectivity help to explain, or does it simply appropriate, aspects of black women's subjectivity? Does psychoanalytic criticism, rarely practiced by black feminists, entail conscription to dominant cultural discourses? Elizabeth's initial desire to write psychoanalytically on *Beloved* evolved into a desire, which she shared with Barbara and Helene, to question what it would mean to revise feminist psychoanalysis as a discourse on the subjectivity of women of color. The prospect of bringing together at a conference several black and white feminist critics—to present work, to brainstorm, and, if necessary, to work through painful disagreements—seemed promising, as well as challenging, to all three.

Not surprisingly, there were problems built into this conception from the start. As the only African American organizer of the conference from which this collection of essays derives, Barbara bore the familiar burden of representing women of color. Even more serious was the way the project reproduced the dominant black-white binary that erases the far more variegated spectrum of racialized female subjectivities. Yet because it seemed impossible to do justice to the complexities of every cultural formation, we decided to structure this discussion by foregrounding two. The exceptionally charged, enduring, and complicated history of black and white women in this country constitutes, we hope, a plausible and productive point of departure for a dialogue on race, psychoanalysis, and female subjectivity that we encourage other voices to disrupt and dispute.

By focusing attention on African American texts and contexts, the conference was designed to force a rethinking of psychoanalytic theory comparable to, yet potentially more disruptive than, the transformations that (white) feminism had produced by centering women in a revised developmental story, foregrounding the differential construction of gendered subjectivities, and revaluing the preoedipal as psychic register. Recognizing that despite these substantial achievements white feminists had unwittingly reaffirmed the determining structure of the middle-class family in their work and had reproduced the dynamic of white self and racialized other, we hoped that the introduction of African American criticism, theory, and fiction would broaden the terms for a collaborative feminist critique.

The conference title, we thought, was clear: "Psychoanalysis in African American Contexts: Feminist Reconfigurations." The invited lecturers all professed more than passing interest in the announced subject, and their lecture titles indicated that our perception of the conference was generally shared. But the conference that took place was not the conference that had been advertised or planned. Rather than the object of interrogation, psychoanalysis proved to be the resisted term. Some papers never mentioned it; others made passing reference to it before proceeding to other concerns. What was of importance to many of the white participants was the range of ways in which they could engage with African American women's texts, whereas for many of the black scholars, the conference provided a space within which they could present critical approaches that had not been easily allowed at conventional literary conferences. In different ways—and for different reasons having to do with race, training, and generation—the participants were testing assumptions about the three prominent words and phrases in the conference title: *psychoanalysis, feminism,* and *African American contexts.*

The tone of the conference was subdued until the Saturday afternoon session (significantly entitled, as it proved, "Spirituality/Psychoanalysis: Cultural Encounters"). In her paper, "Channeling the Ancestral Muse: Lucille Clifton and Dolores Kendrick," Akasha (Gloria) Hull emphasized the well-known fact that Clifton and Kendrick, like any number of African American women writers, foregrounded spirituality in their themes and accounts of poetic inspiration. What made her paper so provocative was that she asked the question, "Where in the current theorizing about poetic form and politics is there space to situate such matters?" What ignited the audience was that Hull introduced a different subject of intellectual inquiry into an academic conference about race and psychoanalysis. This affirmation of African American women's spirituality signaled the return of the repressed.

There were few women of color nonparticipants at the conference. Most of those who were there had come not because they were particularly concerned about the revamping of psychoanalysis, but because they were interested in seeing so many black women scholars in the flesh. Hull's paper brought home to them the extent to which they felt that metaphoric systems from which they might derive original ways of reading had been suppressed or denigrated by the academy. Like the African American women writers who were their counterparts, many of these critics thought (whether they believed in these systems or not) that spirituality could provide new access to certain African American texts. But unlike their writing sisters, they did not feel free to examine spiritual discourses and practices within the university. Hull's paper offered them a way to come out of the closet and question the languages available for representing unconscious processes, modes of healing, and the social formation of the female subject. Was psychoanalysis just another cultural narrative whose self-bestowed claim to universality had been fortified by the interest of literary critics in the academy?

The ensuing debate sharply highlighted the consequences of differently disseminated and institutionalized cultural perspectives. Since African belief systems for negotiating the inexplicable were transmitted orally among, and often guarded carefully within, denigrated New World cultural groups, these systems have typically been ignored or dismissed as superstition by humanistic academic disciplines willing to grant psychoanalysis the status of (at least) a powerful representational system. The institutionalization of psychoanalysis as a theory of textuality (in effect, the legitimation of particular psychoanalytic perspectives) allows us to distinguish between an interpretive method (which we came at the conference to call "psychoanalytics")—a practice of reading for repressions, contradictions, repetitions, and displacements —and a more culturally specific psychoanalytic thematics drawn from the Western family romance. But whatever distinctions we make, these interpretive strategies derive from and reinforce a particular construction of the unconscious more useful in exposing fissures in the dominant cultural texts than in interrogating the discourse of the dominated. Filtering texts by subjugated groups through a psychoanalytic "hermeneutics of suspicion" tends to subvert their specific kinds of social knowledge and authority.

If psychoanalysis has entered and been reconstituted within the academy under the aegis of the humanities, "race" has been institutionally positioned as an object of primarily sociological inquiry. Most visibly manifested through reactive practices such as social movements, race has been most thoroughly examined in terms of domination and agency rather than subjectivity. As is vividly exemplified by the contrast in Stuart Hall's foundational essay, "Cultural Studies and its Theoretical Legacies," between the restrained account of the "profound theoretical struggle" required to put race on the agenda of cultural studies and the near-hysterical narrative of the violent disruption produced by feminism—"As the thief in the night, it broke in; interrupted, made an unseemly noise, seized the time, crapped on the table of cultural studies"—the discourse of social theory has been better able to assimilate race, perceived as a (masculine) political formation, than to accommodate the feminist "'re-opening' of the closed frontier between social theory and the theory of the unconscious—psychoanalysis."[1] Although cultural studies has proved increasingly capable of incorporating gender and psychoanalysis, Hall's split between an implicitly white psychoanalytic feminism and an implicitly masculine discourse on race points to a more stubborn difficulty: the lack of discursive ground for the black female subject who stands at the crossroads of these terrains.

This anthology cannot by itself remedy this lack. Rather than attempting to construct a metalanguage that might mediate among—at the cost of flattening—the discourses of spirituality, psychoanalysis, gender, and race, we hope these essays provide richer accounts of each discourse's possibilities, limitations, and internal heterogeneity. Instead of proposing a grand design, we generate multiple opportunities for particular local exchanges. For as the concluding conference session made clear, each discourse is itself a site of contestation: rather than the summing up we envisaged, this final event erupted into a heated exchange about the politics of self-naming. Yet the disputes between the advocates of "Black" versus "African American" were no more intense than the controversies between the Lacanians and object relations theorists. Members of all discursive camps, themselves multiply and shiftingly determined by specific incidents and debates, frequently felt embattled or suppressed. Far from perceiving themselves privileged as purveyors of "theory," many of the white psychoanalytic feminists felt under attack from materialist critics, as well as from adherents of competing psychoanalytic schools; African American psychoanalytic feminists felt as marginalized within their own cultural cohort as critics who wanted to examine spirituality felt within the academy at large; senior feminists, black and white, felt threatened (and thereby ideologically reunified) by a younger generation, black and white, who were astonished to discover their power to intimidate established scholars; and all of us were at least fleetingly allied by the racist treatment inflicted on African American participants by a local hotel manager. The anthology, we realized, had to complicate substantially the vision of the conference represented by its poster, which foregrounded an African American woman whose quizzical gaze at the viewer partially eclipsed yet nevertheless was framed by the shadowy outline of Freud. Each term needed to be problematized: Freud could not stand for psychoanalysis, an anonymous black woman could not stand for race, and the invisible but shaping presence of the white feminism that had positioned these two figures against each other needed to be overtly thematized.

On the last night of the conference, Helene held a party for the participants at her house. At some point in the evening, Barbara went out on the deck to have a cigarette. Hortense Spillers and Mae Henderson drifted out to continue talking with her. As they discussed the situations at their different campuses, as well as their ideas about where black feminism might be going, they were joined by younger scholars who were also concerned about directions and trends in the profession. Suddenly, Helene and Elizabeth looked at one another in a moment of guilty and nervous recognition: the party had split along racial lines; the black women were all out on the deck; the white women had either gone home or were sitting indoors in the living room. To those on the inside, which now appeared an outside, it seemed the inevitable had happened; they had been found out and excluded from the inner circle that the margin had now become.

After a period of anxious waiting, Elizabeth went outside to ask if the group in the living room could join the group on the deck. "In a little while," she was told; a critical discussion was just underway. After waiting another half an hour, the white women could stand it no longer and burst out on the deck with their paranoia, their wounded feelings, their sense of just but nonetheless painful exclusion. But no: the black feminists on the deck said they had not been talking about or consciously excluding them; indeed, they had not registered their absence, or had not read it in racialized terms. Intensely engaged in debating complex theoretical and political differences and power relations among themselves, they were protecting their discussion against interruption. Although the white feminists had believed their black colleagues to be part of a closed but close community, few of the black women at the conference had actually known one another in the past. Though each of them had often been invited to represent black feminism at one or another conference over the years, they had generally been invited as individuals, alone. Perceived from the outside as part of an exclusive community, each felt her isolation painfully. This meant that younger black academics had rarely met those who had acted, in a crucial sense, as mentors, both through their work and by virtue of their active professional presence. Ironically, Helene's deck—and the larger conference—represented a landmark occasion: an opportunity for intra- and intergenerational bonding that had everything to do with the black scholars themselves and nothing to do with their white counterparts.

Retrospectively, this incident made clear that the subtext of cross-racial anxieties and fantasies that pervaded the public and private spaces of the conference needed to be specifically theorized in the anthology, as did the racially charged division between spiritual and psychoanalytic discourses. It is for this reason that we frame the anthology with two sections that are in implicit dialogue with one another: an opening section on the racial politics of reading, "Crossdressing, Crossreading, or Complementary Theorizing?" which foregrounds the motives for and problems with the current white feminist investment in black women's texts; and a concluding section, "Healing Narratives," which features essays primarily by black feminists on African-derived alternatives to and interconnections with the European discourse of psychoanalysis. Within this frame, the two middle sections explore ways that questions of racial difference engage and challenge diverse schools of psychoanalytic theory. "Representing the Unrepresentable: The Symbolic and the Real" examines the problems and possibilities of representing race within a primarily Lacanian frame; "Race, Psychoanalysis, and Female Desire" probes the racial dimensions of the female desires posited by Freudian and object relations theory. These middle sections, although unavoidably selective in their coverage, together address both the dominant psychoanalytic metadiscourse on representation and the prevailing thematic focus of psychoanalytic feminism.

Our first section opens with Ann duCille's essay, "The Occult of True Black Womanhood: Critical Demeanor and Black Feminist Studies," which decries the status of black women as the "quintessential site of difference" and fetishized object of contemporary critical inquiry. Placing the Victorian cult of true womanhood, denounced by white feminists, against the postmodern exoticizing of black women's textual bodies, in which white feminists are deeply complicit, the essay uncovers the primitivizing critical fantasies that motivate and shape white and masculine readings of black women's textual bodies, readings that occult and consequently maintain power relations in the academy. Dwelling on white feminists (while including representative white and black male critics), duCille dissects the construction of black women's literary and critical texts as mammies who initiate, nurture, and legitimate the aspiring critic by teaching her or him the secrets and values of endurance. Their conscious intentions notwithstanding, white feminists repeatedly demonstrate an unacknowledged sense of racial entitlement. They treat the field of black feminist studies "not like a discipline with a history and a body of rigorous scholarship and distinguished scholars underpinning it, but like an anybody-can-play pick-up game performed on a wide-open, untrammeled field," or like a bridge that is "walked on over and over and over again" by critics seeking solid ground. As an antidote to the critic "who views the objectified [black feminist] subject from a position of unrelinquished authority," duCille tentatively proposes "the strategy of black and white women working together on intellectual projects," the "complementary theorizing" we have borrowed as the utopian name for the critical essays that initiate this volume.

Tania Modleski's essay, "Doing Justice to the Subjects: Mimetic Art in a Multicultural Society: The Work of Anna Deavere Smith," might be considered a response to duCille's call. Thinking with and through Anna Deavere Smith's strategies of "mimetic identification" in *Fires in the Mirror* and *Twilight*, Modleski works along with Smith to unfix the racial definitions that generate territorial strife and mimetic rivalry. By bringing together such theorists as Daniel and Jonathan Boyarin and Cornel West to articulate Smith's commitment to "deterritorialization" and "diasporic consciousness," "sharing space with others, devoid of exclusivist and dominating power," Modleski reenacts at the level of theory Smith's performative unsettling of cultural oppositions between Jews and blacks. Modleski does not, however, merely imitate or celebrate

Smith; she also criticizes what she sees as Smith's subordination of gender to racial oppression, her failure to engage the historic rivalries and partnerships between black and white women (as she does between blacks and Jews), and her scapegoating of white women as the voice of racism. "If Smith wasn't going to acknowledge my oppression as a woman," Modleski remarks in a decidedly nonfetishizing moment, "I would not recognize hers as an African American." By reflecting on, rather than merely enacting or denying, the mimetic rivalry between them, Modleski, like Smith, refuses to be fixed, opening instead an exchange as mobile as Smith's own location, "'on the road,' in a kind of permanent exile, hammering out justice."

Whereas Modleski challenges Smith's subordination of gender to race, Margaret Homans strives to produce a gender alliance across race in her essay, "'Racial Composition': Metaphor and the Body in the Writing of Race." Seeking to further a "mutually instructive relation between feminisms" engaged with the ways the body, black or white, tends to be derogatively troped as female, Homans highlights the gender dimensions of critical debates in the late 1980s between African American feminists and prominent male African American theorists, especially Henry Louis Gates Jr. and Houston Baker, concerning the figurative versus the literal or embodied character of race. Pointing to the masculinist assumptions of the poststructuralist theory of language on which Gates and Baker rely (assumptions deriving most centrally from Lacan's "positioning of the mother's body as the absence that makes language's substitutions possible and necessary"), Homans joins those black feminists who refuse simply to repudiate the claims of the literal, the body, and the female. Tracing the "sustained though deeply ambivalent interest in the racially marked body" through several 1980s fictional and autobiographical texts by Maya Angelou, Alice Walker, and Toni Morrison, she examines the interplay between relatively literal and conspicuously figurative language in order to reveal the tension that exists between race as body and race as metaphor. She demonstrates that a revision of the fall as a story of interdependent racial and sexual division recurs in these texts, suggesting the "failure of embodiment adequately to represent a prior condition of wholeness. As narratives of embodiment, stories of the fall explain why the literal is always accompanied by its opposite: figuration names the gap that embodiment seeks but fails to close." Body and figuration are inextricable, yet only the women writers affirm the body and the literal. In the two 1994 memoirs with which Homans's essay concludes, however, both sides of the debate have come to coexist, as the maternal body shifts for both the male and female author from a unified, originary, and consequently unrepresentable black materiality to the source of the knowledge of division.

Responding to Homans's discussion (among others), the final essay in this section returns to the questions raised by Ann duCille. In "Black Writing, White Reading: Race and the Politics of Feminist Interpretation," Elizabeth

Abel examines the desires and fantasies that mark recent white feminist readings of black women's texts. She argues, in agreement with duCille, that despite their wide range of critical strategies, these readings emerge from a desire to share the cultural authority produced in part by black women's enforced experience of embodiment. The essay begins by teasing out the fantasies evoked by Toni Morrison's story "Recitatif," in which the race of the two female protagonists is at once strongly marked and deeply ambiguous. After contrasting her own reading of embodiedness as a signifier of blackness with a black feminist identification of race through political and cultural signifiers, Abel analyses the rhetoric of race in three contemporary critical discourses frequently deployed in white feminist readings of black women's texts. Proceeding from deconstruction to psychoanalysis and then to cultural criticism, she concludes that "however interwoven with and ruptured by other differences, race remains a salient source of the fantasies and allegiances that shape our ways of reading." Nevertheless, she endorses "crossing racial boundaries in reading" because "our inability to avoid inscribing racially inflected investments and agendas" contributes, however inadvertently, to "the racialization of whiteness. As masculinity takes shape in part through its constructions of femininity, whiteness—that elusive color that seems not to be one—gains materiality through the desires and fantasies played out in its interpretations of blackness, interpretations that, by making the unconscious conscious, supplement articulated ideologies of whiteness with less accessible assumptions."

The essays in "Crossdressing, Crossreading, or Complementary Theorizing?" work variously with the Imaginary processes of dyadic mirroring, of constantly renegotiated boundaries between two imperfectly yet insistently differentiated terms. Yet despite its status as the central trope for the production of subordinate and dominant racial identities in the heavily masculine tradition of postcolonial psychoanalysis extending from Franz Fanon through Homi Bhabha, the cross-racial mirror operates in these essays consistently in only one direction. Positioned in contemporary cultural politics as the object more often than the agent of imitation, African American feminists, two and a half decades after Toni Morrison's *Bluest Eye,* rarely invoke the ahistorical apparatus of the mirror stage. The essays in the next section, "Representing the Unrepresentable: The Symbolic and the Real," engage the full range of Lacanian registers in an attempt to open psychoanalysis to history. Shifting from recent reading relations between white and black feminists to the challenges of theorizing African American subjectivity, this section also marks a shift from the fantasmatic and repetitive cycles of the Imaginary to the ways that the Symbolic engages and refuses history. Haunting this section is the elusive Lacanian category of the Real, associated here with the burden of a negated history.

The section opens with Hortense Spillers's meditation on the intersections through which the discourses of "race" and "psychoanalysis," each traditionally structured through the other's exclusion, destabilize each other's certitudes and conceptual boundaries. Her project is to displace the African American "community," traversed in her account by the dominant culture and consequently riddled with ambivalence, from its stable position as an object of social science inquiry to a more uncertain locus as the subject of a psychoanalytic culture criticism. "'All the Things You Could Be by Now, If Sigmund Freud's Wife Was Your Mother': Psychoanalysis and Race" initiates a shift from a familiar historical narrative of collective progress from slavery to liberation, to a less transparent emancipatory story. That story focuses not on the collective but on the "one" that, constituted through intersubjective symbolic matrices and consequently different from the singular, self-determined individual, is possessed nevertheless of particularity and some degree of agency. As a "discipline in self-reflection," psychoanalysis for Spillers helps articulate the "interior intersubjectivity" of an African American subject formed through deeply social symbolic processes. By insisting on the processes of negation that found the Symbolic register, psychoanalysis posits a subject re-presented beyond the fixed corporeality that the dominant culture assigns to race. A psychoanalytic culture criticism propels racial subjectivity from the historically given, the always already known, and consequently "the perfect affliction . . . destiny in the world we have made," to a shifting effect of complex mediations between imposed meanings and cultural self-reflexivity. Reconceptualizing agency for African Americans as "self-consciously assertive reflexivity" constitutes for Spillers a project that is inextricably psychoanalytic and political.

It is possible to understand Spillers's goal as shifting the subject of race from the register of the Real, understood as the status quo of psychic immobility, to the mediations and modulations of the Symbolic. In "Seeing Sentiment: Photography, Race, and the Innocent Eye," Laura Wexler argues, in contrast, that the Real offers interpretive leverage by exceeding both the endless repetitions of the Imaginary and the structures of the Symbolic. Rather than the racist immobilization of history, the Real is "the violent, unsustainable, unthinkable possibility that nonetheless *is, has* happened, and must be endured . . . a kind of wounding" that "opens Freud to history." Consequently, "it is the wounding that we must seek in a psychoanalysis of the Real, so as to know it, so as to touch it, so as to set ourselves free." Utilizing Roland Barthes's notion of the photographic *punctum* as "this element which rises from the scene, shoots out of it like an arrow, and pierces me . . . this wound, this prick, this mark made by a pointed instrument," Wexler tries to induce a "rupture of the Real" by penetrating the sentimental visual rhetoric of George Cook's 1865 photograph of an African American nursemaid holding a white child. By following the "subliminal message" of the nursemaid's striped dress to "read between the lines" of the white photographer's sub-

jugating gaze, Wexler detects signs of the nursemaid's resistance to her assigned function: enhancing by contrast the white mother's sentimental authority. Rather than pursuing the impossible project of recovering the nursemaid's voice or interiority (perhaps a more familiar version of the
psychoanalytic project), Wexler furthers what she calls the "cognitive appropriation of the Real" by examining the historical circumstances under
which the nursemaid's image, and photographic images more generally, circulate and determine how social relations of race, gender, and class are en-
visioned and rendered invisible.

Wexler reads through the image of a black nursemaid the historical
wounds that photography conceals and reinflicts; Spillers reads the substitutions of the Symbolic register as a reprieve from the givens of history. In
"'Beyond Mortal Vision': Harriet E. Wilson's *Our Nig* and the American Racial
Dream-Text," Katherine Clay Bassard negotiates between these positions
through her reading of the first novel by an African American woman novelist. Choosing as her governing metaphor the "shadows" of slavery that according to Wilson fall even in the north, Bassard reads *Our Nig* as both an
expose of white American culture's repressed relation to what Toni Morrison has called "American Africanism" and as an exploration of the particular challenges and possibilities of cultural production for the African Americans who inhabit those cultural shadows. For Frado, the novel's mulatta
narrator, indentured as a child to an abusive white family, these shadows become a privileged interpretive locus from which to read the racial and gender power relations incorporated into the double stories of the "Two-Story
White House, North," whose social margins she inhabits and disturbs. Although Frado's position recalls that of the nursemaid photographed six years
later by George Cook, she is endowed with interpretive authority. Through
her eyes, we as readers "*see* what is supposed to remain unseen . . . *race* as the
underside of the American dream or nightmare," the Real story glimpsed
in the gaps, displacements, and silences of the national social narrative. Like
Joseph, the Biblical prototype that Wilson invokes, Frado becomes an interpreter of dreams: here, the American dream-text of color, "black, white
and yeller," not an individual but a social text that both encodes and represses
the violence of race. As the child of a white mother and black father, a reversal of the normative structure of racialized sex in antebellum America,
Frado, constructed as a "Nig" and used as a slave by the white family she
serves, implicitly calls into question the 1662 Virginia law of *partus sequitir
ventrem*. In Bassard's interpretation, this law—that "children got by an Englishman upon a Negro woman shall be bond or free according to the condition of the mother"—constitutes a "peculiarly twisted myth of origins"
through which "the black woman becomes the origin of the 'fall' of millions
of black children (male and female) into perpetual slavery." Bassard argues
that, by splitting servitude from the black maternal body, Wilson destabilizes

the equation of race and condition, severs the social symbolic from the biology it claims as ground, and fissures white America's image of itself as coherent, legitimate, and whole. Reading the American social dream against the political unconscious it generates, Bassard suggests how to put into practice Spillers's conception of psychoanalytics.

For both Wexler and Bassard, the racially fractured mother-child relation is the site at which we can glimpse the wounds of history. Similarly, in the final essay in this section, Helene Moglen reads the narrative of a black woman forced by the violence of slavery to assume the mythic function of primal mother as an exposure of the ways that seemingly timeless modes of psychic functioning are constructed and enacted in history. Continuing the gesture toward the Real initiated by the two preceding essays, "Redeeming History: Toni Morrison's *Beloved*" directs our attention to the psychic register evoked and obscured by the "hallucinatory delusions" of the Imaginary and the "shared psychosis of the cultural Symbolic." "To travel back through the mirror of the Imaginary toward that primal space" of the Real, Moglen argues, is "to claim another dimension of self-formation that underlies and resists the dynamic of othering" which propels Imaginary fantasies of gender and racial opposition that are given social shape in the Symbolic. From the vantage point of the Imaginary, whose narrative mode is the fantastic, the feared and desired moment prior to differentiation is identified ambivalently with the primal mother, who "is thought to mark all difference that is the absence of differentiation," who "holds the promise of all meaning that is also the threat of meaninglessness. . . . Asocial, she is outside of history. Apolitical, she neither changes nor can she be responsible for change." *Beloved,* in Moglen's reading, "removes this omnipotent and yet powerless mother from the place before desire and brings her into history in the figure of the black woman whose children are born into the alienated relations of slavery." By "radically interrogating the fantastic tradition within which she also writes," Morrison undoes the conventional oppositions between fantastic and realist narrative modes, and between psychoanalysis and history.

The essays in "Representing the Unrepresentable: The Symbolic and the Real" interrogate and extend a Lacanian discourse on representation by forcing a confrontation with the historical crisis of slavery. Those in "Race, Psychoanalysis, and Female Desire" draw upon and revise Freudian and object relations theory by placing the psychoanalytic narratives of (white) femininity that emerged in the 1920s against mostly contemporaneous black women's texts that show how the desiring female subject is culturally embedded and socially produced. Explicitly rejecting the exclusivity or dominance of gender difference in the construction of subjectivity, these essays track the elaborate dynamic through which categories of race, class, and sexuality interact with those of gender to constitute complex representational systems. Centrally, they reveal the extent to which racial specificities, while overtly absent from, have also been powerfully influential in, the construction of the psychoanalytic subject. Hence, both the unspoken whiteness of the (heterosexual, narcissistic, masochistic) female subject of psychoanalysis, and alternative constructions of femininity, come newly into focus. Eroding the boundaries between theory and fiction, this section brings to the surface hidden assumptions of both, demonstrating how a historicized psychoanalytic discourse can enrich and be enriched by a revisionary reading of literary texts.

The section opens with Jean Walton's "Re-Placing Race in (White) Psychoanalytic Discourse: Founding Narratives of Feminism," an essay that enables us to see how the assumptions that have limited the revisionary project of contemporary white feminists also shaped the interpretive work of early women analysts and their patients, who ignored the decisive influence of race in the construction of women's sexual and gender identities. Participating in a racialized discourse that overlooked the desires, identifications, and experiences of women who are not white, they all assumed whiteness to be fundamentally constitutive of female subjectivity. For example, although Joan Riviere deconstructed the essentialist notion of femininity in her influential essay, "Womanliness as Masquerade," she ignored the fact that the female subjectivity on which her essay's reconceptualization is based is specifically white and depends for its coherence on the figuration of black men and the elision of black women. In a similar vein, Walton shows that Melanie Klein's theorization of a female creativity that makes reparation for aggressive wishes directed at the mother relies on the evocation and dismissal of a black woman in the fantasy of a female analysand. In making visible the racialized aspect of psychoanalytic discourse itself—specifically the psychoanalytic discourse of white feminists—Walton significantly opens that discourse to further interventions that take race as their central analytic term.

Shifting to a fictional narrative by an African American woman who was a contemporary of the early white female analysts, Barbara Johnson insists, in "The Quicksands of the Self: Nella Larsen and Heinz Kohut," that a focus on intrapsychic structures can provide insight into the intersecting relations of race, class, gender, and sexuality. Using Kohut's theory of narcissism to analyze Larsen's protagonist, Helga, whose desires are represented as contradictory and self-destructive, Johnson also deploys her reading of Helga to force a reconsideration of Kohut's "selfpsychology." In her view, Kohut's definition of narcissistic personality disorder does not merely reflect entrapment in a fiction of the autonomous self generated by the mirror stage, as Lacanians have maintained, but offers a richer exploration of complex structures of mirroring, of which the mirror stage is only one example. To explain Helga's recurrent inconsistency and ultimate paralysis, Johnson applies and extends Kohut's theory, suggesting how the mirroring environment of the nuclear family interacts with that of the larger society to influence the construction of the self. Because the narcissistic psychic formation "is also a social, economic and political structure in the world," race can serve as a "self-object" from which the self derives positive and negative mirroring, often simultaneously—as in the case of Larsen's biracial protagonist. Finally, by showing how the frameworks that both Larsen and Kohut employ are themselves artifacts of a middle-class consciousness that commodifies and fetishizes the decontextualized self, Johnson emphasizes how class complicates racial difference and shapes the assumptions of theory as well as those of fiction.

Through an intricate close reading of Larsen's other novel, *Passing*, Judith Butler explicitly challenges two assumptions that have marked psychoanalytic feminism (and Freudian theory generally) as white: that sexual difference is more basic than other differences in the constitution of the subject and that some forms of sexual difference are not tinged by race. In "Passing, Queering: Nella Larsen's Psychoanalytic Challenge," Butler shows that sexual and racializing norms not only coexist in the social field but also are articulated in relation to and through one another. She argues that in *Passing*, cultural prohibitions against miscegenation and homosexuality converge in order to produce a normative heterosexuality (with its gender differences) that guarantees the reproduction of racial purity. In her reading, the complex nodes of power in the fiction are mediated by Clare, the "passing" mulatta who rejects sexual and racial taboos. For her white husband, Bellew, Clare is "the necessary and impossible object of desire . . . the fetish in regard to which his own whiteness is anxiously and persistently secured." For Irene, Clare's rediscovered mulatta childhood friend who clings to the passionless bourgeois identity that secures her social position, Clare is the desired, feared, and even hated Other. Though the revealed impossibility of Clare's situation ultimately enables the consolidation of racist, homophobic, and elitist values, the "muted homosexuality" within the text functions as a persistent excess: a political promise that Butler herself attempts to keep, not only through her interpretation of *Passing*, but also in her use of Larsen's novel to produce a revisionary reading of the psychic economy of Freud.

The final essay in this section both advances the historical frame and returns it to the context of slavery in order to examine the interrelations among violence, enslavement, and sexuality. In "The Stories of O(Dessa): Stories of Complicity and Resistance," Mae G. Henderson explores the intertextual relations between Sherley Anne Williams's contemporary rendition of a slave narrative, *Dessa Rose*, and two precursor texts: William Styron's *Confessions of Nat Turner* and Pauline Réage's *Story of O*. Williams's revision of Styron's "historical novel" about the slave insurrection led by Nat Turner protests the "racial masquerade" through which the white male author articulates his own subjectivity rather than that of his black male subject, who is consequently dispossessed of political agency and transformed into a spectacle of black emasculation. In her more extended engagement with *The Story of O*, Williams reconstructs Réage's infamous narrative of female erotic submission as "an allegory of white female complicity with patriarchy . . . a hazardous alliance in which the patriarchy is further institutionalized by the integration of the white woman into its fundamental structures." By having Dessa Rose refuse to cooperate with her white male would-be captors and repudiate the *O* (sign of emptiness, openness, and self-negation) with which her white interrogators repeatedly attempt to preface her name, Williams both invokes and rewrites the story of white feminine pleasure in surrender as a narrative of black feminist resistance to that masochistic scenario. Exposing (along with Williams) the pornographic subtext of slavery, Henderson also exposes the racial assumptions underlying discussions of female masochism. To reveal, without reproducing, the power dynamics that produce ideologies of desire is the critical challenge that Henderson detects in Williams's text. Shifting at the conclusion of her essay from scenes of writing to scenes of reading, Henderson proposes a critical practice that resists the positions of submission and conquest in our engagement with literary and critical texts.

Henderson decenters the white woman as the representative figure of a psychoanalytic discourse on female sexuality. Our final section, "Healing Narratives," completes that decentering by examining the status of African spiritual and cultural systems in theorizing diasporic subjectivities. The section begins by returning to a critical turn-of-the-century moment in American culture, in which spirituality and psychology could still be perceived as two interconnected discourses of the unconscious. In "Pauline Hopkins and William James: The New Psychology and the Politics of Race," Cynthia D. Schrager examines the ways in which Pauline Hopkins used late-nineteenth-century discourses of the unconscious (particularly the writings of William James) to explore the political situation and complex subjectivity of African Americans in post-Reconstruction America. Focusing on *Of One Blood, Or the Hidden Self,* Schrager traces the development of two contradictory positions in Hopkins's fiction, contradictions that the title itself implies. On the one hand, as Schrager demonstrates, Hopkins employs an intrapsychic model in shaping her three protagonists: white characters whose "hidden selves" are revealed, in the course of the story, to be black. Emphasizing the pervasiveness of miscegenation, this model asserts the inevitable indeterminacy of racial identity. On the other hand (perhaps, as Schrager suggests, because the depth model lends itself to appropriation by a white racializing discourse), Hopkins introduces a Pan-African perspective in the second half of her story. Transferring the concept of the "hidden self" from an intrapsychic to a social field, she affirms the essentialism of an African identity that underlies and redeems oppressed blackness.

Defining unconscious states broadly enough to include spiritistic possession (now called channeling), James was among the most extreme of the new psychologists in his refusal to distinguish between the rational and the irrational, the secular and the mystical, the transpersonal and the personal.

As Schrager demonstrates, James's approach was particularly valuable to W. E. B. Du Bois, who was attempting to define a form of subjectivity that reflected the particular experience of African Americans. Drawing simultaneously on a religious discourse of spiritual possession and a psychological discourse of multiple personality, Du Bois characterized African American subjectivity as an experience of "double-consciousness": a state marked both by interior struggle and by privileged access to the spiritual domain. Whereas most of the essays in this collection employ or at least assume the discourse of the unconscious that, aligned with Freud, ultimately emerged as dominant, the final three essays return to or examine the validity of the perspective shaped by Du Bois and James. They implicitly suggest that if the revisionary project initiated by our conference is to be successful, we must directly engage the debate that the new psychologists began and that psychoanalytic theory subsequently suppressed.

In her essay, "Channeling the Ancestral Muse: Lucille Clifton and Dolores Kendrick," Akasha (Gloria) Hull considers the ways in which the work—and lives—of two African American women poets have been shaped by a form of spiritual receptivity that, rooted in African practice and belief, provides significant continuity for the African American community. For her, the creative sensibility made possible by channeling is validated by New Age awareness but remains unrecognized and untheorized within the academy. Following the lead of Clifton and Kendrick—and many other African American women writers—Hull insists on breaking the silence that has surrounded spiritualism, denying its validity as a mode of knowledge and expression. By affirming the "transmission of female ancestral energy as a vital force" in the lives and poetry of these and other writers, she makes a critical contribution toward defining an African American poetics.

Carolyn Martin Shaw engages Hull's argument from the perspective of an anthropologist, insisting that spiritualism does not connect African Americans with an ancestral past but unites them with others—especially New Age religionists—who "identify differently." In her essay, "The Poetics of Identity: Questioning Spiritualism in African American Contexts," she links spiritualism and Africanity to identity politics, examining them all as postmodern phenomena that reflect a need for origin stories and celebrate local knowledges. Specifically considering how spirit mediumship functions in contemporary Zimbabwe, she distinguishes the separate paths that African and African American spirituality have taken. She proposes that in most African contexts, ancestors' messages are not inevitably positive for women, nor are women who serve as mediums for spirits necessarily honored in their everyday lives: "In African societies, spirit mediumship may be a form of social control, means of self-aggrandizement, or an affirmation of group solidarity." From Shaw's perspective, the value of the spirituality that Hull celebrates finally derives from the fact that the racial trauma that connects African Americans is symbolically summoned by its message: "creating a kinship of blood but not in blood."

It is the story of shared trauma that Barbara Christian finds at the heart of Toni Morrison's *Beloved*, and the argument of her essay, "Fixing Methodologies: *Beloved*," is located somewhere between the position occupied by Hull and the one finally advanced by Shaw. For Christian, Morrison's unique accomplishment derives from her focus on the actual and symbolic meaning of the Middle Passage, the historical moment that divided the condition of being African from that of being African American. In order to understand the trauma of that disjunction, Christian reads Morrison's novel from the perspective of an African cosmology that affirms the continuity of past and present in the naming and nurturing of embodied spirits. For her, *Beloved* serves as a "fixing" ceremony: an act of remembrance that initiates the healing of a psychic wound that was originally inflicted by an enforced and collective act of forgetting. "In acknowledging and naming our holocaust, we feed, remember, and respect those forgotten, raging spirits whom we call the past, whose bodies and blood fed, and continue to feed, the ground on which we walk." In its emphasis upon the trauma of forgetting and the healing nature of memory, Christian's argument suggests a definition of the unconscious in which the spiritual and the psychoanalytic once again converge.

Barbara Christian's essay returns us, on one level, to the place where Ann duCille's opening critique left off. Implicitly, Christian reiterates the need for white feminist critics to be attentive to and respectful of the cultural and historical contexts of African American women's texts. But considered in the context of the essays that have intervened between the introduction and conclusion, the return also seems to signal an advance. The project of complementary theorizing, undertaken in however initiatory a way, has produced an expanded set of questions, intersections, and concerns. Other voices, engaged in similar conversations, will continue to complicate these debates. We hope this volume fulfills the paradoxical promise of its opening epigraphs, which assert both the potential and the limits of psychoanalysis—but not from the predictable points of view. If this inquiry into female subjects reopens questions we have come to think are closed, it serves at least some common goals of psychoanalysis and feminism.

NOTE

1. Lawrence Grossberg, Cary Nelson, and Paula Treichler, eds., *Cultural Studies* (New York: Routledge, 1992), 282.

I

Crossdressing, Crossreading, or Complementary Theorizing?

The Occult of True Black Womanhood
Critical Demeanor and Black Feminist Studies

Ann duCille

The Black Woman; The Black Woman: An Anthology; The Black Woman in America;
The Black Woman in American Society; The Black Woman Cross-Culturally; Black
Women in America; Black Women in White America; Black Women in the Nineteenth
Century; Black Women in Nineteenth-Century American Life; Black Women Writers;
Black Women Writers at Work; Black Women Writing Autobiography; Black Women
Writing the American Experience; Black Women Novelists; Black Women Novelists
in the Wake of the Civil Rights Movement; Black Women, Fiction, and Literary
Tradition; The Sexual Mountain and Black Women Writers; Ain't I a Woman?;
Arn't I a Woman?

For reasons that may already be obvious, the books named above and numerous others like them have led me to think of myself as a kind of sacred
text. Not me personally, of course, but me black woman object, Other. Within
and around the modern academy, racial and gender alterity has become a
hot commodity that has claimed black women as its principal signifier. I
am alternately pleased, puzzled, and perturbed—bewitched, bothered, and
bewildered—by this, by the alterity that is perpetually thrust upon African
American women, by the production of black women as infinitely decon-
structable "othered" matter. Why are black women always already Other? I
wonder. To myself, of course, I am not Other; to me it is the white women
and men so intent on theorizing my difference who are the Other. Why are
they so interested in me and people who look like me (metaphorically speaking)? Why have we—black women—become the subjected subjects of so
much contemporary scholarly investigation, the peasants under glass of intellectual inquiry in the 1990s?

The attention is not altogether unpleasant, especially after generations
of neglect, but I am hardly alone in suspecting that the overwhelming interest in black women may have at least as much to do with the pluralism

and perhaps even the primitivism of this particular postmodern moment as with the stunning quality of black women's accomplishments and the breadth of their contributions to American civilization. It is not news that by virtue of our race and gender, black women are not only the "second sex"—*the Other*, in postmodern parlance—but we are also the last race, the most oppressed, the most marginalized, the most deviant, the quintessential site of difference. And through the inversionary properties of deconstruction, feminism, cultural studies, multiculturalism, and contemporary commodity culture, the last shall be first. Perhaps.

I say perhaps because we have experienced the problematic of such inversions before: the preoccupation with black women, with the blues, the black folk, the authentic, the real colored thing in the 1920s, for example, a preoccupation fueled at least in part by the primitivist proclivities of the historical moment. In the twenties, the fascination with the black female body, in particular, and the primitive sexual anatomy and appetite attributed to the African woman increased the degree to which the black female functioned as an erotic icon in the racial and sexual ideology of Western civilization.

Black feminist theorist bell hooks calls the contemporary version of this preoccupation with alterity "the commodification of Otherness" or "eating the Other." "Within commodity culture," she writes in *Black Looks*, "ethnicity becomes spice, seasoning that can liven up the dull dish that is mainstream white culture." Mass culture, then, in hooks's view, perpetuates the primitivistic notion "that there is pleasure to be found in the acknowledgment and enjoyment of racial difference" (21).

Where gender and racial differences meet in the bodies of black women, the result is the invention of an other Otherness, a hyperstatic alterity. Mass culture, as hooks argues, produces, promotes, and perpetuates the commodification of Otherness through the exploitation of the black female body. In the 1990s, however, the principal sites of exploitation are not simply the cabaret, the speakeasy, the music video, the glamour magazine; they are also the academy, the publishing industry, the intellectual community. In the words of black male theorist Houston Baker, who is among those who have recently taken up African American women (and taken on black feminist critics): "Afro-American women's expressivity and the analyses that it has promoted during the past two decades represent the most dramatically charged field for the convergence of matters of race, class, and gender today" (1–2). Of course, one of the dangers of standing at an intersection—particularly at such a suddenly busy, three-way intersection—is the likelihood of being run over by oncoming traffic. Michele Wallace likens the traffic jam that has built up around Zora Neale Hurston, in particular, to a "rainbow coalition" of critics, who, "like groupies descending on Elvis Presley's estate," are engaged in "a mostly ill-mannered stampede to have some memento of the black woman" (174), who is, at least to some degree, a figment of their individual and collective critical imaginations.

Precisely the question I want to explore in this essay is what it means for black women academics to stand in the midst of the "dramatically charged field"—the traffic jam—that black feminist studies has become. Are we in the way of the critical stampede that accompanies what I am calling here "the occult of true black womanhood"? Are we in danger of being trampled by the "rainbow coalition" of critics—"black, white, male, female, artists and academics, historicists and deconstructionists"—that our own once isolated and isolating intellectual labors have attracted to the magnetic field of black feminist studies?

"HURSTONISM" AND THE BLACK FEMINIST PHENOMENON

In her foreword to the 1978 University of Illinois Press reprint of *Their Eyes Were Watching God*, black poet, novelist, and critic Sherley Anne Williams tells of first encountering Zora Neale Hurston and *Their Eyes* while a graduate student enrolled in a two-semester survey of black poetry and prose. "Afro-American literature was still an exotic subject then," Williams writes, "rarely taught on any regular basis" (vi). She goes on to describe how she and her classmates fought over the pitifully few copies of African American texts, long out of print, that they were able to beg, borrow, and otherwise procure from musty basements, rare book collections, and reserved reading rooms. When it finally became her turn to read *Their Eyes Were Watching God*, Williams says she found in the speech of Hurston's characters her own country self and, like Alice Walker and numerous others, became Zora Neale's for life.

For many of us who came of intellectual age in the late sixties and early seventies, Sherley Anne Williams's "discovery" of Zora is an almost painfully familiar textual encounter of the first kind. Though Hurston was not the first black woman writer I encountered or claimed as my own (that was Ann Petry), it was during this same period—1971, in fact—that I, too, discovered Zora. I was introduced to her and to her work by my friend and fellow graduate student, another gifted black woman writer, Gayl Jones. When I began my teaching career a few years later at a college in upstate New York, Gayl was again generous enough to lend me her well-worn, oft-read copy of *Their Eyes*. Only a lingering fear of being prosecuted for copyright infringement prevents me from detailing how I went about sharing among the dozen or so students in my seminar, none of whom had heard of Hurston, the fruits that bloomed within the single, precious, tattered copy of *Their Eyes Were Watching God*.

Twenty years later, African American studies courses and black women writers such as Hurston are once again exotic subjects. They are exotic this time out, however, not because they are rarely taught or seldom read, but because in the midst of the present, multicultural moment, they have become politically correct, intellectually popular, and commercially precious sites of literary and historical inquiry. Long either altogether ignored as historical and literary subjects or badly misfigured as magnanimous mammies, man-eating matriarchs, or immoral Jezebels, black women—that is, certain black women—and their texts have been taken up by and reconfigured within the academy, elevated and invoked by the intellectual elite as well as the scholarly marginal. Currently in print in several editions, *Their Eyes Were Watching God* has become quasi-canonical, holding a place of honor on syllabi of mainstream history, social science, literature, and American studies courses, as well as of perhaps more marginalized disciplines such as African American studies and women's studies. Much the same holds true for Alice Walker's *Color Purple* and Toni Morrison's *Beloved,* each of which has been awarded the Pulitzer Prize for fiction.

It is important to note that black women critics and scholars have played a crucial role in bringing to the academic fore the works of "lost" writers such as Hurston and Nella Larsen and in opening up spaces within the academy both for the fiction of contemporary African American women writers and for the study of black and other women of color more generally. Though I am usually suspicious of efforts to define benchmarks and signposts, there are nevertheless a number of important essays, anthologies, and monographs that I think can be rightly claimed as the founding texts of contemporary black feminist studies. Toni Cade Bambara's anthology *The Black Woman* (1970)—which showcased the prose and poetry of writers such as Nikki Giovanni, Audre Lorde, Paule Marshall, Alice Walker, and Sherley Anne Williams—stands as a pivotal text along with critical essays and literary, historical, and sociological studies by Barbara Smith, Barbara Christian, Frances Beal, Joyce Ladner, Jeanne Noble, Darlene Clark Hine, Angela Davis, Frances Foster, Filomina Chioma Steady, Sharon Harley and Rosalyn Terborg-Penn, and Mary Helen Washington.[1]

Whereas keepers of (dominant) culture have given the lion's share credit for the development of black literary and cultural studies to male scholars such as Houston Baker, Henry Louis Gates, and Cornel West, Mary Helen Washington nevertheless has been a key player in efforts to define and institutionalize the fields of African American literature and black feminist studies for more than twenty years.[2] Among my most precious personal possessions is a tattered copy of the August 1974 issue of *Black World,* which contains an article by Washington entitled "Their Fiction Becomes Our Reality: Black Women Image Makers." In this article, one of the first pieces of black feminist criticism I "discovered" and learned from (and in others that began appearing in *Black World* in 1972), Washington read, reviewed, and critiqued the works of black women writers such as Gwendolyn Brooks, Maya Angelou, Ann Petry, and Toni Cade Bambara, as well as Walker, Marshall, and Morrison.

Much the same can and must be said of Barbara Christian and Barbara Smith, whose essays on African American women writers began appearing in print in the 1970s. Christian's first book, *Black Women Novelists: The Development of a Tradition, 1892–1976*, which brilliantly analyzed the work of black women writers from Frances Harper to Marshall, Morrison, and Walker, remains a foundational text—"the Bible in the field of black feminist criticism," according to Michele Wallace (184). Nor have the more than fifteen years since its publication dulled the impact and significance of Barbara Smith's pivotal essay "Toward a Black Feminist Criticism" (a widely reprinted, often anthologized black lesbian feminist critical declaration that, as Cheryl Wall points out, gave name, definition, and political persuasion to the perspective from which Bambara, Washington, and others had been writing (Wall 45). Smith's work in literary criticism and that of her sister Beverly Smith in the area of black women's health have played crucial roles in developing the fields of black feminist and black lesbian feminist studies.

Within the realm of literary studies alone, the names making up even a partial list of pioneering black feminist scholars are, as Houston Baker has said, "legion" (10): Deborah McDowell, Nellie McKay, Hortense Spillers, Gloria Hull, Patricia Bell Scott, Cheryl Wall, Valerie Smith, Mae Henderson, Gloria Wade-Gayles, Thadious Davis, Trudier Harris, Frances Smith Foster, Hazel Carby, Joyce Joyce, and Claudia Tate, as well as Christian, Washington, Smith, and many many others.[3] Both as an inspiration to aspiring young black women writers and as an editor at Random House in the 1970s, Toni Morrison, too, has played a particularly dramatic role in opening up spaces for and directing critical attention toward African American women.

As a beneficiary of their research and writing, I am anxious to give credit where credit is long overdue, but this essay is not intended as a praisesong for black women scholars, critics, and artists, or even as a review of the literature they have generated.[4] Rather, I examine critically some of the implications and consequences of the current explosion of interest in black women as literary and historical subjects. Among the issues I explore are the ways in which this interest—which seems to me to have reached occult status—increasingly marginalizes both the black women critics and scholars who excavated the fields in question and their black feminist "daughters" who would further develop those fields.

What does it mean that many prestigious university presses and influential literary publications such as the *New York Times Book Review* regularly rely not on these seasoned black women scholars but on male intellectuals— black and white—to read, evaluate, and review the book manuscripts of young black women just entering the profession? What does it mean for the black female professoriate that departments often ask powerful senior black male scholars to referee the tenure and promotion cases of the same black women scholars who have challenged or affronted these men in some way?

What does it mean for the field in general and for junior African Americanists in particular that senior scholars, who are not trained in African American studies and whose career-building work often has excluded (or at least not included) black women, are now teaching courses in and publishing texts about African American literature and generating supposedly "new scholarship" on black women writers? What does it mean for the future of black feminist studies that a large portion of the growing body of scholarship on black women is now being written by white feminists and by men whose work frequently achieves greater critical and commercial success than that of the black female scholars who carved out a field in which few "others" were then interested?

My questions are by no means new; nor do I claim to have any particularly insightful answers. I only know that as an African Americanist who has been studying the literature and history of black women for almost thirty years and teaching it for more than twenty, I have a burning need to work through on paper my own ambivalence, antipathy, and, at times, animosity over the new-found enthusiasm for these fields that I readily—perhaps too readily—think of as my own hard-won territory. I feel a little like the parent who tells the child she is about to reprimand that "this hurts me more than it hurts you." But lest anyone think that this is an easily authored Portnoy's complaint in blackface—yet another black womanist indictment of white feminists who can do no right and men who can do only wrong—I want to make explicit my own dis-ease with the antagonism to which I have admitted and by which I am myself somewhat baffled.

Elsewhere I have argued against territoriality, against racial, cultural, and gender essentialism, against treating African American studies as the private property of what Gayatri Spivak calls "black blacks."[5] Yet questions of turf and territoriality, appropriation and co-optation persist within my own black feminist consciousness, despite my best efforts to intellectualize them away. Again, this is not a new dilemma. The modern, academic version of the ageless argument over who owns the sacred text of me and mine is at least as old as the work of white anthropologists Melville and Frances Herskovits dating back to the 1920s and reaching a controversial peak in 1941 with the publication of *The Myth of the Negro Past,* a study of African cultural retentions scorned by many black intellectuals (Herskovits, *American Negro, Dahomey,* and *Myth*; Herskovits and Herskovits). It was in the fifties, however, that white scholars began to loom large in the realm of black historiography and literary criticism, often receiving within the academy an attention and credibility that the pioneering work of many black historians and literary critics had not enjoyed. Black historian Darlene Clark Hine noted in 1980 that "most of the highly-acclaimed historical works were, with few exceptions, written by white scholars." In fact, in her estimation, the legitimization of black history as a field proved a "bonanza for the [white] professional historians already in positions [as university professors and/or recognized scholars] to capitalize from the movement" (Hine, *Four Black* 115, as quoted in Meier and Rudwick 294).

One hundred thirty years ago, former slave Harriet Jacobs was able to publish her life's story only with the authenticating stamp of the well-known white abolitionist Lydia Maria Child as editor and copyright holder. "I have signed and sealed the contract with Thayer & Eldridge, in my name, and told them to take out the copyright in my name," Child wrote in a letter to Jacobs in 1860. "Under the circumstances *your* name could not be used, you know" (Jacobs 246). The circumstances to which Child alluded (but did not name) were of course the conditions of slavery under which Jacobs had lived for most of her life and from which she had not completely escaped. Now, as then, it often seems to take the interest and intervention of white scholars to legitimize and institutionalize African American history and literature or such "minority discourses" as postcoloniality and multiculturalism. Let me offer two examples: Gerda Lerner's *Black Women in White America* and Shelley Fisher Fishkin's *Was Huck Black?*

Black feminist critic Gloria Wade-Gayles has identified Toni Cade Bambara's *Black Woman* as "the first book that pulled together black women's views on black womanhood" and Jeanne Noble's *Beautiful, Also, Are the Souls of My Black Sisters* as the "first history of black women in America written by a black woman" (Wade-Gayles 41–42). Yet, despite the recovery and reconnaissance missions of Bambara, Noble, Joyce Ladner, and other black women intellectuals who did groundbreaking work in the seventies, it is white feminist historian Gerda Lerner whom the academy recognizes as the pioneer in reconstructing the history of African American women.

With the 1972 publication of her documentary anthology *Black Women in White America,* Lerner became by many reckonings the first historian to produce a book-length study devoted to African American women. Her goal, as she outlined in her preface, was to call attention to such "unused sources" as black women's own records of their experiences and "to bring another forgotten aspect of the black past to life" (xviii). In drawing on such first-person accounts as diaries, narratives, testimonies, and organizational records and reports, Lerner endeavored in her volume, she says, "to let black women speak for themselves" (xx).

Though the notion of letting someone speak for herself is surely problematic, I want to note as well that Lerner was by no means the first to draw on what she implies were unexamined resources. Black artists, activists, and intellectuals had made use of these resources since the nineteenth century. Former slave William Wells Brown, for one, drew on such sources in the many novels, narratives, and histories he published between 1847 and his death in 1884. Although written in a vein admittedly different from Lerner's work, Mrs. N. F. Mossell's *Work of the Afro-American Woman,* first published in 1894,

represents an early effort on the part of an African American woman to acknowledge the accomplishments and contributions of her black sisters. Black
activist, educator, and "race woman" Anna Julia Cooper wrote of the "long
dull pain" of the "open-eyed but hitherto voiceless Black Women of America" in *A Voice from the South,* published in 1892. In fact, the longevity of the
insider-outsider debate is reflected in Cooper's one-hundred-year-old pro-
nouncement: "Only the BLACK WOMAN can say 'when and where I enter,
in the quiet, undisputed dignity of my womanhood, without violence and
without suing or special patronage, then and there the whole *Negro race enters with me*'" (31). Their own travails, joys, sorrows, and the testimonies and
plaintive cries of other African American women, poor women, and working women were the imperatives that propelled much of the political activism
among black clubwomen at the turn of the century.

To take up a more contemporary example, I might point out that for
Nor should we ignore the intellectual labors of black literary scholar
Charles Nichols, whose masterwork *Many Thousand Gone: The Ex-Slaves' Account of Their Bondage and Freedom* has directed two generations of researchers
interested in slavery to a significant source: the "forgotten testimony of its
victims" (ix).[6] In fact, the methodology Lerner employed in *Black Women in
White America* is one perfected by Nichols.

To take up a more contemporary example, I might point out that for
decades black writers, critics, and scholars have attempted to delineate the
tremendous impact African American culture has had on the mainstream
American literary tradition. Their efforts, however, have received little
attention from the academy. But when a white scholar recently asked, "Was
Huckleberry Finn Black?" the academy, the publishing industry, and the
media sat up and took notice. I am referring, of course, to the hoopla over
Shelley Fisher Fishkin's book *Was Huck Black?* As much as a year before it appeared in bookstores, Fishkin's study was lauded in such influential publi-
cations as the *New York Times, Newsweek,* and the *Chronicle of Higher Education.*
In fact, according to the London *Times,* more than fifty news items on the
book appeared across the country, sporting such headlines as: "Scholar Concludes That Young Black Was Model for Huck Finn's Voice; Huck Finn Speaks
'Black,' Scholar Says; and Theory Might Warm Foes to Twain's Novel"
(Fender 27). I quote from one such article that appeared in the *Chronicle:*
"Ms. Fishkin's book, *Was Huck Black?: Mark Twain and African-American Voices,*
is likely to have a major impact, not just on the way scholars interpret a main-
stay of the American literary canon, but also on the way scholars define that
canon. By calling attention to the way multicultural voices have influenced
mainstream literature, it suggests that traditional views of the dichotomy between majority and minority cultures may be flawed. In so doing, the book
gives the term multiculturalism a new meaning" (Winkler A6).

I do not mean to make little or light of Shelley Fishkin's research and conclusions: hers is important and provocative work. What I am intrigued by,

however, is the response from the white intellectual establishment. Why is the conclusion that we need to pay more attention to African American culture, even when we study the canon, suddenly being greeted as news? Haven't black scholars long argued the reflexive nature of cultural appropriation and the interrelatedness of so-called minor and major traditions? Speaking at a socialist conference in 1917, James Weldon Johnson, whom David Levering Lewis calls the "dean of Afro-American letters," reportedly shocked his audience by declaring that "'the only things artistic in America that have sprung from American soil, permeated American life, and been universally acknowledged as distinctively American' were the creations of the Afro-American." No African Americanist I know has been surprised at being told at this late date what many of us have argued for a long time: that Twain, like many major white American writers, drew canon fodder from "the black experiences" that are a fundamental, if often unacknowledged, part of American culture.

These and numerous other examples suggest to me a color line and intellectual passing within and around the academy: black culture is more easily intellectualized (and canonized) when transferred from the danger of lived black experience to the safety of white metaphor, when you can have that "signifying black difference" without the difference of significant blackness. Fishkin's work, like Lerner's, is undeniably important, but it does not stand alone as revolutionary. "Sociable Jimmy," the young black boy on whose vernacular speech Twain may have based Huck's colorful language, may never have gotten to speak for himself in print, but black women had been speaking for themselves and on behalf of each other long before Gerda Lerner endeavored "to let" them do so.

As I have suggested, the question of who speaks for me, who can write my sacred text, is as emotionally and politically charged as it is enduring and controversial. Asked about the explosion of interest in the lives and literature of black women among male scholars and white feminists, Barbara Christian responded in part:

> It is galling to me that after black women critics of the 1970s plowed the neglected field of Afro-American women's literature when such an act was academically dangerous, that some male and white feminist scholars now seem to be reaping the harvest and are major commentators on this literature in influential, though not necessarily feminist journals such as *The New York Review of Books*. Historical amnesia seems to be as much a feature of intellectual life as other aspects of American society. (Christian et al. 61)

Historical amnesia may displace her at any time, but for this moment anyway, the black woman writer has become a bonanza. Her near phenomenal popularity as subject matter has spawned a wealth of critical scholarship and has spontaneously generated scores of scholars determined to claim her material and cultural production—what Houston Baker calls "Afro-American women's expressivity"—as their intellectual discourse. But as Barbara Christian's remarks imply, black women's expressivity is not merely discourse; it has become lucre in the intellectual marketplace, cultural commerce. What for many began as a search for our mothers' gardens, to appropriate Alice Walker's metaphor, has become for some a Random House harvest worth millions in book sales and prestigious university professorships. Sensitive as the issue is, it must be said even at the risk of hurt feelings that the explosion of interest in the black female subject is at least in some measure about economics—about jobs. White feminist scholar Elizabeth Abel has acknowledged as much. "This new attentiveness [to texts by women of color] has been overdetermined," she argues, "by the sheer brilliance and power of this writing and its escalating status in the literary marketplace and, consequently, the academy; [and] by white feminist restlessness with an already well-mined white female literary tradition" (478). For many scholars trained in these well-mined fields, the shift to African American studies has yielded more prominent positions at more prestigious institutions.

But is this, as it seems to be for Barbara Christian, necessarily a bitter harvest? We—"we" being here African American women scholars—have complained long and loud about exclusion, about the degree to which white feminists and male critics have ignored the work of black women. Can we now legitimately complain that they are taking up (and taking over?) this important work? And what do such complaints tell us about ourselves and our relationship to what many of us continue to speak of as *our* literature?[7]

As I have acknowledged, I, too, am troubled, even galled by what at times feels like the appropriation and co-optation of black women by white feminists and by men. But what I ultimately want to get at in this article is not simply about property rights, about racial or gender territoriality. It is by no means my intention to claim Hurston, Morrison, Walker, and others as the private property of black women readers who, like Sherley Anne Williams, see themselves in their characters. In fact, I have argued elsewhere that rather than liberating and valorizing black female voices, the celebration of African American women's literature and history as the discursively familiar, as a "truth" to which black women scholars have privileged access rooted in common experience, both delimits and demeans those discourses. For, however inadvertently, it restricts this work to a narrow orbit in which it can be readily validated only by those black and female for whom it reproduces what they already know.[8]

Undeniably critical contributions to the study of black women and their literature and history have been made by scholars who are neither black nor female. The name of William L. Andrews comes to mind immediately, as does that of Robert Hemenway. That we have increased access to the autobiographical writings of nineteenth-century African American women is a result in part of Andrews's effort. That Hurston's work is now so readily accessible is a result in no small measure not only of the efforts of black feminist writer Alice Walker, but also of those of white male scholar Robert Hemenway. Through the research and publishing efforts of white feminist scholar Jean Fagan Yellin and black male theorist Henry Louis Gates, to cite two other examples, we now have authentication of and access to two fundamental texts from the nineteenth century: Harriet Jacobs's *Incidents in the Life of a Slave Girl, Written by Herself* and Harriet Wilson's *Our Nig*. Moreover, since 1988 the Schomburg Library of Nineteenth-Century Black Women Writers, of which Gates is general editor, has made available to critics and scholars dozens of previously lost texts. The recent work of white feminist scholar Elizabeth Ammons also represents a positive turn in literary studies. In its intercultural readings of works by African, Asian, Native, Jewish, and white American women, her book *Conflicting Stories: American Women Writers at the Turn into the Twentieth Century* represents a model we all would do well to follow.

Surely this is great work and good news. Why, then, am I and so many other black feminist scholars left wrestling with enduring questions about co-optation and exploitation? Why are we haunted by a growing sense that we are witnessing (and perhaps even have inspired in some way) the commodification of the same black womanhood we have championed? It is a mistake, I think, to define this persistent (but perhaps inherently unresolvable) debate over who can read black female texts as strictly or even perhaps primarily racial or cultural or gendered: black versus white, male versus female, insider versus outsider, our literature versus your theory, my familiar versus their foreign. The most important questions, I have begun to suspect, may not be about the essentialism and territoriality, the biology, sociology, or even the ideology about which we hear so much but, rather, about professionalism and disciplinarity; about cultural literacy and intellectual competence; about taking ourselves seriously and insisting that we be taken seriously not as objectified subjects in someone else's histories—as native informants—but as critics and as scholars reading and writing our own literature and history.

DISCIPLINARY MATTERS: WHEN DEMEANOR DEMEANS

So I have arrived at what for me is at the heart of what's the matter. Much of the newfound interest in African American women that seems to honor the field of black feminist studies actually demeans it by treating it not like a discipline with a history and a body of rigorous scholarship and distinguished scholars underpinning it, but like an anybody-can-play pick-up game performed on a wide-open, untrammeled field. Often the object of the game seems to be to reinvent the intellectual wheel: to boldly go where in fact others have gone before, to flood the field with supposedly new "new scholar-ship" that evinces little or no sense of the discipline's genealogy. Moreover, many of the rules that the academy generally invokes in doing its institutional business—in making appointments, assigning courses, and advancing faculty —are suddenly suspended when what is at stake is not the valorized, tradi-tional disciplines of Western civilization but the more marginal, if extremely popular, fields within African American studies.

Among those elements considered when English departments hire Me-dievalists, Victorianists, Americanists, and so on, at least in my experience in the academy, are school(s) attended, the nature of one's graduate train-ing, the subject of one's dissertation, and not only what one has published but where one has published as well. Were the articles refereed? Were they published in reputable academic journals? Are the journals discipline-specific, edited and juried by experts in the candidate's field, scholars who know whereof they read? I have seen these valorized criteria relaxed time and time again, however, when these same traditionally trained, nonblack scholars are being hired not in the fields in which they were educated but in African American studies. Interestingly enough, the same loosening of standards does not readily occur when black scholars—particularly young black scholars—apply for positions as generalists in American or world lit-erature. The fact that the educational system is such that it is still largely im-possible to specialize in African American literature without first being trained in the European and Anglo-American canons does not keep the pow-ers that be from questioning the preparedness of blacks who apply for jobs as generalists. A dissertation on Toni Morrison or C. L. R. James or W. E. B. Du Bois does not necessarily qualify one as an Americanist, but a thesis on Chaucer or the Brontës or Byron is not an impediment to an appointment as an African Americanist.

Indeed, the question of who is authorized to teach African American dis-course is riddled with ironies, paradoxes, and contradictions. Black scholars duly and properly trained and credentialed in traditional fields—medieval studies, for example—are often assumed or expected to be ready, willing, and able to teach black studies courses. African American studies programs and department are not supposed to be intellectual ghettos populated ex-clusively by black scholars, particularly when white scholars want to enter such programs, but the field of African American studies often is treated like a black ghetto—like the one right and proper place for black intellectuals— when black scholars dare to step out of it, dare to be Medievalists or classi-cists or British Victorianists.

Moreover, despite the fact that many of our white colleagues and admin-istrators may theorize African American and black feminist studies as open fields, as acquirable tastes ("You don't have to be one to teach one," as some-one put it), this intellectual position often is not lived up to in institutional practice. For when these same individuals want someone to provide a black reading of their work or black representation on a committee or black resources for their students or information about a particular black author or details about an event in black history, more times than not it is to black faculty that they turn, and not to the white Victorianists they have hired as African Americanists and have authorized to teach courses in black literature and history.

So here we have another paradox of critical demeanor: the difference between authority and authenticity. Black scholars on predominantly or overwhelmingly white campuses are rarely authorized simply as scholars. Rather, our racial difference is an authenticating stamp that, as Indira Karamcheti has argued, often casts us in the role of Caliban in the classroom and on the campus. Speaking of minority scholars in general, Karamcheti writes:

> We are sometimes seen, it seems to me, as traveling icons of culture, both traditional (as long as we're over there) and nontraditional (when we're right here), unbearably ancient in our folk wisdom and childlike in our infantile need for the sophistication of the West. We are flesh and blood information retrieval systems, native informants who demonstrate and act out difference, often with an imperfectly concealed political agenda. We are the local and the regional opposed to the universality of the West, nature to its culture, instinct to its intellect, body to its brain. We are, in fact, encased in the personal and visible facts of our visible selves, walking exemplars of ethnicity and of race. (13)

Walking exemplars of ethnicity and race. It seems to me that this is particularly true for black women scholars on white college campuses where they experience both a hypervisibility and a superisolation by virtue of their racial and gender difference. Unfortunately, icons are not granted tenure automatically; when their canonical year rolls around, all too often these same black women faculty members who have been drawn on as exemplars and used up as icons will find themselves chewed up and spit out because they did not publish. (Consider the startling number of brilliant black women scholars who have produced only one book or no book.) Sympathetic white colleagues lament their black colleagues' departures from the university: "Why didn't she just say 'no'?" they ask each other, rarely remembering the many times they implored her to just say "yes," the numerous occasions on which they sent her students with questions only she could answer or problems only she could solve, or the many instances in which they treated her not like a colleague but like their personal research assistant or native informant.

Given the occult of true black womanhood, to be (not so) young, female, and black on today's college campuses is difficult. But more troubling still is the fact that commodified, Calibanized black women intellectuals, whose authority as academicians often has been questioned at every turn in their careers, are not supposed to resent, or even to notice, the double standard that propels others forward even as it keeps them back. For the most part, however, black women in the academy not only have noticed, we have refused to suffer in silence; our complaints are by now old news. Many ears, once sympathetic to "the black woman's plight," her "double jeopardy," her "exceptional burdens," have been frozen by the many winters of our discontent. Our grievances have begun to be heard only as "anti-intellectual identity politics" and "proprietary claims." What Houston Baker describes as our "black feminist manifestos"—our "admonitions, injunctions, and cautions to those who wish to share the open road" (11)—reveal us to be, even to our most supportive colleagues, small-minded, mean-spirited, and downright petty.

Of course, my point is that for many of us, for many black women scholars, questioning the race, ethnicity, culture, and credentials of those the academy authorizes to write our histories and to teach and interpret *our* literature is anything but petty. Rather, it is a concern that rises from the deepest recesses of who we are in relation to where we live and work. Black women have pioneered a field that even after more than twenty years remains marginalized within the university, regardless of how popular both the field and its black women practitioners are with students. Our at once precarious and overdetermined positions in the academy and our intimate knowledge of social, intellectual, and academic history prompt us not simply to guard our turf, as often accused, but also to discipline *our* field, to preserve its integrity and our own.

I have emphasized the pronoun *our* in order to problematize the admitted possessiveness of our disciplinary concerns. For no matter how compelling—no matter how historically resonant—the sense of personal stake that permeates the scholarship by black women about black women just may be an aspect of the insider-outsider problematic for which African American women academics have to take responsibility. It may be time for us to interrogate in new and increasingly clinical ways our proprietary relationship to the field many of us continue to think of as *our own*.

Such internal review presents its own problematic, however. To claim privileged access to the lives and literature of African American women through what we hold to be the shared experiences of our black female bodies is to cooperate with our own commodification, to buy from and sell back to the dominant culture its constitution of our always already essentialized identity. Yet to relinquish claim to the experiences of the black body and to confirm and affirm its study purely as discourse, simply as a field of inquiry equally open to all, is to collaborate with our own objectification. We become objects of study where we are authorized to be the story but have no special claim to decoding that story. We can be, but someone else gets to tell us what we mean.

This conundrum operates, of course, in realms beyond the either-or options I have established here. But how to find the middle ground, that happier medium? How do we negotiate an intellectually charged space for experience in a way that is not totalizing and essentializing—a space that acknowledges the constructedness of and the differences within our lived experiences while at the same time attending to the inclining, rather than the declining, significance of race, class, culture, and gender?

I ONCE WAS BLIND, BUT NOW I SEE—YOU

By and large, it is only those who enjoy the privileges of white skin who can hold matters of race at arm's length. White feminist theorist Jane Gallop, for instance, can say that "race only posed itself as an urgent issue to me in the last couple of years" (Gallop et al. 363), but race always has been an urgent issue for Mary Helen Washington, Barbara Christian, and Barbara Smith—indeed for most, if not all, black feminist critics. Gallop can say that she did not feel the need to discuss race until the focus of her work shifted from French poststructuralist theory to American feminist literary criticism. But Gayatri Spivak and other Third World women know only too well the fallacies and consequences of treating race as something only other (nonwhite) people own and racism as a problem particular to the United States. As Spivak writes in *In Other Worlds:* "In the matter of race-sensitive analysis, the chief problem of American feminist criticism is its identification of racism as such with the constitution of racism in America. Thus, today I see the object of investigation to be not only the history of 'Third World Women' or their testimony but also the production, through the great European theories, often by way of literature, of the colonial object" (81).

The colonial object is furthered not only by the canonical literature of the West, as Spivak suggests, but also by a would-be oppositional feminist criticism whose practitioners continue to see whiteness as so natural, normative, and unproblematic that racial identity is a property only of the nonwhite. Unless the object of study happens to be the Other, race is placed under erasure as something outside immediate consideration, at once extratextual and extraterrestrial. Despite decades of painful debate, denial, defensiveness, and color-consciousness-raising, "as a woman" in mainstream feminist discourse all too often continues to mean "as a white woman." White feminist philosopher Elizabeth Spelman calls this enduring, thoroughly internalized myopia the "Trojan horse of feminist ethnocentrism" (13).[9] Indeed, for women of color who are often asked to prove their feminism by placing their gender before their race, the exclusionary ethnocentrism of seemingly innocent constructions such as "women and minorities" is at once as hollow and as loaded as the Greeks' wooden horse.

But there is a larger and somewhat more convoluted point I want to get at here, and maybe I can use Jane Gallop's words to make it for me. In the conversation previously referred to, Gallop confesses that African American women have become for her what French men used to be: the people she feels inadequate in relation to and tries hardest to please in her writing. This fear of black feminists "is not just idiosyncratic," Gallop believes—not just hers alone—but a shared anxiety among white women academics. She traces her own awareness of this anxiety to what she calls a "non-encounter" with black feminist critic Deborah McDowell, who teaches at the University of Virginia where Gallop once gave a talk. "I had hoped Deborah McDowell would come to my talk," she says; "she was there, she was the one person in the audience that I was really hoping to please" (Gallop et al. 363–64). Gallop goes on to explain that as part of her lecture she read from the manuscript that became *Around 1981: Academic Feminist Literary Theory,* after which someone in the audience asked if she was including any black feminist critical anthologies in her study. "I answered no and tried to justify it, but my justifications rang false in my ears," she admits. She continues:

> Some weeks later a friend of mine showed me a letter from McDowell which mentioned my talk and said that I was just doing the same old thing, citing that I was not talking about any books edited by black women. I obsessed over McDowell's comment until I decided to add a chapter on Pryse and Spillers's *Conjuring.* I had already vowed not to add any more chapters out of fear that I would never finish the book. As powerful as my fear of not finishing is, it was not as strong as my wish for McDowell's approval. For McDowell, whom I do not know, read black feminist critic. (Gallop et al. 363)

Gallop ends her commentary on what might be called "the influence of anxiety" by noting that McDowell ("read black feminist critic") has come to occupy the place of Lacan in her psyche in much the same way that "emphasis on race has replaced for [her] something like French vs. American feminism" (364). It is interesting that although she clearly desired McDowell's approval, like the white child who insults its mammy one moment and demands a hug from her the next, Gallop seemed to expect that approval without having to do the thing most likely to win it: include McDowell and other black women scholars in the category of feminist theorists or treat black feminist critics as colleagues to be respected for the quality of their scholarship rather than as monsters to be feared for the quantity of their difference.

Gallop's confessional narrative—and McDowell's nonspeaking part in it—is problematic on so many levels that it is difficult to unpack and isolate its multiple fractures. Among other things, her remarks seem to me to exoticize, eroticize, anomalize, and masculinize (if not demonize) Deborah McDowell and the whole category of "black feminist critic" for which she is made to stand. Just what are the implications of conflating white French men and black American women as thorns in the side of white feminists, as Father Law? Gallop's transference is all the more vexed because she and her collaborators define "the men"—"them"—as "the enemy" throughout their conversation. In fact, as Nancy K. Miller puts it at one point, where feminist critique and French male theorists meet, the result is a "David and Goliath thing, with little Jane Gallop from Duluth taking out her slingshot to use on the great man" (Gallop et al. 358).

Not-so-little (academically speaking) Jane Gallop wields words like a slingshot; but McDowell, daunting as her scholarly accomplishments are, is no Goliath. There is a very different power relation in play. McDowell, whom I believe Gallop means in some way to honor, is actually demeaned by a narrative that casts her (and, by virtue of Gallop's own symbolic action, "the black feminist critic") somewhere between monster and mammy: demanding, demeaning, impossible to please, but at the same time possessing irresistible custodial power and erotic allure as the larger than life (racialized) Other.

I must rush to insert that mammy is my metaphor, not Gallop's. In fact there is nothing in Gallop's commentary that defines McDowell as anything other than "black feminist critic"—nothing that describes her work or that explains why she looms so large in Gallop's psyche while writ so small in her text. McDowell, the black feminist critic, is never anything other than *the Other* in "Criticizing Feminist Criticism." Race enters the conversation between these three white feminists only through the referenced bodies of objectified black women and only in those moments when the speakers tally their own and each other's sins of omission against women of color and their irritation at being chastised or, as they say, "trashed" for those exclusions.

Spurred by McDowell's criticism, Jane Gallop did indeed go on to add the Pryse and Spillers anthology *Conjuring* to her study of academic feminist theory, with quite interesting results. Provocative if tentative, Gallop's critique is at its most incisive where it attends to the tensions between the different organizing principles set out in the coeditors' individually authored introduction and afterword. Her critique is, for me anyway, most engaging where it claims and attempts to explain that *Conjuring* comes with its own deconstruction.

As Gallop reads it, Marjorie Pryse's introduction argues for a continuum of black women writers—a single, unified tradition rooted in and passing on what Pryse describes as the magic, folk wisdom, and "ancient power" of black women. Hortense Spillers's afterword, in contrast, foregrounds crosscurrents and discontinuities—differences within a tradition that is itself always in flux. Gallop concludes that Pryse frames and Spillers reframes. Whereas Spillers's reframing turns the reader's expectations inside out, Pryse's introductory framing, according to Gallop,

> corresponds to and evokes in the reader, at least in the white female academic, a fantasy which orients our reading of black women. I want the conjure woman; I want some ancient power that stands beyond the reaches

> of white male culture. I want black women as the idealized and exoticized
> alternative to European high culture. I want some pure outside and am fool
> enough to think I might find it in a volume published by Indiana University
> Press, with full scholarly apparatus. (*Around 1981* 169)

Again, this is a difficult passage to unpack, made even more so by the author's subsequent admission that she was disappointed that the book was "so
'academic'" and that she attributed its particularly erudite essays, with their
classical allusions, to critics she imagined to be white. Surely Gallop does not
mean what she seems to me to say here. Is she really admitting in print that
she expected a critical anthology subtitled *Black Women Fiction, and Literary
Tradition*—a book edited by two university professors, one of whom has long
been regarded as one of the deans of black feminist criticism—to be other
than scholarly, literate, and intellectually sophisticated?

To be fair, I think Gallop's tone is meant to be ironic, to point out—and
perhaps even to poke fun at—the essentializing fantasies of "the white female academic" reader who desires the Other to be other, who brings to the
text of the Other a different set of assumptions, who in effect expects to leave
high theory behind when she goes slumming in low culture. Hers is a dangerous strategy, but one that seems to be popular among white readers of
"black texts," who feel compelled to supplement their critiques with exposes
of their former racism (or sexism) in a kind of I-once-was-blind-but-now-I-
see way. (It worked for the composer of "Amazing Grace," a reformed slave
trader.) I will have more to say about this strategy in a moment, but for now
I want to linger over what is for me as much a critique of "the white female
academic" reader as of *Conjuring*.

Gallop in terms perhaps a bit too subtle for the subject is telling us that
she, as a white woman reader, wanted to find in this black book the exotic
black female Other, the "new delight," the "spice," to liven up the dull dish
of Western culture she as an academic usually consumes. "Since I am a white
academic," she writes, "what sort of fantasy not only renders those attributes
contemptible but, from an imagined identification with some righteous outside, allows me to cast them as aspersions on others?" (*Around 1981* 169).
In this instance, anyway, Gallop's anomalizing and exoticizing movements
are not entirely unselfconscious, as they seemed to be in "Criticizing Feminist Criticism." As her self-reflective question suggests, her essay is under-
pinned by an implicit critique of the primitivistic assumptions and expectations that "the white female academic" (I would be more generous and
say *some* white female academics) brings to the reading of texts by or about
black women.

Even more interesting, however, is Gallop's contention that Pryse's introduction invokes and evokes such desires in the reader, especially the white
reader. She says that reading *Conjuring* for a second time, even knowing that

Spillers's corrective essay lay ahead, she still nearly gave herself over to the introduction's romantic vision of the black female folk. "In this chapter I wanted to transmit this illusory take on the anthology," Gallop writes, "because I consider this illusion central to *our* reading of black women. *We* must confront *our* wish to find this ancient power, this pure outside of academic culture, before *we* deconstruct or correct *our* illusion" (170; emphasis added). In other words, the reader needs to absorb Pryse's framing before Spillers's reframing can take effect.

I am not quite sure how this follows: why do we need this critical *felix culpa*, this happy fall into what Gallop describes as the folk fantasies of Pryse before *we* can be rescued by the refined vision of Spillers? But perhaps my failure to follow Gallop's logic fully here stems from the fact that her "we" and "our" are at least as problematic as the ones I used earlier. I am not a part of her "we," and she is not a part of mine. Pryse's introduction did not evoke in *me* as a reader the desires Gallop evidently assumes it evokes in her universal "we." Although I cannot appropriate her "we," her larger point about the opposing strategies of Pryse's introduction and Spillers's afterword is one I want to take up and to politicize.

What happens if we add to Gallop's notion of the framing versus reframing, idealizing versus realizing, "good cop" versus "bad cop" routine of the coeditors the fact that Marjorie Pryse is white and Hortense Spillers black? What does it mean, then, that Spillers both brings up the rear and has the last word and, according to Gallop, "deconstructs or corrects" not only Pryse's romantic vision of a black female folk but the primitivistic expectations of the "white female academic"? Can one correct where there has been no error? Perhaps because she does not quite dare to play critical hardball with those whom she seems to take to be two black feminist critics, Gallop bends over backward to soft-pedal away the very ideological disjuncture she has so astutely identified. If the coeditors are simply playing out a well-rehearsed, mutually agreed upon routine, as Gallop ultimately concludes, why has Pryse positioned herself as the essentializing, idealizing white woman academic and left the real, corrective black feminist criticism to Spillers?

Gallop's reading of editorial matters in *Conjuring* unwittingly plays into my hand and punctuates my principal point about the dangers of a critical demeanor that demeans its subject in the very act of analyzing it. It is, of course, no better for me to use Gallop (or Pryse) as a metonym for white feminist critics than it is for Gallop to so use Deborah McDowell. Yet the wide-eyed wonderful illusions Gallop attributes to Pryse's introduction and the closed-eyed myopia of her own remarks in "Criticizing Feminist Criticism" demonstrate precisely why it remains so difficult for some black feminist scholars to entrust the texts of our familiar to the critical caretaking of white women (and men) for whom black women are newly discovered foreign bodies, always already Other.

CRITICAL APOLOGIA: THE *DRIVING MISS DAISY* CRAZY SYNDROME

Yet. Still. And but. If a Ph.D. in British literature is not a title deed to the African American text, neither is black skin. Romantic fantasies of an authentic, cohesive, magical, ancient, all-knowing black female folk are certainly not unique to white academics who would read black women. Some might argue that what is at issue is not simply the color or culture of the scholar but the kind, quality, and cultural competence of the scholarship. Black historian Carter Woodson reportedly welcomed the contributions of white scholars, "so long as they were the products of rigorous scholarship and were not contaminated by the venom of racial [and, I would add, gender] bias" (quoted by Meier and Rudwick 289). Unfortunately, however, such biases are ideologically inscribed and institutionally reproduced and as such are not easily elided—not even by the most liberal, the most sensitive, the most well-intentioned among us. I think, for example, of Adrienne Rich.

I had long been a fan of Rich's poetry, but I was rather late in coming to her prose. *Of Woman Born: Motherhood as Experience and Institution,* originally published in 1976, was more than a dozen years old before I gave myself the pleasure of reading it. For once, however, my timing could not have been better, for I "discovered" this essential book at a critical moment in my life and in the development of my feminism: on the eve of my fortieth birthday, as I wrestled with the likelihood of never having a child. Rich's brilliant analysis of motherhood as an instrument of patriarchy helped me come to terms with the constructedness of what I had been reared to believe were natural maternal instincts without which I was no woman. But for all that Rich's book gave me, it also took something away; and what it snatched from me, ironically and perhaps a little unfairly, has come to mean almost as much to me as what it gave.

For a moment in the penultimate chapter of this passionate and painful critique of motherhood, Rich turns her remarks toward the black woman who helped raise her. To this woman, who remains nameless, Rich assigns the designation "my Black mother." "My Black mother was 'mine,'" she writes, "only for four years, during which she fed me, dressed me, played with me, watched over me, sang to me, cared for me tenderly and intimately" (254). Rich goes on to describe poetically the physical presence of her Black mother, from whom she "learned—*nonverbally*—a great deal about the possibilities of dignity in a degrading situation" (254; emphasis added). Unaware of the degrading situation she creates with her words, she continues: "When I began writing this chapter I began to remember my Black mother again: her calm, realistic vision of things, her physical grace and pride, her beautiful soft voice. For years, she had drifted out of reach, in my searches backward through time, exactly as the double silence of sexism and racism intended her to do. She was meant to be utterly annihilated" (254–55).

THE OCCULT OF TRUE BLACK WOMANHOOD   *41*

To the double silences of sexism and racism Rich adds a third: the silence (and the blindness) of feminism. Like Jane Gallop, who I am sure meant to praise Deborah McDowell, Adrienne Rich no doubt means to honor the woman who cared for her as a child. But the poetry of her prose should not disguise the paternal arrogance of her words or mask the annihilating effect of her claim on the being she resurrects and recreates as "my Black mother." Silent and nameless in Rich's book, "my Black mother" has no identity of her own and, in fact, does not exist beyond the care and nurture she gave exclusively to the young Adrienne.

"'Childless' herself, she was a mother," Rich writes of her objectified subject. Her claim to "my Black mother" and her attempt to thrust motherhood upon a childless black woman domestic worker are all the more ironic because of what she claims for all women in the introduction to the anniversary edition of *Of Woman Born:* "The claim to personhood; the claim to share justly in the products of our labor, not to be used merely as an instrument, a role, a womb, a pair of hands or a back or a set of fingers; to participate fully in the decisions of our workplace, our community; to speak for ourselves, in our own right" (xxviii). Even in the midst of her own extended critique of the mystification of motherhood and the objectification of women as mothers, Rich has both mystified and objectified someone she can see only in the possessive case as "my Black mother." "My Black mother" is a role, a pair of hands; her function is to instruct the white child "nonverbally" in the ways of the world, even as she cannot speak "in [her] own right."[10]

The kind of transformative move Rich makes in invoking the silent racial, maternalized Other is in no way unique to her prose. The child may be father of the man in poetry, but frequently when white scholars reminisce about blacks from their past it is black mammy (metaphorically speaking, even where the mammy figure is a man) who mothers the ignorant white infant into enlightenment. Often as the youthful, sometimes guilty witness to or cause of the silent martyrdom of the older Other, the privileged white person inherits a wisdom, an agelessness, perhaps even a racelessness that entitles him or her to the raw materials of another's life and culture but, of course, not to the Other's condition.

Such transformative moves often occur in the forewords, afterwords, rationales, even apologias white scholars affix to their would-be scholarly readings of the black Other—discussions that methinks just may protest too much, perhaps suggesting a somewhat uneasy relationship between author and objectified subject. These prefaces acknowledge the "outsider" status of the authors—their privileged positions as white women or as men—even as they insist on the rightness of their entry into and the significance of their impact on the fields of black literature and history.

Gerda Lerner offers such a rationale in her preface to *Black Women in White America:* "Black people at this moment in history need above all to define themselves autonomously and to interpret their past, their present and their future" (xviii). Having called upon the black "physician" to heal her- or himself, Lerner then goes on to explain her presence in the operating room:

> Certainly, historians who are members of the culture, or subculture, about which they write will bring a special quality to their material. Their understanding and interpretation is apt to be different from that of the outsider. On the other hand, scholars from outside a culture have frequently had a *more challenging vision* than those closely involved in and bound by their own culture. Both angles of vision are complementary in arriving at the truth about the past and in finding out 'what actually happened." (xix; emphasis added)

A more challenging vision? Why does the perspective of the white scholar reading "the black experience" represent a more challenging vision?

Lerner is not alone in prefacing her work with such a self-serving claim. For reasons that I hope will become clear, I am reminded of "Who You For?"—the opening chapter of John Callahan's study *In the African-American Grain: Call-and-Response in Twentieth-Century Black Fiction*. In this chapter, Callahan takes us on a sentimental journey through his Irish American youth, which was *colored* not only by his being likened to niggers—"'Do you know the definition of an Irishman?'" the eight-year-old Callahan was asked by a much bigger Italian boy. "'A Nigger turned inside-out'" (5)—but also by the black male guardians and protectors who "taught [him] a great deal about the hard work of becoming a man" (9). The teaching tools used by one of these guardians—Bill Jackson, the chauffeur for the insurance company for which Callahan worked while in college—include a "prolonged *silent* challenge" after Callahan called him a black bastard (9; emphasis added) and his "trickster's way" of teaching Callahan certain lessons.

Like Adrienne Rich, Callahan describes his black guide as "silent," even as he credits the chauffeur with teaching him many things "essential to [his] own evolving voice and story" (10). Indeed Bill Jackson, the stereotypical black trickster, remains silent as he is employed by Callahan to claim not only Callahan's own Irish American voice but also entitlement to African American fictions of voice, fictions that in the author's words "connect and reconnect generations of Americans—African-American, yes and preeminently, but all others too, Irish-Americans like me, for instance—with those past and present oral traditions behind our evolving spoken and written voices" (21).

Here again a critical posturing that means to celebrate a literature to my mind actually demeans it by leveling and universalizing it. Callahan's introduction suggests that we are all brothers not only under the skin but under the book jacket as well. The white scholar understands "the African American experience" not in its own right, not on its own terms, but because he can make it like his own. With his voice, he can translate another's silence into his speech. He speaks through and for the Other. Bill Jackson's silence is telling in this translative move, but so too is his profession. It is altogether fitting and proper that Jackson is a chauffeur, for indeed Callahan's introduction and Jackson's role in it invoke for me what I call the *Driving Miss Daisy* syndrome: an intellectual slight of hand that transforms power and race relations to make best friends out of driver and driven, master and slave, boss and servant, white boy and black man.

When Callahan overhears the company vice president lumping together Irish and African Americans as "contemptible, expendable lower caste," he wishes for the craft, strength, skill, and smarts of a black football player he admires from a distance to help him speak up for himself (though apparently not for the niggers with whom he is compared). "My fate linked to African-Americans by that Yankee bank officer," Callahan writes, "I became more alert and sympathetic to black Americans my own age and younger who, though cursed, spat upon, and beaten, put their lives and voices on the line to uphold the law of the land and integrate public schools in the South" (8)

I feel as if I am supposed to applaud this declaration of allegiance, empathy, and understanding, but instead the claim of fellow feeling and universality—of linked fates and shared voice—makes me profoundly angry and mars my reading of what is actually a very fine book. Ultimately, Callahan's personal narrative, like Rich's, takes symbolic wealth from the martyred, romanticized black body but retains the luxury of refusing, erasing, or ignoring its material poverty. Twenty-five years later, John Callahan is a well-respected university professor, whereas, as he tells us in his introduction, Roy Fitch—the protective black mailroom manager under whom he once worked—"looks after" a building near the "plebeian end" of the city green (xi). Intent as he is on using Fitch to tell his story, Callahan does not comment on or I suspect even see the historical irony of their relative positions. Nor does he grasp the ironic implications of his own storytelling. "Don't climb no mountain on my back," he recalls Fitch saying to him years before in response to his awkward attempt to apologize for yet another racial slur. Had Callahan understood the signifying significance of Fitch's word—were he as good at interpreting speech as silence—he could not possibly have written the introduction he did.

However troubling Rich's and Callahan's apologias may be to me as a black woman reader, white British Victorianist Missy Dehn Kubitschek acknowledges an indebtedness to the latter for the inspiration behind the personal commentary that opens her own study of black women writers. "My admiration for 'Who You For?'" she writes in the preface to *Claiming the Heritage: African-American Women Novelists and History*, "led me to consider voicing my own simultaneously social and psychic travels as a prelude to this study of African-American women's novels" (xii).

Following Callahan's lead, Kubitschek opens her study with what she calls

"A Personal Preface," in which she offers a firsthand account (complete with family history) of how she as a white woman British Victorianist came to write a book about African American women novelists. Hers is a long story, but, briefly told, one of the principal players in her disciplinary conversion was her grandmother, a longtime armchair racist, who "changed her mind about race" after watching a television program about the "dangerous urban black ghetto" of East St. Louis. Mediated through the medium of television, urban blacks became objects of pity for Mrs. Dehn rather than fear. The possibilities of Grandmother Dehn's "impossible" change of heart at such an advanced age were "seismic" for Kubitschek, who was a graduate student at the time and who found in her grandmother's conversion the seeds of her own (xviii).

But other transformative encounters lay ahead for Kubitschek in her graduate student years—experiences that not only helped her get over her family's racism but over her own as well. Arriving early and alone for work one morning in the basement office of the English department building, Kubitschek was terrified first by a male voice and then by the sudden appearance of a black man. Reading her horror writ large across her face, the man, a construction worker apparently also early on site for the task of renovating the building, "quickly" and "quietly" explained that he just wanted to use the phone. "Of course, I had been afraid before I had seen that he was black," Kubitschek writes. "Rape is always a threat to women, always a possibility" (xxi). But seeing his black skin heightened her fear, she admits, and revealed her racism. Because she had recently read Richard Wright's "Big Boy Leaves Home," she knew, she says, the historical implications of her reaction. "'Race' ceased to be something that had constructed other people, especially blacks," as she began to understand herself as a racial as well as gendered being.

Rape is always a threat to women, particularly to a woman alone with a man. Black man, white man, green man from Mars, I darn well would have been afraid in Kubitschek's shoes, too. Her fear feels far more legitimate to me than the white liberal guilt that I suspect leads her to call that fear racism and to apologize for it in her preface to a book that is supposed to be about African American women writers. Through yet another troubling slight of text, Kubitschek's articulated awareness of her former racism becomes the authorizing agent behind her strange metamorphosis from British Victorianist to African Americanist.

I know I am misbehaving. I know I should be more patient, more sisterly, more respectful of other people's discoveries. I know my bad attitude comes from what in this instance might be called the arrogance of "black privilege": after all, I—whose earliest childhood memories include finding a snake in our mailbox shortly after we moved into an all-white neighborhood and being called "nigger" on my first day at an all-white elementary school—did not learn my racial consciousness from reading Richard Wright's "Big Boy Leaves Home" as an adult. But I mean my criticism as a kindness. Perhaps if I can approximate in words—however haltingly—what is so inexplicably problematic and profoundly offensive about these *Driving-Miss-Daisy*, some-of-my-best-friends-are-black, I-once-was-a-racist confessionals, I will do the field and all those who want to work in it a genuine favor. Perhaps if I can begin to delineate the difference between critical analysis that honors the field and guilty conscience rhetoric that demeans it, I can contribute something positive to the future production of scholarship on African American women. Unfortunately, the words do not come easily and the heart of what's the matter is a difficult place to get to. How do you tell people who do not get it in the first instance that it is only out of the arrogance of white privilege or male prerogative that they assume that it is an honor for a black woman to be proclaimed their black mother or their black friend or their black guardian or their black conscience?

It would be a mistake, however, for me to imply that these demeaning gestures are solely the product of white privilege and racial difference. For my money, the occult of true black womanhood has generated few more offensive renderings of African American women writers and critics than that offered by black literary theorist Houston Baker in *Workings of the Spirit: The Poetics of Afro-American Women's Writing*. Having largely ignored black women as cultural producers throughout his long and distinguished career, Baker suddenly takes them up in *Workings*. And like Missy Dehn Kubitschek, for whom the writing of African American women is a kind of survival kit,[11] Baker tells us in his conclusion that the shared horror of a friend's rape led him to seek solace in the "expressive resistances of Afro-American women's talking books." The writings of black women authors like Hurston, Morrison, and Shange helped teach him and his friend to move beyond being victim to being survivor. "The texts of Afro-American women writers," Baker says, "became mine and my friend's harrowing but sustaining path to a new, common, and, we thought, empowering discourse and commitment. To 'victim,' in my friend's semantics, was added the title and entitlement 'survivor.' Are we not all only that? Victim/Survivors?" (208–9).

Both Kubitschek and Baker seem unaware of the ways in which their survival-kit-claims to the black texts they critique potentially reinscribe African American women writers and their characters as magnanimous mammies who not only endure like Faulkner's Dilsey but whose primary function is to teach others to do the same as well. Although Baker is certainly entitled to tell his story, using his friend's rape to claim entitlement to the texts of black women writers—to authorize his entry into a field he has virtually ignored—makes for a story that I, for one, resent being asked to read as part of his critical discourse. For me, this maneuver compromises the integrity of his intellectual project; it makes the feminist concept that the personal is political a kind of bad joke. Like the some-of-my-best-friends-are-black tone of Kubitschek's preface, Callahan's introduction, and Rich's chapter, Baker's conclusion makes me distrust not his cultural competence, perhaps, but his gender sensibility—his ability to handle with care the sacred text of me and mine.

But I was made suspicious of *Workings of the Spirit* long before I got to its conclusion. For, like Lerner, Kubitschek, and Callahan, Baker also has included an introduction that calls attention to himself as outsider. He begins his study by acknowledging the prior claim and what he calls the justifiably "cautious anxieties" of black feminist critics such as Barbara Smith, Barbara Christian, and Mary Helen Washington, who long ago mined the "provinces of Afro-American women's expressivity" that he is just now entering. A "blackmale" scholar "will find cause to mind his steps in a demanding territory," he asserts, seemingly unaware of the step he misses with his province-metropole metaphor. Baker's language here works linguistically to confirm him in the very role he wants most to avoid—that of colonizing, come-lately "blackmale" critic. His diction is a small example of what I found to be a big problem with *Workings of the Spirit:* the hierarchical relation between what he inevitably treats as master (male) and minor (female) narrative traditions, even in this book dedicated to exploring black female expressivity. Rather than building on the work of black women scholars who excavated the field he is just now entering, Baker, for the most part, either ignores or dismisses what he implies is their primarily historical (as opposed to theoretical) feminist criticism in favor of his own masculinist theorizing and the black male writers and white male theorists he champions.

In *Workings of the Spirit,* our mothers' gardens are populated by what Baker terms *phenomenological* white men such as Gaston Bachelard along with the phenomenal black women—Hurston, Morrison, and Shange—who are the book's announced subjects. Indeed, Baker's study of black women writers marginalizes its female objectified subjects; male writers, critics, theorists, and male experience prevail as the text's principal referents. In *Workings*'s third chapter, for example, to even get to Baker's reading of Toni Morrison's *Sula,* one must first wade through thirty pages on Richard Wright. The attention to Wright (and other male artists and intellectuals) is justified, Baker argues, because "classic Afro-American male texts" provide a touchstone from which "to proceed by distinctions" in exploring the provinces of black female expressivity.

Baker's posterior positioning of Morrison within a chapter supposedly devoted to her work intersects the problematic I have been working with here. Like much of the new "new scholarship" that has come out of the occult of true black womanhood, Baker's book fails to live up to its own postmodern, deconstructive principles. It achieves neither inversion nor subversion; black women writers and the black feminist critics who read them remain fetishized bodies juxtaposed against analytical white or superior male minds. As objects of investigation in studies like Baker's, black women are constructed in terms of their difference from or (in the name of sisterhood) similarity to the spectator, whether the spectator is a black male theorist or a white feminist critic. In other words, the black female Other is made only more Other by the male theorist or by the "white female academic" (to use Jane Gallop's phrase) who views the objectified subject from a position of unrelinquished authority.

This failure of inversion is particularly alarming in Baker's case because of the enormous power he wields in the academy and the publishing industry. That *Workings of the Spirit* was published as part of a series Baker edits under the University of Chicago imprint suggests just how absolutely absolute power authorizes and reproduces itself. For black feminist studies, the ramifications of this power dynamic are potentially devastating: black feminist critics can be de-authorized with a roll of the presses, even as black women are deployed in a decidedly masculinist project that claims to "enter into dialogue" with them.

Baker is, of course, free to disagree with black women scholars (as we frequently do with each other), but his failure to take seriously their critical insights ultimately undermines his effort to enter into what he acknowledges is an already established dialogue. His privileging of male subjects in this book supposedly about black women writers becomes an act of silencing and makes his text the victim of its own intentional phallacy. By "intentional phallacy," I mean the gap between Baker's stated wish to avoid appropriating and objectifying the work and images of African American women through a "blackmale" gaze and the degree to which his text fosters rather than avoids such appropriations.

His essential and, I think, essentializing metaphors—black women as "departed daughters" and "spirit workers"—taken together with the uncontextualized photographs of black women interspersed throughout his book, raise questions about the gaze, about specularization and objectification, that Baker, despite his desire not to "colonize" the female subject, does not address or, I suspect, even see. This is both ironic and unfortunate, since Mae Henderson—one of the black feminist critics Baker faintly praises for her "fine theorizing"—called his attention to the problematic of the gaze generated by his work in a critique of an earlier essay of his that was the prototype for *Workings of the Spirit*. The danger, she warned, "is not only that of essentializing but of reinforcing the most conventional constructs of (black) femininity." Henderson was troubled in particular by the "*specularity* of [Baker's] rather spectacular theory" of black female spirituality. She cautioned him to rethink his treatment of black women in terms that would not objectify and idealize them (159).

Though the words of praise from Henderson excerpted on *Workings*'s back cover imply her endorsement of Baker's finished project, she in fact has offered the author both an elegantly incisive critique and an eloquently pointed admonition. Her cautionary tale has been little heeded, however;

Workings of the Spirit, I would argue, continues the idealization and specularization of black women that its prototypical essay began. The book's complementary phototext seems to me, in fact, to evoke precisely what Henderson identified as "the male activity of scopophilia." Largely unremarked
except for occasional captioned quotations from Baker's written word, the
images of black women interspersed throughout the text objectify graphi-
cally those whom the book objectifies linguistically. But in another example
of Baker's strategic deployment of women, this objectification is made
"okay" by the author's claim that the phototext is the handiwork not of senior "blackmale" theorist Houston Baker but of junior female scholars Elizabeth Alexander and Patricia Redmond. This, in fact, is Baker's final point,
his "last word":

> The phototext is the artistry of two young scholars. Their complementary
> text is a rich enhancement of the present work, and I cannot thank Eliza-
> beth Alexander and Patricia Redmond enough for their collaboration. It
> seems to me that the intertextuality represented by their effort makes the
> present work more engaging than it would otherwise have been. My initial
> idea was that such a text would comprise a type of countercurrent of signi-
> fication, soliciting always my own words, qualifying their "maleness." What
> emerged from the labors of Redmond and Alexander, however, is a visuali-
> zation of an Afro-American women's poetics. Eyes and events engage the
> reader/viewer in a solicitous order of discourse that asks: "Who reads here?"
> (212)

If these photos indeed could ask such a question, I suspect that their answer would be, "A man." Baker means for the photographs to speak for themselves of "the space, place, and time of Afro-American women" (213), but it
is unclear how they are to do so placed unproblematically in the midst of
what is—despite his claims about the collaborative efforts of Alexander and
Redmond—*his* project. Whose project the phototext is becomes even clearer
when we know that at the time the book was compiled Alexander and Redmond were graduate students to whom Baker assigned the task of assembling
a complementary photo essay. The image that Alexander and Redmond presented to Baker as the "parting shot" of his book is of a young black woman,
her mouth open wide as if in a scream. I wonder what it means that the black
woman depicted in midscream is literally, physically, clinically mute.

TOWARD A CONCLUSION

I am not quite certain what to make of the ground I have covered in this article or where to go from here. More bewitched, bothered, and bewildered
than ever by my own problematic, I find myself oddly drawn to (gulp) William
Faulkner. The griefs of great literature, Faulkner suggested in his Nobel Prize

acceptance speech, must grieve on universal bones. I realize that I have heard this before—and not just from Faulkner. The Self recognition spontaneously generated by the literature of the ennobled Other is the essence of Callahan's professed link to African American "fictions of voice" and the medium of Baker's and Kubitschek's claimed connection to the texts of black women. And they are not alone in this kind of association with the ennobled Other. In the words of three white feminist academics who claim to identify closely with the explicit depiction of physical and psychic abuse in the fiction of black women writers such as Toni Morrison, Alice Walker, and Gayl Jones: "We, as white feminists, are drawn to black women's visions because they concretize and make vivid a system of oppression." Indeed, they continue, "it has not been unusual for white women writers to seek to understand their oppression through reference to the atrocities experienced by other groups" (Sharpe et al. 146). For these feminists, as for Baker and Kubitschek, the lure of black women's fiction is, at least in part, its capacity to teach others how to endure and prevail, how to understand and rise above not necessarily the pain of black women but their own.

Is this usage of black women's texts a bad thing? If Faulkner is right—if it is the writer's duty to help humankind endure by reminding us of our capacity for courage and honor and hope and pride and compassion and pity and sacrifice and survival—black women writers have done the job particularly well. The griefs of African American women indeed seem to grieve on universal bones—"to concretize and make vivid a system of oppression." But it also seems (and herein lies the rub) that in order to grieve "universally," to be "concrete," to have "larger meaning," the flesh on these bones ultimately always must be white or male.

This, then, is the final paradox and the ultimate failure of the evidence of experience: to be valid—to be true—black womanhood must be legible as white or male; the texts of black women must be readable as maps, indexes to someone else's experience, subject to a seemingly endless process of translation and transference. Under the cult of true black womanhood, the colored body, as Cherríe Moraga has argued, is "thrown over a river of tormented history to bridge the gap" (xv), to make connections—connections that in this instance enable scholars working in exhausted fields to cross over into the promised land of the academy.

Both black women writers and the black feminist critics who have brought them from the depths of obscurity into the ranks of the academy have been such bridges. The trouble is that, as Moraga points out, bridges get walked on over and over and over again. This sense of being a bridge—of being walked on and passed over, of being used up and burnt out, of having to "publish while perishing," as some have described their situations—seems to be a part of the human condition of many black women scholars. Though neither the academy nor mainstream feminism has paid much attention to the crisis of black female intellectuals, the issue is much on the minds of black feminist scholars, particularly in the wake of the Thomas-Hill hearings, the critique of professional women and family values, and the loss of Audre Lorde and Sylvia Boone in a single year. So serious are these issues that the state and fate of black women in and around the university were the subjects of a national conference held at the Massachusetts Institute of Technology in January 1994. Entitled "Black Women in the Academy: Defending Our Name, 1894–1994," this conference, the first of its kind, drew together nearly two thousand black women from institutions across the country. The conference organizers have said that they were overwhelmed by the response to their call for papers: they were instantly bombarded by hundreds of abstracts, letters, faxes, and phone calls from black women describing the hypervisibility, superisolation, emotional quarantine, and psychic violence of their precarious positions in academia.

I do not mean to imply that all black women scholars see themselves as what Hurston called "tragically colored," but I think that it is safe to say that these testimonies from across the country represent a plaintive cry from black women academics who see themselves and their sisters consumed by exhaustion, depression, loneliness, and a higher incidence of such killing diseases as hypertension, lupus, cancer, diabetes, and obesity. But it also seems to me that Jane Gallop's anxieties about African American women, Nancy K. Miller's fear that there is no position from which a middle-class white woman can speak about race without being offensive, and Houston Baker's desire for dialogue with black women scholars also represent plaintive cries. Clearly both white women and women and men of color experience the pain and disappointment of failed community.

As much as I would like to end on a positive note, I have little faith that our generation of scholars—black and nonblack, male and female—will succeed in solving the problems I have taken up here. We are too set in our ways, too alternately defensive and offensive, too much the products of the white patriarchal society that has reared us and the white Eurocentric educational system that has trained us. If ever there comes a day when white scholars are forced by the systems that educate them to know as much about "the Other" as scholars of color are required to know about so-called dominant cultures, perhaps black women will no longer be treated as consumable commodities.

Until that day, I see a glimmer of hope shining in the bright eyes of my students who seem to me better equipped than we to explore the intersection of racial and gender difference. I was impressed by the way young women—black and white—and one lone white man in a seminar I offered on black feminist critical theory were able to grapple less with each other and more with issues, to disagree without being disagreeable, and to learn from and with each other. I wonder if there is a lesson for us older (but not necessarily wiser) academics in their interaction. I wonder what it would mean for feminist scholarship in general if *woman* were truly an all-inclusive category, if "as a woman" ceased to mean "as a white woman." I wonder what it would mean for women's studies, for black studies, for American studies, if women of color, white women, and men were truly able to work together to produce the best of all possible scholarship.

Although the editorial scheme of *Conjuring* may employ different, even contradictory notions of text and tradition, as Jane Gallop suggests, perhaps the strategy of black and white women working together on intellectual projects is one that we should embrace. I do not mean to suggest that we can or should police each other, but I wonder about the possibilities of what my colleague Sharon Holland calls "complementary theorizing."[12] I wonder what shape Gallop's conversation with Nancy K. Miller and Marianne Hirsch might have taken were women of color talked with rather than about. I wonder what kind of book *Workings of the Spirit* might have been were it truly a collaborative effort with black women or even with one black woman—perhaps the woman with whom Baker says he first discovered the healing powers of African American women's fiction. I have never met Adrienne Rich, but if we had been friends or colleagues, if I had had the honor of reading *Of Woman Born* in manuscript, perhaps I could have given back to her some of what her book gave me by pointing out to her (rather than to the readers of this book) the problems of "my Black mother." However idle they may appear, for me these speculations about what might have been offer a measure of hope about what yet might be.

NOTES

"The Occult of True Black Womanhood: Critical Demeanor and Black Feminist Studies" was originally published in *Signs* 19.3 (1994): 591–629. (U of Chicago P. Reprinted by permission of the University of Chicago Press.

1. See, among many others, Bambara; Beal; Davis "Reflections" and *Women;* Ladner; Washington "In Pursuit," "Introduction," "Their Fiction," and "Zora Neale Hurston"; Foster; Skeeter; Christian *Novelists* and "Images"; B. Smith "Notes" and "Toward"; Harley and Terborg-Penn; Noble; Bell, Parker, and Guy-Shaftall; Dill "Across," "Dialectics," and "Race"; Hine and Wittenstein; Hine "Four Black" and *When the Truth;* hooks *Ain't I;* Steady; and Hull, Scott, and Smith.

2. For whatever it may suggest about the crisis and the production of the black intellectual, it is interesting to note that the intellectual labors of Baker, Gates, and West have been chronicled and lauded in cover stories and feature articles in publications such as the *New York Times,* the *Boston Globe, Newsweek,* the *Washington Post,* and *Time* magazine. I recall seeing only one article on Mary Helen Washington, in the "Learning" section of the Sunday *Globe* (although, of course, there may have been others). The article was dominated by a stunning picture of Washington, ac-

companied by a caption describing her as a scholar-teacher who "helps restore sight to the 'darkened eye' of American literary tradition." Despite this very fitting and promising caption, the article went on to say remarkably little about Washington's actual scholarship and its impact on American literary studies (see Weld).

3. Most of the black feminist critics Baker lists have produced essays, articles, and books too numerous to name. In addition to a wealth of critical essays, Thadious Davis, Trudier Harris, and Deborah McDowell have made tremendous contributions to the fields of African American and black feminist literary studies through their editorial work on a number of important projects, including volume 51 of the *Dictionary of Literary Biography* (Harris) and Beacon Press's Black Women Writers Series (McDowell). See among many other pivotal essays, introductions, and books, McDowell "New Directions"; Tate; Hull, Scott, and Smith; Wall "Poets"; McKay; Wade-Gayles; Carby "It Jus' Be's" and *Reconstructing;* Joyce; V. Smith; and Spillers.

4. For such a review of the critical literature, see Carby *Reconstructing* and Wall "Taking Positions."

5. See, for example, the introduction and conclusion to my study *The Coupling Convention: Sex, Text, and Tradition in Black Women's Fiction* (1993).

6. Lerner does mention Nichols briefly in the bibliographical essay at the end of *Black Women in White America*. Nichols's book, she writes, "offers an excellent synthesis of the literature of slave narratives and evaluates their authenticity" (620).

7. White deconstructivist Barbara Johnson has called Henry Louis Gates on his repeated use of the term "our own." Johnson notes that in a single discussion "Gates uses the expression 'our own' no fewer than nineteen times." She goes on to query the meaning behind his ambiguous phrase: "Does Gates mean all black people (whatever that might mean)? All Afro-Americans? All scholars of Afro-American literature? All black men? All scholars trained in literary theory who are now interested in the black vernacular? See Gates; and Johnson.

8. For those of us tempted to make common (black female) experience the essence of critical interpretation or to view black women's fiction as expressive realism, Belsey's words may be prohibitively instructive: "The claim that a literary form reflects the world is simply tautological," she writes. "What is intelligible as realism is the conventional and therefore familiar. . . . It is intelligible as 'realistic' precisely because it reproduces what we already seem to know" (47).

9. Echoing the complaint that women of color have leveled for some time (at least since Sojourner Truth's public query, "Ain't I a woman," first asked more than 140 years ago), Spelman argues that holding their own experiences to be normative, many white feminists historically have given little more than lip service to the significance of race and class in the lives of women.

10. In the tenth anniversary revised edition of *Of Woman Born,* a wiser, reflective Adrienne Rich attempts to expand and adjust her vision in light of 1980s concerns and considerations. To her discussion of "my Black mother" she appends a footnote that reads in part: "The above passage overpersonalizes and does not, it seems to me now, give enough concrete sense of the actual position of the Black domestic worker caring for white children" (255). Even ten years later, Rich has failed to recognize that she is talking about another woman—another woman who is not her black mother but a laborer whose role as mammy is also socially, politically, and economically constructed.

11. In the final moments of her personal preface, we learn that the lessons of Grandma Dehn and the black construction worker notwithstanding, it was actually the survival strategies embedded in black literature that ultimately led Kubitschek to the work of African American women writers. "The stories that constitute African-American literature say that oppression kills and that people survive oppression," she tells us. "Wanting to know more about survival brought me here" (xxiii).

12. Sharon Holland, letter to the author, September 1993.

WORKS CITED

Abel, Elizabeth. "Black Writing, White Reading: Race and the Politics of Feminist Interpretation." *Critical Inquiry* 19 (1993): 470–98.

Ammons, Elizabeth. *Conflicting Stories: American Women Writers at the Turn into the Twentieth Century.* New York: Oxford UP, 1992.

Andrews, William L., ed. *Sisters of the Spirit: Three Black Women's Autobiographies of the Nineteenth Century.* Bloomington: Indiana UP, 1986.

Baker, Houston, Jr. *Workings of the Spirit: The Poetics of Afro-American Women's Writing.* Chicago: U of Chicago P, 1991.

Bambara, Toni Cade. *The Black Woman.* New York: New American Library, 1970.

Beal, Frances. "Double Jeopardy: To Be Black and Female." *Sisterhood Is Powerful.* Ed. Robin Morgan. New York: Random House, 1970. 340–52.

Bell, Roseanne P., Bettye J. Parker, and Beverly Guy-Sheftall, eds. *Sturdy Black Bridges: Visions of Black Women in Literature.* Garden City, N.Y.: Anchor, 1979.

Belsey, Catherine. *Critical Practices.* New York: Routledge, 1980.

Brown, William Wells. *Clotel; or, The President's Daughter: A Narrative of Slave Life in the United States.* With an introduction by William Farrison. 1853. New York: Carol Publishing, 1989.

Callahan, John F. *In the African-American Grain: Call-and-Response in Twentieth-Century Black Fiction.* 2nd ed. Middletown, Conn.: Wesleyan UP, 1989.

Carby, Hazel. "It Jus' Be's Dat Way Sometime: The Sexual Politics of Women's Blues." *Radical America* 20.4 (1986): 9–22.

———. *Reconstructing Womanhood: The Emergence of the Afro-American Woman Novelist.* New York: Oxford UP, 1987.

Christian, Barbara. *Black Women Novelists: The Development of a Tradition, 1892–1976.* Westport, Conn.: Greenwood, 1980.

———. "Images of Black Women in Afro-American Literature: From Stereotype to Character." 1975. *Black Feminist Criticism: Perspectives on Black Women Writers.* New York: Pergamon, 1985. 1–30.

Christian, Barbara, Ann duCille, Sharon Marcus, Elaine Marks, Nancy K. Miller, Sylvia Schafer, and Joan W. Scott. "Conference Call." *differences* 2 (1990): 52–108.

Cooper, Anna Julia. *A Voice from the South.* With an introduction by Mary Helen Washington. 1892. New York: Oxford UP, 1988.

Davis, Angela. "Reflections on the Black Woman's Role in the Community of Slaves." *Black Scholar* 3 (1971): 3–15.

———. *Women, Race, and Class.* New York: Random House, 1981.

Dill, Bonnie Thornton. "Across the Barriers of Race and Class: An Exploration of the Relationship between Female Domestic Servants." Diss. New York U, 1979.

———. "The Dialectics of Black Womanhood." *Signs* 4 (1979): 543–55.

———. "Race, Class, and Gender: Prospects for an All-inclusive Sisterhood." *Feminist Studies* 9 (1983): 131–50.

duCille, Ann. *The Coupling Convention: Sex, Text, and Tradition in Black Women's Fiction.* New York: Oxford UP, 1993.

Fender, Stephen. "African Accents, Tall Tales." Rev. of *Was Huck Black? Mark Twain and African American Voices,* by Shelley Fisher Fishkin, and *Mark Twain and the Art of the Tall Tale,* by Henry B. Wonham. *Times Literary Supplement* 16 July 1993: 27.

Fishkin, Shelley Fisher. *Was Huck Black? Mark Twain and African American Voices.* New York: Oxford UP, 1993.

Foster, Frances. "Changing Concept of the Black Woman." *Journal of Black Studies* June 1973: 433–52.

Gallop, Jane. *Around 1981: Academic Feminist Literary Theory.* New York: Routledge, 1992.

Gallop, Jane, Marianne Hirsch, and Nancy K. Miller. "Criticizing Feminist Criticism." *Conflicts in Feminism.* Ed. Marianne Hirsch and Evelyn Fox Keller. New York: Routledge, 1990. 349–69.

Gates, Henry Louis, Jr. "Canon-Formation and the Afro-American Tradition." *Afro-American Literary Studies in the 1990s.* Ed. Houston Baker Jr. and Patricia Redmond. Chicago: U of Chicago P, 1989. 13–49.

Harley, Sharon, and Rosalyn Terborg-Penn, eds. *The Afro-American Woman: Struggles and Images.* New York: Kennikat, 1978.

Harris, Trudier, ed. *Afro-American Writers from the Harlem Renaissance to 1940.* Detroit: Gale Research, 1986. Vol. 51 of *Dictionary of Literary Biography.*

Hemenway, Robert. *Zora Neale Hurston: A Literary Biography.* Urbana: U of Illinois P, 1977.

Henderson, Mae. "Commentary on 'There Is No More Beautiful Way: Theory and the Poetics of Afro-American Women's Writing,' by Houston Baker." *Afro-American Literary Studies in the 1990s.* Ed. Houston A. Baker Jr. and Patricia Redmond. Chicago: U of Chicago P, 1989.

Herskovits, Melville J. *The American Negro: A Study in Racial Crossing.* 1928. Westport, Conn.: Greenwood, 1985.

———. *Dahomey.* New York: Augustin, 1938.

———. *The Myth of the Negro Past.* Boston: Beacon, 1941

Herskovits, Melville J., and Frances Herskovits. *Suriname Folklore.* New York: Columbia UP, 1936.

Hine, Darlene Clark. "The Four Black History Movements: A Case for the Teaching of Black History." *Teaching History: A Journal of Methods* 5 (1980): 115.

———. *When the Truth Is Told: A History of Black Women's Culture and Community in Indiana, 1875–1950.* Indianapolis: National Council of Negro Women, 1981.

Hine, Darlene Clark, and Kate Wittenstein. "Female Slave Resistance: The Economics of Sex." *Western Journal of Black Studies* 3.2 (1979): 123–27.

Hirsch, Marianne, and Evelyn Fox Keller. *Conflicts in Feminism.* New York: Routledge, 1990.

hooks, bell. *Ain't I a Woman?* Boston: South End, 1981.

———. *Black Looks: Race and Representation.* Boston: South End, 1992.

Hull, Gloria, Patricia Bell Scott, and Barbara Smith, eds. *All the Women Are White, All the Blacks Are Men, but Some of Us Are Brave.* Old Westbury, N.Y.: Feminist P, 1982.

Jacobs, Harriet. *Incidents in the Life of a Slave Girl, Written by Herself.* 1861. Ed. Jean Fagan Yellin. Cambridge, Mass.: Harvard UP, 1987.

Johnson, Barbara. "Response to Gates." *Afro-American Literary Studies in the 1990s.* Ed. Houston Baker Jr. and Patricia Redmond. Chicago: U of Chicago P, 1989. 39–44.

Joyce, Joyce A. "The Black Canon: Reconstructing Black American Literary Criticism." *New Literary History* 18 (1987): 335–44.

Karamcheti, Indira. "Caliban in the Classroom." *Radical Teacher* 44 (1993): 13–17.

Kubitschek, Missy Dehn. *Claiming the Heritage: African-American Women Novelists and History.* Jackson: UP of Mississippi, 1991.

Ladner, Joyce. *Tomorrow's Tomorrow: The Black Woman.* New York: Doubleday, 1972.

Lerner, Gerda. *Black Women in White America: A Documentary History.* New York: Random House, 1972.

Lewis, David Levering. "Parallels and Divergences: Assimilationist Strategies of Afro-American and Jewish Elites from 1910 to the Early 1930s." *Journal of American History* 71 (1984): 543–64.

McDowell, Deborah. "New Directions for Black Feminist Criticism." 1980. *The New Feminist Criticism: Essays on Women, Literature, and Theory.* Ed. Elaine Showalter. New York: Pantheon, 1985.

McKay, Nellie. *Jean Toomer, Artist: A Study of His Literary Life and Work, 1894–1936.* Chapel Hill: U of North Carolina P, 1984.

Meier, August, and Elliot Rudwick. *Black History and the Historical Profession, 1915–1980.* Urbana: U of Illinois P, 1986.

Moraga, Cherrie. Preface. *This Bridge Called My Back: Writings by Radical Women of Color.* Ed. Cherrie Moraga and Gloria Anzaldua. New York: Kitchen Table, Women of Color P, 1981. xiii–xix.

Mossell, Mrs. N. F. *The Work of the Afro-American Woman.* 1894. With an introduction by Joanne Braxton. New York: Oxford UP, 1988.

Nichols, Charles. *Many Thousand Gone: The Ex-Slaves' Account of Their Bondage and Freedom.* Bloomington: Indiana UP, 1963.

Noble, Jeanne. *Beautiful, Also, Are the Souls of My Black Sisters.* Englewood Cliffs, N.J.: Prentice-Hall, 1978.

Pryse, Marjorie, and Hortense Spillers, eds. *Conjuring: Black Women, Fiction, and Literary Tradition.* Bloomington: Indiana UP, 1985.

Rich, Adrienne. *Of Woman Born: Motherhood as Experience and Institution.* 1976. New York: Norton, 1986.

Sharpe, Patricia, F. E. Mascia-Lee, and C. B. Cohen. "White Women and Black Men: Different Responses to Reading Black Women's Texts." *College English* 52 (1990): 142–53.

Skeeter, Sharon J. "Black Women Writers: Levels of Identity." *Essence* 4 (1973): 3–10.

Smith, Barbara. "Notes for Yet Another Paper on Black Feminism, or Will the Real Enemy Please Stand Up?" *Conditions: Five* (1979): 123–27.

———. "Toward a Black Feminist Criticism." 1977. *The New Feminist Criticism: Essays on Women, Literature, and Theory.* Ed. Elaine Showalter. New York: Pantheon, 1985.

Smith, Valerie. *Self-Discovery and Authority in Afro-American Narrative.* Cambridge, Mass.: Harvard UP, 1987.

Spelman, Elizabeth. *Inessential Woman: Problems of Exclusion in Feminist Thought.* Boston: Beacon, 1988.

Spillers, Hortense. "Mama's Baby, Papa's Maybe: An American Grammar Book." *Diacritics* 17 (1987): 65–81.

Spivak, Gayatri Chakravorty. *In Other Worlds: Essays in Cultural Politics.* New York: Routledge, 1988.

———. "In Praise of *Sammy and Rosie Get Laid.*" *Critical Quarterly* 31.2 (1989): 80–88.

Steady, Filomina Chioma, ed. *The Black Woman Cross-Culturally.* Cambridge, Mass.: Schenkman, 1981.

Tate, Claudia. *Interviews with Black Women Writers.* New York: Continuum, 1981.

Wade-Gayles, Gloria. *No Crystal Stair: Visions of Race and Sex in Black Women's Fiction.* New York: Pilgrim P, 1984.

Walker, Alice. "In Search of Our Mothers' Gardens." *Ms.* May 1974: 64–70, 105.

Wall, Cheryl A. "Poets and Versifiers, Singers and Signifiers: Women Writers of the Harlem Renaissance." *Women, the Arts, and the 1920s in Paris and New York.* Ed. Kenneth W. Wheeler and Virginia Lee Lussier. New Brunswick, N.J.: Transaction, 1982. 74–98.

———, ed. "Taking Positions and Changing Words." *Changing Our Own Words: Essays on Criticism, Theory, and Writing by Black Women.* New Brunswick, N.J.: Rutgers UP, 1989. 1–15.

Wallace, Michele. "Who Owns Zora Neale Hurston? Critics Carve Up the Legend." *Invisibility Blues.* New York: Verso, 1990. 172–86.

Washington, Mary Helen. "In Pursuit of Our Own History." *Midnight Birds: Stories of Contemporary Black Women Writers.* Ed. Mary Helen Washington. Garden City, N.Y.: Anchor, 1980. xiii–xxv.

———. Introduction. *Black-Eyed Susans: Classic Stories by and about Black Women.* Ed. Mary Helen Washington. Garden City, N.Y.: Anchor, 1975. ix–xxxii.

———. "Their Fiction Becomes Our Reality: Black Women Image Makers." *Black World* August 1974: 10–18.

———. "Zora Neale Hurston: The Black Woman's Search for Identity." *Black World* August 1972: 68–75.

Weld, Elizabeth New. "The Voice of Black Women." *Boston Globe* 14 February 1988: 98, 100.

Williams, Sherley Anne. Foreword. *Their Eyes Were Watching God.* By Zora Neale Hurston. Urbana: U of Illinois P, 1978.

Wilson, Harriet. *Our Nig; or, Sketches from the Life of a Free Black.* 1859. New York: Vintage, 1983.

Winkler, Karen J. "A Scholar's Provocative Query: Was Huckleberry Finn Black?" *Chronicle of Higher Education* 8 July 1992: A6-A8.

Doing Justice to the Subjects

Mimetic Art in a Multicultural Society: The Work of Anna Deavere Smith

Tania Modleski

1

In *Fires in the Mirror,* her smash hit one woman show performed at New York's Public Theater in the summer of 1992, African American performer Anna Deavere Smith plays the parts of twenty-nine people whom she interviewed about the Crown Heights riots that occurred in Brooklyn the previous year. She invited people who were directly involved in the Crown Heights events to discuss their experiences and asked others—people like Angela Davis and Ntzoake Shange—to reflect more generally on issues of racial identity. Although Smith excerpted the remarks of her subjects, she aimed for complete fidelity to their speech acts, repeating their words verbatim and even including slips of speech and stammerings. Later Smith designed a similar piece, *Twilight: Los Angeles, 1992* about the Rodney King beating incident and the turmoil that ensued. This piece was first performed at the Mark Taper Forum in Los Angeles. It was then revised for a run at the New York Public Theater and revised again for Broadway's Cort Theater. Both of these theatrical pieces not only concern public events but have *become* major public events, often uncannily producing and reproducing the politics reflected in the works and revealing with exceptional clarity that socially engaged criticism must understand how the media and other institutions shape interpretation. Before proceeding to a discussion of Smith's work itself, therefore, I want to analyze the responses of the critics to Smith's performances. In what follows I focus more on *Fires in the Mirror* than on *Twilight* because as a more reflexive text that aims to account for the complex processes of identity formation, *Fires in the Mirror* clues us into the theoretical and political issues at stake in Smith's work as a whole.

Smith's performances are part of an ongoing series of pieces entitled *On the Road: A Search for American Character.* Typically Smith constructs her pieces as follows: having been invited to come into a specific community to inter-view people about a controversial event, usually one involving racial conflict and sometimes gender antagonism as well, she records interviews with the people involved, memorizes their words, and "performs" them on stage. The interviewees are invited to attend the performance. In her earlier work, au-dience awareness that the interviewees were present had a very unsettling ef-fect, particularly because audiences often responded in ways that seem to have been unanticipated by the subjects—for example, bursting into laughter over something said with great earnestness or passion.[1] In the earlier work too, au-diences often knew the people whom Smith impersonated, but as the work gained international attention, it inevitably changed, so that the "communi-ties" being investigated are major metropolises and the events are of cata-clysmic proportions; the people being performed are thus most likely un-known to audience members, or known only through media representations.

In some ways, Smith's work marks her as an exemplary postmodern artist. She problematizes the authority of the speaking subject, foregrounding the split between the way people consciously present themselves and the way they appear. Other postmodern aspects of Smith's art include the reliance on quo-tation and allegory (by including the observations of critics and theorists, the work may be said to contain an interpretation of itself) and the site-specific nature of the performances.[2] Indeed, as regards this latter aspect, Smith is a pioneer and the theater owes her a great debt on this account alone, for although site-specificity is common in the visual arts, it has hith-erto not characterized contemporary theatrical practice. Yet its postmod-ernism notwithstanding, there is something about the work that induces even sophisticated poststructuralist critics to lapse into older critical vocabularies in analyzing it. For example, Barbara Johnson, while insisting on the craft involved in putting the piece together, can nevertheless speak of the way "'Fires in the Mirror' holds its mirror up to America" (10). Certain questions thus inevitably arise about the work's relation to theoretical issues concern-ing art and representation. Does this almost "purely" mimetic art, hailed by so many critics in the mainstream press as presenting "the true words of real people," testify to a naive belief in the myth of presence, or to the belief in language's function to mime or mirror "a pre-given reality," or to the belief in the artist's representativity, her ability to speak for, or in this case *as,* the subaltern? These are questions with both metaphysical and political di-mensions, which we might sum up in a single question: In light of the de-mands of black America for justice ("no justice, no peace") during the re-cent political strife in Crown Heights and in Los Angeles, can Smith's representations ever (as we say of photographs with especially fair likenesses) hope to do "justice" to their subjects?

Certainly, the overwhelmingly white male critical establishment has pic-tured Smith in terms that evoke the very emblem of liberal justice, the woman with the scales, and have continually pronounced her to be "fair," "impartial," "balanced." Frank Rich wrote of *Fires in the Mirror*, "Her show is a self-contained example of what one person can accomplish, at the very least, in disseminating accurate, unbiased inside reportage." The highest praise thus came in the narcissistic form of journalists lauding Smith's skills as a journalist, praise that in an ironic kind of postmodern reciprocity offset the press's earlier characterization of the riot-torn Crown Heights, with its angry inhabitants and "outside agitators" commandeering the airwaves, as "theater" (Klein 28). Smith herself has sometimes seemed to acquiesce in the assessment of her work as uncommitted to a particular viewpoint. In a *Newsweek* review, Smith discusses with Jack Kroll her reluctance to drop from *Twilight*'s final script Stanley Sheinbaum's account of how his attempt to talk to gang members aroused the fury of the police: "'Stanley said, "F— you! I'll talk to whoever I like. Why do I have to be on one side?"'" Smith says: "'It broke my heart to lose that, because it helps me to make the point of why do *I* have to be on one side?'" ("Fire" 63). And, of course, this passage helps Kroll to make the point of why does *he* have to be on one side (when even the black female author isn't)? Thus by mimicking the mimic, the media reviewers avoid having to deal with the political issues at the heart of Smith's work.

From the view that truth lies "in the balance" of the opposite sides of what Jean-François Lyotard calls the postmodern agon, it is but a step to declaring that the struggles (between blacks and Jews, blacks and Koreans, blacks and whites, and so on) are meaningless in their own terms. Observe the contortions of thought in the following remarks of a *New York Times* discussion of *Fires in the Mirror:*

> With the rioting in Los Angeles fresh in our minds, the obvious remark
> to make about "Fires in the Mirror" is that it couldn't be more timely. Yet
> the timelessness of the piece is what impressed me. Put the specifics aside
> and you have a view of people so at odds with one another that human
> nature itself seems to be to blame. We are stubborn creatures, claiming
> right for ourselves and wrong for the other guy, and that stubbornness
> repeatedly dooms us to violence. Nonetheless, we advance a thousand
> and one reasons, grand and pitiful, to explain why giving an inch just
> isn't possible. (D. Richards H5)

And so, a work which started out scrupulously to reproduce the specifics of people's opinions, utterances, and mannerisms and to locate itself in the time and place of the struggle it documents ends by being acclaimed in terms that evacuate all politics and "set aside" all specifics.

Doubtless this move is facilitated by the fact that the work in question is a one-person show and "specifically" (to invoke the word some are so eager to set aside) a one-woman show—and even more specifically, a one-woman show by an African American. Because Smith plays all the parts herself, her body seems for many of the reviewers to contain—in various senses of the word—the conflicts she acts out, emblematizing our national motto, "In Many One." Indeed, Kroll's review of *Fires in the Mirror* begins by quoting Whitman, "I am large, I contain multitudes" (Kroll, "A Woman" 74). John Lahr also compares Smith to Whitman, to the latter's disadvantage: "Whitman's great poem, of course, invoked the voices of America but celebrated only himself" (90). Yet surely there are significant differences between the self-description of a white man who says he "contains multitudes" (or even who says he's large) and the designation of a black woman as a container of the teeming multitudes. Does not this line when it is applied to an African American woman conjure up the notion of the black woman as the archetype of the maternal, as, in the words of one reviewer, "a vessel of empathy for people caught in some of life's inexplicable situations"? (Clines C9).

The view that female actors are "vessels of empathy" is not new. Diderot in his writings on the theater consigned women to the category of "passive mimesis," evoked by "pity or sympathy, compassion, the first and most primitive moral and social aptitude." As opposed to the male actor whose work involves "active, virile, formative, properly artistic . . . mimesis," women according to Diderot "alienate, split or alter themselves . . . only in passion and passivity, in the state of being possessed or being inhabited" (Lacoue-Labarthe 263).[3] In this regard, we might note the tendency of reviewers to use language about Smith that conjures up the image of her as a kind of spiritual medium: "A Seance with History" blares the headline of one review (Wright). This image, needless to say, is doubly fraught when used to describe a black woman.

As medium, the woman's body becomes coextensive with the theater itself. Jack Kroll, at the conclusion of his review of *Twilight,* quotes Rodney King's aunt, who says she has learned about love from watching Smith's show, and then observes, "That's a lot of power for theater to have. The name of this theater is Anna Deavere Smith" ("Fire" 63). The association of the female body with the space of theater, some have argued, goes far back in Western thought. Luce Irigaray argues that Plato's cave is a figure for the female body, the womb. The cave, we remember, is a kind of theater, a deceptive shadow world where men are transfixed by images projected on a wall, images that are mere copies of the material world, itself a copy of the ideal world that the mind of the philosopher strives to apprehend. The magicians who project these images are like the artists who would be banished from the just society for keeping men enthralled with the world of seductive imitations. For the philosopher, then, art and the feminine must be left behind.

Irigaray condemns the Platonic idealism the parable is meant to illustrate, the philosophical tendency to impose sameness and identity on all things, making them into more or less good copies of Truth: "No two ways about it, a form, even if it be a shadow, must be sired by, standardized against *one* face, *one* presence, *one* measure: that of Truth" (292). The operation by which everything in this world is made into a reflection of the ideal is metaphor: "the 'like,' the 'as if' of that masculine representation dominated by truth, light, resemblance, identity" (265).[4] Here we encounter the familiar terrain of humanism, so vividly illustrated in the passage I quoted from Richards's *New York Times* article: racial difference is subsumed by human nature so that racial conflict is attributable to human beings' *natural* tendency to be "at odds" with one another. "A thousand and one reasons" for racial animosity, a thousand and one grievances, are reduced to one cause, one motive: the stubbornness of humanity as a species.

As I have said, Smith's work, in immersing itself in the details of specific racial conflicts, hardly endorses the humanist approach of the *Times* writer. It insists on our confronting the pervasiveness of racism while at the same time showing how strict adherence to racial identity impedes our understanding of one another, and it offers by way of example the possibility of crossing racial boundaries to put oneself in someone else's "skin." Smith's approach vividly illustrates the practice Irigaray counsels women and other "inferior species" to adopt in order to avoid the obliteration of human differences that occurs in the process of creating metaphoric equivalencies: the practice of *mimesis.* Drucilla Cornell defines this practice: "*Mimesis*, understood as a non-violent ethical relation to what is Other, and not as a mode of artistic representation that supposedly . . . mirrors . . . the real in art, is an expression of Adornian non-identity in which the subject does not seek to identify or categorize the object, but rather to let the object be in its difference. [*Mimesis*] identifies with, rather than identifying as" (148). Now, this description of "mimetic identification" applies almost uncannily to Smith's performance, which involves more than almost any other conceivable performance an "identification with" the Other. Smith's work thus seems to represent a challenge to racial essentialisms ("identifying as" an African American, as a Latino, and so on) and to affirm the specificity and uniqueness of the human subject. The performance indeed approaches the state of what Philippe Lacoue-Labarthe has called "absolute vicariousness . . . the very lapse of essence" (116).

We can begin to understand the breadth of the praise Smith's work has received, both from the mainstream press and from postmodern critical quarters—camps that might be expected to be "at odds" with one another. On the one hand, the work evokes a humanist fantasy of the kind anatomized by Irigaray, whereby the maternal body becomes the ground of representation. For some, the body in Smith's performance presents a welcome image of plenitude and wholeness in a society that has been rent asunder by contending elements. Hence, the frequency with which Smith's work is seen as contributing to the "healing" of a racially divided America, despite her frequent disclaimers to the contrary. Smith's body becomes a utopian image of the body politic, and her work is affirmed in the name of the nation: *E Pluribus Unum*. Thus John Lahr concludes his review in the *New Yorker*, "'Twilight' goes some way toward reclaiming for the stage its crucial role as a leader in defining and acting out that ongoing experiment called the United States" (94). Yet one might counter this remark with Gayatri Spivak's trenchant observation that "women can be ventriloquists, but they have an immense *historical* potential of *not* being (allowed to remain) nationalists; of knowing in their gendering, that nation and identity are commodities in the strictest sense: something made for exchange. And that they are the medium of that exchange" (803). In this country black women have had to bear the greatest burden as mediums of exchange, their bodies frequently becoming the site for the playing out of racial and sexual tension. Anita Hill is only the most recent example of such a woman, pressed into the service of the collective national psyche.

On the other hand, Smith's work plays into a posthumanist fantasy of the sort Cornell indulges, a fantasy that also grounds itself in the maternal body but that explicitly opposes, as Spivak suggests we must oppose, the concept of identity: the maternal body, says Cornell, is "a 'subject of heterogeneity' in which the One is tied to the Other and, therefore, is not truly One. [The] 'maternal body' presents us with an image of love through non-identity" (185). But if the metaphoric process condemned by Irigaray obliterates the object by appropriating it, mimetic identification endangers the subject, who, as Cornell approvingly notes, "loses control" in being "taken over" by the Other (149). Such language powerfully returns us to the image of the black female medium.

And, indeed, Cornell recognizes that mimesis is based on stereotypes associated with femininity but argues that for this very reason it should be adopted as a means of turning "subordination into affirmation" (148). However, to notice the difference between mere subordination and subordination turned into affirmation, one would require a self-consciousness about gender and an acceptance of identity politics—affirming oneself as a woman or, in Smith's case, as a black woman. In this regard, we might recall John Lahr's implicit praise of Smith's subordination of herself to her subjects: "Whitman's great poem . . . invoked the voices of America but celebrated only himself"; and we might reply: But isn't it time the black woman celebrated herself? Unfortunately, the celebration of black womanhood (*as* black womanhood) is the least developed aspect of Smith's work.

In any case, I hope it is obvious by now that what the rhetoric of the actress as medium obscures is the extent to which Smith has been subject to media-tion—in part, ironically enough, through the very process of the media's granting her a privileged contact with the "real" (rather than focusing on her artistry). This insistence on the real further obscures the extent to which at its most sophisticated the work functions as a complex commen-

tary on the impossibility of accessing the real through language and representation: the author, in this regard, is no passive medium but a complex
mediator. One brilliant moment in the play has Smith portraying Jewish
writer Letty Cottin Pogrebin, who is represented as speaking on the phone
(to Smith). Pogrebin has apparently been invited to speak about her uncle
Isaac's experience of the Holocaust, and she says, "Well, it's hard for me to
do that because I think there's a tendency to make hay with the Holocaust,
to push all the buttons. And I mean this story about my uncle Isaac—makes
me cry and it's going to make your audience cry and I'm beginning to worry
that we're trotting out our Holocaust stories too regularly and that we're going to inure each other to the truth of them." Pogrebin decides to read from
her own book an account of Isaac, "the designated survivor" of the Holocaust whose mission was to "stay alive and tell the story": staying alive meant
passing as an Aryan and, among other atrocities he had to perform, being
required to shove his own wife and children into the gas chamber. Later Isaac
told his account, which Pogrebin heard "translated from his Yiddish" by her
mother, to dozens of agencies and community leaders, and after "speaking
the unspeakable" for months "when he finished telling everything he knew,
he died."

We might say that the story of Isaac as told by Pogrebin illustrates what
Shoshana Felman, analyzing the testimonial accounts of Holocaust survivors,
calls "the crisis of witnessing": the conflict between the necessity of telling
all and the impossibility of "speaking the unspeakable"—to say nothing of
the obscenity of our desire to hear the unspeakable (to "make hay with the
Holocaust").[5] This conflict is self-consciously reflected in Smith's own rendering of Pogrebin's story, which is characteristically reproduced with what
appears to be absolute fidelity but is also delivered over the phone, a device
which, along with the book from which Pogrebin reads and the mother's English translation of Isaac's Yiddish, provides one more layer of mediation between us and the horror experienced by Isaac.

Indeed, all of Smith's work in her *On the Road* series may be said to negotiate this conflict and to oscillate with great artistry between the desire to
capture the real and the awareness of the difficulties and even dangers of attempting to do so. Perhaps, however, the decision in *Fires in the Mirror* to end
with Gavin Cato's father mourning the death of his son tips the balance rather
too far in one direction, so that the tears shed on stage seem to offer a guarantee of the real—of raw human emotion—and to provide the cathartic comfort that Pogrebin wanted to avoid, thus lending support to the humanist
position that the politics of the event can be peeled away to manifest the authentic human tragedy underneath.

Yet even here, Cato's parting line (the final line of the play) in which,
scorning the supposed power of the Jews to prevent his speaking out, he says,
"No there's nothing to hide, you can repeat every word I say," contains a re-

flexive turn that invites us to ponder the meaning of the strategy of repetition governing the work as a whole, rather than allowing us to rest in the illusion of transparency. It is to this issue and to a consideration of the function of repetition in art created for a multicultural society that I now turn.

2

Recently, theorists of colonialist discourse have developed a line of thought analogous to Irigaray's. Homi Bhabha's work in particular addresses itself to the question of mimesis, or what he calls *mimicry*. Both Irigaray and Bhabha attempt to understand how people who have had an alien language and culture imposed on them (by men, by whites, by colonizers) may be said to use language in such a way as to signal that their speech emanates from an "elsewhere"—a place outside the master discourse. In a recent article of particular interest for discussing Smith's work, Bhabha looks at the question of repetition through an analysis of the poem "Names" by Derek Walcott. The poem begins, "My race began as the sea began / with no nouns, and with no horizon / with pebbles under my tongue, / with a different fix on the stars." Walcott's poem goes on to tell of the colonial encounter, of the way the colonialist named places in the new land after those in his home land, applying "belittling diminutives" to them: "then, Little Versailles meant plans for the pigsty, names for the sour apples / and green grapes / of their exile." But the African, who seemed to acquiesce in these names, "repeated, and changed them" (Bhabha 51–52).

Analyzing this poem for the light it sheds on the question of identity politics, Bhabha sees two versions of language being articulated in it: the imperialist project of naming, which rests on the presupposition of the ability of language to "mirror a pre-given reality," and another process on the part of the African who "in repeating the lessons of the masters, changes their inflections" (53). Bhabha seizes on the transformative potential of repetition as it is poetically affirmed by Walcott to point to "another destiny of culture as a site—one based not simply on subversion and transgression, but on the prefiguration of a kind of solidarity between ethnicities that meet in the tryst of colonial history" (51).

What Bhabha's analysis does not bring out in Walcott's poem, however, is the triple notion of mimeticism at work in it. First, as Bhabha notes, is the view of language as mirroring reality. On a second level, though, there is the imitative naming practiced by the colonist, who is exiled from, and envious of those who are privileged in, his own country—and no doubt envious as well of the new culture in which he is an alien: hence, the "sour apples" and "green grapes," denoting the envy that leads him to apply "belittling diminutives" to the country he now inhabits. And finally, on a third level, there is the transformative potential of the mimicry practiced by the colonized people: "Listen, my children, say: *moubain:* the hogplum, / *cerise:* the wild cherry, / *baie-la:* the bay, / with the fresh green voices they were once themselves / in the way the wind bends / our natural inflections" (52). In the poem the color green marks the shift in levels of repetition, from the second meaning to the third: from suggesting the envy at the heart of mimetic rivalry, the "green" as it recurs in the phrase "fresh green voices" comes to signify a culture no less "natural" or "authentic" and certainly no less creative than any other for having passed through a colonial culture that has commanded its subjects to "mimic" its alien language and customs. As we shall see Smith's work brilliantly oscillates between these two modes of repetition: repetition in the form of mimetic rivalry, rooted in envy and anger, and repetition as a transformative process, yielding complex surprises and illustrating how repetition is always repetition with a difference. Moreover, by mimicking not just members of the dominant culture but various ethnic groups as well, Smith does indeed prefigure, to quote Bhabha again, "a solidarity between ethnicities that meet in the tryst of colonialist history."

In our own society, minstrelsy as a popular, peculiarly American form of entertainment has historically been a principle means by which the dominant culture "belittled" African American culture through mimicry (and recent analyses like those of Erik Lott have shown how envy and desire are components of the attraction minstrelsy held for so many whites). Smith's work, which involves figuratively adopting whiteface, blackface, brownface, and so on can be interestingly situated within the tradition of minstrelsy because it plays so close to the edges of caricature, sometimes pulling back in time and sometimes not. Indeed, to the extent that reviewers criticized the show, their reservations had to do with their feelings that it too frequently fell into caricature (Wood 12). These reviewers neglected to see the dynamism of Smith's portrayals, the ceaseless volatility of the process whereby types dissolve into individuals and individuals crystallize into types. In Smith's acting style, her tendency to place excessive stress on individual speech mannerisms (accents and the like) continually threatens to topple her impersonations over into caricature. Just when people are presented as most themselves, they suddenly seem like "types," our laughter as suddenly seems to border on ridicule, and we find ourselves confronting our own racism. Yet a laugh, a subtle gesture, a vocal inflection will give us a glimmer of an individual behind the type (for example, the black nationalist Leonard Jeffries's wry tone of voice that seems to mock his own infamous megalomania when he remarks that there might not have been a *Roots* without him—since he found the lost manuscript in the Philadelphia airport). Here we see the dual aspect of mimicry: its aggressive aspect, so obvious in minstrelsy, which reduces people to stereotypes and robs them of their complexity, and the utopian aspect Bhabha assigns to the mimicry—the promise of solidarity embedded in Smith's artistic practice of identifying with an "other" whose differences are scrupulously observed and preserved. We have simultaneously imitation as theft and imitation as the sincerest form of flattery.

Smith not only practices mimicry in such a way as to prefigure solidarity between ethnicities, but her text also contains a complex commentary on how mimetic processes function—always unstably—in the constitution of identity. In a section on "Hair" in *Fires in the Mirror,* for example, Al Sharpton defends his hair style against those who see it as imitating the hair of white people. He angrily insists that he wears his hair like James Brown because Brown was a kind of surrogate father to him and not because he wants to look like whites. "I mean in the fifties it was a slick. It was acting like White folks. But today people don't wear their hair like that. James and I the only ones out there doing that. So it's certainlih [*sic*] not a reaction to Whites. It's me and James's thing" (22).[6] Bhabha's thesis is strikingly illustrated by this example: although Sharpton seems caught in that "inauthentic repetition" to which the dominant culture appears to doom the subordinate one, in actuality he is engaged in an intraracial play of male mimetic desire that not only remains in a resistant relation to white culture but, insofar as it attests to a tension between individual and group identity, links him to members of other subordinate groups, other ethnicities within our society who also struggle with questions of authenticity and inauthenticity—like the Lubavitcher woman who immediately follows Sharpton and speaks of her ambivalence about wearing wigs. At odds with their respective groups over the question of adopting the customs and styles that signal their difference from the dominant culture, the militant black minister and the Lubavitcher woman appear for a moment to have more in common with each other than with members of their own groups.

In his book *Typography: Mimesis, Philosophy, Politics,* Philippe Lacoue-Labarthe has written that "every culture . . . is built violently upon the ground—and the threat—of a *generalized* state of competition," of violent "mimetic rivalry" (102). Though this may be true, what it neglects is the way subordinate cultures have been forced into particularly virulent forms of mimetic rivalry with each other through divide and conquer strategies practiced by the dominant group. At no time in American history has the virulence reached greater heights than it sometimes has in the relation between blacks and Jews. Yet solidarity between ethnic groups has probably never been stronger between any other two groups. Seeing a history of shared oppression, blacks and Jews have worked in civil rights coalitions together, but such solidarity has sometimes broken down into rivalry when it appears to one group that the other is receiving preferential treatment. One of the most obvious examples of this is the break between blacks and Jews over the question of affirmative action. Many Jews have opposed affirmative action programs on the grounds that they themselves have managed to achieve their successes without such programs and that their own gains would be eroded as African Americans progress.

The territory of Crown Heights, where warring factions accused each other during the riots of receiving preferential treatment, is a perfect site for the study of the relations between blacks and Jews, for understanding the mimetic rivalry that has driven these two groups apart and the forces that have contributed or might contribute to drawing them together. During the middle part of the century, when Caribbean immigrants began moving into middle-class Jewish neighborhoods as the latter were moving out to Queens and the suburbs, blacks aspiring to the status of property owners began to "imitate the Jew," as Mary Helen Washington puts it in an afterward to Paule Marshall's *Brown Girl, Brownstones,* a novel set in Brooklyn during this period (312). The Lubavitchers, however, halted the process of upward mobility, of white flight from a Brooklyn as blacks moved in. In 1969 the Grand Rebbe, Joseph Schneerson, ordered the Lubavitchers to remain in Crown Heights and, according to one Lubavitcher, to "'make linkages' and establish a relationship with their new neighbors" (Noel 38). Whatever the original intention, the Lubavitch community, which has acquired a great deal of political power over the years, has grown to the point where, as some commentators have remarked, they "steadily harass" their black neighbors to sell their property (Logan 105). "Nothing's wrong with that," one rabbi says about pressuring blacks to sell their homes at a profit. "That's the American business market" (Noel 39).

The rabbi's remark allies him with the mother in Paule Marshall's novel. To be sure, the latter in her obsession with becoming a property holder in Brooklyn, with Crown Heights as her ultimate goal, is more brutally direct in her defense of the American way. Commenting on the inevitability of mimetic rivalry, the mother asserts, "Power, is a thing that don really have nothing to do with color. . . . Take when we had to scrub the Jew floor. He wasn't misusing us so much because our skin was black but because we cun do better. And I din hate him. All the time I was down on his floor I was saying to myself: 'Lord, lemme do better than this. Lemme rise!'" She maintains that "people got a right to claw their way to the top and those on top got a right to scuffle to stay there." And though the world "won't always be white," people of color once they get on top "might not be so nice either 'cause power is a thing that don make you nice" (224–25).

Selina, the novel's heroine, resists this philosophy, dimly envisioning another truth and going off on her own at the end of the novel to seek it out. Embracing the condition of exile, Selina as a doubly displaced person (from Barbados and from Brooklyn) may be said to embody the kind of "diasporic consciousness" recently theorized by Daniel Boyarin and Jonathan Boyarin in an article written for *Critical Inquiry.* The Boyarins, like Smith in *Fires in the Mirror* and like so many thinkers addressing questions of race and ethnicity today, set out to think through the problems of integration and difference, and in particular they ask how Jews may hold on to "ethnic, cultural specificity but in a context of deeply felt and enacted human solidarity" (720). They argue that at certain moments in Jewish history when Jews and Jewish identity have been endangered, an insularity has helped preserve group identity; at such times it might have been necessary for Jews "to undertake the education, feeding, providing for the sick, and the caring for Jewish prisoners, to the virtual exclusion of others" (and here one can't help recall the ambulance that was widely said to have abandoned the dying Gavin Cato—in reality, the police ordered the ambulance to leave with the Jewish driver, for the crowd was angry and city ambulances were coming on the scene; but the fact that people were all too ready to believe the worst attests to the widespread perception of Jews as chiefly concerned with "their own") (712). However, the Boyarins maintain that under conditions of Jewish hegemony, where Jews claim sole right to the land, diasporic consciousness—"a consciousness of a Jewish collective as one sharing space with others, devoid of exclusivist and dominating power"—is the only way of achieving "a species-wide care without eradicating cultural difference" (713).

"Race and space," the Boyarins write, "together form a deadly discourse" (714). They point out that Abraham, the father of Jewry, was "deterritorialized" when he was told to leave his own land for the promised land, and they call for a "prophetic discourse" that evinces "preference for 'exile' over rootedness in the Land" (718). This is not to deny the importance of attachment to the land, they say, but it is to recognize the attachment others have to it as well. (The final image of Selina in *Brown Girl, Brownstones,* who as she leaves Brooklyn throws back one of the two bangles worn by girls in Barbados, suggests this attachment to two places at the very moment of exile.) In stressing "deterritorialization" and rejecting myths of autochthony, the Boyarins align themselves with many leaders in the African American community, who increasingly question notions of black "authenticity" as the grounds of political practice, stressing instead the "political and ethical dimensions of blackness" and what Cornel West, using the same term as the Boyarins, calls the "prophetic nature" of a discourse based on new and different coalitions (26).

Within Smith's text, Angela Davis similarly calls for a rejection of a politics grounded exclusively in race, which she claims is too static a concept; instead of remaining anchored in a single community, she recommends using the "rope" of the anchor to move across communities. Smith's mimetic practice, which consists of juxtaposing voices from these various communities, works to realize in aesthetic form the movement across borders, signifying a refusal to stay in place or to be fixed, in the way Bhabha says the stereotype is always fixed and rendered immobile. Thus the very premise of Smith's performances is diasporic consciousness.[7] Further, *Fires in the Mirror* suggests that what blacks and Jews have in common is the condition of diaspora; their common ground is their "groundlessness." Ironically, this condition has been the source of intense mimetic rivalry between the two groups, particularly over the question of whose experience in the diaspora has been worse. Thus in Smith's text Conrad Mohammed argues that slavery was infinitely more brutal than the Holocaust. Obviously, diasporic consciousness should not be invoked to avoid the understanding that people in the here and now live unequally in the diaspora and that inequalities—such as the Jews having more political power in Crown Heights than blacks—need to be worked out. Yet insofar as it disputes the validity of claims to original rights and original wrongs, diasporic consciousness marks a shift from mimetic rivalry to solidarity—a shift, again, that is inherent in the very concept of Smith's work, one of the most intriguing aspects of which is its undermining of certainty about origins. Part of the unsettling effect of the performances is that although some of the figures Smith mimics are familiar to us (if only from their media representations), in many cases we are acutely aware of watching imitations without knowing the originals. Giving priority, as it were, to the copy over the original, Smith radically and viscerally contests ideals of authenticity, in effect "deterritorializing" her characters and getting them to act on new common ground—the stage.

3

Mimetic rivalry came into play in various ways around the production and reception of Smith's performances. When it was announced that Smith would be coming to Los Angeles to do a show on the L.A. uprising, modeled after the work she did on Crown Heights, local artists wrote a letter of protest to the Mark Taper Forum that was headlined in the local media. The artists complained that the Taper, which commissioned the piece, never features L.A. artists on the main stage, unless those artists have first gained celebrity in the New York theater world. As people of color living in Los Angeles, these artists argued, they were in a unique position to create art about the violence that had occurred in their own community.

It is interesting to note how these protests mimicked on the artistic plane the mimetic strife at the heart of Smith's performances. People from various ethnic and racial backgrounds turned their anger on another person from a marginalized group who possessed an advantage they did not. Although most of those who protested were careful to emphasize that the Taper was the target of their anger, not Smith herself, the press obviously relished the racial dimension of the controversy (it is hard to believe the press would have been as interested in a letter to the Taper protesting its marginalization of people of color if Smith hadn't been perceived as the target.) Being judged as a kind of "outside agitator" in the theater world, Smith found herself in the midst of interracial and intraracial conflict, as artists of color from Los Angeles temporarily asserted their identity in terms of community as well as race—not unlike the blacks who lived in Crown Heights during the time in which Marshall's novel is set.

Struggles akin to those Smith's work represents arose also at the level of reception in numerous postplay discussions, both those held at the Taper and those that took place more informally among theater-goers. The discussions revealed much resentment because Smith appeared to slight certain groups (such as non-Korean Asians) or to caricature a given group more than others. One person who was outraged over the way she was represented was Judith Tur, the only white woman in the Los Angeles version of *Twilight* and the character who expresses the most undisguised racist views in the play: "Let them go out and work for a living. / I'm sick of it. / We've all had a rough time in our life. / I've had a major rough time." Such sentiments are familiar to us by now as the very stuff of mimetic rivalry—the perception that one's own oppression ("rough time") is equal to or greater than that of the other.

I must confess that I was disturbed by Smith's choice of a woman to be the voice of racism—after all, we live in a white patriarchy, not a matriarchy. I felt that Smith was not willing to consider how, like Jews, women as women have a history of oppression. Nor did she appear to recognize the fact that, like Jews and blacks, white women and black women have sometimes been partners and sometimes rivals in the struggle against oppression. An acknowledgment of the historic tensions between these groups would, I thought, have been more in keeping with Smith's overall project. On the contrary, however, it seemed to me that in its treatment of white women, Smith's text did not so much analyze the dynamics of scapegoating as enact it: whereas the white men interviewed for *Twilight* exhibit an entire range of human responses to the beating of Rodney King and its aftermath except the most virulent form of racism that, for example, led one of the policemen who beat Rodney King to joke about "gorillas in the mist," white women remain unrehabilitated.[8] This is especially evident in the Broadway version, which contains the portraits of two additional rather ghastly white women. Here I have to admit to my own implication in the rivalry inspired by Smith's work in *Twilight:* after seeing the way white women were portrayed in this version my first reaction was one of anger. I did not initially consider my privileged relation to women of color, but rather thought primarily about my own oppression. I even briefly considered withdrawing my article from this collection. If Smith was not prepared to acknowledge my oppression as a woman, I felt, I would not recognize hers as an African American.

Both of the white female characters who have been added to the text are upper-middle-class women (class is a category that complicates the binaries of racial difference but is not brought to bear sufficiently in Smith's choice of interviewees). One of these is a Brentwood mother who worries that the threat of gang violence interferes with prom night—and lest we miss the message that this woman is a tad out of touch with the real victims of police brutality and gang violence, a video image of a gated community is projected behind Smith when she mimes this character.[9] The other woman added to the latest version of *Twilight* is a real estate agent, portrayed in an extremely caricatured way, who laments the closing of the Polo Lounge at the Beverly Hills Hotel, where during the "riots" she and her friends would "huddle together" until two or three in the morning (153). This woman, whose name is Elaine Young, is a figure of ridicule in part because of the plastic surgery problems she has had: silicone implanted in her cheeks exploded, causing her to have thirty-six operations to restore her face. As a result, she has become an activist in the war against silicone implants.[10]

Though Young's plight as Smith performs it is played largely for comic effect (thus inviting us to see the woman's problems as the grotesque consequence of vanity and privilege), one can detect faintly in the text a thread with which one could construct a more feminist analysis. The thread would link the aging white woman, Elaine Young, to the baby girl of Elvira Evers, a Panamanian woman from Compton who was shot during the uprising and whose baby while still in the womb received the bullet in her elbow. Shortly after the child was born, her mother subjected her to another kind of body piercing: "We don't like to keep the girls without earrings. We like the little / girls / to look like girls from little" (in other words, from a very early age); "she was seven days, / and I / pierced her ears." There is a hint here and in Elaine Young's story of a violence different from the choke-holds, baton blows, and drive-by shootings that preoccupy the media in times of racial strife, a violence inflicted by patriarchy—even when enacted by women— on the female body to brand it with the mark of gender. (Chinese footbinding is a classic example of violence against women and is surely no less a feminist issue for being practiced on aristocratic women.) Such violence, often more sanctioned than the violence done to Rodney King or Gavin Cato or Yankel Rosenbaum, is less likely to be perceived as the stuff of drama, especially by male theater reviewers and male-dominated award committees.

As a consequence of Smith's privileging of racial hierarchy over gender hierarchy, issues of gender return to haunt the text with the specter of mimetic rivalry. But if the work does not extricate itself from the dynamics it illustrates, it does point the way out. In particular, it suggests the necessity for us, on the one hand, to remain judicious in our assessments of blame for our various oppressions and, on the other hand, to recognize not just the wrongs that are done to us but the privileges that make our lives so enviable to those without our advantages.

In focusing on individual responses to Smith's work, we must not overlook the institutional forms of mimeticism at play around Smith's performances— evidenced, for example, in the Mark Taper Forum's unabashed desire to follow the New York theater scene rather than attempt to foster artists closer to home. What complicated the straightforward workings of mimetic desire in this case, however, was the fact that *Fires in the Mirror* had such an impact in New York partly because it opened around the same time that the uprising in L.A. occurred—a fact that reviewers seldom failed to notice. In one sense then, *Twilight,* commissioned with the idea that Smith would do L.A.'s very "own" riot, was a copy of a work that already seemed to mirror that riot. Yet when *Twilight* was nominated for a Tony Award, the director of the Taper, Gordon Davidson, crowed: "We're the most active and productive theater in the area of new and challenging work in the United States. Somebody else can add 'the world.'" In a gesture of artistic imperialism that is strikingly ironic in light of Smith's project, the white producer implicitly denies all debts, blithely treading on the sensitivities of the people of color who felt overlooked by his choice in the first place, and explicitly puts himself solidly at the point of origin.

The feeling of ownership that many of us who live in Los Angeles experienced after the uprising (a friend told me she never felt that Los Angeles was really "her" city until those explosive days in April 1992) had positive aspects to it insofar as it gave rise to a sense of responsibility at the local level on the part of people who had previously lacked commitment to the city. However, such commitment needs to be accompanied by an awareness not only of the differences between any two places in the way racism is experienced—say, between Crown Heights Brooklyn, and Los Angeles, California (in Crown Heights two groups appeared to be locked in an agonistic struggle with one another; in Los Angeles, as *Twilight* brings out, many ethnic groups were involved in events that seemed far less centered than those that occurred in Crown Heights)—but also of the similarities. After all, racism in this country is a transcommunal phenomenon—as the numerous "copycat riots" following in the wake of the L.A. uprising attest.

The phrase "copycat riot" is obviously a dismissive one, particularly as it is taken up in journalistic practice; it implies that such uprisings are "mere copies," without their "own" rationale and specificity—a view that never stands up under rigorous analysis. To repeat: repetition is always repetition with a difference, and as we have seen throughout, it is necessary to adopt a double vision, seeing the sameness and the uniqueness in various experiences of oppression and of protests against oppression. Each of the two models I began by outlining—the humanist, which stresses identity, and the posthumanist, which stresses difference—is thus inadequate for theorizing this approach.

Speaking of Plato's banishment of the artist from the republic, Christopher Prendergast writes that the mimetic artist through "his doublings and multiplications . . . introduces 'improprieties' (a 'poison') into a social system ordered according to the rule that everything and everyone should be in its/his/her 'proper' place. He disturbs *both* the law of identity *and* the law of differentiation," and in short is "excommunicated not because [his work] is a threat to truth, but because it is a threat to order" (10; emphasis added). Insofar as Smith's performances were comforting to some precisely because she seemed to stay in her "proper place," the space of the maternal, it is necessary to add one more variable to the Boyarins' formula and say that race, space, and *gender* make for a "deadly discourse." We could cite the black nationalist Leonard Jeffries, who in *Fires in the Mirror* laments the censoring of the term "Mother Africa" from the television version of *Roots:* the nationalist fantasy is often a gendered fantasy, and women must resist not only staying in place, but allowing themselves to be represented *as* space.

Yet the view of Smith as "container" of the multitudes is, as I suggested earlier, in part belied by the nature of the project itself, which involves her in a constant traversal of borders. One might in this light see Smith's continual deflection of the question so frequently posed to her by journalists, "Where are *you* in this piece?" not as a refusal to take a political position but a refusal to be pinned down. If, as I would argue, the black woman has traditionally occupied the most fixed place in this country's representational practices, her departure from that role constitutes perhaps the most threatening sign of disorder, more threatening certainly than the work of the implicitly white male artist evoked by Plato and Prendergast. In this regard, we might look at a revealing moment in the Los Angeles version of *Twilight*, when Stanley Sheinbaum tells of driving on the freeway the night of the riots and receiving his first clue that something was wrong when he saw a black woman in a Mercedes carrying a hammer.[11] This account invariably provoked a response of hilarity in audiences (and indeed was mentioned again by Sheinbaum in the *Los Angeles Times* in a letter attempting to defend Smith's use of humor in *Twilight*). The laughter was undoubtedly a response to what seems a carnivalesque crossing of borders involving unexpected intersections of class, gender, and race (presumably the sight of black men driving expensive cars and bearing submachine guns would be less apt to signal something oddly out of place). I think we can take this image of the woman on the freeway as emblematic of Smith's artistry, which also involves such carnivalesque crossings. And in response to the journalists' recurrent question, "Where are you in all this?" we might recall the title of Smith's series and say that she is "on the road," in a kind of permanent exile, hammering out justice.

NOTES

1. See S. Richards for an illuminating discussion of Smith's early work.
2. Craig Owens's is the most cogent description of postmodern art that I've read. See especially "The Allegorical Impulse: Toward a Theory of Postmodern Art," parts 1 and 2, 52–87.

3. For a discussion of the Ancient Greek's view of woman as "the mimetic creature *par excellence*," see Zeitlin 79.

4. For an excellent application of Irigaray's reading of Plato to the issue of women and theater, see Diamond.

5. It is extraordinary that in Felman's book, which explores the "crisis of witnessing" opened up by the Holocaust, the obscenity of our eagerness to consume Holocaust stories, photographs, and so on, is not considered to be part of this crisis.

6. See Mercer for a discussion of how even before the Afro, black hair style, which appeared to imitate white styles, was actually more independent of these styles than later generations of African Americans tended to believe.

7. Unfortunately, Smith's decision to emphasize only the divisions between blacks and Jews around the Crown Heights incidents meant passing up an opportunity to reveal aspects of solidarity that actually existed at the time of the Crown Heights riots. Cornel West in a discussion of Black-Jewish relations castigates the media for perpetuating the belief of most Americans "that the black community has been silent in the face of Yankel Rosenbaum's murder." The media "seem to have little interest in making known to the public the moral condemnations" emanating from black ministers in particular. West concludes, "Black anti-Semitism is not caused by media hype—yet it does sell more newspapers and turn out attention away from those black prophetic energies that give us some hope" (78–79). In Smith's case it is not media hype so much as the demands of drama that seem to require the agonistic structure.

8. Yet Smith could have chosen to include an interview with the female CHP officer who broke the code of silence during the second federal trial of the police officers and cried on the witness stand over what she witnessed of the King beating—thus providing key testimony that resulted in the guilty verdict against Sergeant Koon and some of his men.

9. This character does not appear in the book *Twilight: Los Angeles, 1992,* which was apparently rushed into print before the Broadway version was completed. The book thus includes, in Smith's words, "some of the material . . . performed both in the play's Los Angeles version for the Taper and in the version presented at the New York Shakespeare Festival. It includes additional interviews that were not included in the stage versions" (xvii).

10. The Broadway version has Young speak at two different times, but only one part of the interview is included in the book. Young's tale of the horrors of plastic surgery does not appear in the printed text of *Twilight.*

11. This does not appear in the printed version.

WORKS CITED

Abatemarco, Tony. "When Will the Taper's Power Brokers Wake Up?" *Los Angeles Times* 17 August 1992: F3.

Bhabha, Homi K. "Freedom's Basis in the Indeterminate." *October* 61 (Summer 1992): 46–57.

Boyarin, Daniel, and Jonathan Boyarin. "Diaspora: Generation and the Ground of Jewish Identity." *Critical Inquiry* 19.4 (1993): 693–725.

Clines, Francis X. "At Work with Anna Deavere Smith." *New York Times* 10 June 1992: C1, C9.

Cornell, Drucilla. *Beyond Accommodation: Ethical Feminism, Deconstruction, and the Law.* New York: Routledge, 1991.

Diamond, Elin. "Mimesis, Mimicry, and the 'True-Real.'" *Acting Out.* Ann Arbor: Michigan UP, 1993. 363–82.

Fanon, Frantz. "West Indians and Africans." *Toward the African Revolution.* London: Writers and Readers, 1980.

Felman, Shoshana, and Dori Laub. *Testimony: Crises of Witnessing in Literature, Psychoanalysis, and History.* New York: Routledge, 1992.

Gates, Henry Louis, Jr. *The Signifying Monkey: A Theory of Afro-American Literary Criticism.* New York: Oxford UP, 1988.

Irigaray, Luce. *Speculum of the Other Woman.* Trans. Gillian C. Gill. Ithaca: Cornell UP, 1985.

Johnson, Barbara. "No Short Cuts to Democracy." *Fires in the Mirror: Essays and Teaching Strategies.* Ed. Pamela Benson. Boston: WGBH Educational Print and Outreach, 1993. 9–11.

Klein, Joe. "Deadly Metaphors." *New York* 9 September 1991: 26–29.

Kroll, Jack. "Fire in the City of Angels." *Newsweek* 28 June 1993: 62–63.

———. "A Woman for All Seasons." *Newsweek* 1 June 1992: 74.

Lacoue-Labarthe, Philippe. *Typography: Mimesis, Philosophy, Politics.* Cambridge: Harvard UP, 1989.

Lahr, John. "Under the Skin." *The New Yorker* 28 June 1993: 90–94.

Logan, Andy. "Around City Hall." *The New Yorker* 23 September 1991: 102–8.

Lott, Erik. *Love and Theft: Blackface Minstrelsy and the American Working Class.* New York: Oxford UP, 1993.

Mercer, Kobena. "Black Hair/Style Politics." *New Formations* 3 (Winter 1987): 33–55.

———. "'1968': Periodizing Postmodern Politics and Identity." *Cultural Studies.* Ed. Lawrence Grossberg, Cary Nelson, and Paula A. Treichler. New York: Routledge, 1992. 442–49.

Noel, Peter. "Crown Heights Burning: Rage, Race, and the Politics of Resistance." *Village Voice* 3 September 1991: 37–41.

Owens, Craig. *Beyond Recognition: Representation, Power, and Culture.* Ed. Scott Bryson, Barbara Kruger, Lynne Tillman, and Jane Weinstock. Berkeley: U of California P, 1992.

Prendergast, Christopher. *The Order of Mimesis: Balzac, Stendhal, Nerval, Flaubert.* Cambridge: Cambridge UP, 1986.

Rich, Frank. "Diversities of America in One-Person Shows." *New York Times* 15 May 1992: C1, C19.

Richards, David. "And Now, a Word from Off Broadway." *New York Times* 17 May 1992: H5, H24.

Richards, Sandra L. "Caught in the Act of Social Definition: *On The Road* with Anna Deavere Smith." *Acting Out: Feminist Performances.* Ed. Lynda Hart and Peggy Phelan. Ann Arbor: Michigan UP, 1993. 35–54.

Sheinbaum, Stanley K. "One-Woman Show Has Message for All of Us." *Los Angeles Times* 5 July 1993: F3.

Shirley, Don. "Tonys Cheer Taper, What's It Mean?" *Los Angeles Times* 18 May 1994: F1, F9.

Smith, Anna Deavere. *Fires in the Mirror.* New York: Doubleday, 1993.

———. *Twilight: Los Angeles, 1992.* New York: Doubleday, 1994.

Spivak, Gayatri Chakravorty. "Acting Bits/Identity Talk." *Critical Inquiry* 18 (Summer 1992): 770–803.

Washington, Mary Helen. Afterword. *Brown Girl, Brownstones.* By Paule Marshall. New York: The Feminist P, 1981.

West, Cornel. *Race Matters.* Boston: Beacon, 1993.

Wood, Daniel B. "Many Voices in One Mouth." *The Christian Science Monitor* 8 July 1993: 12.

Wright, Damon. "A Seance with History." *The New York Times* 10 May 1992: H14.

Zeitlin, Froma I. "Playing the Other: Theater, Theatricality, and the Feminine in Ancient Greek Drama." *Representations* 2 (1985): 63–94.

"Racial Composition"

Metaphor and the Body in the Writing of Race

Margaret Homans

The discourses of race and of gender in this country have historically been characterized by debates about the body: about the ontological status as well as the interpretability of biological difference. This essay investigates a moment —the mid and late 1980s—when debates about embodied race and embodied gender came into rhetorically charged conflict.[1] For Henry Louis Gates Jr., in his writings of this time, any hint of essentialism with respect to race— racial definition through biology—was equivalent to a return to slavery, for it had been on the grounds of suppositional "natural" difference that whites justified slavery. It seemed that there could be no benefit from noticing biological racial difference, and in any case, according to Anthony Appiah, there is little difference to notice: perhaps none at all.[2] These arguments appeared to have brought the debate about racial biology to a close, to render it purely a phenomenon of the historical past. In contrast, the debate over the status of the body within U.S. feminist theory remained a lively and complicated one, a debate that could be oversimplified as follows: is sexual difference of primary importance in the creation and maintenance of gender categories and to be celebrated as the source of women's distinctive experiences? Or is gender difference a cultural and social construction, and the function of feminist theory to minimize biological difference so as to maximize the possibility of social change? As Linda Alcoff wrote in 1988, although feminists now recognize that we must "deconstruct and de-essentialize" the category "woman," it remains nonetheless the "concept [in which] our very self-definition is grounded."[3] Although these different debates about difference took different aspects of the body as synecdoches for it, their historical coincidence produced a contested question: what meaning does the difference between these two debates about the body have—the former dominated by black men, the latter by white women—when the subject is the bodies of African American women?

In discounting the body in this apparently appropriate way, Gates's African Americanist theory made a move familiar from the white European theory that he took as his starting point, a move that was familiar in its implicit or explicit positioning of women and in its disregard for what some women were saying. Although Gates's paradigms of the Signifyin(g) Monkey for the practice of black writing and of the god Esu-Elegbara for the literary critic derived from African and African American religion and folkways, his discovery of the value of these figures was prepared for (according to his account) by his education in the deconstructive and psycholinguistic theories of Lacan, Derrida, and de Man, whose shared view of language as a system of differences and displacements was of particular use to a critic trying to move away from "the idea of a transcendent signified, a belief in an essence called 'blackness.'"[4] Whereas for some feminists such a view of language led the way as well to an escape from biological essentialism in the realm of gender, for others it meant hostility to the female body.

The liberatory power of the deconstructive view of language derives from the perception that a gap lies between signifier and signified and between word and referent. Hence the liberatory understanding that gender is not the same as biological sex—indeed that sex is an effect produced by gender —or that race is an idea or metaphor. The problem lies in Lacan's positioning of the maternal body as the absence that makes language's substitutions possible and necessary. Like Freud's claim that patriarchal religions are superior to matriarchal ones because they substitute the difficult belief in an invisible paternity for the relatively easy belief in visible maternity, the position that Gates inherited from poststructuralism can be seen to identify and celebrate the abstract as masculine and devalue embodiment as female. It is for this reason (among others) that, despite the appeal of deconstructive ways of thinking about gender, the issue of the female body wouldn't (and still won't) go away in feminist theory. To quote from Alcoff again on the category "woman," "If gender is simply a social construct, the need and even the possibility of a feminist politics becomes immediately problematic. . . . How can we speak out against sexism as detrimental to the interests of women if the category is a fiction?" (420). For some of the same reasons (and some others), the female body and the body troped as female won't go away in African American studies as well. Gates's effort to disarticulate race and the body didn't take into account a long cultural tradition, both inside and outside of the deconstructive position he occupied, that, for good or ill, identifies women with the body.

When Gates celebrated African American writing and criticism for saving black Americans from reduction to "nature" and "essence," he substituted, in the undesirable position of the referent or ground from which language differentiates itself, female for black. If, in Gates's revision of a traditional saying, "figuration [for 'signification'] is the nigger's occupation," then writing as figuration as uplift was still paradigmatically a male—if now black male—province, with the female ground still subordinate.[5] What Gates dismissed as "essence," the body and the referential, or racially marked experience as bodily experience, some African American women writers were still adhering to, and this adherence sometimes took the form of embracing (both thematically and rhetorically) a relatively literal language, in striking contrast to Gates's celebration of figuration. Their reasons for adhering to the body and to the literal intersect—in what I hope is a mutually instructive relation between feminisms—with the reasons for the equivocal status of the body within what had been a white-dominated corner of feminist theory. These writers refused to allow racist as well as sexist biologism to determine their thinking: they valued the body regardless of the degraded position to which androcentric culture had assigned it, and to which their categorical association with it doubly relegated them.

I will begin by discussing places where this difference of view appears explicitly in the heated 1980s debate over the usefulness of poststructuralist theory for the study of African American literature. But I also argue that this debate emerges implicitly in African American women's fiction of the same time: that an equivocation over figurative (especially metaphoric) language versus (relatively) literal language is the rhetorical form in which the debate over racial and gendered "essence" was worked out. The use or representation of a relatively literal language corresponds to and puts into practice a belief in the embodiedness of race and of gender (a belief that race and gender are experienced in the body), whereas the view that race is figurative coincides with and is performed as a celebration of language as figuration and a tendency to use conspicuous metaphors. Neither belief, along with its corresponding rhetorical form, can be easily dislodged, as the texture of these critical and fictive writings shows.

A painful debate appeared in a 1987 issue of *New Literary History* between Gates and Houston A. Baker Jr., on the one hand, and Joyce A. Joyce, on the other, on the subject (among others) of Gates's claim that race is a metaphor. That this debate touched a powerful chord in many readers earns it the close scrutiny I give it here. In her critique of the current state of African American literary criticism, Joyce's initial objection is to the willing assimilation of black critics like Gates and Baker into white middle-class styles of thought, typified by their embrace of poststructuralism. To adopt that theory's difficult vocabulary, she argues, is an elitist "rejection of race."[6] Pivotal in her argument are two statements by Gates, one quoted at the outset and one quoted in her reply to Gates's and Baker's responses:

> "Blackness" is not a material object or an event but a metaphor; it does not have an "essence" as such but is defined by a network of relations.[7]

> Race, as a meaningful criterion within the biological sciences, has long been recognized to be a fiction. When we speak of "the white race" or "the black race," "the Jewish race" or "the Aryan race," we speak in biological misnomers and, more generally, in metaphors.[8]

In her comments on these passages, Joyce first calls Gates's equation of race with metaphor his "denial of blackness or race as an important element of literary analysis of Black literature" (337). Later she describes it as an instance of "the prevalent, malevolent, unconscionable, illusionary idea that race and (it goes unsaid) racism have ceased to be the leading impediments that thwart the mental and physical lives of Black people" (373). Thus she identifies Gates's view of race as metaphor as central to his assimilation into white middle-class values, the assimilation that is the object of her more general critique.

As the debate continues, it emerges that Joyce and Gates are not as far apart as each appears to believe. When Joyce concludes by calling race an "inane, illogical concept" (377), she would seem to agree with Gates's statement, quoted by her, that "the relation between a sign, such as blackness, and its referent, such as absence" is arbitrary.[9] What he means by *metaphor* is this arbitrary assignment of cultural meanings to nature. Both, it appears, want to deny the validity of culturally imposed racial boundaries while accepting their present political reality. Nonetheless, Joyce's reasons for objecting to Gates's view of race as metaphor are of particular interest to feminist readers. To say that race is a metaphor is, for her, a denial of the body. Of Gates's poststructuralist masters, such as de Man and Derrida, she writes: "Their pseudo-scientific language is distant and sterile. These writers evince their powers of ratiocination with an overwhelming denial of most, if not all, the senses. Ironically, they challenge the intellect, 'dulling' themselves to the realities of the sensual, communicative function of language" (339–40). Of critics prior to Gates, she writes favorably that they "saw a direct relationship between Black lives—Black realities—and Black literature" (338). With these references to the senses, the sensual, and "realities," Joyce makes the body the ground of contention, the body that is troped as female in the poststructuralist theory Gates uses and whose absence that theory requires.

It is important to note that the body Joyce defends here is not simply "essence." For Joyce, and for the other black women writers I discuss here, the body is experiential, including but not limited to the erotic, and context-bound.[10] It bears the traces of remembered histories and is not separable from the mind (as in her expression, "the mental and physical lives of Black people"). What she is defending is not the body alone, but the inseparability of body and mind, against a philosophical tradition that depends on a mind-body split.[11] Nonetheless, the body in Joyce's sense of it is closer to the category excluded in poststructural systems than to the position of authority within those systems. Hazel Carby (see the following) links experience negatively to essentialism in a way that supports my interpretation here. For the sake of coalition politics, we might provisionally align two rather different definitions of the female body, coming from what have historically been white and black feminisms.

That it is gender as well as race that is under contention becomes clearer in Gates's and Baker's responses to Joyce. Gates attributes to Joyce's essay a "keyword" that Joyce does not actually use: "integrity."[12] *Integrity*, in the sense of "the absence of violation and corruption, the preservation of an initial wholeness or soundness" (349), is for him a conservative concept—especially because of its resonance with the Southern Agrarians' idea "that texts are 'wholes'" (350)—in contrast to the "exhilarating speculation and experimentation" that for him characterizes "Afro-American criticism . . . at the present time" (348–49). Oddly, however, Gates goes on to use the term favorably in reference to himself: "those of us who respect the sheer integrity of the black tradition . . . must, above all, respect the integrity, the wholeness, of the black work of art." This aim, stated repeatedly—"to preserve the integrity of these texts, . . . to protect the integrity of our tradition"—is to be accomplished "by bringing to bear upon the explication of its meanings . . . any tool of sensitivity to language that is appropriate," that is, the contemporary literary theory he favors (351–52). Rather than rejecting the notion of integrity altogether, Gates is only rejecting Joyce's right to defend it and her manner of doing so.

As Deborah McDowell remarks about this debate, in "this already fixed match between black men and black women . . . the bodies/texts of black women have become the 'battlefield on and over which men, black and white, [fight] to establish actual and symbolic political dominance and to demonstrate masculine' control."[13] Gates deploys a sexualized language that metaphorically renders black literature as a helpless woman's body and himself as her true and only champion, whose privilege as champion is exclusive access to her body. Not to use contemporary literary theory is to "inflict upon our literary tradition the violation of the uninformed reading. We are the keepers of the black literary tradition" (353). Joyce's suspicion that poststucturalism is a "denial of . . . the senses" is verified here, in the particular sense that it is a denial or curtailment of the body troped as female and specifically of the female body, by Gates's definition of criticism as a masculine project and literature as the objectified female body to which other women, as speaking subjects, cannot have access. She is responding, it would seem, to the poststructuralist critic's hierarchical understanding of his relation to the body of literature.

Baker's response to Joyce also finds the activity of women's bodies threatening to the male preserve of criticism. He begins not by responding to

Joyce's writing but by describing a face-to-face encounter with "a black woman" (whom Joyce later identifies as Deborah McDowell), who he claims launched a conservative "attack" on his redefinition of the Harlem Renaissance at a conference shortly before he received Joyce's essay.[14] Linking the two episodes, Baker asserts that "my response is not directed against a group" but then proceeds in the rest of the essay to refer categorically to "a black woman critic" and "black women critics." Baker like Gates seems to view African American criticism as an endangered male preserve and justifies, perhaps more that Gates's text, Joyce's description of the replies as "misogynist" and "paternalistic." For Baker, Joyce and McDowell "represent what I can only call a new black conservatism, one that ironically derives from black women critics. I say 'ironically' because in the world of avant-garde literary study today, it is possible to think that black women, above all others perhaps, should be in the vanguard of one of the most exciting areas of literary criticism and theory in the United States" (367). One man's conservatism, however, may be another woman's radicalism: Joyce's version of the episode differs entirely from Baker's and portrays Baker as the conservative.[15]

Baker aligns Joyce's attention to the senses with an old-style racist stereotype of "the negro" that represents, for him, everything that black critics should reject: "assertions of a 'noble savagery,' sensually humanistic delightfulness, and monosyllabic clarity . . . achieve nothing but a pat on the head and a reinforcement of a Howellsian minstrel sensibility in the academy" (367). For Baker, who sees the "complexity" of poststructuralist theory raising African American culture up from "sensual" simplicities, Joyce's championing of the senses, along with McDowell's in-the-body "attack," represents a valuation of ground over figure, and this alignment can only have been determined by their gender, as "black women critics." Blacks have wrongly been called "sensual" by Howells and his like, but women, Baker implies, really are "sensual" and would drag the race back towards the body's ground.

Despite the starkness of the critical opposition Joyce, Baker, and Gates enact, it is interesting to note that each concludes by returning to the position he or she denounces. Gates and Baker both end by laying claim to the senses and to the material of African American culture; Joyce ends with an extravagant and phallocentric metaphor: "[T]hese final comments water the seeds that I have planted throughout this essay" (382). The constitution of this debate is such that it is almost impossible to sustain only one side of it, rhetorically or thematically.

To say so is, however, to imply, erroneously, that the debate is symmetrical. The material and institutional circumstances of the debate are germane to its content and reception. Gates and Baker were and are celebrity professors at topflight research universities, and they dominate their field; Joyce was not, at the time, so well-known or so prestigiously placed.[16] This asymmetry reflects the relative prestige of "high theory" and "practical criticism" throughout the academy, and it reflects as well the structure of metaphor itself, the metaphoricity that Gates and Baker champion and that Joyce finds oppressive. This situation puts the differential power of the sexes at the forefront of the debate's significance. Women such as Joyce may continue to take an interest in the position of ground or body, but in the current situation they will generally suffer for it. Gates and Baker accuse her of doing what she claims to do, but her motives are inscrutable to them and different from the ones they ascribe to her.

Echoes of the debate between Joyce and Gates and Baker can be heard in the considerably more constructive and egalitarian conversation about the place of white "theory" that was taking place at the same time among African American women critics. Fundamental to this discussion was the following question: does the term *black feminist criticism* refer literally to writing produced only by black women, or can the term be metaphoric, referring to criticism by anyone so long as it bears a certain orientation and subject matter? The most prevalent view on this subject in the 1970s and early 1980s was, as Cheryl Wall pointed out in 1989 with reference to a statement by Mary Helen Washington, that the function of black feminist criticism was to establish a correct representation of black women; and, as Hazel Carby pointed out in 1987 about Barbara Smith's influential 1977 "Toward a Black Feminist Criticism," that only black women can, or should, undertake this task, on the grounds that their experience is unique and nontransferable.[17] Carby also notes that in 1980 Deborah McDowell defined the term as "Black female critics who analyze the works of Black female writers from a feminist or political perspective."[18]

This set of views was reformulated in 1989 by Patricia Hill Collins, who argued that all thought, black or white, derives from the standpoint of the thinker, which in turn derives from that thinker's experience. As a consequence, "living life as an African American woman is a necessary prerequisite for producing black feminist thought."[19] In 1984 bell hooks criticized white women academics for writing about black women: "They make us the 'objects' of their privileged discourse on race. As 'objects,' we remain unequals, inferiors."[20] Despite their differences, these two statements share a wariness about anyone but black women themselves speaking either for or about black women and an implicit identification of black feminism with the persons of black women. In 1989, however, hooks modified her position not only to allow for but to require white women's writing on black women (so long as their point of view as whites is made explicit and so long as they do not claim to be authoritative).[21] And Hazel Carby included others besides black women in the black feminist project. After critiquing the early statements by Smith and McDowell she writes, "Black feminist criticism has too frequently been reduced to an experiential relationship that exists between black women as critics and black women as writers who represent black women's reality. Theoretically this reliance on a common, or shared, experience is essentialist and ahistorical" (16). To call experience an "essentialist" category equates it with biology and links it to Gates's condemnation of "belief in an essence called 'blackness'" as the echo of racist biologism. Following Carby, Valerie Smith in 1989 defined the term *black feminist theory* as "a way of reading inscriptions of race . . . gender . . . and class in modes of cultural expression" and not solely as theory produced by black women.[22] Both Valerie Smith and Carby sought to detach the term *black feminist theory* or *black feminist criticism* from the experiential bodies of black women. They made the term figurative in contrast to the literal or referential use of it by Collins and others.

In including whites in this way, Smith struck a note that curiously echoed hooks's original exclusion of them. Hooks took exception to the way white women "make [black women] the objects of their privileged discourse"; similarly, Smith criticizes the use of black women, by white women and black men, "to rematerialize the subject of their theoretical positions" (44). Black women turn up in the writings of white women and black men, she points out, only when they want to defend themselves against the charge of being ahistorical, because ahistorical writing can be identified by its assumption that "all the women are . . . white, all the blacks male." For Smith, this use of black women to rematerialize critical discourse only reiterates the stereotypical association of black women with "the body and therefore with animal passions and slave labor" (45), an association whose history has been explored by Carby and more recently by Harryette Mullen and others.[23] Black men and white women, Smith argues, retain black women in the position of the ground from which feminist criticism has ostensibly been trying to rescue all women, revealing that it was only white women whom white feminists were trying to rescue. Making *black feminist* figurative rather than literal (as she does when she calls black feminist theory "a way of reading") would, in Smith's view, help to counter this tendency.

The position taken by Valerie Smith and by Carby, then—and to their work we might add the poststructuralist work of Hortense Spillers and Mae Henderson—might seem aligned with that taken contemporaneously by Gates and Baker: that nature, essence, and ground are the wrong identifications for African Americans and that dismantling the heritage of slavery means converting race from a literal designation to a metaphor. The published positions taken by Barbara Smith, McDowell (1980), and Collins—and by Barbara Christian, whose 1987 attack on theory ("The Race for Theory") was reprinted in 1989—might be seen to parallel Joyce's defense of the senses and of the responsibility of black writers to black experience. And yet the lines cannot be so neatly drawn. There was institutional prestige on both sides; more important, individual writers adopted positions on either side at different times, even at the same time. We have already discussed hooks in this regard; McDowell, for another example, concludes the paragraph (and the essay) in which she mentions the Joyce debate by borrowing from Alice Jardine to distinguish, and to link, "black women's written *bodies* and their *written* bodies." For some reason, it remained among these critics a legitimate topic of debate to focus, however intermittently and ambivalently, on the body and the literal and to identify racially marked experience as bodily and black literature as referential, when for Gates and Baker these views had become out of the question.

That each side of the debate remained a legitimate option for at least some black women writers is underscored by certain literary works central to black feminist criticism. In the readings that follow, I trace the sustained though deeply ambivalent interest in the racially marked body in fiction and autobiography by African American women writers and the way in which the debate between race as body and race as metaphor is played out in their balancing of figurative and literal language. Because the debate between experience and theory, or between race as body and race as metaphor, takes form in the language in which the debate is phrased, we should expect to find this debate informing the stylistic texture of contemporaneous writings that are not ostensibly concerned with it. Reading a few passages from 1980s writings by Alice Walker, Maya Angelou, and Toni Morrison will help us see not only that, but also why, some black women writers continued to link race to the body and to relatively nonfigurative language.

For Walker in the late 1980s as for Joyce, race and the writing of race are very physical matters. In a journal entry in *Living by the Word,* from which I take the title of this essay, Walker writes that she once wrote herself this note:

> I am Nicaraguan; I am Salvadorean; I am Grenadian; I am Caribbean; and I am Central American.
> For the past several days I have been thinking about this sentence, and wondering what I mean by it. I am also Norte Americana, an African-American, even an African-Indian-Gringo American, if I add up all the known elements of my racial composition.[24]

Because the people of Central America are likewise racially mixed, she goes on, "when I look at those people . . . I see myself. I see my family, I see my parents, I see the ancestors" (176–77). The writing or "composition" of race is distinctly physical here. *I am Nicaraguan* is a sentence, a deliberate composition and an object for subsequent interpretation; but it is at the same time an assertion of bodily identity.

In many of the essays in *Living by the Word,* Walker mentions her claim to embody the "ancestors" whose blood runs in her veins. "In the Closet of My Soul" discusses the consequences of her having not only a Cherokee grandmother and many former slaves live on in her, but also a white slaveowner.

Her poetry and fiction, she writes, are in part outlets for the voices of these ancestors. Celie "speaks in the voice . . . of my step-grandmother, Rachel"; Mister's slaveowner father "was also my great-great-grandfather" (63, 82). In another journal entry in *Living by the Word,* Walker stresses the specific physicality of "the ancestors" when, just after the controversial publication of *The Color Purple,* they visit her in dreams. A woman fieldworker, missing two fingers, "was only one of a long line of ancestors who came to visit and take my hand that night. . . . I remembered her distinctly next morning because I could still feel her plump hand with its missing fingers gently but firmly holding my own" (67). The explicitly tactile quality of this "contact" with ancestors grounds Walker's writing in the most physical way.

Walker's most splendid invention in her otherwise poorly received novel *The Temple of My Familiar* wildly extends her essays' and journals' claims about the embodiment of ancestors and others. This invention is the series of incarnations experienced, recalled, recounted, and still embodied by the elderly Miss Lissie. Not only has she been various black women throughout human history, but also, shockingly, "I was a white man. . . . I was also, once upon a time, a very large cat."[25] This aspect of the novel would appear to constitute an extravagant fictionalization or figuration of Walker's own claim to embody her ancestors, including the white rapist slaveowner. At the same time, because the novel compels belief in the concreteness of Lissie's experience and memory and because Lissie embodies not ancestors but her own past selves, the novel also literalizes what is, it must be admitted, Walker's fictive conceit about her relation to the past. Lissie's past selves include an African girl sold into slavery; a pygmy in prehistoric Africa; a wife in a harem; a Mooress burnt at the stake as a witch; and, finally and dramatically, a white woman slaveowner, a white Adam (in a rewritten Genesis story), and a lion. "I can still sometimes feel the sun on my fur, the ticks in my mane, the warm swollen fullness of my tongue" (357). Lissie's remembered lives represent a kind of racial memory, in the sense that they constitute a world history of black people as well as a history of interracial (or interspecies) conflict.

Although most of her past selves are black, that she can recall being white and even an animal exposes narrowly biological definitions of race as the fiction Gates emphasizes they are. And yet, just as Lissie seems to bear a simultaneously figurative and literalizing relation to Walker's own self-writing, the insistently physical nature of Lissie's memories—the continued bodily presence of those past selves—corresponds to definitions of race as bodily experience if not as bodily essence. That Lissie not only "was" but still "is" these various beings, in her body, is dramatized by a series of photographs. As her husband Hal cryptically explains to Suwelo (their young acquaintance who has just inherited the house of Lissie's lover, Suwelo's Uncle Rafe) when he discovers pictures of people he doesn't recognize,

"Most of the women are Lissie. . . ."
"But there're a lot of women."
"Lissie is a lot of women." (38)

Instead of "the same woman dressed to make herself appear different [he saw] thirteen pictures of thirteen entirely different women. One seemed tall, another very short, one light-skinned, with light eyes, another dark with eyes like obsidian" (89). These pictures, Lissie later explains to Suwelo, were taken by a photographer who (to his own bafflement) "was able to photograph the women I was in many of my lifetimes before" (90), images not available to the eye alone. After years of confusing and difficult "memory excavation," the photographs "corroborated" the fact that "I had been these people, and they were still somewhere inside of me. . . . The selves I had thought gone forever, existing only in my memory, were still there! Photographable" (90). Two of the pictures, Suwelo discovers, represent the past selves Lissie has so far narrated to him. Later Lissie reveals that there were also photographs of her looking white and looking "feline" (360), which she destroyed because Hal would not have been able to believe or bear them.

Why aren't words and memory enough to establish Lissie's history; why must Walker devise this ingenious method for confirming Lissie's tales? Crucial to Walker's conception of past lives is the bodily memory of them, their continued physical presence. And yet looked at another way, this emphasis on physical evidence functions as a supplement to expose anxieties about the language in which Lissie's memories first emerge. Language risks betraying the things it refers to because of the inevitable gap between word and referent. As physical artifacts that put things themselves before the viewer, favoring ground over figure, or "the senses" over "metaphor" (to return to the terms of Joyce's debate with Gates and Baker), the photos seem to define the linguistic acts they supplement as figural and untrustworthy. Nonetheless, even though photography may be the most literal form of visual representation, it is still representational, black and white and color on paper. That the novel emphasizes photography's mediation as a representational form as much as its capacity to make the body present in a relatively unmediated way is dramatized by the availability of Lissie's bodies only to the camera's lens and not to the bodily eye. Thus, again, Lissie's embodiments suggest figuration as well as the literal, just as they suggest the fictiveness of racial categories as well as the bodily nature of racially marked experience.

The visual representations with which the novel closes summarize this equivocation between body and metaphor, between literal and figurative representations. Arranged around Hal's bed in the nursing home where Suwelo visits him are the paintings Lissie made just before her death. Because he cannot accept what he sees in them, Hal has gone blind. Of the very last two paintings, one represents Lissie as a lion wearing a "very gay, elegant, and shiny red high-heeled slipper" (403), and one represents what Suwelo thinks of as "the tree of life," a tree with all of Lissie's various selves in its branches, or as the uncomprehending Hal describes his memory of it, "That big tree with all the black people and funny-looking critters, and snakes and everything . . . and even a white fellow in it. Then all those lions . . ." (400; ellipses in text).

Whereas the lion painting is, like the photographs, a relatively literal representation of a particular incarnation (and in Gates's account of the paradigmatic tale of "signifying," "the Lion interprets or 'reads' literally" and thus gets duped by the "Monkey [who] speaks *figuratively*"),[26] the tree painting is not. The image constitutes the transformation into metaphor—"family tree," "tree of life," or "evolutionary tree"—of an actual, remembered tree: the plum tree in the background of Lissie's story of her life as the first white man. In the paradisal world in which this story begins, a world in which black is the only skin color and animals and humans coexist in peace, the adolescent Adam and Eve have been sent, with her familiar, a serpent, to pick plums. The two humans make love, and when he wakes up she tells him what he had not understood before, that he is white, a genetic freak. "You look like you don't have a skin" (353), she says; in the mirror of a pool "there I was— a ghost," with pale skin and yellow hair. In his anger and shame at this "hideous personal deficiency" he chases the girl away and kills the serpent, thus inaugurating the fall simultaneously into racial and sexual division and violence.

From this revision of the fall to Lissie's tree painting, the merely scenic plum tree has become figuralized. (That it is this tree that reappears in Lissie's painting is made clear by an intervening episode involving an imaginary plum tree.) In the tree painting, in contrast to the lion painting, the representation is of a conception, the idea that human and animal life form an interconnected whole. Memory is confirmed not by relatively literal representation but by metaphor. The tree painting also gestures towards the high valuation of figuration in Hurston's *Their Eyes Were Watching God*, where the tree, in Gates's reading, is Janie's "master trope," the metaphor that signifies metaphoricity itself.[27] The blooming pear tree that provides Janie with her first vision of sexual delight speaks to her in a way that is clearly not intended as literal, despite the rich physicality of the scene: "It has called her to come and gaze on a mystery. . . . This singing she heard that had nothing to do with her ears."[28] By ending with the two paintings, of the conspicuously figurative tree and of the literal lion, the novel leaves suspended the question of race and figuration: race is either a matter of bodily being (Joyce) or a "metaphor" (Gates), but not both at the same time. If, in this equivocation, Walker may be said to prefer one side to the other, it would be that of the body: it is the painting of the literal-minded lion that is described in the novel's very last words.

Walker's ending both pays homage to Hurston's tree trope and dislodges metaphoricity's centrality by countering the tree with the lion. Walker's tree may allude not only to Hurston's but also to the tree figure in *Beloved,* through which Toni Morrison makes a kindred critique of metaphoricity. Sethe tells Paul D that she has a tree on her back, one she has never seen but that Amy Denver described to her: "That's what she said it looked like. A chokecherry tree. Trunk, branches, and even leaves. Tiny chokecherry leaves."[29] Paul D, deeply sympathetic, "rubbed his cheek on her back and learned that way her sorrow, the roots of it; its wide trunk and branches" (17). Between these two passages, the tree has grown doubly figurative. A figure for "her sorrow," now, not just for the scar that could be said to represent that sorrow, the tree acquires its own figurative elaboration as "sculpture . . . the decorative work of an ironsmith." And yet after Sethe and Paul D make love, this highly complex figure collapses into its referent, which Paul D now sees as "in fact a revolting clump of scars. Not a tree" (21).

The career of Morrison's tree figure shares in the meaning of the juxtaposed tree and lion paintings in *The Temple of My Familiar,* a move from figurative to literal but with an inflection that reveals even more distinctly the political meanings of that move. To see the scar as a beautifully wrought tree risks, perhaps, the danger of forgetting the appalling violence that made the scar eighteen years before. Though Paul's second vision of the scar is as much about the vicissitudes of his feeling as it is about slavery, it also warns the reader not to become mesmerized by the novel's power to generate beautiful figures. Sometimes a scar is a scar and needs to be seen that plainly; figuration, although it assists the grace of love and healing, may conceal the horror of slavery, just as Sethe resents her memory for producing the pastoral pleasantness of Sweet Home more readily that its pain. Moreover, figuration can hide historical truth. Because of the tree figure, Paul D can imagine he knows "the roots," that is, the origins, "of her sorrow," and this false certainty means that the deepest horror in Sethe's history will later take him horribly by surprise. Still, by making the "revolting clump of scars" an effect of Paul D's postcoital depression, the novel suggests that the choice is not between true and false but between kinds of representation that both have their value.

This choice between the values of figurative and literal appears movingly, and with a similar slight weighting towards the literal, in the 1986 fifth volume of Maya Angelou's autobiography, *All God's Children Need Travelling Shoes,* in two haunting scenes from Angelou's poignant attempt to recover her origins in Africa. Like other returned African Americans in the early 1960s, she has not found easy acceptance among the people she nonetheless feels are hers, and she dwells on the possibility that her forebears were sold into slavery by the ancestors of her African contemporaries. Living and working temporarily in Ghana, Angelou describes two trips into the countryside. During the first she arrives in the evening at a remote town, Dunkwa, where, because of "my skin color, features, and the Ghana cloth I wore. . . . I could pass if I didn't talk too much."[30] Unable to find a hotel, she finds herself instead welcomed, fed, and housed by friendly townspeople. She identifies herself in Fanti as a "stranger," although because "only Whites could be strangers" she is accepted as an African of uncertain background. Her clan and racial identity are established in the following conversation with the old man who arranges her housing:

> "Aflao?"
> I said, "No."
> "Brong-ahafo?"
> I said, "No. I am—." I meant to tell him the truth, but he said, "Don't tell me. I will soon know." He continued staring at me. "Speak more. I will know from your Fanti."
> "Well, I have come from Accra and I need to rent a room for the night. I told that woman that I was a stranger . . . "
> He laughed. "And you are. Now, I know. You are Bambara from Liberia. It is clear you are Bambara." He laughed again. "I can always tell. I am not easily fooled." (100–101)

Angelou lets the mistake stand, enjoys the evening in the role of "Bambara Auntie," and concludes the episode with these words: "In Dunkwa, although I let a lie speak for me, I had proved that one of [the slaves'] descendants, at least one, could just briefly return to Africa, and that despite cruel betrayals, bitter ocean voyages and hurtful centuries, we were still recognizable" (105). Her use of the word *pass* to indicate her African appearance ironically reverses the term's ordinary meaning in the U.S. Passing for African goes some way toward compensating for the pain of needing or wanting or being forced to pass for white in the U.S., and it also calls attention, as does *passing for white,* to the arbitrariness or figurativeness of racial categories.[31]

In contrast to this scene stands the volume's final and climactic episode, Angelou's second excursion out of Accra. As she and her traveling companions draw near the coastal town of Keta, they come to a "sturdy and graceful bridge" over a river. Suddenly, and with the violent physical symptoms of racing heart and gasping breath, Angelou becomes possessed by the idea that she and the others must walk across the bridge. She cannot explain this feeling; "I only knew that the possibility of riding across that bridge so terrified me that had the driver refused to stop, I would have jumped from the still moving car" (199). Once on the other side, one of her companions explains to her that "a century ago" this river was spanned by poorly built bridges susceptible to being washed away and that passengers "in conveyances of any kind" would alight and cross by foot to avoid the danger of drowning. Angelou knows that she has never heard this story before; the explanation, left implicit and drawing on conventions of "magic realism," is that a deep and physical memory has been reawakened. She does not need language to explain her bodily relation to this place.

When they reach Keta, a town once notorious as a slave depot, Angelou finds herself addressed, in Ewe, by a woman with "a voice somewhat similar to my own" (202). Although Angelou explains in several languages that she does not speak Ewe, the woman grows angrier and angrier until Angelou calls on her friend to interpret. Before Angelou offers an account of their words, she reveals an astonishing physical fact. Unable previously to get a good look at the woman, "When she raised her head, I nearly fell back down the steps: she had the wide face and slanted eyes of my grandmother." And she is "over six feet tall," like Angelou herself. She makes a gesture of mourning and then introduces the mystified Angelou to other women in the market, who all offer her their produce and repeat the sign of mourning. Finally her friend, very moved, explains. At one point in Keta's history all the adults were killed or forced into slavery. Only a few children escaped, to be rescued by nearby villagers and to keep alive the horrific story. To the women in the market, "descendants of those orphaned children," Angelou, he explains, "look[s] so much like them, even the tone of your voice is like theirs. They are sure you are descended from those stolen mothers and fathers. That is why they mourn. Not for you but for their lost people" (206). Angelou comments: "A sadness descended on me, simultaneously somber and wonderful. I had not consciously come to Ghana to find the roots of my beginnings, but I had continually and accidentally tripped over them or fallen upon them in my everyday life. Once I had been taken for Bambara. . . . And here in my last days in Africa, descendants of a pillaged past saw their history in my face and heard their ancestors speak through my voice" (206–7). Angelou's language here is notably similar to Walker's claim that she embodies and speaks for her ancestors, and to the claim, grounded in her "racial composition," that "I am Nicaraguan." Weeping with her kinswomen, Angelou nonetheless silently ("in my heart") celebrates her people's survival; "Although separated from our languages, our families and customs, we had dared to continue to live." And here, after a last page on her departure at the airport, the autobiography ends, as if in confirmation of language's irrelevance to Angelou's most valued experience.

In the first of these episodes, Angelou discovers her identity as an African only by "let[ting] a lie speak for me," a lie founded on the way she uses words. An act of language establishes identity, but, because untrue—like metaphor, which is a kind of lying—the identification is temporary and unstable. In contrast, when she visits Keta it is physical sensation, physical memory, and physical resemblance—"their history in my face"—that give her a deep and reliable identity as African descendent, and this is Joyce Joyce's sense of body too: the body that remembers experience and is located in a specific history and place. And in further contrast to the "Bambara Auntie" episode, Angelou is nearly speechless: none of her several languages helps her understand a situation whose mysteriousness her account draws out dramatically. Whereas in the "Bambara Auntie" episode fictive language is needed and suffices to create a provisional sense of belonging, when she finds her blood ancestry, language of every kind fails her and also becomes unnecessary. For Angelou, the body speaks racial identity more truly than does fallen language, but with the consequence that the autobiography ends, either in the silence of rest after labor achieved, or in the silence of recognizing language's limits.

Like Lissie's bodily memory of being the first white man and committing the first acts of violence, Angelou's bodily memory of her ancestors at the moment of their enslavement is a memory of the fall. For Angelou as for other descendants of slaves, the violent capture of her ancestors and their expulsion from Africa is the beginning of fallen history. In the scenic arrangement of the episode, a dangerous bridge divides Angelou from her prelapsarian past, just as for her ancestors crossing a dangerous water was the beginning of "life separated from our languages." Each of these falls identifies racial division—the violence between black and white—as the division of fallen language, the splitting of an original unified language into words and bodily referents and even into the black and white that makes words legible on the page.[32] This is the splitting that makes figurative language and that makes all postlapsarian language figurative. The tree that comes to stand for the fall in Walker's novel also becomes the novel's terminal figure for metaphoricity itself. The use or thematization of a relatively literal language is then the attempt to heal the consequences of the fall by healing the dividedness of language, an attempt to return, by way of rhetoric, to Eden.

To these revisionary accounts of the fall, in which the fall is primarily a story about race and language, we could add an anecdote of Walker's in *Living by the Word* about killing a "snake person" in her garden (143). By having the snake "be" a person, Walker rhetorically enacts an Edenic unity between animal and human. Her murder of the snake in the garden (like her Adam's in *The Temple of My Familiar*) is an act at once of physical and of rhetorical violence, for it reveals that the snake is only metaphorically a person. *Is* falls into its component parts, exposing as fallen metaphor what Walker tries to present as the literal designation of identity.

A crucial scene in *Beloved* likewise represents racial opposition as the source and locus of divided, arbitrary language and identifies racial sameness with a prelapsarian literal language. Sethe is recalling the time when her mother, whom she scarcely knew, showed her the brand under her breast that should, with a horrible irony, enable Sethe to recognize her if "you can't tell me by my face" (61). Poignantly, the young girl asks, "But how will you know me? . . . Mark the mark on me too." Her mother slaps her. In her yearning for a bodily link between them, strangers who should be mother and daughter, Sethe mistakes the arbitrary and hated sign of enslavement for the body it defaces, for the breast (under which the scar lurks) she was denied almost from birth. This memory calls up another more deeply buried one. In her mother's own African tongue, which Sethe has now forgotten (a language that stands in the same place that psychoanalysis reserves for the vanished preoedipal stage), Sethe's foster mother once recounted Sethe's conception and survival. The memory of this "message" now returns to Sethe in a medium that is not language, even if the novel must translate it into words. Raped by a series of white men during and after the journey from Africa, Sethe's mother threw away each baby so conceived and kept Sethe alone, the only child conceived with a black man, the only man "she put her arms around" (62). Sethe's memory of a bogus link to the mother—through the sign, the brand—overlays the memory of their real link: their shared bodily blackness.

Although blackness represents shared culture and experience too, it is the absolute terms of physical racial opposition that Nan emphasizes in her telling: "The others from more whites she also threw away. . . . You she gave the name of the black man" (62). As in Angelou's two memories, the establishment of racial identity as bodily is represented as more deep and complete, if also more disturbing, than the establishment of identity by way of arbitrary signs, whether of language or of branding. Whereas the brand signifies fallen language and alludes to the postlapsarian mark of Cain, Sethe's origin, narrated in the language spoken before the fall (before the diaspora, and by Sethe before losing her mother), is one moment in which that racial marking is a true mark, a literal and unfallen sign, like prelapsarian language in Genesis—the blackness that enables love, despite all odds, between mother, daughter, and father.

In these scenes, Walker, Angelou, and Morrison keep suspended as far as possible the choice between race as body and race as metaphor, although each finally gives an edge to the body and bodily memory. Perhaps what is most significant is that each concludes by representing the necessity of choice: figuration or the authentic body, but not both at the same time. What these inconclusive conclusions suggest about the contemporaneous critical debate with which we began is that it was not quite susceptible to closure in the terms in which it was then formulated. Both sides may have been right, but in a way that did not allow them easily to be reconciled or synthesized. The texts by Walker, Angelou, and Morrison discussed here tend to acknowledge that this is so but also to make something fruitful out of the dilemma. By extending their definitions of the body to include history and experience, as does Joyce, they could give serious consideration to bodily definitions of race that might have seemed, to Gates and Baker, "conservative."

I have emphasized that Walker, Angelou, and Morrison see racial iden-

tity and interracial violence as the meaning of language's splittings and attempted unities; racial division brings about or reflects the division between
figuration and the body, and it is a desire to heal the wounds made by racial
imperialism (slavery's wounds) that motivates the rejection of metaphor and
the embrace of a relatively literal language. In the critical debates, however,
gender was as much a point of contention as race. In the sexualized language
Gates uses about his relation to black culture and in Baker's generalizations
about black women critics, gender is a conspicuous subtext in which figuration is either white (for Joyce) or black (for Gates and Baker) but always
masculine, and ground is always female. Valerie Smith shows that in the debate among black feminists the reasons for choosing a figurative or a literal
definition of black feminist theory derive from the gender associations of
those rhetorical modes. And indeed in Walker, Angelou, and Morrison gender is central as well. Angelou's real identification in the Keta episode is as
an African woman with other African women, whereas a man with a comi-
cally inflated sense of his authority invents for her the fiction of "Bambara
Auntie." Walker's Lissie rewrites Genesis so that the violence is not only white
against black but also male against female, and so that the human who first
falls is a man as well as white, his victim a woman as well as black. Morrison's
Sethe is violated and healed as a daughter and a mother; whatever prelapsarian language Sethe can imagine is her mother's.

It is significant, as regards intersections of race and gender, that revisions
of the fall are so pivotal to the novels and autobiographic texts we have sur-
veyed. By rewriting the fall as a story of racial division (as a story of the acts
of racist imperialism known as slavery), these writers do not cancel its traditional meaning of sexual division; rather, sexual and racial division are represented as interdependent. And in the manner of Genesis itself, these revisions are about language by being about sexual and racial division. In each
scene, the fall is the moment at once of embodiment (entrance into history)
and of the failure of embodiment adequately to represent a prior condition
of wholeness. As narratives of embodiment, stories of the fall explain why
the literal is always accompanied by its opposite: figuration names the gap
that embodiment seeks but fails to close. Wherever body and figuration pull
against each other, wherever word divides from meaning, what is at stake is
not only the race but also and inextricably the gender of power. The difficult tension between figuration and the body comes neither from racial division alone, nor from sexual division alone, but from racial division as it is
complicated by sexual division.

If Walker, Angelou, Morrison, and scholars such as Collins and Joyce were
unfashionably defending definitions of race as bodily, it may be because
white-dominated, androcentric U.S. society offers them, as black women, no
position from which to enjoy an illusion of their own universality, such as
the figurative with its safe distancing of the categorically "not-male" offers

men of all races. Gates and Baker, occupying the traditionally empowered side of sexual division (if not of racial division), could see figuration's inscription of sexual division, linking them to powerful white male theorists, as beneficial. The African American women writers discussed here, however, had good reason to find that neither sexual nor racial division gains them anything and good reason therefore to have attempted to heal these divisions in one of the places where they find them, in language. This healing, I have been arguing, took the form of their valorizing relatively literal language, even as they also recognized the necessity and value of figuration.

I wish to return briefly to the late-1980s debate among African American feminists about the status of nonblack women writing about black women. My standing to comment on these matters—then or now—would seem to depend on the very overvaluation of the figurative that many African American women writers tended then to question. That is, according to Valerie Smith, the extension of the term *black feminist theory* from black women to whites requires deciding that the term is metaphoric, not (or as well as) literal. And yet, because I have been arguing that the figurative was not the exclusive source of value for black women writers, as it was for Gates and Baker, I am uncomfortable in claiming that metaphoric title when I write about these issues, even at the distance of several years. Nor, however, could I wish to be understood as doing what Valerie Smith said white feminists tend to do, use black women to "rematerialize the subject of [my] theoretical position." In the present case that would mean my identifying African American women writing in the 1980s, and my own position on their work, wholly with the literal, something I have not done here. Perhaps it would be more fair to say that I have used African American women writers not to "rematerialize [my] discourse but to revalorize its materiality."[33] Neither literally nor figuratively a black feminist (nor even figuratively literally), I am obliged—if I am to choose from the options available within the debate I discuss—to follow bell hooks's 1989 recommendation and identify my perspective as that of a white feminist—that is, as that of someone whose immersion in white feminist debates about the body contributed to my perception that there were two sides to the debate over the embodiedness of race.

Rather than attempting to show what has become recently of the critical debates discussed here, I would like to conclude by looking briefly at two 1994 memoirs, one by Henry Louis Gates Jr. and the other by Shirlee Taylor Haizlip, works that suggest how deeply and productively entangled in each other the two sides of the debate about racial embodiedness have become. This change is accompanied—and possibly enabled—by a new way of deploying the mother's body.

Both of these books understand race to be culturally produced. For Gates, Piedmont, West Virginia, is "the place where I learned how to be a colored boy."[34] Haizlip's book is about the ambiguity of the color line for those of mixed race, a family story about those who passed and those who remained black that "suggests that race and color in America are not interchangeable."[35] For both writers, however, the body is crucial as a site of racial meanings.

For Haizlip, tracking the ancestors of her pale-skinned but black-identified mother and locating her living white-identified relatives, genetics matter and are understood to "shape" more than just physical appearance. Painful though it is to seek out those who crossed the color line, "my children and I need to know the rest of what has shaped us. Simply put, part of their genetic codes belong to us as well" (34). The book is haunted by the possibility of family resemblance: "Whenever I see a tall white man with the slightly kinky golden brown hair, subtly flared nostrils and large ears of my brother, I say, 'There's a Morris'" (13). Even so, race does not follow other inherited traits. In this family, to be black or to "become white" (266) is a cultural choice. "My family had many features in common with these relatives from the other side. And yet as I looked at them I thought to myself, But they are different from me, they are white—whatever that is" (248). Perceived "color" is in fact produced by racial choice, not the other way around. When Angelou sees herself in a long-lost relative's face, her story is complete; but for Haizlip this recognition is only part of a larger story.

Gates's book opens with two epigraphs suggesting that, in this book, race—as for Haizlip—is at once learned and very real: "I remember the very day when I became colored," writes Zora Neale Hurston; but "How dare anyone, parent, schoolteacher, or merely literary critic, tell me not to act *colored?*" answers Arna Bontemps. The preface meditates on the felt reality of racial identity, a reality that implicates the body. Closing a passage on his "divided" wishes about his own racial identifications, Gates writes, "Part of me admires those people who can say with a straight face that they have transcended any attachment to a particular community or group . . . but I always want to run around behind them to see what holds them up" (xv; ellipsis in text). A mellowed continuation of Gates's final claim in his response to Joyce Joyce, the book delights in recalling the material features of an all-black world. As in Haizlip, exact registration of physical appearance matters, and descriptions ring the changes on what *colored* can mean: the Colemans' "colors ran the full spectrum of brown, like the whole race in miniature, from the richest dark chocolate to the creamiest cafe au lait" (58). Of his mother's generation —the last to experience the joys and sorrows of "cradle-to-grave segregation" (64)—he writes, "The soul of that world was colored." Nevertheless, as a memoir of the next generation, the book traces the story of discovering that this culture is learned and thus chosen, not an inevitable consequence of skin color, a discovery made possible by the defamiliarizing perspective of integration and eventually of life beyond Piedmont.

Episodes about hair in both books suggest how the body matters: as the site not of natural race but of a chosen racial culture. The most celebrated episode in *Colored People,* the chapter about hair titled "In the Kitchen," memorializes a sensuous world associated with his mother's body. Remembering the hot smell of his mother's iron curlers heating in the gas fire, Gates writes, "I liked what that smell meant for the shape of my day. There was an intimate warmth in the women's tones as they talked with my mama while she did their hair" (40). Paradoxically, what is most sensuous in the scene is the labor of denying genetic race, and yet the result of that labor is troped as more natural than nature itself. His mother is an artist: "Slowly, steadily, with deftness and grace, Mama's hands would transform a round mound of Odetta kink into a darkened swamp of Everglades" (41). Similarly, two opposite things are "miracles." "How that scorched kink could be transformed through grease and fire into a magnificent head of wavy hair was a miracle to me." Two paragraphs later, however, "it was another miracle how hair so 'straight' would so quickly become kinky again once it even approached some water" (41). *The kitchen* is a term doubly and again paradoxically nostalgic: not only the place where his mother performed her transformative art, it is also "the very kinky bit of hair at the back of the head" that always resists straightening, "unassimilably African" (42).

Turning to his own and other male efforts at hair straightening, the narrator recalls his admiration for Nat King Cole's hair, "a beautifully sculptured work of art"; the chapter closes with the narrator, in Zanzibar many years later, suddenly hearing a Nat King Cole song on the radio and blinking back "tears" (49). Racial identification, felt in the body, means connecting with a body transformed into art, and the book's final episode extends this paradoxical definition of the racially identified body. "The Last Mill Picnic" mourns the passing of one of the pleasurable features of segregation, the annual picnic for colored workers at the town's paper mill ("Who in their right mind wanted to attend the mill picnic with white people, when it meant shutting the colored one down?" [211]). As "these hundreds of Negroes gathered to say goodbye to themselves, their heritage, and their sole link to each other" (216), "natural" hair looks wrong. "All of the people under thirty-five or so sported newly coiffed Afros, neatly rounded and shiny with Afro-Sheen. There were red and black and green dashikis everywhere. . . . I found myself looking for silk socks and stocking-cap waves" (213). Afros require art just as much as "stocking-cap waves" do. It is the Afros that seem artificial and out of place in this scene, and the stocking-cap waves that—like the elegantly straightened heads in Mama's kitchen long ago—stand in here for the natural, the way things were.

Haizlip, who had always lived in a "brown community" but whose pale skin would allow her to pass or "become white" if she "chose" (188), finds that her ambiguous appearance needs artificial definition during her 1960s campaign "to integrate New York City" (209). Learning that she will be profiled in the *New York Times* as "a young black woman doing good works," she is "pleased with what I saw as an opportunity for advocacy" (210). But recalling that her 1959 engagement picture "did not suggest that I was black," she "purchased the biggest Afro wig I could find for the *Times* photograph." Associated with Angela Davis, the Afro wig "make[s] a visual . . . statement." Later Haizlip meets "a fair-skinned girl with a small, neat Afro" who tells her "that picture had changed her physical appearance" when it caused her parents to "relent" about her hair. Here again, as in Gates's memoir, African-looking hair is the product of art, a statement with social causes and effects rather than a natural expression. Perhaps even more radically than in Gates, what might really be natural remains unknowable. Still, the book ends with a double assertion: that color is produced by racial ideas (her dark-skinned husband convinces a waiter to seat him in a whites-only restaurant by asking "'Who told you I was colored?'" [266]) and that "I will never lose my black feelings" (267). The final image is of a black mother's body, but this black mother sponsors an infinitude of racial mixings: "Lucy, that ancient group of fossil bones in Africa, the mother of us all" (268).

Both Gates and Haizlip record experiences of the fall: the change from a comfortably all-"colored" world in childhood to the mixed blessing of integration (Gates) or to the painful exploration of racial division within the family (Haizlip). In both cases the fall brings both difficulty and knowledge. In the passages about the fall that we examined in Walker, Angelou, and Morrison, the text seeks to heal division by turning to relatively literal uses of language. But Gates and Haizlip instead accept and keep open what the fall has made: a personal world of mixed and culturally created racial identifications that are nonetheless felt in the body. What enables them to accept the fall so readily? In these recent memoirs the mother does not represent an essential and unrepresentable blackness, as she does for Sethe in *Beloved* and for Angelou encountering her ancestors in Keta, a blackness that the fall violates. Instead she represents the knowledge that division was present from the beginning, even before what felt to the child like the fall. Gates's mother is both the origin of sensuous nostalgia and the artist who magnificently denatures hair; it is the sadness of Haizlip's mother, unable to shake her rejection by her "white" relatives in childhood, that provokes Haizlip to undertake her genealogical quest; and again Lucy, forebear of us all, who shows that racial multiplicity was intrinsic to the human race from the start. If the mother knows self-division, if the mother in her body knows race as a cultural invention, then the child's fall connects him or her to that mother rather than dividing them. Consequently the mother's body need be neither reduced to sheer body nor renounced. To return to the critical debate of the 1980s, the black mother is no longer caught between the impossible options of being used to "rematerialize" something else (Valerie Smith's complaint) or of being dematerialized altogether; in these memoirs she figures as the source, not the object, of a powerfully critical discourse.

NOTES

1. This essay was originally written in 1989 to comment on a debate then currently vivid. That draft was quoted and critiqued by Elizabeth Abel in "Black Writing, White Reading: Race and the Politics of Feminist Interpretation," *Critical Inquiry* 19 (1993): 470–98, reprinted in this volume. It was also presented at the 1992 conference on which this volume draws. Revising it in late 1995 for publication, I find it necessary to recast it as a discussion of a debate that occurred in the past. I wish to thank the following for their careful readings and generous suggestions: Elizabeth Abel, Harriet Chessman, Susan Stanford Friedman, Marianne Hirsch, Patricia Klindienst, Valerie Smith, and Laura Wexler.

2. See Anthony Appiah, "The Uncompleted Argument: Du Bois and the Illusion of Race," *Critical Inquiry* 12 (1985): 21–37.

3. Linda Alcoff, "Cultural Feminism versus Post-Structuralism: The Identity Crisis in Feminist Theory," *Signs* 13 (1988): 405–36, quotation p. 406.

4. Henry Louis Gates Jr., "Criticism in the Jungle," in *Black Literature and Literary Theory*, ed. Henry Louis Gates Jr. (New York: Methuen, 1984), 7; see also chapter 1 of Gates, *The Signifying Monkey* (New York: Oxford University Press, 1988).

5. Gates, "Criticism in the Jungle," 6. For a fuller account of the associations between, on the one hand, metaphor and an oppressive heterosexuality and, on the other, literal (but less articulate) language and the purely and physically female, see my "'Her Very Own Howl': The Ambiguities of Representation in Recent Women's Fiction," *Signs* 9 (1983): 186–205.

6. Joyce A. Joyce, "The Black Canon: Reconstructing Black American Literary Criticism," *New Literary History* 18 (1987): 335–44, quotation p. 337.

7. Henry Louis Gates Jr., "Preface to Blackness: Text and Pretext," in *Afro-American Literature: The Reconstruction of Instruction*, ed. Dexter Fisher and Robert B. Stepto (New York: Modern Language Association of America, 1979), 67, quoted in Joyce, "The Black Canon," 337.

8. Henry Louis Gates Jr., "Writing 'Race' and the Difference It Makes," *Critical Inquiry* 12 (1985): 4, quoted in Joyce A. Joyce, "'Who the Cap Fit': Unconsciousness and Unconscionableness in the Criticism of Houston A. Baker, Jr., and Henry Louis Gates, Jr.," *New Literary History* 18 (1987): 371–84, quotation p. 373.

9. Quoted in Joyce, "The Black Canon," 341; Gates, "Criticism in the Jungle," 7.

10. I am grateful to Susan Stanford Friedman for clarifying this distinction for me. "The literal body is significant here . . . not as the only source of 'meaning,' but rather [because] *within a given historical setting* (with its particular historical construction of gender and the meaning of a body) it has a set of consequences." Friedman, letter to the author, October 1990.

11. In an attack on "theory" that resembles Joyce's in some regards, Barbara Christian makes a similar point about "the split between the abstract and the emotional

in which Western philosophy inevitably indulges." "The Race for Theory," *Cultural Critique* 6 (1987): 51–63, quotation p. 56.

12. Henry Louis Gates Jr., "'What's Love Got To Do with It?': Critical Theory, Integrity, and the Black Idiom," *New Literary History* 18 (1987): 345–62, quotation p. 348.

13. Deborah E. McDowell, "Reading Family Matters," in *Changing Our Own Words*, ed. Cheryl Wall (New Brunswick, N.J.: Rutgers University Press, 1989), 96–97; McDowell quotes Anthony Barthelemy, "Mother, Sister, Wife: A Dramatic Perspective," *Southern Review* 21 (July 1985): 787.

14. Houston A. Baker Jr., "In Dubious Battle," *New Literary History* 18 (1987): 363–69, quotation p. 363.

15. Joyce learned that McDowell directed her question to any of three panelists, not to Baker alone, and that what she queried was not Baker's particular redefinition of the Harlem Renaissance but rather the "implications of [all three] definitions of that Renaissance . . . in relation to the study of Black women writers," since none of the three speakers discussed any woman writer. Joyce, "Who the Cap Fit," 373–74.

16. Barbara Christian too critiques the "hegemonic" status of theory in the academy ("The Race for Theory" 55, 57).

17. See Cheryl Wall, "Introduction: Taking Positions and Changing Words," in Wall, *Changing Our Own Words*, 4; and Hazel Carby, *Reconstructing Womanhood* (New York: Oxford University Press, 1987), 9.

18. Deborah McDowell, "New Directions for Black Feminist Criticism," in *The New Feminist Criticism*, ed. Elaine Showalter (New York: Pantheon, 1985), 191; quoted and discussed by Carby, *Reconstructing Womanhood*, 12.

19. Patricia Hill Collins, "The Social Construction of Black Feminist Thought," *Signs* 14 (1989): 770; later incorporated in her book, *Black Feminist Thought* (Boston: Unwin Hyman, 1990). To readers steeped in white feminist theory, as Susan Stanford Friedman pointed out to me, Collins's position may recall white feminist responses to a claim such as Jonathan Culler's that a man can "read as a woman." For Tania Modleski, when Culler critiques Freud's privileging of hypothetical paternity over visible maternity, that critique must be turned against Culler's own claim that a man can be a "hypothetical" woman reader. "[A] genuinely feminist literary criticism might wish to repudiate the *hypothesis* of a woman reader and instead promote the 'sensible,' visible, actual female reader." "Feminism and the Power of Interpretation: Some Critical Readings," in *Feminist Studies/Critical Studies*, ed. Teresa de Lauretis (Bloomington: Indiana University Press, 1986), 133. Ironically, the similarity between Modleski's and Collins's positions is exactly what must divide, not affiliate them, as each speaks for experiential specificity.

20. bell hooks, *Feminist Theory from Margin to Center* (Boston: Southend Press, 1984), 12.

21. See bell hooks, *Talking Back* (Boston: Southend Press, 1989), chap. 7.

22. Valerie Smith, "Black Feminist Theory and the Representation of the 'Other,'" in Wall, *Changing Our Own Words*, 39.

23. Harryette Mullen, "'Indelicate Subjects': African American Women's Subjugated Subjectivity," in *Sub/versions: Feminist Studies* (Santa Cruz: University of California, 1991).

24. Alice Walker, *Living by the Word: Selected Writing 1973–1987* (New York: Harcourt Brace Jovanovich, 1988), 176.

25. Alice Walker, *The Temple of My Familiar* (New York: Harcourt Brace Jovanovich, 1989), 360.

26. Henry Louis Gates Jr., "The Blackness of Blackness: a Critique of the Sign and the Signifying Monkey," in *Black Literature and Literary Theory*, 289; emphases are his.

27. Gates, *The Signifying Monkey*, 186.

28. Zora Neale Hurston, *Their Eyes Were Watching God* (1937; reprint, Urbana: University of Illinois Press, 1978), 23.

29. Toni Morrison, *Beloved* (New York: Knopf, 1987), 16.

30. Maya Angelou, *All God's Children Need Travelling Shoes* (New York: Random House, 1986), 99.

31. I am grateful to Patricia Klindienst for suggesting this reading.

32. The racial coding of black figure or print on white ground or paper is suggested also by a scene in Alice Walker's *The Third Life of Grange Copeland* (New York: Harcourt Brace Jovanovich, 1970).

33. Elizabeth Abel, letter to the author, October 5, 1990.

34. Henry Louis Gates Jr., *Colored People: A Memoir* (New York: Knopf, 1994), 4.

35. Shirlee Taylor Haizlip, *The Sweeter the Juice: A Family Memoir in Black and White* (New York: Simon and Schuster, 1994), 34.

Black Writing, White Reading
Race and the Politics of Feminist Interpretation

Elizabeth Abel

1

I realize that the set of feelings that I used to have about French men I
now have about African-American women. Those are the people I feel
inadequate in relation to and try to please in my writing. It strikes me
that this is not just idiosyncratic.
—JANE GALLOP, "CRITICIZING FEMINIST CRITICISM"

Twyla opens the narrative of Toni Morrison's provocative story "Recitatif"
(1982) by recalling her placement as an eight-year-old child in St. Bonaventure, a shelter for neglected children, and her reaction to Roberta Fisk, the
roommate she is assigned: "The minute I walked in . . . I got sick to my stom-
ach. It was one thing to be taken out of your own bed early in the morning—
it was something else to be stuck in a strange place with a girl from a whole
other race. And Mary, that's my mother, she was right. Every now and then
she would stop dancing long enough to tell me something important and
one of the things she said was that they never washed their hair and they
smelled funny. Roberta sure did. Smell funny, I mean."[1] The racial ambiguity so deftly installed at the narrative's origin through codes that function
symmetrically for black women and for white women ("they never washed
their hair and they smelled funny") intensifies as the story tracks the encounters of its two female protagonists over approximately thirty years. Unmediated by the sexual triangulations (the predations of white men on black
women, the susceptibility of black men to white women) that have dominated
black women's narrative representations of women's fraught connections
across racial lines, the relationship of Twyla and Roberta discloses the operations of race in the feminine.[2] This is a story about a black woman and a
white woman; but which is which?

102

I was introduced to "Recitatif" by a black feminist critic, Lula Fragd. Lula was certain that Twyla was black; I was equally convinced that she was white; most of the readers we summoned to resolve the dispute divided similarly along racial lines. By replacing the conventional signifiers of racial difference (such as skin color) with radically relativistic ones (such as who smells funny to whom) and by substituting for the racialized body a series of disaggregated cultural parts—pink-scalloped socks, tight green slacks, large hoop earrings, expertise at playing jacks, a taste for Jimi Hendrix or for bottled water and asparagus—the story renders race a contested terrain variously mapped from diverse positions in the social landscape. By forcing us to construct racial categories from highly ambiguous social cues, "Recitatif" elicits and exposes the unarticulated racial codes that operate at the boundaries of consciousness. To underscore the cultural specificity of these codes, Morrison writes into the text a figure of racial undecidability: Maggie, the mute kitchen worker at St. Bonaventure, who occasions the text's only mention of skin color, an explicitly ambiguous sandy color, and who walks through the text with her little kid's hat and her bowed legs "like parentheses," her silent self a blank parenthesis, a floating signifier ("R" 245). For both girls a hated reminder of their unresponsive mothers, Maggie is not "raced" to Twyla (that is, she is by default white); to Roberta, she is black. The two girls' readings of Maggie become in turn clues for our readings of them, readings that emanate similarly from our own cultural locations.

My own reading derived in part from Roberta's perception of Maggie as black; Roberta's more finely discriminating gaze ("she wasn't pitchblack, I knew," is all Twyla can summon to defend her assumption that Maggie is white) seemed to me to testify to the firsthand knowledge of discrimination ("R" 259). Similarly, Roberta is skeptical about racial harmony. When she and Twyla retrospectively discuss their tense encounter at a Howard Johnson's where Twyla was a waitress in the early 1960s, they read the historical context differently: "'Oh, Twyla, you know how it was in those days: black—white. You know how everything was.' But I didn't know. I thought it was just the opposite. Busloads of blacks and whites came into Howard Johnson's together. They roamed together then: students, musicians, lovers, protesters. You got to see everything at Howard Johnson's and blacks were very friendly with whites in those days" ("R" 255). In the civil rights movement that Twyla sees as a common struggle against racial barriers, Roberta sees the distrust of white intervention and the impulse toward a separatist Black Power movement: she has the insider's perspective on power and race relations.

It was a more pervasive asymmetry in authority, however, that secured my construction of race in the text, a construction I recount with considerable embarrassment for its possible usefulness in fleshing out the impulse within contemporary white feminism signaled by the "not just idiosyncratic" confession that stands as this section's epigraph. As Gallop both wittily acknowledges the force of African American women's political critique of white academic feminism's seduction by "French men" and, by simply transferring the transference, reenacts the process of idealization that unwittingly obscures more complex social relations, I singled out the power relations of the girls from the broader network of cultural signs. [3] Roberta seemed to me consistently the more sophisticated reader of the social scene, the subject presumed by Twyla to know, the teller of the better (although not necessarily more truthful) stories, the adventurer whose casual mention of an appointment with Jimi Hendrix exposes the depths of Twyla's social ignorance ("'Hendrix? Fantastic,' I said. 'Really fantastic. What's she doing now?'" ["R" 250]). From the girls' first meeting at St. Bonaventure, Twyla feels vulnerable to Roberta's judgment and perceives Roberta (despite her anxiety about their differences) as possessing something she lacks and craves: a more acceptably negligent mother (a sick one rather than a dancing one) and, partially as a consequence, a more compelling physical presence that fortifies her cultural authority. Twyla is chronically hungry; Roberta seems to her replete, a daughter who has been adequately fed and thus can disdain the institutional Spam and Jell-O that Twyla devours as a contrast to the popcorn and Yoo-Hoo that had been her customary fare. The difference in maternal stature, linked in the text with nurture, structures Twyla's account of visiting day at St. Bonaventure. Twyla's mother, smiling and waving "like she was the little girl," arrives wearing tight green buttocks-hugging slacks and a ratty fur jacket for the chapel service and bringing no food for the lunch that Twyla consequently improvises out of fur-covered jelly beans from her Easter basket ("R" 246). "Bigger than any man," Roberta's mother arrives bearing a huge cross on her chest, a Bible in the crook of her arm, and a basket of chicken, ham, oranges, and chocolate-covered graham crackers ("R" 247). In the subsequent Howard Johnson scene that Twyla's retrospective analysis links with the frustrations of visiting day ("The wrong food is always with the wrong people. Maybe that's why I got into waitress work later—to match up the right people with the right food" ["R" 248]) the difference in stature is replayed between the two daughters. Roberta, sitting in a booth with "two guys smothered in head and facial hair," her own hair "so big and wild I could hardly see her face," wearing a "powder-blue halter and shorts outfit and earrings the size of bracelets," rebuffs Twyla, clad in her waitress outfit, her knees rather than her midriff showing, her hair in a net, her legs in thick stockings and sturdy white shoes ("R" 249). Although the two bodies are never directly represented, the power of metonymy generates a contrast between the amplitude of the sexualized body and the skimpiness and pallor of the socially harnessed body. Twyla's sense of social and physical inadequacy vis-à-vis Roberta, like her representation of her mother's inferiority to Roberta's, signaled Twyla's whiteness to me by articulating a white woman's fantasy (my own) about black women's potency.[4] This fantasy's tenaciousness is indicated by its persistence in the face of contrary evidence. Roberta's mother, the story strongly implies, is mentally rather than physically ill, her capacity to nurture largely fictional; Roberta, who is never actually represented eating, is more lastingly damaged than Twyla by maternal neglect, more vulnerable as an adult to its memory, a weakness on which Twyla capitalizes during their political conflicts as adults; the tenuousness of the adult Roberta's own maternal status (she acquires stepchildren, rather than biological children, through her marriage to an older man) may also testify figuratively to a lack created by insufficient mothering.

Pivoting not on skin color, but on size, sexuality, and the imagined capacity to nurture and be nurtured, on the construction of embodiedness itself as a symptom and source of cultural authority, my reading installs the (racialized) body at the center of a text that deliberately withholds conventional racial iconography. Even in her reading of this first half of the story, Lula's interpretation differed from mine by emphasizing cultural practices more historically nuanced than my categorical distinctions in body types, degrees of social cool, or modes of mothering. Instead of reading Twyla's body psychologically as white, Lula read Twyla's name as culturally black; and she placed greater emphasis on Roberta's language in the Howard Johnson scene—her primary locution being a decidedly white hippie "Oh, wow"—than on the image of her body gleaned by reading envy in the narrative gaze and by assigning racial meaning to such cultural accessories as the Afro, hoop earrings, and a passion for Jimi Hendrix that actually circulated independently of race throughout the counterculture of the 1960s; as Lula knew and I did not, Jimi Hendrix appealed more to white than to black audiences.[5] Roberta's coldness in this scene—she barely acknowledges her childhood friend—becomes, in Lula's reading, a case of straightforward white racism, and Twyla's surprise at the rebuff reflects her naïveté about the power of personal loyalties and social movements to undo racial hierarchies.

More importantly, however, this scene was not critical for Lula's reading. Instead of the historical locus that was salient for me—not coincidentally, I believe, since the particular aura of (some) black women for (some) white women during the civil rights movement is being recapitulated in contemporary feminism (as I discuss later)—what was central to her were scenes from the less culturally exceptional 1970s, which disclosed the enduring systems of racism rather than the occasional moments of heightened black cultural prestige. In general, Lula focused less on cultural than on economic status, and she was less concerned with daughters and their feelings toward their mothers than with these daughters' politics after they are mothers.

When Twyla and Roberta meet in a food emporium twelve years after the Howard Johnson scene, Twyla has married a fireman and has one child and limited income; Roberta has married an IBM executive and lives in luxury in the wealthy part of town with her husband, her four stepchildren, and her

Chinese chauffeur. Twyla concludes in a voice of seemingly racial resentment: "Everything is so easy for them. They think they own the world" ("R" 252). A short time later the women find themselves on opposite sides of a school integration struggle in which both their children are faced with bussing: Twyla's to the school that Roberta's stepchildren now attend, and Roberta's to a school in a less affluent neighborhood. After Twyla challenges Roberta's opposition to the bussing, Roberta tries to defuse the conflict: "'Well, it is a free country.' 'Not yet, but it will be,'" Twyla responds ("R" 256). Twyla's support of bussing, and of social change generally, and Roberta's self-interested resistance to them position the women along the bitter racial lines that split the fraying fabric of feminism in the late 1970s and early 1980s.[6]

Privileging psychology over politics, my reading disintegrates in the story's second half. Lula's reading succeeds more consistently, yet by constructing the black woman (in her account, Twyla) as the politically correct but politically naive and morally conventional foil to the more socially adventurous, if politically conservative, white woman (Roberta), it problematically racializes the moral (op)positions Morrison opens to revaluation in her extended (and in many ways parallel) narrative of female friendship, *Sula*.[7] Neither reading can account adequately for the text's contradictory linguistic evidence, for if Twyla's name is more characteristically black than white, it is perhaps best known as the name of a white dancer, Twyla Tharp, whereas Roberta shares her last name, Fisk, with a celebrated black (now integrated) university. The text's heterogeneous inscriptions of race resist a totalizing reading.

Propelled by this irresolution to suspend my commitment to the intentional fallacy, I wrote to Toni Morrison. Her response raised as many questions as it resolved. Morrison explained that her project in this story was to substitute class for racial codes in order to drive a wedge between these typically elided categories.[8] Both eliciting and foiling our assumption that Roberta's middle-class marriage and politics, and Twyla's working-class perspective, are reliable racial clues, Morrison incorporated details about their husbands' occupations that encourage an alternative conclusion. If we are familiar (as I was not) with IBM's efforts to recruit black executives and with the racial exclusiveness of the firemen's union in upstate New York, where the story is set, we read Roberta as middle-class black and Twyla as working-class white. Roberta's resistance to bussing, then, is based on class rather than racial loyalties: she doesn't want her (middle-class black) stepchildren bussed to a school in a (white) working-class neighborhood; Twyla, conversely, wants her (white) working-class child bussed to a middle-class school (regardless of that school's racial composition). What we hear, from this perspective, in Twyla's envy of Roberta, "Everything is so easy for them," and in her challenge to the status quo—it's not a free country, "but it will be"—is class rather than (or perhaps compounded by) racial resentment, the adult economic counterpart to Twyla's childhood fantasy of Roberta's plenitude.

By underscoring the class-based evidence for reading Twyla as white, Morrison confirms at once my own conclusion and its fantasmatic basis. Morrison's weighting of social detail, her insistence on the intersections, however constructed, between race and class, are more closely aligned with Lula's political perspective than with my psychological reading, fueled by racially specific investments that the text deliberately solicits and exposes. By both inviting and challenging racialized readings that are either "right" for the "wrong" reasons or "wrong" for the "right" ones, "Recitatif" focuses some questions to address to the massive, asymmetrical crossing of racial boundaries in recent feminist criticism. If white feminist readings of black women's texts disclose white critical fantasies, what (if any) value do these readings have—and for whom?[9] How do white women's readings of black women's biological bodies inform our readings of black women's textual bodies? How do different critical discourses both inflect and inscribe racial fantasies? What rhetorical strategies do these discourses produce, and (how) do these strategies bear on the value of the readings they ostensibly legitimate?

Black feminists have debated the politics and potential of white feminists' critical intervention, but they have not compared or critiqued specific reading strategies, which is perhaps more properly a task of white self-criticism.[10] This essay attempts to contribute to this task by examining signal moments, across a range of discourses, in the white critical texts emerging with such volume and intensity within contemporary feminism. By "contemporary" I mean since 1985, a watershed year that marked the simultaneous emergence of what has been called postfeminism and, not coincidentally, of pervasive white feminist attention to texts by women of color.[11] This new attentiveness was overdetermined: by the sheer brilliance and power of this writing and its escalating status in the literary marketplace and, consequently, the academy; by white feminist restlessness with an already well-mined white female literary tradition; and by the internal logic of white feminism's trajectory through theoretical discourses that, by evacuating the referent from the signifier's play, fostered a turn to texts that reassert the authority of experience, that reinstate political agency, and that rearticulate the body and its passions. The end of the most confident and ethnocentric period of the second wave (roughly 1970–1985) has interestingly collapsed postfeminism and prefeminism as the ideological frameworks in which white women turn to black women to articulate a politics and to embody a discursive authority that are either lost or not yet found. Like Frances D. Gage's perception of Sojourner Truth rescuing the faltering 1851 Women's Rights conference in Akron through the power of her physical presence and resounding question, "A'n't I a woman?" which took "us up in her strong arms and carried us safely over the slough of difficulty turning the whole tide in our favor"; or, in one of the generative contexts for the second wave of feminism, like Jane Stembridge's discovery of a miraculously unashamed mode of female speech in Fanny Lou

Hamer's proud bearing and voice at a 1964 SNCC rally—"Mrs. Hamer . . . knows that she is good. . . . If she didn't know that . . . she wouldn't stand there, with her head back and sing! She couldn't speak the way that she speaks and the way she speaks is this: she announces. I do not announce. I apologize"; the postfeminist turn to black women novelists enacts an anxious transference onto black women's speech.[12]

As Valerie Smith has eloquently argued, the attempt to rematerialize an attenuated white feminism by routing it through black women's texts reproduces in the textual realm white women's historical relation to the black female bodies that have nurtured them.[13] This relation unfolds along a spectrum of materiality. More complex than its prefeminist analogue, contemporary white feminism invokes black women's texts not only to relegitimate the feminist agenda called into question by poststructuralism but also, paradoxically, to relegitimate poststructuralism by finding its prefiguration in black women's texts. Yet whether as a corrective difference or a confirming similarity, as a sanction for a renewed or a resuspended referentiality, black women writers are enlisted to bestow a cultural authority that derives in part from their enforced experience of embodiment.

To attempt to do justice to the spectrum of white feminist approaches, I focus on three case studies that, although far from exhaustive, nevertheless offer a range of influential discourses: deconstruction, psychoanalysis, and cultural criticism. This sequence traces a trajectory from a strategy that seems able to escape my own fantasmatic production of an embodied Other to one that unexpectedly reproduces it. In the end, I turn to the conclusion of "Recitatif" to reopen the question of reading and race.

2

> The nonblack feminist critic/theorist who honestly engages his or her own autobiographical implication in a brutal past is likely to provide nuances such as that of the black feminist critic. What, however, are the preconditions and precautions for the nonblack feminist critic/theorist who dares to undertake such a project?
> —MAE G. HENDERSON, RESPONSE TO HOUSTON A. BAKER JR.,
> "THERE IS NO MORE BEAUTIFUL WAY"

Through the exchanges between Derrida and Lacan, we have become familiar with the debate between deconstruction and psychoanalysis over the discursive construction of subjectivity. Recent work by two prominent white feminist theorists, Barbara Johnson and Margaret Homans, suggests how this debate plays out in the related question of the discursive construction of race: a question especially urgent for critics reading and writing across racial lines.

Because it directly poses the question of the white reader's relation to the African American text and because it has widely influenced readings of Zora

Neale Hurston in particular, and of race in general, "Thresholds of Difference: Structures of Address in Zora Neale Hurston" is an apt focus for a study of Barbara Johnson's textual strategies.[14] "Thresholds" mounts an enormously complex and brilliant critique of the belief in essential racial differences that for Johnson is the substance of racism. (Arguing that black representations of a black essence always operate within a "specific interlocutionary situation" and are "matters of strategy rather than truth," Johnson brackets the question of a possible black belief in, or desire for belief in, a black identity ["T" 285]). Through a reading of three Hurston texts—"How It Feels to Be Colored Me" (1928); "What White Publishers Won't Print" (1950); and *Mules and Men* (1935)—Johnson maps the interlocutionary situations that generate Hurston's ambiguous and contradictory representations of racial identity and difference. Rather than being a constant, color (which figures race for both Hurston and Johnson) varies with positions in discursive exchanges whose subversion of the difference between inside and outside, self and other, is detailed in Johnson's reading of Hurston's complex relation as a northern anthropologist to the southern black communities whose folklore (or "lies") she represents in *Mules and Men*. By anticipating and legitimating the project of dereferentializing race and by relocating differences between the races as internal differences (as in her celebrated figure of resemblances among the heterogeneous contents of differently colored bags), Hurston—or the Hurston represented by these particular texts—is a deconstructive critic's dream.[15]

In the body of the essay, Johnson and Hurston seem to speak in a single voice, but the two voices occasionally diverge, and through their divergence the essay interrogates the politics of interracial reading. Paralleling the "multilayered envelope of address" with which Hurston frames the folktales of *Mules and Men*, Johnson frames her own readings with an analysis of her position as a "white deconstructor" interpreting a "black novelist and anthropologist" ("T" 278). As her language indicates, the frame deploys the rhetoric of racial essences the rest of the essay deconstructs. In addressing (as does Hurston's frame) the politics of a discourse on race, the frame also demonstrates their effects: the interlocutory situation of a white reading of a black text demands some acknowledgment of racial differences. The essay thus deploys a schizophrenic discourse, split between a first-person discourse on the politics of discourse across race and a third-person discourse on the discursive (de)construction of race. The discursive position of a "white deconstructor" of race is self-different, embracing both the assertion and the deconstruction of difference, positions that the text constructs as white and black, respectively.

These positions, however, are themselves unstable. Through what becomes an excess of politicized rhetoric in the frame, read retrospectively against the text's interior, the differences between outside and inside, first person

and third person, white and black, collapse and with them the tension between politics and deconstruction. If the questioning of motive and audience in the frame's opening paragraph are to be taken straight, the response
the next paragraph offers is far more problematic: "It was as though I were
asking her [Hurston] for answers to questions I did not even know I was unable to formulate. I had a lot to learn, then, from Hurston's way of dealing
with multiple agendas and heterogeneous implied readers" ("T" 278). The
deference to Hurston seems as disingenuous as Hurston's comparably located and requisite expressions of gratitude to her white patron, Mrs. Os-
good Mason; for as much as Johnson has to learn from Hurston about strategic discursive constructions of race, she has little to learn from her about
strategies of discourse generally; far from a humble student or innocent
reader with no anterior agendas of her own, she constitutes Hurston as much
in her own deconstructive image as she is herself reconstituted by Hurston's
texts.[16] Yet read in the context of Johnson's reading of *Mules and Men,* the
dissembling rhetoric of the frame becomes a deliberate imitation of Hurston's imitation of the strategy of "lying" that she learns from the Eatonville
residents who, weary of white folks prying into their ways, set verbal "'toy[s]'"
"'outside the door[s]'" of their minds to distract and deceive their white in-
vestigators ("T" 286). If, as Johnson argues, "it is impossible to tell whether
Hurston the narrator is *describing* a strategy [of lying] or *employing* one" since
"Hurston's very ability to fool us—or to fool us into *thinking* we have been
fooled—is itself the only effective way of conveying the rhetoric of the 'lie,'"
Johnson's ability to fool us functions analogously as a rhetorical tool that,
once we have understood its calculated impact, transports us along with both
Hurston and Johnson from the outside to the inside of Eatonville's discur-
sive universe ("T" 286, 289).

   The fluidity of this boundary transgression, however, conceals an important difference between Hurston crossing the boundaries between subject
and object, North and South, literate and oral communities, and Johnson
or her white readers crossing a racial boundary. In the course of Johnson's
essay, a discourse on positionality comes to displace, as well as to produce, a
discourse on race. As the frame slides into the interior, the questions it raises
disappear. There is no further problem about a white deconstructor writing
about, or writing as, a black novelist and anthropologist, since position has
come to stand for race. This erasure of conflict is clear when the frame briefly
returns at the end, merging Johnson's and Hurston's voices in the single
conclusion that "the terms 'black' and 'white,' 'inside' and 'outside,' continue
to matter" only as diversely inhabited and mutually constitutive positions on
a signifying chain ("T" 289). By dislocating race from historically accreted
differences in power, Johnson's deconstructive reading dovetails with Hurston's libertarian politics.[17]

In contrast, Johnson's feminist politics in her discourse on gender enforce a distinction, political rather than metaphysical, between the positions inhabited by men and women: "Jacques Derrida may sometimes see himself as philosophically positioned as a woman, but he is not *politically* positioned as a woman. Being positioned as a woman is not something that is entirely voluntary." The shift from gender to race in the next sentence—"Or, to put it another way, if you tell a member of the Ku Klux Klan that racism is a repression of self-difference, you are likely to learn a thing or two about repression"—places the white deconstructor in a position of vulnerability akin to (rather than politically distinct from) the black person's position, bypassing the racial analogy to the problematic masculine (equated to white) assumption of a figuratively feminine (equated to black) position.[18] Similarly, Johnson distinguishes more firmly between the figurative and the literal in relation to gender than to race: "the revaluation of the *figure* of the woman by a male author cannot substitute for the actual participation of women in the literary conversation. Mallarmé may be able to speak from the place of the silenced woman, but as long as he is occupying it, the silence that is broken in theory is maintained in reality."[19] Johnson's relentlessly deconstructive discourse on race subverts the equivalent gestures that would subject her own role as a white deconstructor to her critique of masculine deconstructions of gender. This difference within her practice of deconstruction, the undoing of a counterpart for race to the feminist resistance to deconstruction, facilitates the project of writing across race. The interlocutory situation that requires the white critic to acknowledge racial difference also requires her to dissolve the tension between literal and figurative, political and philosophical, voluntary and involuntary modes of sameness and difference.

Johnson's essay first appeared in the 1985 special issue of *Critical Inquiry* entitled "'Race,' Writing, and Difference," edited by Henry Louis Gates Jr., whose position on the figurative status of race is signaled by the quotation marks with which he encloses the word; Johnson's essay conforms clearly to that volume's ideology. Gates has been criticized for the politics of his deconstruction of race, and some of the most passionate criticism has been launched by black feminists. Aligning herself with these critics, Margaret Homans argues compellingly in her essay in this volume, "'Racial Composition': Metaphor and the Body in the Writing of Race," that Gates's, and thus by extension Johnson's, deliteralization of race is effectively a masculinist position.[20] The difference between Johnson and Homans derives to a significant degree from the shift from deconstruction to psychoanalysis and the consequent shift from the inside-outside opposition privileged by deconstruction to that between body and language, or the literal and the figurative, which psychoanalysis genders oppositely from deconstruction. Whereas for Johnson, playing primarily off Derrida, figuration enacts an emancipatory feminine displacement of phallogocentric reference, for Homans, playing off Lacan and Chodorow, figuration enacts a masculine displacement of the specifically female (maternal) body whose exclusion founds the symbolic register. Whereas for Johnson the figurativeness of race is enabling for all races, for Homans it enables only men, since women across race accede to figuration only by devaluing the femaleness that is culturally conflated with the body. Paradoxically, however, both positions serve to legitimate white feminist readings of black women's texts: privileging the figurative enables the white reader to achieve figurative blackness; privileging the literal enables the white *woman* reader to forge a gender alliance that outweighs (without negating) both racial differences within gender and racial alliances across gender.

"'Racial Composition'" takes as one of its starting points the debate on black literary criticism carried out in four texts in a 1987 issue of *New Literary History:* the original essay by Joyce A. Joyce, "The Black Canon: Reconstructing Black American Literary Criticism," criticizing the deliteralization of race in Gates and Houston A. Baker Jr.; the responses by Gates and Baker; and Joyce's response to them.[21] Building on her premises that "the position Gates inherited from poststructuralism identifies and celebrates the abstract as masculine and devalues embodiment as female" and that Gates "substituted, in the undesirable position of the referent or ground from which language differentiates itself, female for black," Homans deftly teases out a gendered subtext in the exchange ("RC" 3–4).[22] In Joyce's critique of the assimilation of black literary criticism to the elite discourse of poststructuralism that, through its esoteric terminology and representation of race as a metaphor, severs its connections with the black reading community, with literary traditions rooted in the lived experience of black people, and with the concrete, sensuous features of black literary language, Homans sees a defense of the "body that is troped as female in the post-structuralist theory Gates uses and whose absence that theory requires" ("RC" 7). In the high-handed and patronizing responses by Gates and Baker, she uncovers these critics' sexualized self-representations as the saviors of a feminized black literary body in danger of a retrograde sensualization at the hands of black feminists. Homans then proceeds, via an analysis of the more egalitarian tone and terms of the debate on essentialism within black feminism, to a powerful analysis of the rhetoric of critical scenes in narratives by Alice Walker, Toni Morrison, and Maya Angelou, where the tension between (relatively) literal and figurative language constitutes the "rhetorical form in which the debate over racial and gendered 'essence' was worked out. The use or representation of a relatively literal language corresponds to and puts into practice a belief in the embodiedness of race and of gender . . . while the view that race is figurative coincides with and is performed as a celebration of language as figuration and a tendency to use conspicuous metaphors" ("RC" 5). While insisting on the necessity of maintaining, at different times, both positions, Homans calls attention to black women writers' continuing and complex commitment to the body and to the literal, a commitment that contrasts in both its substance and its ambivalence with Gates's and Baker's unequivocal endorsement of the figurative and that reiterates, within a different context, Homans's own perspective in *Bearing the Word*.[23] As Johnson extends and reauthorizes deconstruction through Hurston, Homans extends and reauthorizes, primarily through Walker, a revaluation of the literal.

Like Johnson, Homans frames her argument by positioning herself in relation to black women's texts. Both frames incorporate acknowledgments of racial difference; but whereas Johnson becomes, in the course of her argument, figuratively black, Homans becomes more emphatically white: "Neither literally nor figuratively a black feminist, then (nor even figuratively literally), I am obliged—if I am to choose from the options available within the debate I discuss—to follow bell hooks' 1989 recommendation and identify my perspective as that of a white feminist" ("RC" 38). Homans's feminist critique of the overvaluation of the figurative demands that, in direct opposition to Johnson, she affirm the literalness of (at least her own) race.

This is a necessary conclusion, in the context of Homans's argument, and also a brave and a problematic one. By embodying her own whiteness, Homans contests the racialization that coexists with the more overt gendering of the symbolic register. In a white feminist counterpart to Gates's strategy of making blackness figurative and figuration black ("figuration is the nigger's occupation"), Homans insistently pinions (female) whiteness to literality, resisting through a different route the dominant culture's splitting of a white symbolic realm from a black materiality.[24] Homans affirms solidarity with black women by asserting a literal difference that is ultimately overridden by the sameness of literality: by the shared association with embodiment.

More problematically, however, literalizing whiteness logically entails reliteralizing blackness as well, and an argument for the literalness of race (or sex) can be safely made only from the position of the subordinated race (or sex), which can define and revalue its own distinctiveness. Speaking for the literal from a position of dominance risks reinscribing the position of the dominated. Homans's position on figuration leads her to an impasse: as a woman she can't ally herself with a (masculine) position on the figurativeness of race; as a *white* woman she can't ally herself with black women writers' (ambivalent) adherence to the embodiedness of race without potentially reproducing the structure of dominance she wants to subvert. There are as serious, although very different, problems with revaluing the literalness of race as with asserting its figurativeness.

3

I began to wonder whether there was any position from which a white
middle-class feminist could say anything on the subject [of race] without
sounding exactly like [a white middle-class feminist]. . . . The rhetorical
predictability of it all. The political correctness. . . . In which case it might
be better not to say anything.
                    —NANCY K. MILLER, "CRITICIZING FEMINIST CRITICISM"

Different as are their consequences for the reading of race, deconstruction
and psychoanalysis are both subjectivist critical ideologies that mandate a
high degree of self-reflexiveness. Materialist feminisms, in contrast, which
have always had priority within black feminist discourse, emphasize the political objectives (and objectivity) of the reading over the question of positionality.[25] Designed to disclose systematically (and ultimately to change) the
intersecting axes of race, class, gender, and sexuality through which women
are multiply and differentially oppressed, materialist feminisms, both black
and white, have de-emphasized the reader's racial location. White readers
within this discourse have paid only perfunctory (if any) attention to the
problem of their own positionality, and black materialists have generally been
hospitable to white women's readings of black texts.[26] It is not coincidental
that Valerie Smith, who insists on the materialist orientation of black feminist theory, also redefines this theory to "refer not only to theory written (or
practiced) by black feminists, but also to a way of reading inscriptions of race
(particularly but not exclusively blackness), gender (particularly but not exclusively womanhood), and class in modes of cultural expression"; or that
Hazel Carby, writing within the discourse of cultural studies, has become one
of the most resolutely antiessentialist and politically exacting black feminist
voices, calling into question simultaneously the presumption of interracial
sisterhood and the presumption of seamless continuity between racial experience, discourse, and interpretation.[27] The de-essentialization of race
among black feminists (in contrast to both white feminists and male Afro-
Americanists) has occurred primarily through the intervention of material
rather than textual differences and under the aegis of Marxism and cultural
studies rather than deconstruction.

    Materialist feminism would appear to be the approach through which
white critics could write about black women's texts with the least self-
consciousness about racial difference and perhaps with the least difference.
Yet white investments in some form of black cultural or social specificity, investments exempted from analysis under the banner of an interracial socialist
feminist sisterhood, tend to intervene in white readings of black texts, substituting racial for class specificity rather than disrupting each with the other.
Racial differences are visibly played out in the critical response to *The Color
Purple*. Both black and white feminists from diverse critical schools have cel-

ebrated the text's subversive stance toward the narrative and rhetorical conventions of epistolary, sentimental, and realist fiction and toward the sexual, domestic, and spiritual institutions of patriarchy.[28] But among materialist feminists, race has made a difference in the assessment of the novel's politics. For example, bell hooks criticizes the novel for isolating individual quests and transformative private relationships from collective political effort, for celebrating the "ethics of a narcissistic new-age spirituality wherein economic prosperity indicates that one is chosen," and for breaking with the revolutionary impulse of the African American literary tradition epitomized by the slave narrative; Cora Kaplan, in an essay entitled "Keeping the Color in *The Color Purple*," defends the novel from accusations of bourgeois liberalism by British socialists who, she feels, have "bleached" the text into "an uncontentious, sentimental, harmless piece of international libertarianism" by failing to understand its relation to "a specifically racial set of discourses about the family and femininity." Kaplan revalues the novel through a black cultural context that hooks claims the novel has repudiated.[29] And whereas Hazel Carby criticizes the critics who, through their celebration of *The Color Purple* (and its line of descent from *Their Eyes Were Watching God*), indulge in a romantic vision of rural black culture that enables them to avoid confronting the complex social crises in the urban black community, Susan Willis praises the novel for contesting industrial capitalism by resurrecting the homestead and cottage industry.[30] The representation of black social relations as utopian alternatives to industrial capitalism or to patriarchal nationalism has appealed more to white than to black materialist feminists.[31]

This appeal and its problems surface clearly in the work of Willis, who deserves special attention as the only white feminist author of a book on black women novelists and of an essay in Cheryl A. Wall's recent anthology of black feminist criticism, *Changing Our Own Words* (1989).[32] In *Specifying: Black Women Writing the American Experience* (1987), Willis maps the ways that twentieth-century black women novelists record through their narrative strategies and subjects the shift from a southern agrarian to a northern industrial economy. Suffused with nostalgia for an agrarian culture that in Willis's opinion supported a "noncommodified relationship" between an author, her language, and her audience, the book insists that "one of the major problems facing black writers today is how to preserve the black cultural heritage in the face of the homogenizing function of bourgeois society."[33] This romanticization of "the" black cultural heritage, whose truth resides in an uncontaminated past to which these novels' protagonists repeatedly return, becomes apparent through the contrast between Willis's study and Hazel Carby's *Reconstructing Womanhood: The Emergence of the Afro-American Woman Novelist*, published the same year, which situates nineteenth-century black women's cultural discourses in relation to hegemonic ideologies.[34] However, in her essay "I Shop Therefore I Am: Is There a Place for Afro-American

Culture in Commodity Culture?" Willis begins to engage this relation by shifting from a strict economic reading of a discrete literary tradition to a more
variegated account of African American participation in the cultural arena
produced by commodity capitalism. The essay, more than the book, positions Willis in a relation to Fredric Jameson analogous to that between Johnson and Derrida, and even more to that between Homans and Lacan, since
Willis, like Homans, prioritizes what is unincorporated by a master system.
"I Shop Therefore I Am" opens up the third term that Jameson brackets in
"Reification and Utopia in Mass Culture," the term representing the possibility of "authentic cultural production" by marginal social groups that inhabit a position outside the dialectic of high culture and mass culture. More
committed than Jameson to criticizing mass culture from a position of estrangement that tends in her work to devolve into a place of authenticity,
Willis both racializes and genders a cultural exterior, relinquishing black men
to an ambiguous dance of subversion and assimilation with mass culture while
retaining black women as unambivalent voices of resistance.[35]

Willis answers her central question—whether it is possible for African
Americans to participate in commodity culture without being assimilated to
it—in gendered terms. The essay plays Toni Morrison, whose Claudia in *The
Bluest Eye* represents for Willis "the radical potential inherent in the position
of being 'other' to dominant society" by repudiating the white-dominated
culture industry epitomized by a Shirley Temple doll, against Michael Jackson, who "states himself as a commodity" through the vertiginous display
of self-transformations and imitations that undo the possibility of authenticity ("I" 174, 187). *"Moonwalker* suggests a split between contemporary black
women's fiction, which strives to create images of social wholeness based on
the rejection of commodity capitalism, and what seems to be a black male
position which sees the commodity as something that can be played with and
enjoyed or subverted" ("I" 195). Although Willis reluctantly admits the subversive possibilities of parody, represented in her essay by Jackson and by the
black film and art critic Kobena Mercer, who argues that commodity culture
heightens the radical potential of artifice, she clearly prefers the authenticity represented for her by Morrison and Walker, with whom the essay begins
and ends. This preference incurs two penalties. First, Willis's analytical inventiveness and subtlety are most impressively released by untangling the contradictions of mass cultural figures: Michael Jackson and his conservative an-
titype Mickey Mouse, on whose genealogical descent from the tradition of
black minstrelsy she brilliantly speculates in an epilogue to a slightly different version of this essay that was published in *New Formations*. The utopian
pressures Willis levies on black women writers, by contrast, simplifies her interpretation. Moreover, by pitting black women novelists against black male
cultural critics and performers, Willis sidesteps an encounter with the black

feminist critics who have endorsed the position she characterizes as "black male." Although there is more of an encounter with black feminist criticism in the essay, where Willis acknowledges her differences from Carby, for example, but doesn't theorize them, than in the book, where she lists black feminists in a general bibliography rather than engaging with them individually, Willis still doesn't interrogate what fuels her own investment in black women writers' representation of "social wholeness," "the autonomous subject," and "fullness of . . . humanity" ("I" 195, 174).[36]

The essay, however, does offer clues. In contrast to Homans, who invokes black women's representations of alliances with white women to underscore the prospects of reciprocity and commonality, Willis enlists black women's representations of white women to suggest women's socially constructed differences. In *The Bluest Eye*'s characterization of "frozen faced white baby dolls" and in *Meridian*'s account of the mummified white female body exhibited for profit by her husband, Willis finds images of the reification white women suffer through immersion (both longer and deeper than black women's) in the culture of commodities. Haunting the white female consumer's version of the cogito, "I shop therefore I am" (parody is apparently a strategy available to white feminists if not to black), the specter of the self's mortification as commodity drives the commitment to the difference of black women's texts, as the title of the other version of this essay indicates: "I Want the Black One: Is There a Place for Afro-American Culture in Commodity Culture?" Overtly, this title replaces the voice of the white female consumer whose identity is shopping with the voice of the black female consumer manipulated into buying black replicants of white commodities, Christie dolls instead of Barbies. Yet the overdetermined referent of the first-person pronoun betrays as well (and this is presumably why this title was not used for the version of this essay in Wall's anthology) the desire of the white feminist critic who also wants "the black one"—the text that promises resistance and integrity, the utopian supplement to her own "deconstruction of commodities."[37] White feminists, like the frozen or mummified white women represented in some black women's texts, seem in Willis's discourse to be corpses finding political energy through the corpus of black women.

Willis's essay brings us back, through a different route, to my reading of Roberta as a site of authority and plenitude figured as a vital, integrated body. In contrast to Johnson and Homans, who locate black and white women on the same (although opposite) sides of the symbolic register's divide, Willis and I operate from a model of difference rather than similarity. The claim for sameness is enabled by, and in turn reauthorizes, belief in a subversive feminine position in language (whether the subversion operates through figuration or literality); the argument for an idealized (biological, social, or literary) difference is fueled by the perception of an increasingly compromised white feminist social position drained by success of oppositionality. But whether argued in terms of sameness or of difference, or in terms of the symbolic or the social domains, these theorizations of reading across race are marked by white desires.

4

> The first thing you do is to forget that i'm Black. Second, you must never forget that i'm Black.
> — PAT PARKER, "FOR THE WHITE PERSON WHO WANTS TO KNOW HOW TO BE MY FRIEND"

How, then, should we evaluate this critical undertaking? The question incorporates two complexly interwoven ones, a hermeneutic question about difference and a political question about legitimacy, that I wish to (re)open briefly in my conclusion by returning to my starting point: reading "Recitatif."

To produce an allegory about reading and race, I omitted aspects of the story—most importantly, its own conclusion—that complicate the division between the characters and, consequently, between their readers. "Recitatif" ends with parallel recognitions by Twyla and Roberta that each perceived the mute Maggie as her own unresponsive, rejecting mother and therefore hated and wanted to harm her. After dramatizing the differences produced by race and class, the story concludes with the shared experience of abandoned little girls who, in some strange twist of the oedipal story, discover that they killed (wanted to kill), as well as loved (wanted to love), their mothers ("R" 261).[38] Sameness coexists with difference, psychology with politics. Race enforces no absolute distinctions between either characters or readers, all of whom occupy diverse subject positions, some shared, some antithetical.[39] By concluding with a psychological narrative that crosses differences (indeed, with a variant of *the* universalizing psychological narrative), "Recitatif" complicates, without canceling, both its narrative of difference and the differences in reading that this narrative provokes.

Race enters complexly into feminist reading. The three case studies examined in this essay indicate certain pervasive tendencies among white feminists, who often read black women's texts through critical lenses that filter out the texts' embeddedness in black political and cultural traditions and that foreground instead their relation to the agendas of white feminism, which the texts alter, or prefigure, but ultimately reconfirm. For despite Jane Gallop's account of the displacement of French men by African American women as figures of authority for white feminists, the discourses produced by French (and German and American) men continue to shape the reading habits of white feminists, who are usually better trained in literary theory than in African American cultural studies. There has been little in white feminism comparable to the detailed reconstructions of black women's literary traditions produced by Barbara Christian, Mary Helen Washington, Deborah E. McDowell, Gloria T. Hull, Nellie Y. McKay, or Margaret B. Wilkerson; or to the mapping of this literature's social and discursive contexts produced by Hazel Carby, Barbara Smith, Valerie Smith, bell hooks, Michele Wallace, Audre Lorde, or June Jordan.[40] Instead, we have tended to focus our readings on the "celebrity" texts—preeminently those by Hurston, Walker, and Morrison—rather than on "thick" descriptions of discursive contexts and have typically written articles or chapters (rather than books) representing black women's texts as literary and social paradigms for white readers and writers. In these texts we have found alternative family structures, narrative strategies, and constructions of subjectivity: alternative, that is, to the cultural practices of white patriarchy, with which literature by white women has come to seem uncomfortably complicit.[41] The implied audience for this critical venture has been white.

The critical picture is not, however, entirely black and white. As the work of Hortense J. Spillers demonstrates especially well, black feminists draw from, as well as criticize, a range of "high" theoretical discourses, including the psychoanalytic discourses that have functioned more prominently within white feminism.[42] Moreover, as Deborah E. McDowell has powerfully argued, white feminist tendencies to construct black feminism as a "high" theory's political "Other" reinscribe, rather than rework, the theory-versus-politics opposition.[43] White feminist criticism is itself fractured by class and generational differences that partially undo the racial divide. As-yet unpublished essays, particularly those by a new and differently educated generation of graduate students, and essays that are published less visibly than those analyzed in this paper, more closely approximate the historical and political concerns of black feminist criticism. Yet however interwoven with and ruptured by other differences, race remains a salient source of the fantasies and allegiances that shape our ways of reading.

Difference, however, paradoxically increases the value of crossing racial boundaries in reading. Our inability to avoid inscribing racially inflected investments and agendas limits white feminism's capacity either to impersonate black feminism, and potentially to render it expendable, or to counter its specific credibility. More important, white feminist readings contribute, however inadvertently, to a project many black feminists endorse: the racialization of whiteness.[44] As masculinity takes shape in part through its constructions of femininity, whiteness—that elusive color that seems not to be one—gains materiality through the desires and fantasies played out in its interpretations of blackness, interpretations that, by making the unconscious conscious, supplement articulated ideologies of whiteness with less accessible assumptions. Reading black women's texts, and reading our readings of

them, is one (although certainly not the only) strategy for changing our ha-
bitual perception that "race is always an issue of Otherness that is not white:
it is black, brown, yellow, red, purple even."[45]

Articulating the whiteness implied through the construction of blackness
approaches, through a different route, the goal of Toni Morrison's recent
critical project: "to avert the critical gaze from the racial object to the racial
subject; from the described and imagined to the describers and imaginers;
from the serving to the served."[46] There is a significant political difference,
of course, between Morrison analyzing European American texts and white
feminist theorists staking critical claims to the African American texts that
constitute a privileged and endangered terrain of black feminist inquiry.[47]
The risks of this intervention have been circumscribed, however, by the effectiveness of black feminists in establishing the authority of their own positions and by the failure of "high" theory to secure unproblematic grounding for white feminists by either resolving or displacing the politics of
reading and race. If we produce our readings cautiously and locate them in
a self-conscious and self-critical relation to black feminist criticism, these risks,
I hope, would be counterbalanced by the benefits of broadening the spectrum of interpretation, illuminating the social determinants of reading, and
deepening our recognition of our racial selves and the "others" we fantas-
matically construct—and thereby expanding the possibilities of dialogue
across as well as about racial boundaries.

NOTES

"Black Writing, White Reading: Race and the Politics of Feminist Interpretation"
was originally published in *Critical Inquiry* 19 (spring 1993): 470–98. University of
Chicago Press. Reprinted by permission of the University of Chicago Press.

1. Toni Morrison, "Recitatif," in *Confirmation: An Anthology of African American
Women,* ed. Amiri Baraka (LeRoi Jones) and Amina Baraka (New York: Quill, 1983),
243, hereafter abbreviated "R." I am deeply indebted to Lula Fragd for bringing this
story to my attention and to Toni Morrison for generously discussing it with me. I
am also very grateful to Margaret Homans for sharing with me an early draft of "'Racial
Composition': Metaphor and Body in the Writing of Race," which became central to
my thinking on writing and race; and to Janet Adelman, John Bishop, Mitchell Breit-
wieser, Carolyn Dinshaw, Catherine Gallagher, Anne Goldman, Crystal Gromer, Dori
Hale, Saidiya Hartman, Marianne Hirsch, Tania Modleski, Helene Moglen, Michael
Rogin, Dianne Sadoff, Susan Schweik, Valerie Smith, Hortense Spillers, and Jean
Wyatt for their helpful comments on this essay.

2. The intervention of white men in relationships between black and white women
is repeatedly represented in slave narratives, best epitomized perhaps by Harriet A.
Jacobs, *Incidents in the Life of a Slave Girl: Written by Herself* (1861; reprint, ed. and with

introduction by Jean Fagan Yellin, Cambridge: Harvard University Press, 1987); the intervention of white women in black heterosexual relationships is most fully explored in the civil rights fiction typified by Alice Walker, *Meridian* (New York: Harcourt Brace Jovanovich, 1976). For a study of American literary representations of the relationships between black and white women in the nineteenth-century South, see Minrose C. Gwin, *Black and White Women of the Old South: The Peculiar Sisterhood in American Literature* (Knoxville, Tenn.: University of Tennessee Press, 1985); for an optimistic characterization of interracial female friendships in recent American women's fiction, see Elizabeth Schultz, "Out of the Woods and into the World: A Study of Interracial Friendships between Women in American Novels," in *Conjuring: Black Women, Fiction, and Literary Tradition*, ed. Marjorie Pryse and Hortense J. Spillers (Bloomington, Ind.: Indiana University Press, 1985), 67–85.

3. *Transference* is Gallop's own term for her relation to black feminist critics. In her *Around 1981: Academic Feminist Literary Theory* (New York: Routledge, 1992), esp. 169–70, Gallop critiques the idealization and exoticization of black women, but she limits herself to making the transference conscious rather than positing alternatives to it. In "Transferences: Gender and Race: The Practice of Theory," delivered at the University of California, Berkeley, Department of African American Studies, 3 April 1992, Deborah E. McDowell, who had inadvertently occasioned Gallop's comments about transference, deliberately spoke back from, and thereby exploded, the position of the transferential object.

4. The "not just idiosyncratic" nature of this fantasy is suggested by Gallop's accounts in "Tongue Work" and "The Coloration of Academic Feminism" in *Around 1981*, 143–76 and 67–74, and, by extension through the analogies she draws between constructions of race and class, in "Annie Leclerc Writing a Letter, with Vermeer," in *The Poetics of Gender*, ed. Nancy K. Miller (New York: Columbia University Press, 1986), 137–56. In her analysis of the black woman's telling role in Joan Micklin Silver's film *Crossing Delancey*, Tania Modleski outlines an especially exploitative enactment of this fantasy; see Tania Modleski, *Feminism without Women: Culture and Criticism in a "Postfeminist" Age* (New York: Routledge, 1991), 129–30. In Richard Dyer, "Paul Robeson: Crossing Over," *Heavenly Bodies: Film Stars and Society* (New York: St. Martin's Press, 1986), Dyer succinctly summarizes the most pervasive, nongendered version of this fantasy: "Black and white discourses on blackness seem to be valuing the same things—spontaneity, emotion, naturalness—yet giving them a different implication. Black discourses see them as contributions to the development of society, white as enviable qualities that only blacks have" (79).

5. On the general phenomenon of black innovation and white imitation in postwar American culture, see Kobena Mercer, "Black Hair/Style Politics," *New Formations* 3 (winter 1987): 33–54.

6. For a particularly powerful statement of the disenchantment bred among women of color by white women's opposition to bussing, see Nikki Giovanni, "Why Weren't Our 'Sisters in Liberation' in Boston?" *Encore*, 6 January 1975, 20.

7. By tracing the course of a friendship from girlhood through adulthood, "R" filters the narrative of *Sula* through the lens of race, replacing the novel's sexual triangulation with the tensions of racial difference. It is hard for me to imagine that the critical question that Sula, Roberta's knowing, transgressive counterpart, poses

to Nel—"How do you know? . . . About who was good. How do you know it was you?"—
could be translated, in "R," into a white woman's challenge to a woman of color (Toni
Morrison, *Sula* [New York: Knopf, 1973], 146).

8. In this exchange (November 1990), Morrison provided a more detailed account of her intentions than she does in her only (and recently) published comment on the story, in the preface to her *Playing in the Dark: Whiteness and the Literary
Imagination* (Cambridge, Mass.: Harvard University Press, 1992): "The kind of work
I have always wanted to do requires me to learn how to maneuver ways to free up
the language from its sometimes sinister, frequently lazy, almost always predictable
employment of racially informed and determined chains. (The only short story I
have ever written, 'Recitatif,' was an experiment in the removal of all racial codes
from a narrative about two characters of different races for whom racial identity is
crucial)" (xi).

9. Although I realize that by isolating white and black dynamics of reading from
white feminist readings of texts by other women of color I am reinforcing the unfortunate collapse of *color* and *black*, encompassing such a diverse textual field within
a single analysis would blur important differences. In contrast, for example, to black
feminist complaints about the white feminist misrecognition of the politics and language of black feminism, Norma Alarcón protests the Anglo-American feminist resistance to granting theoretical status to the multiple-voiced subjectivity of women
of color; see Norma Alarcón, "The Theoretical Subject(s) of *This Bridge Called My
Back* and Anglo-American Feminism," in *Making Face, Making Soul: Haciendo Caras*,
ed. Gloria Anzaldua (San Francisco: Aunt Lute Foundation, 1990), 356–69. For a
different perception of white feminism's response to the multiple voicing charac-
terizing texts by women of color, see Teresa de Lauretis, "Eccentric Subjects: Feminist Theory and Historical Consciousness," *Feminist Studies* 16 (spring 1990): 115–50.

10. The strongest questions about, although not unqualified opposition to, white
feminist readings of black women's texts have been posed by bell hooks. See, for example, bell hooks [Gloria Watkins], "Critical Interrogation: Talking Race, Resisting
Racism," *Inscriptions* 5 (1989): 159–62, and "Feminism and Racism: The Struggle Continues," *Zeta* (July-August 1990): 41–43. See also Patricia Hill Collins, "The Social
Construction of Black Feminist Thought," *Signs* 14 (summer 1989): 745–73. For more
positive perspectives, see Valerie Smith, "Black Feminist Theory and the Representation of the 'Other,'" in *Changing Our Own Words: Essays on Criticism, Theory, and Writing by Black Women*, ed. Cheryl A. Wall (New Brunswick, N.J.: Rutgers University Press,
1989), 38–57; Hazel V. Carby, *Reconstructing Womanhood: The Emergence of the Afro-American Woman Novelist* (New York: Oxford University Press, 1987), chap. 1; Michele Wallace, "Who Owns Zora Neale Hurston? Critics Carve Up the Legend," in *Invisibility
Blues: From Pop to Theory* (London: Verso, 1990), 179–80; Barbara Christian, "But What
Do We Think We're Doing Anyway: The State of Black Feminist Criticism(s) or My
Version of a Little Bit of History," in Wall, *Changing Our Own Words*, 67, 73; and hooks,
Talking Back: Thinking Feminist, Thinking Black (Boston: South End Press, 1989), chap.
7. For a trenchant black male critique of the racial privilege concealed behind the
self-referential gestures of some white male commentators on African-American texts,
see Michael Awkward, "Negotiations of Power: White Critics, Black Texts, and the
Self-Referential Impulse," *American Literary History* 2 (winter 1990): 581–606. See also
Kenneth W. Warren, "From under the Superscript: A Response to Michael Awkward,"

and Awkward, "The Politics of Positionality: A Reply to Kenneth Warren," *American Literary History* 4 (spring 1992): 97–109.

11. In "Feminism, 'Postfeminism,' and Contemporary Women's Fiction," in *Tradition and the Talents of Women,* ed. Florence Howe (Urbana, Ill.: University of Illinois Press, 1991), 268–91, Deborah Silverton Rosenfelt proposes 1985 as the date of postfeminism's emergence and defines the phenomenon succinctly as the "uneven incorporation and revision [of feminism] inside the social and cultural texts of a more conservative era" (269). For a more negative assessment of postfeminism, and a broader location of its origins in the mid-1980s, see Gayle Greene, *Changing the Story: Feminist Fiction and the Tradition* (Bloomington, Ind.: Indiana University Press, 1991), esp. pt. 3. In selecting 1985 as the watershed year in white feminists' engagement with questions of racial location, I am building on Miller's suggestion in the conversation held between Miller, Marianne Hirsch, and Jane Gallop, published under the title "Criticizing Feminist Criticism," in *Conflicts in Feminism,* ed. Hirsch and Evelyn Fox Keller (New York: Routledge, 1990), 359. In 1985 Pryse and Spillers's *Conjuring,* the first anthology of literary criticism coedited by a black woman and a white woman, was published. The same year Alice Walker's *The Color Purple* (New York: Harcourt Brace Jovanovich, 1982) was selected as the focus for a collective presentation at the sixth annual British conference on "Literature/Teaching/Politics"; this presentation culminated in several white feminist essays on the novel. This year also witnessed the first serious white British feminist response to critiques by women of color; see Michele Barrett and Mary McIntosh, "Ethnocentrism and Socialist-Feminist Theory," *Feminist Review,* no. 20 (June 1985): 23–47; for four different responses to this essay, see Caroline Ramazanoglu, Hamida Kazi, Sue Lees, and Heidi Safia Mirza, "Feedback: Feminism and Racism," *Feminist Review,* no. 22 (February 1986): 83–105, and Kum-Kum Bhavnani and Margaret Coulson, "Transforming Socialist-Feminism: The Challenge of Racism," *Feminist Review,* no. 23 (June 1986): 81–92. Another way to mark the shift occurring in 1985 is to contrast the semantic fields of two identical titles: *Between Women: Biographers, Novelists, Critics, Teachers, and Artists Write about Their Work on Women,* ed. Carol Ascher, Louise DeSalvo, and Sara Ruddick (Boston: Beacon Press, 1984), about the enabling identification between women writers and the women about whom they write, and Judith Rollins, *Between Women: Domestics and Their Employers* (Philadelphia: Temple University Press, 1985), about the conflicts between white women and the black women who work for them.

12. I am following Phyllis Marynick Palmer's wonderful reading of Sojourner Truth's role at the Akron Women's Rights convention in "White Women/Black Women: The Dualism of Female Identity and Experience in the United States," *Feminist Studies* 9 (spring 1983): 151, 153. Palmer quotes from Frances D. Cage, "The Akron Convention," in *The Feminist Papers: From Adams to de Beauvoir,* ed. Alice Rossi (New York: Northeastern University Press, 1974), 429. Paula Giddings cites Jane Stembridge's reaction to Fanny Lou Hamer in her *When and Where I Enter: The Impact of Black Women on Race and Sex in America* (New York: W. Morrow, 1984), 301. For SNCC's complex role in catalyzing the second wave of a white feminist movement, see chap. 17 in Giddings, *When and Where I Enter,* and Sara Evans, *Personal Politics: The Roots of Women's Liberation in the Civil Rights Movement and the New Left* (New York: Knopf, 1979). In *Meridian* and in "Advancing Luna—and Ida B . Wells," in *You Can't Keep a Good Woman Down* (New York: Harcourt Brace Jovanovich, 1981), 85–104, Walker offers

narrative accounts of white women's predatory relation to a movement that gave them the illusion of purposefulness.

13. See Valerie Smith, "Black Feminist Theory and the Representation of the 'Other,'" 38–57.

14. See Barbara Johnson, "Thresholds of Difference: Structures of Address in Zora Neale Hurston," *Critical Inquiry* 12 (autumn 1985): 278–89, hereafter abbreviated "T." For evidence of this essay's influence, see Angela P. Harris, "Race and Essentialism in Feminist Legal Theory," *Stanford Law Review* 42 (February 1990): 581–616; Priscilla Wald, "Becoming 'Colored': The Self-Authorized Language of Difference in Zora Neale Hurston," *American Literary History* 2 (spring 1990): 79–100; Wallace, "Who Owns Zora Neale Hurston?" 172–86; Tamar Katz, "'Show Me How to Do Like You': Didacticism and Epistolary Form in *The Color Purple*," in *Alice Walker*, ed. Harold Bloom (New York: Chelsea House, 1989), esp. 191–92. The race of the reader is not an issue in "T"'s companion piece, published the year before, "Metaphor, Metonymy, and Voice in *Their Eyes Were Watching God*," in *Black Literature and Literary Theory*, ed. Henry Louis Gates Jr. (New York: Methuen, 1984), 205–15, in which gender performs a more critical role than race. In Johnson's "Apostrophe, Animation, and Abortion," in *A World of Difference*, ed. Barbara Johnson (Baltimore: Johns Hopkins University Press, 1987), 184–99, another outstanding essay on structures of address, differences in gender again occlude racial differences, which are theorized for neither the poets nor the critic. In Johnson's other African American essays, such as "Euphemism, Understatement, and the Passive Voice: A Genealogy of Afro-American Poetry" and "The Re(a)d and the Black," in *Reading Black, Reading Feminist: A Critical Anthology*, ed. Henry Louis Gates Jr. (New York: Meridian, 1990), 204–11 and 145–54, the racial position of the reader is similarly bracketed.

15. The Hurston represented by other texts fulfills other critical dreams. See Mary Helen Washington, foreword to *Their Eyes Were Watching God* (1937; reprint, New York: Perennial Library, 1990), vii–xiv; Alice Walker, "On Refusing to Be Humbled by Second Place in a Contest You Did Not Design: A Tradition by Now" and "Looking for Zora," in *I Love Myself When I Am Laughing . . . and Then Again When I Am Looking Mean and Impressive: A Zora Neale Hurston Reader*, ed. Alice Walker (New York: The Feminist Press, 1979), 1–5, 297–313; and Alice Walker, "Foreword: Zora Neale Hurston—A Cautionary Tale and a Partisan View," in *Zora Neale Hurston: A Literary Biography*, by Robert E. Hemenway (Urbana, Ill.: University of Illinois Press, 1977), xi–xviii. In *I Love Myself When I Am Laughing*, Walker describes "How It Feels to Be Colored Me" as "an excellent example of Zora Neale Hurston at her most exasperating" (151). For a black feminist reading that is closer to Johnson's but is routed through Bakhtin instead of Derrida, see Mae Gwendolyn Henderson, "Speaking in Tongues: Dialogics, Dialectics, and the Black Woman Writer's Literary Tradition," in Wall, *Changing Our Own Words*, 16–37.

16. For a similar critique, see Tzvetan Todorov, "'Race,' Writing, and Culture," in *Race, Writing, and Difference*, ed. Henry Louis Gates Jr. (Chicago: University of Chicago, 1986), 379–80.

17. Hurston's resistance to considering race a sociopolitical obstacle to success recurs throughout her writing. For example, she asserts: "I do not belong to the sobbing school of Negrohood who hold that nature somehow has given them a lowdown dirty deal and whose feelings are all hurt about it. . . . I have seen that the world is

to the strong regardless of a little pigmentation more or less. No, I do not weep at the world—I am too busy sharpening my oyster knife" (Hurston, "How It Feels to Be Colored Me," 153). Similar claims pervade her autobiography, *Dust Tracks on a Road,* ed. Robert E. Hemenway (Urbana: University of Illinois Press, 1984). For an analysis of Hurston's racial politics, see Hemenway, *Zora Neale Hurston,* esp. chap. 11. For a different reading of Johnson's position in this essay, see Awkward, "Negotiations of Power," 603–4.

18. Johnson, introduction to *A World of Difference,* 2–3.

19. Johnson, "Les Fleurs du Mal Armé: Some Reflections on Intertextuality," in *A World of Difference,* 131. As the paragraph continues, Johnson qualifies but does not undo the distinction between figurative and literal. The pressures created by Johnson's racial position are visible in her differences of emphasis from the Afro-Americanist whose position on race is closest, indeed very close, to her own: Henry Louis Gates Jr.; see, for example, her response to Gates's "Canon-Formation, Literary History, and the Afro-American Tradition: From the Seen to the Told," in *Afro-American Literary Study in the 1990s,* ed. Houston A. Baker Jr. and Patricia Redmond (Chicago: University of Chicago, 1989), 14–38, 39–44.

20. "'Racial Composition': Metaphor and the Body in the Writing of Race," hereafter abbreviated "RC." My discussion here is based on the earlier draft of Homans's essay that was delivered at the Psychoanalysis in African-American Contexts conference in Santa Cruz. In the substantially revised version of the essay that appears in this volume, Homans explicitly historicizes the positions assumed in the 1987 critical debate that had constituted a springboard for her argument and updates the discursive options available at that time by including the analysis of two recent African American memoirs. In the current version, Homans persuasively asserts the inextricability of figurative and literal constructions of race, complicates the range of meanings associated with the body, and de-emphasizes the psychoanalytic framework for gendering figuration masculine. By foregrounding the status of the literal in her analysis, I do not mean to minimize the other side of her complexly nuanced and carefully historicized argument, but to clarify some of the stakes of the positions assumed by Johnson and Homans, both of whom have in fact been influenced by both deconstruction and psychoanalysis. For earlier examples of Homans's writing on African American women's texts, see Margaret Homans, "'Her Very Own Howl': The Ambiguities of Representation in Recent Women's Fiction," *Signs* 9 (winter 1983): 186–205, which is primarily concerned with negotiating tensions between Anglo-American and French feminist positions on language and women's experience; "The Woman in the Cave: Recent Feminist Fictions and the Classical Underworld," *Contemporary Literature* 29 (fall 1988): 369–402, which, by reading Gloria Naylor's *Linden Hills* with Luce Irigaray's *Speculum of the Other Woman,* also foregrounds the compatibility of French feminist discourse and fiction by African American women; and "'Women of Color': Writers and Feminist Theory," *New Literary History* 25 (fall 1994): 73–94, which examines white feminist uses of writing by women of color.

21. See Joyce A. Joyce, "The Black Canon: Reconstructing Black American Literary Criticism," *New Literary History* 18 (winter 1987): 335–44; Henry Louis Gates Jr., "'What's Love Got to Do with It?': Critical Theory, Integrity, and the Black Idiom," *New Literary History* 18 (winter 1987): 345–62; Houston A. Baker Jr., "In Dubious Battle," *New Literary History* 18 (winter 1987): 363–69; and Joyce, "'Who the Cap Fit':

Unconsciousness and Unconscionableness in the Criticism of Houston A. Baker, Jr.,
and Henry Louis Gates, Jr.," *New Literary History* 18 (winter 1987): 371–84. In a re-
cent interview with Charles H. Rowell ("An Interview with Henry Louis Gates, Jr.,"
Callaloo 14 [1991]: 444–63), Gates qualifies and clarifies the basis for his response to
Joyce (451–52). For a different configuration of race, gender, and reading in the *New
Literary History* (and other) critical debates, see Michael Awkward, "Race, Gender,
and the Politics of Reading," *Black American Literature Forum* 22 (spring 1988): 5–27.
Rather than gendering the dispute between Joyce and Baker and Gates, Awkward
allies Joyce's position on race with Elaine Showalter's position on feminism as
reductively sociopolitical modes of criticism and contrasts both with the more fluid
poststructuralist approaches represented by Baker and Gates, on the one hand, and
by Mary Jacobus on the other. One uncomfortable consequence of Awkward's
construction is that, by using white feminism as his frame of reference, he erases
Joyce's participation in the discourse of black feminism. For yet another account of
the *New Literary History* debate, see Diana Fuss's chapter, "'Race' under Erasure? Post-
Structuralist Afro-American Literary Theory," in *Essentially Speaking: Feminism, Nature
and Difference* (New York: Routledge, 1989), 73–96; Fuss sides primarily with Gates
and Baker and mentions the gender implications of the debate only in passing.

22. Homans focuses appropriately on Gates rather than Baker, since the label *poststructuralist* applies far more accurately to Gates. In "Caliban's Triple Play," Baker's
response to Gates's special issue of *Critical Inquiry,* Baker sounds at times uncannily
like Joyce in criticizing Anthony Appiah, and implicitly Gates as well, for belittling
the visible, biological signs of race that function so perniciously in the "real" political world; see Houston A. Baker Jr., "Caliban's Triple Play," in *"Race," Writing, and Difference*, 381–95. For a critique of Baker's "essentialism," see Elliott Butler-Evans, "Beyond Essentialism: Rethinking Afro-American Cultural Theory," *Inscriptions* 5 (1989):
121–34. For a defense of Baker's "materialism," see Fuss, *Essentially Speaking*, 86–93.
Baker is definitely an "essentialist" when it comes to gender, as is clear in his recent
book, *Workings of the Spirit: The Poetics of Afro-American Women's Writing* (Chicago: University of Chicago Press, 1991), and from Mae Gwendolyn Henderson's response to
Baker's essay, "There Is No More Beautiful Way: Theory and the Poetics of Afro-American Women's Writing," in Baker, *Afro-American Literary Study in the 1990s*, 135–63. In
her response to the panel on "Black Feminism" at the Wisconsin Conference on Afro-
American Studies in the Twenty-First Century (April 1991), Carby singled out for
criticism Baker's idealization of black women writers and erasure of black feminist
critics.

23. See Margaret Homans, *Bearing the Word: Language and Female Experience in Nineteenth Century Women's Writing* (Chicago: University of Chicago Press, 1986), esp. chap.
1, which juxtaposes Lacan and Chodorow to explore the association of the literal
with the feminine.

24. For Gates's revision of the traditional saying "signification is the nigger's occupation" to "figuration is the nigger's occupation," see "Criticism in the Jungle" and
"The Blackness of Blackness: A Critique of the Sign and the Signifying Monkey," in
Black Literature and Literary Theory, 1–24, 285–321. For the cultural splitting of a disembodied white femininity from a black female materiality, see Barbara Christian,
Black Feminist Criticism: Perspectives on Black Women Writers (New York: Pergamon Press,
1985), chap. 1, and Carby, *Reconstructing Womanhood,* chap. 2.

25. For an especially powerful and influential account of black materialist feminism, see The Combahee River Collective, "A Black Feminist Statement," in *All the
Women Are White, All the Blacks Are Men, But Some of Us Are Brave: Black Women's Studies,* ed. Gloria T. Hull, Patricia Bell Scott, and Barbara Smith (Old Westbury, N.Y.:
Feminist Press, 1982), 13–22. See also Bonnie Thornton Dill, "Race, Class, and Gender: Prospects for an All-Inclusive Sisterhood," *Feminist Studies* 9 (spring 1983): 131–50.
For a warning against eclipsing the formal and imaginative qualities of literature by
privileging sociopolitical analysis, see Christian, "But What Do We Think We're Doing Anyway?"

26. Two examples of white materialist feminist criticism that either do not consider the critic's racial position an obstacle, or consider it a readily surmountable obstacle, are Lauren Berlant, "Race, Gender, and Nation in *The Color Purple,*" *Critical Inquiry* 14 (summer 1988): 831–59, and Anne E. Goldman, "'I Made the Ink': (Literary)
Production and Reproduction in *Dessa Rose* and *Beloved,*" *Feminist Studies* 16 (summer
1990): 313–30. For examples of black materialist feminist willingness to entertain readings by white feminists, see Carby, *Reconstructing Womanhood,* chap. 1; Carby's argument that there are no "pure, autonomous cultures that belong to particular groups
or classes of people" implicitly opens the analysis of cultural struggles and articulations to a diverse materialist readership (Hazel V. Carby, "The Canon: Civil War and
Reconstruction," *Michigan Quarterly Review* 28 [winter 1989]: 42). See also hooks, *Talking Back,* chap. 7, and Valerie Smith, "Black Feminist Theory and the Representation
of the 'Other.'"

27. Valerie Smith, "Black Feminist Theory and the Representation of the 'Other,'"
39. See Carby, *Reconstructing Womanhood,* chap. 1.

28. See Deborah E. McDowell, "'The Changing Same': Generational Connections
and Black Women Novelists," *New Literary History* 18 (winter 1987): 281–302; Henderson, "*The Color Purple:* Revisions and Redefinitions," *Sage* 2 (spring 1985): 14–18,
reprinted in Bloom, *Alice Walker,* 67–80; Thadious M. Davis, "Alice Walker's Celebration of Self in Southern Generations," *Southern Quarterly* 21 (summer 1983): 39–53,
reprinted in Bloom, *Alice Walker,* 25–37; Barbara Christian, "Alice Walker: The Black
Woman Artist as Wayward" and "No More Buried Lives: The Theme of Lesbianism
in Audre Lorde's *Zami,* Gloria Naylor's *The Women of Brewster Place,* Ntozake Shange's
Sassafrass, Cypress and Indigo, and Alice Walker's *The Color Purple,*" in *Black Feminist
Criticism: Perspectives on Black Women Writers,* ed. Barbara Christian (New York: Pergamon Press, 1985), 81–102 and 187–204; Katz, "'Show Me How to Do Like You,'"
185–94; Jean Wyatt, "Eros as Creativity: The Extended Family in *The Color Purple,*" in
Reconstructing Desire: The Role of the Unconscious in Women's Reading and Writing (Chapel
Hill, N.C.: University of North Carolina Press, 1990), 164–85; and Molly Hite, "Romance, Marginality, Matrilineage: *The Color Purple,*" in *The Other Side of the Story: Structures and Strategies of Contemporary Feminist Narrative* (Ithaca, N.Y.: Cornell University
Press, 1989), 103–26. It is interesting to note, nevertheless, a difference in emphasis: some black feminists (preeminently McDowell) have emphasized the novel's subversion of the conventions of characterization and diction governing black literature,
whereas most white feminists have located the novel in relation to the dominant traditions of white literature.

29. bell hooks, "Writing the Subject: Reading *The Color Purple,*" in Bloom, *Alice
Walker,* 223; Cora Kaplan, "Keeping the Color in *The Color Purple,*" in *Sea Changes: Es-*

says on Culture and Feminism (London: Verso, 1986), 182, 187. Focusing on twentieth-century black male discourses on gender and the family, Kaplan is foregrounding a different black literary tradition from hooks, yet, as the title of her essay indicates, she insists that the novel's value resides in its relation to specifically black cultural traditions. In Alison Light, "Fear of the Happy Ending: *The Color Purple,* Reading and Racism," in *Plotting Change: Contemporary Women's Fiction,* ed. Linda Anderson (London: Edward Arnold, 1990), 85–96, the novel's "imaginary resolution of political and personal conflicts" (87), which hooks protests in relation to a black audience, is endorsed in terms of the political importance of utopianism for a (white) feminist audience. Black discursive specificity enables Kaplan's rehabilitation of the text; white reading specificity implicitly enables Light's.

30. See Hazel V. Carby, "It Just Be's Dat Way Sometime: The Sexual Politics of Women's Blues," *Radical America* 20, no. 4 (1986): 11, and Susan Willis, *Specifying: Black Women Writing the American Experience* (Madison, Wis.: University of Wisconsin Press, 1987), chaps. 5 and 7.

31. The tendency toward idealization troubles even the most brilliant materialist reading of the text, Berlant's, "Race, Gender, and Nation in *The Color Purple.*" For although Berlant ultimately repudiates the novel's (in her view inadequate) "womanist" alternative to patriarchal nationalism, her struggle to endorse this alternative contrasts with her less ambivalently negative representation of white women's privatized cultural bonds and identifications in her essay "The Female Complaint," *Social Text,* no. 19–20 (fall 1988): 237–59. Despite her political critique of Walker's text, Berlant is more sympathetic to it than either hooks or Carby.

32. See Susan Willis, "I Shop Therefore I Am: Is There a Place for Afro-American Culture in Commodity Culture?" in Wall, *Changing Our Own Words,* 173–95, hereafter abbreviated "I".

33. Willis, *Specifying,* 16, 72.

34. See Hazel V. Carby, "Reinventing History/Imagining the Future," a review of *Specifying* by Willis, *Black American Literature Forum* 23 (summer 1989): 381–87. In this detailed and largely favorable review, Carby criticizes only the romanticization of rural black folk culture, which for Carby typifies a misleading trend in contemporary African American cultural history. Willis's book has received extensive and largely favorable reviews from black feminists. Although several have decried its arbitrary historical boundaries and selection of texts, they have mostly found her historically grounded readings provocative and illuminating. See, for example, Barbara Christian, "Connections and Distinctions," a review of *Specifying* by Willis, *The Women's Review of Books* 4 (July-August 1987): 25–26; Cheryl A. Wall, "Black Women Writers: Journeying along Motherlines," a review of *Specifying* by Willis, *Callaloo* 12 (1989): 419–22; and Deborah E. McDowell, a review of *Specifying* by Willis, *Color, Sex, and Poetry: Three Women Writers of the Harlem Renaissance* by Hull, and *The Character of the Word* by Karla Holloway, *Signs* 14 (summer 1989): 948–52. One critic with nothing good to say about this "odd Marxist colonization (domestication? deflowering?) of black women writers" is Wallace, "Who Owns Zora Neale Hurston?" 184.

35. Fredric Jameson, "Reification and Utopia in Mass Culture," *Social Text* 1 (winter 1979): 140; Jameson devotes only a paragraph to this possibility. In his later essay, "Postmodernism, or, The Cultural Logic of Late Capitalism," *New Left Review* 146 (July-August 1984): 53–92, he greatly complicates the position from which might

emanate a political art no longer tied to cultural enclaves whose marginality is representable in two-dimensional space; there is no longer any position unincorporated within "the truth of postmodernism, that is, . . . the world space of multinational capital" (92); Willis, however, is responding primarily to "Reification and Utopia in Mass Culture." For Willis, the utopian possibilities of marginal space are available to diverse groups. In her "Gender as Commodity," *South Atlantic Quarterly* 86 (fall 1987): 403–21, children play the role that black women writers play in "I Shop Therefore I Am"; in Susan Willis, *"Fantasia:* Walt Disney's Los Angeles Suite," *Diacritics* 17 (summer 1987): 83–96, the nature represented in the "Nutcracker" sequence images the utopian social relations of a space outside of capitalist production. In *"Fantasia,"* Willis begins with the perspective of historical estrangement that the film offers for critiques of contemporary mass culture but slides into the utopian position offered by the "Nutcracker" sequence. In her discourse on black women's writing, estrangement is consistently utopian.

36. Willis's footnote to Carby painfully reveals her struggle to agree and disagree simultaneously rather than to analyze the sources of their differences. Carby's position in general is closer to Kobena Mercer's than to Willis's, calling Willis's gender analysis into question. Similarly, although Willis cites Sylvia Wynter's essay on minstrelsy as parody (see Sylvia Wynter, "Sambos and Minstrels," *Social Text* 1 [winter 1979]: 149–56), she doesn't speculate about why Wynter is so much less ambivalent about the subversive power of parody than Willis is. Michele Wallace's essay on Michael Jackson, "Michael Jackson, Black Modernisms and 'The Ecstasy of Communication,'" in *Invisibility Blues,* 77–90, which appeared about the same time as Willis's, is closer to Wynter's analysis than to Willis's, further problematizing the gender alliance across racial lines. About her resistance to grappling with individual black feminist critics in her book, Willis explains: "Taken as a whole, these [black feminist] books define the critical context for my thinking about the literature. None of these texts is directly cited in my interpretations because I chose not to speak to the criticism. Such a method would have produced a very different book" (183). This "very different book" might have beneficially entailed some dialogue about differences rather than a construction of difference based on the desire for a vision of "transformed human social relationships and the alternative futures these might shape" (159).

37. Susan Willis, "I Want the Black One: Is There a Place for Afro-American Culture in Commodity Culture?" *New Formations,* no. 10 (spring 1990): 96.

38. I am borrowing, with thanks, Sue Schweik's insights and formulation.

39. For a powerful statement of a similar conclusion about race and reading, see Mary Helen Washington, "How Racial Differences Helped Us Discover Our Common Ground," in *Gendered Subjects: The Dynamics of Feminist Teaching,* ed. Margo Culley and Catherine Portuges (Boston: Routledge, 1985), 221–29. Washington decides: "I will never again divide a course outline and curriculum along racial lines (as I did in 'Images of Women') so that the controlling purpose is to compare the responses of white women and black women, because I see how much the class imitates the syllabus. I do not want to see black women in opposition to white women as though that division is primary, universal, absolute, immutable, or even relevant" (227–28).

40. This is not an inclusive list of black feminist critical projects, practitioners, or texts; it merely calls attention to some influential examples of black feminist writing on, or collections of, black women writers, such as Barbara Christian, ed., *Black Women*

Novelists: The Development of a Tradition, 1892–1976 (Westport, Conn.: Greenwood Press, 1980); Christian, *Black Feminist Criticism;* Mary Helen Washington, ed., *Black-Eyed Susans: Classic Stories by and about Black Women* (Garden City, N.Y.: Anchor Books, 1975), *Midnight Birds: Stories by Contemporary Black Women Writers* (Garden City, N.Y.: Anchor Books, 1980), and *Invented Lives: Narratives of Black Women 1860–1960* (Garden City, N.Y.: Anchor Books, 1987); Deborah E. McDowell, "New Directions for Black Feminist Criticism," in *The New Feminist Criticism: Essays on Women, Literature, and Theory,* ed. Elaine Showalter (New York: Pantheon, 1985), 186–99; Deborah E. McDowell and Arnold Rampersad, eds., *Slavery and the Literary Imagination* (Baltimore: Johns Hopkins University Press, 1989); Gloria T. Hull, *Color, Sex, and Poetry: Three Women Writers of the Harlem Renaissance* (Bloomington, Ind.: Indiana University Press, 1987) and *Give Us Each Day: The Diary of Alice Dunbar-Nelson* (New York: W. W. Norton, 1984); Nellie Y. McKay, ed., *Critical Essays on Toni Morrison* (Boston: G. K. Hall, 1988); Margaret B. Wilkerson, ed., *Nine Plays by Black Women* (New York: New American Library, 1986); Carby, *Reconstructing Womanhood;* Barbara Smith, "Toward a Black Feminist Criticism," in Hull, Scott, and Smith, *All the Women Are White, All the Blacks Are Men, But Some of Us Are Brave,* 157–75; Valerie Smith, "Black Feminist Theory and the Representation of the 'Other'" and *Self-Discovery and Authority in Afro-American Narrative* (Cambridge, Mass.: Harvard University Press, 1987); bell hooks, *Ain't I a Woman: Black Women and Feminism* (Boston: South End Press, 1981), *Feminist Theory from Margin to Center* (Boston: South End Press, 1984), *Talking Back,* and *Yearning: Race, Gender, and Cultural Politics* (Boston: South End Press, 1990); Wallace, *Invisibility Blues;* Audre Lorde, *Sister Outsider: Essays and Speeches* (Trumansburg, N.Y.: Crossing Press, 1984); and June Jordan, *Civil Wars* (Boston: Beacon, 1981).

41. For some recent white feminist accounts of the alternatives offered by black women's texts, see Elizabeth Abel, "Race, Class, and Psychoanalysis? Opening Questions," in *Conflicts in Feminism,* ed. Marianne Hirsch and Evelyn Fox Keller (New York: Routledge, 1990), 184–204; Marianne Hirsch, *The Mother/Daughter Plot: Narrative, Psychoanalysis, Feminism* (Bloomington, Ind.: Indiana University Press, 1989), esp. 176–99; Hite, *The Other Side of the Story,* 103–26; Elizabeth Meese, *(Ex)Tensions: Re-Figuring Feminist Criticism* (Urbana, Ill.: University of Illinois Press, 1990), 129–54 (and, for other women of color, chaps. 2 and 5); Roberta Rubenstein, *Boundaries of the Self: Gender, Culture, Fiction* (Urbana, Ill.: University of Illinois Press, 1987), 125–63 (and all of pt. 2 for other women of color); and Wyatt, *Reconstructing Desire,* 164–209.

42. For examples of Spillers's revisionist use of psychoanalytic theory, see her "Interstices: A Small Drama of Words," in *Pleasure and Danger,* ed. Carole S. Vance (Boston: Routledge, 1984), 73–100; "Mama's Baby, Papa's Maybe: An American Grammar Book," *Diacritics* 17 (summer 1987): 65–81; and her essay in this volume. Spillers's work productively complicates the distinction Susan Thistlethwaite draws in her *Sex, Race, and God: Christian Feminism in Black and White* (New York: Crossroad, 1989) between the psychological focus of white feminism and the sociopolitical focus of black feminism.

43. McDowell made this argument in a paper entitled "Residues," delivered at the Wisconsin Conference on Afro-American Studies in the Twenty-First Century, Madison, Wis., March 1991.

44. Carby and hooks have both written pervasively and eloquently about this need; for recent examples, see Hazel V. Carby, "The Politics of Difference," *Ms.* (Septem-

ber-October 1990): 84–85, and hooks, "Critical Interrogation." On whiteness as "the metaphor for the metaphorical production of the Subject as one devoid of properties," see David Lloyd, "Race under Representation," *Oxford Literary Review,* no. 1–2 (1991): 13. On the asymmetry of the system of racial marking, which "inscribes the system of domination on the body of the individual, assigning to the individual his/her place as a dominated person" while not assigning "any place to the dominator," who remains unmarked, see Colette Guillaumin, "Race and Nature: The System of Marks," *Feminist Issues* 8 (fall 1988): 41.

45. hooks, "Critical Interrogation," 162.

46. Morrison, *Playing in the Dark,* 90.

47. In "The Race for Theory," *Cultural Critique* 6 (spring 1987): 51–63, Christian powerfully demonstrates the distorting effects of literary theory's intervention in the reading of black women's texts. Although she does not hold white feminists responsible for this intervention, her argument clearly applies to white feminist (as well as masculinist) theoretical discourses.

II

Representing the Unrepresentable
The Symbolic and the Real

"All the Things You Could Be by Now, If Sigmund Freud's Wife Was Your Mother"

Psychoanalysis and Race

Hortense J. Spillers

1

The view from here is old-fashioned. One might even call it lame, predicated as it is on the proposition that self-knowledge has its uses. From here, we might be invested in a reinvigorated social practice, whose aim is ethical and restorative. But to say so is to start at the end of this piece, where and when and if the writing has not only congealed, but explained itself. We have now to do with beginnings.

A framework that would properly contextualize a confrontation between "psychoanalysis" and "race" is not imaginable without a handful of prior questions, usually left unarticulated, that set it in motion in the first place. The new social practices toward which I have gestured cannot proceed, however, unless we are willing to pose the not quite thinkable on which bases the converging issues have previously rested. In other words, culture theorists on either side of the question would rule out, as tradition has it, any meeting ground between race matters and psychoanalytic theories. But I want to shift ground, mindful of this caveat: Little or nothing in the intellectual history of African Americans within the social and political context of the United States suggests the effectiveness of a psychoanalytic discourse, revised or classical, in illuminating the problematic of "race" on an intersubjective field of play, nor do we yet know how to historicize the psychoanalytic object and objective, invade its hereditary premises and insulations, and open its insights to cultural and social forms that are disjunctive to its originary imperatives. How might psychoanalytic theories speak about "race" as a self-consciously assertive reflexivity, and how might "race" expose the gaps that psychoanalytic theories awaken? Neither from the point of view of African Americans' relationship to the dominant culture, nor, just as important, from that of the community's intramural engagements have we been obliged in our analytical and critical writings to consider the place of fantasy, desire, and the "un-conscious," of conflict, envy, aggression, and ambivalence in the repertoire of elements that are perceived to fashion the life-world. Only a handful of writers of fiction—Ralph Ellison, Toni Cade Bambara, Alice Walker, David Bradley, and Toni Morrison, among them—have posed a staging of the mental theater as an articulate structure of critical inquiries into the "souls of black folk," though my having recourse to W. E. B. Du Bois's 1903 work indeed suggests that the black New Englander was on course nearly a century ago. I think it is safe to say, however, that the psychoanalytic object, subject, and subjectivity constitute the missing layer of hermeneutic and interpretive projects of an entire generation of black intellectuals now at work. The absence is not only glaring but also perhaps most curious in its persistence. There are genuine costs as a result, whose upshot may be observed in what I would consider occasional lapses of ethical practice in social relations among black intellectuals themselves. Such lapses are most painfully obvious and most dramatically demonstrable in cross-gender exchanges within this social formation, although this outcome is not the only way to read the picture. Within genders, the black intellectual class is establishing few models of conduct and social responsibility, but perhaps change is in the making.[1] Relatedly, we appear to be at a crossroads in trying to determine who "owns" African American cultural production as an "intellectual property," in brief, who may "speak" for it, and whether or not possession itself is the always exploitative end of access, even when the investigator looks like me.

Though a sustained reading of this manifestation is beside the point of this essay, it hovers in the background as precisely the sort of problem that a revised and corrected social political practice might field, if not solve, might mobilize to pointed attention, if not drive out altogether. Psychoanalytic discourse might offer a supplementary protocol to consider. This essay attempts to provide such an opening.

2

By juxtaposing "psychoanalysis" and "race," is one bringing them into alignment in the hope that these structures of attention will be mutually illuminating and interpenetrative? Or does one mean to suggest the impossibility of the latter, which reinforces the impression that these punctualities are so insistently disparate in the cultural and historical claims that they each invoke that the ground of their speaking together would dissolve in conceptual chaos? "Race" speaks through multiple discourses that inhabit intersecting axes of relations that banish once and for all the illusion of a split between "public" and "private." The individual in the collective traversed by "race"—and there are no known exceptions, as far as I can tell—is covered by it before language and its differential laws take hold. It is the perfect affliction, if by that we mean an undeniable setup that not only shapes one's view of things but also demands an endless response. Unscientific in the eyes of "proofs," governed by the inverted comma, unnatural and preponderant in its grotesque mandates on the socius, "race" is destiny in the world we have made. What is this thing called "race"?[2] Our deadliest abstraction? Our most nonmaterial actuality? Not fact, but our deadliest fiction that gives the lie to doubt of ghosts? In a word, "race" haunts the air where women and men in social organization are most reasonable.

"Race," therefore, travels: though we are confronted, from time to time, with almost-evidence that the age of the post-race subject is upon us, we are just as certain that its efficacies can and do move from one position to another and back again. "Race" is both concentrated and dispersed in its localities. In other words, "race" alone bears no inherent meaning, even though it reifies in personality; it gains its power from what it signifies by point, in what it allows to come to meaning, such as the synonymity struck between Africanness and enslavement by the close of the seventeenth century in the English colonies, which marked the boundary of freedom and decided in turn a subject's social and political status. In the context of the United States, "race" clings, primitively, to a Manichaean overtness—"black'' and "white." But it is evident that "race" by other names may operate within homogeneous social formations that lose their apparent similarity under hierarchical value: "race" is not simply a metaphor. It is the outcome of a politics, and for one to mistake it is to be politically stupid and endangered. But it is also a complicated figure or metaphoricity that demonstrates the power and danger of difference, that signs and assigns difference as a way to situate social subjects. If we did not already have "race" and its quite impressive powers of proliferation, we would need to invent them. The social mechanism at work here is difference in and as hierarchy, although "race" remains one of its most venerable master signs.

The problem is how to explain the way by which "race" translates into cultural self-production at the same time that it is evidently imposed by agencies (agentification) that come to rest in the public and administrative sphere, or what we understand as such. The provocation is to grasp its self-reflexivity that is presumptively "private" and "mine." But the relay between self-fashioning and "out there" is only intricately revealed. As seems clear to me at the moment, the African American collective denotes the quintessential object of the discourses of social science, insofar as the overwhelming number of commentaries concerning it have to do with the "findings" of the sociological and the collective situation within the economy. Naming here becomes destiny to the extent that the social formation, or individual communities within it, comprehend themselves almost entirely as an innocence or a passivity worked upon, worked over by others. Whereas it would be simplistic and erroneous to say, "all we have to do," we can guess without apology that there is an aspect of human agency that cannot be bestowed or restored by others, even though the philosopher's recognition or lack of recognition will in fact support it, and it is this aspect of the historical and cultural apprenticeship—strategies for gaining agency—that we wish to describe in a systematic way.

A psychoanalytic culture criticism, or psychoanalytics, would establish the name of inquiry itself as the goal of an interior intersubjectivity that I would in turn designate as the locus at which self-interrogation takes place. It is not an arrival but a departure, not a goal but a process, and it conduces toward neither an answer nor a cure because it is not engendered in formulae and prescriptions. More precisely, its operations are torquelike to the extent that they throw certainty and dogma (the static, passive, monumental aim) into doubt. This process situates a content to work on as a discipline, as an ascesis, and I would specify it on the interior because it is found in economy but is not exhausted by it. Persistently motivated in inwardness, in-flux, it is the "mine" of social production that arises, in part, from interacting with others, yet it bears the imprint of a particularity. In the rotations of certainty, this "mine" gets away with very little, scot-free, and that rebounds back upon the ethical wish that commences this writing.

I would say from my limited acquaintance with classical psychoanalytic theory that the missing pieces that help us to articulate a protocol of healing in reference to the African American life-world involve the dimensions of the socioethical. Even though the Freudian archive offers a rich itinerary of narratives and their context, beginning with Fräulein Anna O's family situation, we cannot trace from there a systematic trajectory of wider social engagement and implication: We cannot tell where a household locates in political economy and the stresses generated by the positioning, although it is clear from the discourse on the early psychoanalytic movement that its initial subjects were, to a degree, quite comfortably situated in the environment, were even "at home" in it.[3] (But was that the problem? That what might have been a rebellion, or the site of an "uncanny," or a "home," reappeared as a symptom instead?) The relationship, then, between the nuclear family and the intervening sociometries of the bourgeois household of Viennese society of that era generated the neurosis and its science out of a social fabric that feminist investigation has been keen to rethread.[4] It seems that Freud wrote as if his man or woman were Everybody's, were constitutive of the social order, and that coeval particularities carried little or no weight. The universal sound of psychoanalysis, in giving short shrift to cultural uniqueness (which it had to circumvent, I suppose, in order to win the day for itself and to undermine, to throw off the track, the anti-Semitic impulses of Freud's era), must be invigilated as its limit: Precisely because its theories seduce us to want to concede, to give in to its seeming naturalness, its apparent rightness to the way we live, we must be on guard all the more against assimilating other cultural regimes to its modes of analyses too quickly and without question, if at all. Freud could not see his own connection to the "race" and culture orbit, or could not theorize it, because the place of their elision marked the vantage from which he spoke. Because it constituted his enabling postulate, it went "without saying." Perhaps we could argue that the "race" matrix was the fundamental interdiction within the enabling discourse of founding psychoanalytic theory and practice itself. But it is the missing element here that helps to define Freud's significance as one of the preeminent modern punctualities of Western time.

I have no evidence that what are for me, at least, the major topics of the psychoanalytic field are not in fact stringently operative in African American community: self-division; the mimetic and transitive character of desire; the economies of displacement—associative and disjunctive; the paradox of the life-death pull; the tragic elements couched in the transfer of social powers from one generation of historical actors to another; the preeminent distinctions that attach to the "Twin Towers" of human and social being— "Mama" and "Papa" (this item invites sustained attention because parenting in black communities is historically fraught with laws that at one time overdetermined the legal status of the child as property, but the question is to what extent the legal relations—a child who neither "belonged" to the mother, nor to an African father—might have been translated into an affective one); the "paradox of the negative,"[5] or the sign's power to delegate by negation; and the special relationship that adheres between exile and writing (which may be retroactively viewed here through the lens of De Certeau). It seems, then, that the life-world offers a quintessential occasion for a psychoanalytic reading, given the losses that converge on its naming, given the historic cuts that have star-crossed its journey. The situation of African American community is more precisely ambivalent than any American case, in light of its incomplete "Americanization" even at this late date. The way it is situated in American culture precisely defines the human social element trapped between divergent cultural mappings, as well as an oppositional and collusive circuit of desire. In the U.S. field of social relations, African American culture is open, by definition, if by that we mean a constant commerce in real and symbolic capital among struggling intersubjectivities. Even though the "neighborhood" that we spoke of earlier comes close, on the mythic level, to the cocoon of kin and relatedness that Fanon imagines for the black-before-going-to-Europe, it was always crossed by something else—the General Motors car, for example, the old assembly-line technologies replaced by automation and the service economy, the ubiquitous television and media-blitz—those metropolitan and urban byways and by-the-ways along the borders of particular cultural enclosure. If we translate these technological means into a figural and semiotic use, then clearly African American personality is situated in the crossroads of conflicting motivations so entangled that it is not always easy to designate what is "black" and "white" here.

The question for this project is not so much why and how "race" makes the difference—the police will see to it—but how it carries over its message onto an interior, how "race," as a poisonous idea, insinuates itself not only across and between ethnicities, but also within. What I am positing here is blankness of "race" where something else ought to be, that emptying out that I spoke of earlier, the evacuation to be restituted and recalled as the discipline of a self-critical inquiry. In calling this process an *interior intersubjectivity,* I would position it as a power that countervails another by an ethical decision, but would this countervalence belong, by definition, to what Freud called the "secondary processes"[6] of consciousness, and would a radical shift of consciousness adequately effect the kind of root change I mean? In my view, classical psychoanalytic theory offers interesting suggestions along this route by way of Lacanian schemes, corrected for what I would call the "socionom," or the speaking subject's involvements with ideological apparatuses, which would embrace in turn a theory of domination (to that extent, Lacanian psychoanalytic theory is simply heavenly, insofar as it has no eyes for the grammar and politics of power). What one anticipates, then, is that a fourth register will be called for in establishing "reality" (of the dominated political position) as the psychic burden, acquired postmirror stage, that reads back onto the Lacanian triangulation a distended organizational calculus.[7]

3

What is missing in African American cultural analysis is a concept of the "one." Though there is a hidden allegiance to the idea of the superstar or hero—the emplotments of both the autobiography and the form of the slave narrative are firmly grounded in old-fashioned notions of bourgeois individualism—it is widely believed that black people cannot afford to be individualistic. I must admit that most of the black people I know who think this are intellectuals, who, in practice, not only insist on their own particularity but in some cases even posit a uniqueness. But if we can, we must maintain a distinction between the "one" and the "individual," even though the positions overlap. The individual of black culture exists strictly by virtue of the "masses," which is the only image of social formation that traditional analysis recognizes. Practically speaking, the masses were all there were against the other great totalizing narratives—"white" and "Indian"—in the historical period stretching from colonization to nationhood. The individual of the life-world does not stand in opposition to the mass, but at any given moment along the continuum might be taken as a supreme instance of its synecdochic representation.[8] In other words, Every Black Man or Woman *is* the "race"— as the logic of slave narratives amply demonstrates—and the elements of the formula are reversible and commensurate. Imagining, then, that African

American culture, under extreme historical conditions, was not merely at odds with the cultural dominant but opposed to it, the intellectual-activist has concluded that African American culture inscribes an inherent and coherent difference. African American culture, on the supposed African model, is advanced as a collective enterprise in strict antinomy to the individualistic synthesis of the dominant culture, as well as a summation and reification of the indigenous mass. The individual-in-the-mass and the mass-in-the-individual mark an iconic thickness: a concerted function whose abiding centrality is embodied in the flesh. But before the "individual," properly speaking, with its overtones of property ownership and access, more or less complete, stands the "one," who is both a position in discourse—the spoken subject of the *énoncé* that figures a grammatical instance—and a consciousness of positionality—the speaking subject of the *énonciation,* the one in the act of speaking as consciousness of position. As the former is mapped onto his or her world by social and discursive practices, the latter comes into the realization that he or she is the "one" who "counts."[9] This one is not only a psychic model of layered histories of a multiform past, but she is the only riskable certainty or grant of a social fiction, insofar as the *point* mimics the place where the speaker or speaking is constituted. *I* grants its validity in assuming the social for itself, and not unlike the Other, whose gaze floods what it grasps and summons the attention at the same time, the "one" is both conceded and not-oneself; it is not to be doubted, in the same sense that its sureness is tentative.[10] To that degree, the mass is the posited belief that empirical data insist on, but where is it? Could we say that "one," by contrast, is always "here" not "there"? That it is concrete and specific, even if anonymous? This is not to choose "one" over the "mass," but to ask a different question, for we know no other gage of the intersubjective than the one who would assure the more. From this view, the mass is not only putative and abstract, but also never emerges otherwise. It would be absurd to say that there is no mass; say rather that its historical and social materiality can be brought to stand, stage by stage, and bit by bit that begins unimpressively on the smaller scale of something local and at hand. For openers, it is exactly too massive and disappears under the weight of report. The picture will change right away when mass movement is required, but that is something else again, and demands several, shouting.

In the meantime, who is this one? I am referring to a structure in this instance: the small integrity of the now that accumulates the tense of the presents as proofs of the past, and as experience that would warrant, might earn, the future. In the classical model, the mental apparatus, Freud argued, can be analogized to a compound microscope or photographic apparatus.[11] Instantly defensive about the "unscientific" status of assertion by analogy, Freud claims that his procedure is permissible so long as the "scaffolding" is not mistaken for the "building." But the single lesson that we take away from

Freud in this case is the split function of subjectivity at the heart of subject formation. The crux of the matter is concentrated in *The Interpretation of Dreams,* which assigns to consciousness itself a relatively minor role in the drama of mind-life. Consequently, Freud apportions a far greater share of mental activity to the functions of the unconscious and the primary processes that suggest their import, he holds, in dreams and the neurosis. Related to the dynamic play of mental forces, Freud contends that "psychotherapy can pursue no other course than to bring the [unconscious] under the domination of the [preconscious]" (578). As Lacan will have it decades later, the particular aim of psychoanalysis is "historically defined by the elaboration of the notion of the subject. It poses this question in a new way, by leading the subject back to his signifying dependence."[12]

The Freudian and Lacanian fields of discourse are not only separated from each other by considerable disparity in time, conditions of material culture, and the narrative and conceptual modalities that would situate and explain them, but also, because they reach subject formation by an act of poetic faith that imagines subjectivity hermetically sealed off from other informing discourses and practices, both are foreign, if not inimical, to subject formations defined by the suppression of discourse. In other words, the social subject of "race" is gaining access not only to her own garbled, private language, as psychoanalysis would have it, but also to language as an aspect of the public trust. The one that I am after, then, must be built up from the ground, so to speak, inasmuch as classical psychoanalytic theory and its aftermath contradictorily point toward it—a subject in its "signifying dependence," which means that the subject's profound engagement with and involvement in symbolicity is everywhere social—yet such theories cannot demarcate it. As far as I can tell, African American cultural analysis, as black intellectuals carry it out, has not explained a subject in discourse crossed by stigmata, or the nonfantastical markings of a history whose shorthand is "race." From that angle, the most promising of trails may be false, since it does not necessarily lead to a destination but circles back to the same place. The problem here, which fractures chaotically in many directions at once, is how to break the circle, how to pursue a theoretical model that might pose the pacing along to the next step, even if such pacing effects a halting progression. The interior intersubjectivity would substitute an agent for a spoken-for, a "see-er," as well as a "seen." Habermas's self-reflection, in which case the laws are operative but do not apply, appears to be predicated on the agency of self-knowing, but Du Bois's figure of the "double consciousness" suggests the complications through which such agency must pass.[13]

When Du Bois spoke earlier in the century about the protocol of "double consciousness," he was gesturing toward the duality of cultural fields metaphorized by "African" and "American." Though the former term had been used in self-reference to the American Negro long before Du Bois's era and would be again in our own, Du Bois was working under the assumption that "Africa" more than vaguely signaled the origins of black culture. It is also noteworthy that his provocative claims, barely elaborated beyond that short paragraph that the student knows virtually by heart, crosses their wires with the specular and the spectacular: the sensation of looking at oneself and of imagining being seen through the eyes of another is precisely performative in what it demands of a participant on the other end of the gaze.[14] Du Bois was trying to discover, indeed, to posit, an ontological meaning in the dilemma of blackness, working out its human vocation in the midst of over-whelming social and political power. It was not enough to be seen; one was called upon to decide what it meant. To that degree, Du Bois's idea posed an instance of self-reflexivity. Addressing the aims and objectives of con-sciousness as it negotiated the terrain of a given reality, Du Bois, writing con-temporaneously with Freud, was interested in providing a new mythography, or a new way of seeing the black problem, for the "souls of black folk."

The subject of double consciousness is divided across cultural valences, but Du Bois did not exhaust the formulation. For him, nothing was hidden from the sight of the man in the mirror, who not only recognized the false-ness of his countenance, as in a kind of theatrical mask, but how he had come to wear it. From that angle, the subject already "knows" as much as he knew, for all intents and purposes, on the day he was born. But Du Bois's economy of doubleness was adequate insofar as it proffered a name for cultural am-bivalence, while seeking a reconciliation of putative opposites; the Du Boisian knot cannot be cut or resolved on the level where Du Bois was pos-ing the question, because the act of seeing oneself rests in the subject's head and is only partially shaped and motivated by the official deed, and the change of seeing mostly depends on a change of mind coming from the di-rection of a power imagined to be entirely other, but an entirely other from outside. Though Du Bois understood quite correctly that an effective polit-ical solution rested in the hands of black community—the Niagara Move-ment and the NAACP springing from it constituted his practical response—the latter was conflated in his scheme with an ontology. He was not so much wrong in making this move as too quick to reach a conclusion. But despite that, the dilemma that Du Bois justly posed is the psychocultural situation of minorities in the West, even though Du Bois specifically targeted the "prob-lem of the color line" as it traversed the body of the seventh son, born with a caul over the face, the American Negro. In working with the Du Boisian double, we recover the sociopolitical dimensions that classical psychoanaly-sis and its aftermath sutured in a homogeneity of class interests, just as Du Bois's scheme must be pressured toward a reopened closure: The subject in the borrowed mirror is essentially mute. Du Bois is speaking for him. But it is time now, if it were not in 1903, for him to speak for himself, if he dares. That this will not be simple is all the more reason why it must be done.

The interior intersubjectivity is predicated, then, on speaking. The un-avoidable contradiction in what I am proposing, which would historically re-semble the Freudian "talking cure" but would also share in the dialectics of Toni Morrison's character called Sethe, is that my solution specifically re-lates to a social positioning vis-à-vis discourse.[15] Perhaps the speaking of in-tersubjectivity effects a kind of mimicry of the professional wordsmith's re-lationship to symbolic capital, but how is the speaking I mean here to be differentiated from professional discourse?

There is much insistence, at least in our customary way of viewing things, that the professional has little in common with the majority of the popula-tion. True enough as far as it goes, this truism is tinged with animus toward activity perceived to be esoteric, elitist, and uncommon. But this simplified reading of the social map, sealing off entire regions and territories of ex-perience from the reciprocal contagion proper to them, offers us slim op-portunity to understand how the social fabric, like an intricate tweed, is sewn across fibers and textures of meaning. There is the discourse in which the professional, as De Certeau observes, dares and labors,[16] the discourse of tra-vail, but there is also the mark of the professional's human striving in terms of the everyday world of the citizen-person—coming to grips with the pains of loss and loneliness; getting from point a to b; the inexorable passing of time, change, and money; the agonies of friendship and love, and so on. *This* speaking, and the one I refer to, is nothing less than the whole measure of the tirelessly mundane element in which ground, we recall, Freud placed the key to the mental theater, the unconscious and the dream life, the ap-parent junk tossed off by the deepest impulses. In that regard, the profes-sional's relationship to discourse is tiered, but it is also imbricated by forms of dialects through which she lives her human and professional calling, as work is rent through with the trace of the uncommon and the more com-mon. On this level, speaking is democratically impoverished for a range of subjects, insofar as it is not sufficient to the greedy urge to revelation of mo-tives that the social both impedes and permits, nor is it adequate to the gaps in kinetic and emotional continuity that the subject experiences as discom-fort. Psychoanalytic literature might suggest the word *desire* here to desig-nate the slit through which consciousness falls according to the laws of un-predictability. In that sense, the subject lives with desire as intrusive, as the estranged, irrational, burdensome ill fit that alights between where she "is at" and wants to be. On this level of the everyday, the professional discourser and the women commandeering the butcher's stand at the A&P have in com-mon a mutually scandalous secret about which they feel they must remain silent, but which speaking, more emphatically, *talking*, about appease, com-pensate, deflect, disguise, and translate into usable, recognizable social en-ergy. I mean, then, this speaking as it turns us off the track of isolation into which the preciosity and lowness of desire, persistent in solid juxtaposition in the same person, might tend to lead. I believe that this arena of the emotionally charged and discharged is not only where the subject lives but also the positions through which she speaks a particular syntax.

Is it not the task of a psychoanalytic protocol to effect a translation from the muteness of desire and wish—that which shames and baffles the subject, even if its origins are dim, not especially known—into an articulated syntactic particularity? An aspect of the emancipatory hinges on what would appear to be simple self-attention, except that reaching the articulation requires a process, that of making one's subjectness the object of a disciplined and potentially displaceable attentiveness. To the extent that the psychoanalytic provides, at least in theory, a protocol for the "care of the self" on several planes of intersecting concern, it seems vital to the political interests of black community, even as we argue (endlessly) about its generative schools of thought. I should think that the process of self-reflection, of the pressing urgency to make articulate what is left in the shadows of the unreflected, participates in a sociopolitical engagement of the utmost importance. If we think of *speaking* along this line of stress, then we cut right through the elitist connotations of *discourse* to the basic uses of literacy, whose attainment is currently regarded by the postmodernists as something of an embarrassment. But if we imagine such achievement as an emancipatory aim, then the perceived advantages of it lose their sting of privilege. Relatedly, both speaking and literacy in the ways I am stipulating might be understood as the right to use, which certain theoreticians regard as one of the premier destinies of property.[17] This entire discussion is caught up in questions of power in the last instance, but I am concerned with only one of its multiple and interpenetrative phases, and that is the power and position of a specific speaking.

To speak is to occupy a place in social economy, and in the case of the racialized subject, history has dictated that this linguistic right to use is never easily granted with human and social legacy but must be earned, over and over again, on the level of a personal and collective struggle that requires in some way a confrontation with the principle of language as prohibition, as the withheld. But an irony here ensues that the researcher-subject must both surmount and ride: the historic prohibition can only be spoken within language, yes, but also within discourse (the particular dialects of criticism, resistance, testimonial and witness, and so on). But what must be emphasized here is the symbolic value of the subject's exchanges with others, and it is within the intersubjective nexus that the inequalities of linguistic use and value are made manifest—what one can do with signs in the presence and perspective of others—and it is only within those circuits that a solution can be worked out. The unalterable difficulty is that such an operation cannot escape the Western context, and this is crucial. As we observed before, the traditional subject of psychoanalytic process was deceptively "at home" in the culture; this subject seemed to believe that he or she "belonged," whereas the minority subject does not start there.

Though a psychoanalytics related to the life-world would implicitly maintain contact with its predecessor texts, with the conceptual horizon that situates it, it is equally true that such a protocol would be guided by a new aim, insofar as the analysis must make a place for it—the speaking that self-reflection begins to demand. The scarcity, the deficit is located in the occasion for this private discourse that is not satisfied by the public forms and proprieties of narrative, autobiographical and otherwise, that remain substantially malleable to market forces and fickle public opinion. A cultural analysis revised and corrected for this most difficult of tasks is called upon to substitute the problematics of culture for that of "race," or a determinate group interest whose outcome is always already known, and to articulate its investigations along three lines of stress: the diurnal or the everyday, the dimension of the practical and pragmatic, and the dimension of the contemplative. Of these three registers of analysis, the third is the least developed in the field.

Currently, the cultural analysis offers no theory of the "everyday" and appears to have no firm grasp of social subjects in relationship to it. Such an understanding would conduce toward a systematic materialist reading, which would establish "race," in turn, in perspective with other strategies of marking and stigmata. Because of its allegiance to ideologies of empiricism, material success, and the transparencies of reading,[18] the analysis provides no clue to the contemplative register of the life-world. I am not talking about the recognition of the significance of rumor, gossip, and jaw-wagging, nor about armchair reading and philosophizing, but rather a name for the sense of time that we could call *distancing*, standing apart momentarily from the roll and moil of event and and finding ways to introduce it to the repertoire of human and social relations that traverse communities of interest. Because our analysis of the fields of the everyday and the contemplative are tangled up in the confusions of crisis-response (the threat to affirmative action policies, for example), we therefore flounder on the pragmatic point, or the realm, of direct political action and engagement. But it seems clear that the dimension of the contemplative practice, contextualized in relationship to the "science of a general economy of practices," must be pronounced as an aspect of cultural continuity and struggle.[19]

Contrary to the position taken by certain black leadership, I would say that "analysis" is not "paralysis," because it certainly seems that the absence of it is a living social death. Practically speaking, the leadership, wherever it arranges itself along the axes of responses, must update its message, send a different one, and link its own destiny more fully to the work of scholarship and reading.[20] (Du Bois remains the exemplary figure in this.) Exactly how today's leadership—and I do not exempt the intellectuals as a social formation from the general charge—is itself an elaboration of the problem it would solve should be thought about with a careful and, where possible, generous attitude, though such an investigation is not my aim here. If the psychoanalytic hermeneutic has any bearing at all on the life-world, and I believe that it does, then it will enter the picture at the third level of stress, even though dynamically speaking these layers of human time are interpenetrative. However, their articulation very much depends on the extent to which we differentiate pieces of the social content and demand.

The formal coherence that we seek for an apposite psychoanalytic practice does not commence in the psychoanalytic at all, but is firmly rooted in habits and levels of communication, reading, and interpretation—in short, how communities are apprenticed in culture and the ways in which such lessons are transmitted. Even though we customarily attribute reading and interpretive activity to an advantageous class position, the conclusion is inaccurate; the wide dissemination of literacies, visual and cybernetic, as well as literary, necessitate the negotiation of signs at whatever level, to whatever degree of competence. Sign reading, or the field of the semiotic, is democratically executed, as the culture worker can do nothing more nor less than point this out as a strategy for opening the way to the third dimension of social engagement.

If we cut through this human section in order to retrieve schematically the contemplative practice as a point of entry to the entire ensemble, then we mean no less than the capacity to detach oneself from the requirements of self-attention long enough to concentrate on something else; transformative labor marks a distinctive activity from that of the everyday and that of the practical and pragmatic, but such labor is contextualized and shaped by both and translates its living in both by other means. In other words, there is a dimension of activity in the life-world that lays claim not only to the materiality and immediacy of labor but also to its difference of perspective. Distancing here might be regarded as the mark of self-displacement in the social given: If the aim of a radical democratization is to free up more and more subjects to their transformative potential—is this not the point of a "pedagogy of the oppressed"?[21]—wresting their time farther and farther away from the necessity to concentrate on the needs of the biological creature and whether or not it is safe and secure, then such an aim will be carried out in the sphere of political practice and engagement. This is not to suggest that the range of cultural expression is apolitical or above the ground, nor is it to contend that access to work is unrelated to the economy and public policy, but it is to insist that each of these temporal emphases of the speaking or historical subject bears significance in relation to the human project. Such an insistence will operate as if we mean in fact a social division of labor, and so be it, but I mean division as the scissiparous effect within subjects rather than between them. Just as the culture worker maintains for himself or herself, so that worker must ever more forcefully hold out for others the subject's right of access to his or her double in the place where it is created.

The double resonates here through intentionalities: It means at once the "add on" that comes to the subject in her access to work and by way of that other scene evoked in the psychoanalytic reading. We must acknowledge what the classical psychoanalytic writers could take for granted, and that is the extent to which information about the other scene was predicated on access to literacy and economic resources. In short, we mean a more or less exact correspondence between the body freed from the harshest, most oppressive labor regime and emancipated to labor abstracted in an intellectual, or imaginative and creative quantum. African American cultural analysis must knot the relations between work—increasingly rationalized in a service economy that counts the turning of alphabets on a television game show as a "career"— and self-reflection or self-knowledge, or end up choked by it. But it would seem odd, if not downright perverse, to insist that only bourgeois subjects operate in the way of the double, although the explanatory discourses and enabling postulates of differentiated speaking and practice are brought about by the same power differential that disperses subjects along the paths of political economy in unequal ways. In that sense, symbolic economies, of which psychoanalytic practice and theories are one, are directly tied to the sociopolitical sphere. The culture worker, because he or she understands this or will soon, is called upon, therefore, to work as though that work carried the ultimately political leaning that it does.

I believe that the problem here has more to do with evolving a language appropriate to the subjects differently constructed from the classical moment of psychoanalytic theory and its postmodern aftermath than deciding "for" or "against" the psychoanalytic aim. This task will eventually require a lengthy and patient revisiting of the key questions of those theories with a result that I certainly cannot predict, except that the main thing appears to be, for the culture critic, the articulation of a position in discourse and practice along the lines of a more carefully modulated reading of human and social performances in the life-world rather than an actual psychoanalytic model for it. I am suggesting that such a model for diasporic communities might initiate its protocols with a practice "on the ground"—the case histories of subjects who speak their word to the analyst, not unlike John Gwaltney's quite different venture in *Drylongso*[22]—and on the other side, as it were, of the "white man." It seems to me that such a model does not commence with and cannot be based in "race" but rather in the intimate spaces where the white man's almighty form is in fact "forgotten" and misbegotten in the funny and satirical. It would be neither accurate nor useful to propose an irreparable split between the intimate and the public, for doing so would simply reverse and compound the error that traditional analysis has made all along. Rather, a subtler modulation of the flows from one to the other must be sought. As the critics have correctly maintained, much of the activity of self-defining, which describes the goal of self-reflection, or what I am calling here the interior intersubjectivity, has occurred in the transgressive unpredictable play of language. For that reason, a psychoanalytic model appropriate to the life-world and courageous enough to forego the refuges of delusion, which wrap around this world like a shroud, would risk its occasions in language, not only the locus of the subject's practice of culture—both the natal and the broader one that traverses it—but also the single feature of cultural apprenticeship that has been the most denied.

4

When I was young and free and used to wear silks (and sat in the front pew, left of center, I might add),[23] I used to think that my childhood minister occasionally made the oddest announcement: Whenever any one of our three church choirs was invited to perform at another congregation, our minister, suspecting that several of his members would stay home or do something else that afternoon, skillfully anticipated them. Those who were not going with the choir were importuned to "send go." The injunction always tickled me, as I took considerable pleasure in conjuring up the image of a snaggle-toothed replica of my seven-year-old self going off in my place. But the minister meant "send money," so pass the collection plate. Decades later, I decided that the "send go" of my childhood had an equivalent in the semiotic and philosophical discourse as the mark of substitution, the translated inflections of selves beyond the threshold of the fleshed, natural girl. It was not only a delightful idea to me that one herself need not always turn up, but also a useful one. One and one did not always make two but might well yield some indeterminate sum, according to the context in which the arithmetic was carried out and, indeed, which arithmetic was performed.

I have been suggesting that we need to work the double in this discussion. Perhaps this is as factual as I know: In any investigatory procedure concerning African American culture, a given episteme fractures into negative and positive stresses that could be designated the crisis of inquiry that reveals where a kind of abandonment—we could also call it a gap—has occurred. Rather than running straight ahead toward a goal, the positivity (a given theoretical instrument) loops back and forward at once. For example, the notion of substitutive identity, not named as such in the literature of social and cultural critique and writing, is analogous to the more familiar concept of "negation." On the one hand, negation is a time-honored concept of philosophical discourse and is already nuanced and absorbed, if not left behind, by linked discursive moves, from Hegel to Marx, from Kojève to Sartre and Lacan.[24] On the other hand, it is a useful concept to "introduce," alongside the psychoanalytic hermeneutic, to a particular historical order located in the postmodern time frame as a move toward self-empowerment, but in an era of discourse that needn't spell out the efficacy of either. (The same might be said for the concept of the "subject.") We are confronted, then, by divergent temporal frames or beats that pose the problem of adequacy—how to reclaim an abandoned site of inquiry in the critical discourse when the very question that it articulates is carried along as a part of the methodological structure, as a feature of the paradigm that is itself under suspicion, while the question itself foregrounds a thematic that cannot be approached in any other way. If one needs a "subject" here, with its repertoire of shifts and transformations, and "negation," with its successive generational closures and displacements, as both might be regarded as a "disappeared" quest-object at best, or a past tense for theory at worst, then we have come to the crisis that I have foretold, the instrument trapped in a looping movement or behind-time momentousness that must jump ahead. One tries in this fog of claims to keep her eyes on the prize: if by substitutive identities—the "send go"—we mean the capacity to represent a self through masks of self-negation, then the dialectics of self-reflection and the strategies of a psychoanalytic hermeneutic come together at the site of a "new woman" or "new man." I believe that that is the aim of the cultural analysis.

A break toward the potentiality of becoming, or the formation of substitutive identities, consists in going beyond what is given; it is also the exceeding of necessity. Though this gesture toward a theory of the transcendent is deeply implicated in the passage and itinerary of modern philosophy and the Cartesian subject, it is not so alien to the narratives and teachings of overcoming not only long associated with native traditions of philosophy in the life-world (via the teachings of the Christian church), but also entirely consonant with the democratic principles on which the nation was founded (though immensely simplified in the discourses of liberal democracy). But the resonance that I would rely on here is less dependent on a narrative genealogy, whose plot line culminates in an epiphany of triumph, than on a different relation to the "Real," where I would situate the politics and the reality of "race."

Even though it is fairly clear that "race" can be inflected (and should be) through the three dimensions of subjectivity offered by Lacanian psychoanalysis, the Symbolic, the Imaginary, and the Real, its face as an aspect of the Real brings to light its most persistent perversity.[25] In Mikkel Borch-Jacobsen's reading of Lacan's "linguisteries," the Real is said to be "'pure and simple,' 'undifferentiated,' 'non-human,' 'without fissure,'" and "'always in the same place.'"[26] As these Lacanian assertions seem to match precisely the mythical behavior of "race," or of any "myth today,"[27] they pointedly refer to the situation of the subject of enunciation—his or her ownmost Real, or the status quo. In the classical narratives of psychoanalytic theory, the status quo, the standing pat, does not by error open onto death's corridor, inasmuch as

it freezes and fixes subjectivity in a status permanently achieved. The outcome breezes by us in the very notion of "status," with its play on *statue, sto,
stant,* and so on. In this sense, "overcoming" is the cancellation of what is
given. Borch-Jacobsen offers this explanation: "Thus language, the manifestation of the negativity of the subject who posits himself by negating (himself as) the Real, works the miracle of manifesting what is not: the tearing
apart, the ek-sistence, and the perpetual self-overtaking that 'is' the subject
who speaks himself in everything by negating everything" (193). "Speaking"
here is both process and paradigm to the extent that signifying enables the
presence of an absence and registers the absence of a presence, but it is also
a superior mark of the transformative, insofar as it makes something by cut-
ting through the "pure and simple" of the "undifferentiated" in the gaps and
spacings of signifiers. If potentiality can be said to be the site of the human
rather than the nonhuman fixedness, more precisely, if it is the "place" of
the subjectivity, the condition of being and becoming subject, then its mission is to unfold—through "words, words, words" (193), yes, but "words,
words, words" as they lead us out to the re-presentational where the subject
commences its journey in the looking glass of the Symbolic.

  Thus, to represent a self through masks of self-negation is to take on the
work of discovering where one "is at"—the subject led back to his or her
signifying dependence. Freud had thought a different idea, as we observed
before, the bringing unconscious under the domination of the preconscious,
whereas Lacan, Freud's post-Sausserian poet, revised the idea as the "mapped"
"network of signifiers" brought into existence at the place where the subject
was, has always been: "Wo es war, soll Ich werden."[28] We could speak of this
process as the subject making its mark through the transitivity of reobjecti-
vations, the silent traces of desire on which the object of the subject hinges.
This movement across an interior space demarcates the discipline of self-
reflection, or the content of a self-interrogation that "race" always covers over
as an already-answered. But for oneself, another question is posed: What might
I become, insofar as? To the extent that "I" "signs" itself "elsewhere," represents itself beyond the given, the onus of becoming boomerangs,[29] Ralph Ellison's word, it rebounds on the one putting the question. But what impedes
the function of the question?

  If we move back in the direction of a prior moment, the seven-year-old
in the front pew, we can go forward with another set of competencies that
originate in the bone ignorance of curiosity, the child's gift for strange dreams
of flying and bizarre, yet correct, notions about the adult bodies around
her—how, for example, her father and brothers bent forward in a grimace
when mischievously struck in a certain place above the knees by a little girl,
propelling off a rollaway bed into their arms. The foreignness had already
begun in the instant grasp of sexual and embodied division. But from that
moment on, the imposition of homogeneity and sameness would also be un-

derstood as the great text of the "tradition" of "race." But before "race," something else has happened both within the context of "race" and alongside it.

Does tradition, then, depositories of discourse and ways of speaking, kinds of social practice and relations, enable some questions and not others? This seems so, but tradition, which hides its own crevices and interstices, is offered as the suture that takes on all the features of smoothness; in order to present itself as transparent, unruffled surface, it absorbs the rejects according to its most prominent configurations. But it seems that the move toward self-reflexivity demands a test of inherited portions of culture content in order to discover not only what tradition conceals but, as a result, also what one, under its auspices, is forced to blindside. Carrying out that line of thinking, we might be able to see in an apposite psychoanalytic protocol for the subjects of "race," broken away from the point of origin, which rupture has left a hole that speech can only point to and circle around, an entirely new repertoire of inquiry into human relations.

5

Among all the things you could be by now, if Sigmund Freud's wife were your mother, is someone who understands "the Dozens," the intricate verboseness of America's inner city. The big mouth brag, as much an art form as a strategy of insult, the Dozens takes the assaulted home to the backbone by "talking about" his mama and daddy. It is a choice weapon of defense and *always* changes the topic; bloodless because it is all wounding words and outrageous combinations of imagery and democratic because anyone can play and *be* played, it outsmarts the uzi—not that it is pleasant for all that—by resiting (and "reciting"?) the stress: the game of living, after all, is played between the ears, up in the head. Instead of dispatching a body, one straightens its posture; instead of offering up a body, one sends one's word. It is the realm of the ludic and the ludicrous that the late jazz bassist, Charlie Mingus, was playing around in when he concocted, as if on the spot, the title of the melody from which the title of this essay is borrowed. Responding to his own question that he poses to himself on the recording—"What does it mean?"—he follows the lines of his own cryptic signature, "Nothing. It means nothing." And what he proceeds to perform on the cut is certainly no thing we know. But that really is the point—to extend the realm of possibility for what might be known, and not unlike the Dozens, it will not be easy to decide if it is fun.

We traditionally understand the psychoanalytic in a pathological register, and there is the real question of whether it remains psychoanalysis without its principal features—a "third ear," something like the "fourth wall," or the speech that unfolds in the pristinely silent arena of two star witnesses—a patient and one "who is supposed to know." The scene of assumptions is completed in the privileged relations of client and doctor in the atmosphere of the confessional. But my interest in this ethical self-knowing is to unhook the psychoanalytic hermeneutic from its rigorous curative framework and recover it in a free-floating realm of self-didactic possibility that might decentralize and disperse the knowing one. We might need help here, but the uncertainty of where we'd be headed makes no guarantee of help. "Out there," the only "music" they are playing is Mingus's or much like it, and I should think that it would take a good long time to learn to hear it well.

NOTES

Another section of this essay appeared in *Critical Inquiry* (summer 1996). The end of the installment in this volume overlaps with the beginning of the *Critical Inquiry* essay. The entire piece, from which the essay in this volume has been excerpted and edited, appeared in *boundary 2* (fall 1996) and will be included in a forthcoming collection of my essays.

1. Perhaps the long-awaited thaw in the recognition of a collective and cooperative interest among African American women in the academy is only now coming about. During the month of January 1994, several hundreds of black women and women of color converged on the campus of the Massachusetts Institute of Technology for four days of meetings devoted to inquiry concerning a range of issues. Organized by MIT Professors Robin Kilson (history) and Evelyn Hammond (the history of science), "Defending Our Name, 1894–1994," taking its title's cue from the *New York Times* advertisement in support of Professor Anita Hill, was keynoted by three leading figures: Dr. Johnetta Cole, president of Spelman College, Professor Angela Davis of the History of Consciousness Board, University of California, Santa Cruz, and law Professor Lani Guinier of the University of Pennsylvania Law School. Prior to the MIT conference, black women graduate students in English and African American studies at the University of Pennsylvania convened a smaller conference of similar design at the Philadelphia campus during the spring of 1993. The MIT symposium was modeled on this idea.

2. For a recent examination of the problematics of "race" in aspects of its loose and strict construction, see Dominick LaCapra, ed., *The Bounds of Race: Perspectives on Hegemony and Resistance* (Ithaca: Cornell University Press, 1991).

3. A good introduction to a study of the social context of emergent psychoanalytic theory is offered in Juliet Mitchell, "Psychoanalysis and Vienna at the Turn of the Century," appendix to *Psychoanalysis and Feminism: Freud, Reich, Laing, and Women* (New York: Vintage Books, 1975), 419–35. Peter Gay's biographical study of Sigmund Freud exhaustively articulates the life with the career and both with the context of Freud's era: *Freud: A Life for Our Time* (New York: W. W. Norton, 1988); see esp. chaps. 5–7, 197–361.

4. A number of important works—both monographs and essay collections—in feminist interventions on the psychoanalytic object have emerged within the last decade and a half, including Charles Bernheimer and Claire Kahane, eds., *In Dora's*

Case—Freud-Hysteria-Feminism, Gender and Culture Series, ed. Carolyn G. Heilbrun and Nancy K. Miller (New York: Columbia University Press, 1985); Mary Jacobus, *Reading Woman: Essays in Feminist Criticism.* Gender and Culture Series, ed. Carolyn G. Heilbrun and Nancy K. Miller (New York: Columbia University Press, 1986); Teresa Brennan, ed., *Between Feminism and Psychoanalysis* (New York: Routledge, 1989); Richard Feldstein and Judith Roof, eds., *Feminism and Psychoanalysis* (Ithaca: Cornell University Press, 1989).

5. Delineating the four realms or regions of linguistic reference, Kenneth Burke speaks of the "paradox of the negative" in that context: it "is simply this: Quite as the *word* 'tree' is verbal and the *thing* tree is non-verbal, so all words for the non-verbal must, by the very nature of the case, discuss the realm of the non-verbal in terms of *what it is not.* Hence, to use words properly, we must spontaneously have a feeling for the *principle of the* negative." Burke, *The Rhetoric of Religion: Studies in Logology* (Berkeley: University of California Press, 1970), 18; emphasis Burke. For all intents and purposes, the classic distinction between sign and thing gained primacy via the field of modern linguistics and one of its most influential teachers of the early twentieth century, Ferdinand de Saussure. Saussure, *Course in General Linguistics,* ed. Charles Bally and Albert Sechehaye in collaboration with Albert Riedlinger, trans. Wade Baskin (New York: McGraw-Hill, 1966). Overlapping Freud's era, Saussure's researches were posthumously introduced to a wider audience of readers by his former students.

On this side of the Atlantic, however, philosopher Charles Sanders Peirce carried out innovative work on semiotics and a theory of signs during the late nineteenth and early twentieth centuries; see Peirce, "Logic as Semiotic: The Theory of Signs," in *Philosophical Writings of Peirce,* ed. Justus Buchler (New York: Dover Publications, 1955), 98–120.

6. Juliet Mitchell offers what appears to be an unobjectionable, perhaps even inevitable, response to notorious penis envy, one of the items that renders feminist theories and indeed some feminists edgy about the entire Freudian protocol: "I think the main problem arises because the suggestion is taken outside the context of the mechanisms of unconscious mental life—the laws of the primary process (the laws that govern the workings of the unconscious) are replaced by these critics by those of the secondary process (conscious decisions and perceptions), and as a result the whole point is missed." (Freud: The Making of a Lady I: Psychoanalysis and the Unconscious," in Feldstein and Roof, *Feminism and Psychoanalysis,* 5–15; passage cited from p. 8).

7. This fourth register would be nothing more nor less than "reality," constructed in relationship to the Lacanian Schema R; see Anthony Wilden, trans., *Speech and Language in Psychoanalysis: Jacques Lacan* (Baltimore: Johns Hopkins University Press, 1968), 294–98. If we think of this encodation as a psychic totality of "one," it might be analogized in accordance with genetic structure as the "socionom."

8. The value of the synecdochic figure rests in its commutability—Kenneth Burke speaks of the "noblest synecdoche" entailed in the identity of "microcosm" and "macrocosm." In this "noblest instance," "the individual is treated as a replica of the universe, and vice-versa . . . since microcosm is related to macrocosm as part to whole, and either the whole can represent the part or the part can represent the whole." Burke, "The Four Master Tropes," appendix D to *A Grammar of Motives* (New York: Prentice Hall, 1952), 508.

9. The speaking subject of enunciation marks two distinctions: The "I" of the enunciation is not the same thing as the "I" of the statement; Jacques Lacan, *The Four Fundamental Concepts of Psychoanalysis*, ed. Jacques-Alain Miller, trans. Alan Sheridan (New York: W. W. Norton, 1978), 138–39. Alan Sheridan translates *énoncé* as the statement, or the "actual words uttered," whereas *énonciation* refers to "the act of uttering them"; Jacques Lacan, translator's note in *Ecrits: A Selection*, trans. Alan Sheridan (New York: W. W. Norton, 1977), ix. The "I" who makes "the statement is the subject of the enunciation (*sujet de l'énonciation*), or what I am calling here the "speaking subject of the enunciation," whereas the "I" that constitutes "the grammatical subject of the statement itself is the subject of the statement (*sujet de l'énoncé*)"; Mikkel Borch-Jacobsen, *Lacan: The Absolute Master,* trans. Douglas Brick (Stanford: Stanford University Press, 1991), 260 n. 20. Now, the consciousness who "counts" is the one who speaks his or her position, whereas the statement does not uniquely define that one by virtue of the shifter "I" that establishes his or her relation in grammatical context—a position in discourse.

10. Jean-Paul Sartre's "bodies" exist in three dimensional space—the "body-for-me," or one's relations with objects of the world, the "body-for-the-other," and "body-as-seen-by-the-other"; Sartre, translator's introduction to *Being and Nothingness: An Essay on the Phenomenological Ontology,* trans. Hazel E. Barnes (New York: Philosophical Library, 1956), xli. Lacan and Sartre might have shared a teacher in Alexandre Kojève, whose lectures on Hegel's *Phenomenology* were delivered at the École des Hautes Etudes between 1933 and 1939; Wilden, *Speech and Language in Psychoanalysis,* 192–93. These lectures became the influential *Introduction to the Reading of Hegel: Lectures on the Phenomenology of Spirit,* assembled by Raymond Queneau, trans. James H. Nicols Jr., ed. Allan Bloom (Ithaca: Cornell University Press, 1980). This passage of the essay is much indebted to the Sartrean body and "look": "What I constantly aim at across my experiences are the Other's feelings, the Other's ideas, the Other's volitions, the Other's character. This is because the Other is not only the one whom I see but the one who sees me. . . . finally in my essential being I depend on the essential being of the Other, and instead of holding that my being-for-myself is opposed to my being for others, I find that being-for-others appears as a necessary condition for my being for myself" (228, 238).

11. Sigmund Freud, *The Interpretations of Dreams,* vols. 4 and 5 of *The Standard Edition of the Complete Psychological Works of Sigmund Freud,* trans. and ed. James Strachey, 24 vols. (London: Hogarth Press, 1953–1974).

12. Lacan, *The Four Fundamental Concepts.*

13. Addressing the project of psychoanalysis related to the critique of ideology, Habermas contends that both take "into account that information about lawlike connections sets off a process of reflection in the consciousness of those whom the laws are about. Thus the level of unreflected consciousness, which is one of the conditions of such laws, can be transformed. Of course, to this end a critically mediated knowledge of laws cannot through reflection alone render the law itself inoperative, but it can render it inapplicable." Jürgen Habermas, appendix to *Knowledge and Human Interests,* trans. Jeremy J. Shapiro (Boston: Beacon Press, 1968), 310. Originally published as *Erkenntnis und Interesse* (Frankfurt: Suhrkamp Verlag, 1965); reprinted as *Technik und Wissenschaft als "ideologie"* (Frankfurt: Suhrkamp Verlag, 1968).

14. W. E. B. Du Bois, *The Souls of Black Folk,* with intro. Henry Louis Gates Jr. (New York: Bantam Books, 1989), 2–3:

After the Egyptian and Indian, the Greek and Roman, the Teuton and Mongolian, the Negro is a sort of seventh son, born with a veil, and gifted with second-sight in this American world,—a world which yields him no true self-consciousness, but only lets him see himself through the revelation of the other world. It is a peculiar sensation, this double-consciousness, this sense of always looking at one's self through the eyes of others.

15. When I refer to "talking," or more exactly "speaking" here, I am far closer to meaning the plain speech of everyday encounter than the particularized discourse of the psychoanalytic hermeneutic. For example, during the long televised ordeal of the O.J. Simpson murder trial, CNN reported on events surrounding the news phenomenon with unrelieved regularity; one of the stories that the cable outlet carried for the customary twenty-four-hour coverage was that of a black medical doctor in Los Angeles who had turned the site of his practice, for a few hours a day, into a sort of neighborhood den, open to members of the community, where talk about the trial occurred. In the footage I saw, the scene was arranged like a classroom, as the doctor himself both talked and listened to what his interlocutors had to say. That is exactly the sort of protocol I would mean for the "talking cure" as a metaphor for exchange that occurs quite a lot less often in black communities than we might imagine. I see no reason why black church congregations cannot convert pulpit and altar into a public forum at least once a week for the exercise of discourse related to events that touch on the lives of the congregants. It seems to me that a few valuable lessons might be conveyed this way, in the undramatic informal analysis of the Event. As the last standing independent organ in black communities, black churches have the stellar occasion to teach attention (as a function of determining how one is situated), criticism (as a function of seeing), and articulation (as a function of saying what is on the mind and the heart). We do not need psychoanalytic training for these tasks, but the simpler will to communicate.

16. In *La culture au pluriel*, Michel de Certeau makes a distinction between discourse as work and discourse as the mark of activity in getting at the problematic of "culture." (Paris: Christian Bourgois Editeur, 1980), 225.

17. For a systematic investigation of various positions on property, see C. B. MacPherson, ed., *Property: Mainstream and Critical Positions* (Toronto: University of Toronto Press, 1978).

18. I am borrowing this notion from Louis Althusser and Etienne Balibar, *Reading Capital*, trans. Ben Brewster (London: Verso Books, 1979); see esp. pt. 1: "From *Capital* to Marx's Philosophy."

19. See Pierre Bourdieu, *Outline of a Theory of Practice*, trans. Richard Nice, Cambridge Studies in Social Anthropology, ed. Jack Goody (Cambridge: Cambridge University Press, 1977). Originally published as *Esquisse d'une théorie de la pratique, précédé de trois études d'ethnologie kabyle* (Paris: Librairie Droz, 1972). Bourdieu argues that aspects of Kabyle anthropological structures: "oblige us to abandon the dichotomy of the economic and the non-economic which stands in the way of seeing the science of economic practices as a particular case of a general science of the economy of practices, capable of treating all practices, including those purporting to be disinterested or gratuitous, and hence non-economic, as economic practices directed towards the maximizing of material or symbolic profit" (183). But I am borrowing his

notion toward different ends by contending that a revised African American culture critique would seek to place the subject in the "totality" of his or her surround, including the interior.

20. During the winter 1995 convocation of the Rainbow Coalition, Rev. Jesse Jackson emphatically addressed the question of "personal responsibility": "We cannot give up any more ground on that word." Jesse Jackson, "Defending the Family: Strategies for Economic Justice and Hope" (speech given at the convocation of the Rainbow Coalition, Washington, D.C., January 1995), broadcast on C-SPAN, 6 January 1995. His remarks were contextualized, indeed necessitated, by what the pundits have called a political "tsunami"—an earthquake at sea—that stunned the nation in November 1994, when less than forty-three percent of the national electorate reporting brought us a Republican majority in Congress and the first so-called revolutionary leader of the new majority in more than four decades, Newton Gingrich of Georgia, newly ascendant Speaker of the House of Representatives. The winter meeting had been called as a signal to the American (to borrow a term from British politicians) "Lib/Lab/Left" coalition to mark this moment as a crucial realignment of the sociopolitical landscape and to think again, as a result, the uses to which the idea of alliance might be put. Jackson's remarks also signaled that he was alert to the question of agency and the imperative to refashion a notion of it.

21. This powerful text, to which title the quoted passage refers, has become a classic tool of thought about the insurgent aims of education; Paulo Freire, *Pedagogy of the Oppressed,* trans. Myra Bergman Ramos (New York: Herder and Herder, 1970). Specifically grounded in the Brazilian situation, Freire's work, in applying the thinking of Fanon and Marx, might be suggestive for other localities.

22. One of the most exciting works in African American culture studies over the last fifteen years has been John Gwaltney's *Drylongso: A Self-Portrait of Black America* (New York: Vintage Books, 1981). A veritable mine of black talk on every conceivable subject, from sex to the economy, *Drylongso* foregrounds ordinary "members of the tribe," as Ralph Ellison might have put it. I am uncertain of the origins of the locution, but it was well-known in my household and neighborhood in Memphis: when someone had not shown particular flair or aplomb in carrying out a task, my mother would describe his or her behavior as "just drylongso." In Gwaltney's book, however, the characters are anything but uninteresting, and they make no pretense, as far as we can tell, to any particular competence or "expertise." I believe that Gwaltney was driving home this point.

23. This sentence alludes to a wonderful collection of short stories by Barbadian-Canadian writer, Austin Clarke, *When He Was Free and Young and He Used to Wear Silks* (Toronto: House of Anancy Press, 1971).

24. For a lucid reading of Jacques Lacan's indebtedness to Hegelian philosophy by way of Alexandre Kojève, see Borch-Jacobsen, *Lacan,* 244 n. 9.

25. Jacques Lacan, *Écrits,* selected from the original *Écrits* (Paris: Éditions du Seuil, 1966). In the translator's note to Jacques Lacan, *The Four Fundamental Concepts,* the three Lacanian dimensions are defined together: Sheridan points out that the Imaginary was the first to appear, prior to the Rome Report of 1953, in which writing the notion of the Symbolic surfaces. The Real was initially "of only minor importance, acting as a kind of safety rail." Gradually developing, its impact shifted over time, from a "function of constancy" as that "which always returns to the same place," to

that "before which the imaginary faltered, that over which the symbolic stumbles"—thus, the "impossible." Sheridan explains that, though linked to the Symbolic and the Imaginary, the Real stands for neither and "remains foreclosed from the analytic experience, which is an experience of speech." In any case, the Real comes about prior to the subject's assumption of the symbolic and "is not to be confused with reality, which is perfectly knowable: the subject of desire knows no more than that, since for it reality is entirely phantasmatic" (280). In J. LaPlanche and J.-B. Pontalis, *The Language of Psychoanalysis,* trans. Donald Nicholson-Smith, with intro. David Lagache (New York: W. W. Norton, 1973), no discussion is found of the Real, but there are entries on the "Reality Principle" and "Reality-Testing"; on the Imaginary (210); and on the Symbolic and its contrastive uses in Freud and Lacan (439–41).

26. Borch-Jacobsen, *Lacan,* 193.

27. Compare Roland Barthes, "Myth Today," in *Mythologies,* trans. Annette Lavers (New York: Hill and Wang, 1975).

28. Lacan, *The Four Fundamental Concepts,* 44.

29. For the "boomerang" effect and an inquiry into it, see Ralph Ellison, *Invisible Man* (New York: The Modern Library, 1992), esp. the prologue.

Seeing Sentiment

Photography, Race, and the Innocent Eye

Laura Wexler

Our white sisters / radical friends / love to own pictures of us / sitting at a factory machine / wielding a machete / in our bright bandanas / holding brown yellow black red children / reading books from literacy campaigns / holding machine guns / bayonets / bombs / knives / Our white sisters / radical friends / should think again.
—JO CARRILLO, *AND WHEN YOU LEAVE, TAKE YOUR PICTURES WITH YOU*

1

As we know, Freudian psychoanalysis operates with a certain picture of the family in mind, an image of the rules and the psychic results of kinship that is not a universally explanatory structure. And in the phrase that Hortense Spillers has taken for the title of her paper published in this volume, "All the Things You Could Be by Now if Sigmund Freud's Wife Was Your Mother," we are reminded once again of that fact. Charlie Mingus's irony gracefully points out that the Freudian matrix, as located in the bourgeois European female subject, has not been the mother of us all. And further, although Mingus doesn't say it explicitly, to be Son of Freud is not everybody's fantasy of inheritance.

Nevertheless, in her essay Spillers suggests that something of Freud does carry over into African American contexts.[1] It is the weight that Freud puts upon the wound, as sign and source of differentiation. This is not, however, the old wound that we are so tired of hearing about—castration, penis envy, lack, the old nemesis of feminism,—but the wound as Spillers has redefined it: a violent jamming, two things enforced together in the same instance, a merciless, unchosen result of the coupling of one into an alien culture that yet withholds its patronym. The oxymoronic figure, the ambivalence induced by a wounding, the array of enunciative registers through which the Invisible Man weaves in and out of visibility—these are some of the multiple traces of the wound that Spillers finds and names. Through her naming, one locates the wound in an African American "rupture of the Real on either side of the Symbolic and the Imaginary."

The Lacanian "Real," as I understand it, is that which is in excess of the endless, delusory self-reflexivity, the repetition *en abyme* that characterizes the Imaginary. And at the same time, the Real is that which is unsubsumed by or even refused by—although not unsubsum*able* by—the Symbolic. The Real occupies, therefore, very much the same terrain as the wound—the violent, unsustainable, unthinkable possibility that nonetheless *is*, *has* happened, and must be endured. Indeed the Real is, in Lacan, a kind of wounding, which is why the Lacanian appropriation of Freud also opens Freud to history. And so, if it is true, as Spillers states, that the intellectual has a responsibility not to be confused about the task, then it is the wounding that we must seek in a psychoanalysis of the Real, so as to know it, so as to touch it, so as to set ourselves free.

In this essay I literalize the Freudian picture of the sentimental family, using pictures and the history of pictures—photographs, actually—to see if one such rupture of the Real out of the literal image cannot be induced. For if, I reason, Freud built his apprehension of the Real partly on a sentimental picture of the family, surely the ubiquitous literal images of the family—the actual litter of such images in the portraits, photographs, lithographs, woodcuts and engravings of nineteenth-century bourgeois life—were one thing that supported him in doing so. And these images are still available as texts for us to read, although, in the main, we have not done so. I attempt to read, therefore, one family's sentimental photograph of an African American "nursemaid" and a white child as an image that occupies a particularly relevant juncture of the Lacanian mirror function—that which serves to propel the sentimental family further and further into its Imaginary—and the Lacanian Symbolic or Law of the Father—that which refuses utterance to the almost impossible to foreground Real. I choose this image not because it is unique, for it is not, but because it has often been reproduced without being attended to. I argue that an utterance of the Real does escape "on either side of the Symbolic and the Imaginary," in signs and traces in this picture. In my view, historical contextualization of this particular photograph opens (or reopens) a kind of wound—a *punctum,* to use Roland Barthes's exquisite term—that offers a way for a subjugated history to be spoken.

In *Camera Lucida,* Roland Barthes distinguishes between two fields of attention to photographs. First, and always, there is a *studium:*

> Thousands of photographs consist of this field, and in these photographs I can, of course, take a kind of general interest, one that is even stirred sometimes, but in regard to them my emotion requires the rational intermediary of an ethical and political culture. What I feel about these photographs derives from an *average* affect, almost from a certain training. I did not know a French word which might account for this kind of human

interest, but I believe this word exists in Latin: it is *studium,* which doesn't mean, at least not immediately, "study," but application to a thing, taste for someone, a kind of general, enthusiastic commitment, of course, but without special acuity. It is by *studium* that I am interested in so many photographs, whether I receive them as political testimony or enjoy them as good historical scenes: for it is culturally (this connotation is present in *studium*) that I participate in the figures, the faces, the gestures, the settings, the actions.

Second, there may also be a *punctum.* Of the *punctum,* Barthes writes:

> The second element will break (or punctuate) the *studium.* This time it is not I who seek it out (as I invest the field of the *studium* with my sovereign consciousness), it is this element which rises from the scene, shoots out of it like an arrow, and pierces me. A Latin word exists to designate this wound, this prick, this mark made by a pointed instrument: the word suits me all the better in that it also refers to the notion of punctuation, and because the photographs I am speaking of are in effect punctuated, sometimes even speckled with these sensitive points: precisely, these marks, these wounds are so many *points.* This second element which will disturb the *studium,* I shall therefore call *punctum;* for *punctum* is also: sting, speck, cut, little hole—and also a cast of the dice. A photograph's *punctum* is that accident which pricks me (but also bruises me, is poignant to me).[2]

The Barthean *punctum* cuts a hole in the "general, enthusiastic commitment [of vision] . . . without special acuity." In the contexts in which it has been reproduced so far, the photograph of the "nursemaid and her charge" has played the part of *studium.* I am trying to find its point, which is also, as I take it, the historical, the photographic, and the psychoanalytic task.

One caveat. I write this essay in the belief that close, attentive readings of historical photographs can restore voice and context to historical knowledge that may have been hidden or repressed. But what I offer is my own reading solely. It is not meant to speak over or foreclose other meanings. Perspectives on photographs, as on history, differ from individual to individual and from social location to social location. Each standpoint—and surely my own, as a white, upper-middle-class educated woman who is a university professor—contains ignorance and blindness. Some of these photographs are painful images. I hope that in drawing attention to them and insisting on reading them, naming the political functions that I see to be at work in them, I add to the power/knowledge that these images make available and that I do not also at the same time objectify their subjects or misname history from my own partial perspective in ways that might invite additional reification.[3]

One alternate reading of the "nursemaid and her charge" that has been suggested to me poses the "nursemaid" as a day laborer in the Cook family who is not at all disturbed by her situation or by the scene of photography. Certainly she herself has been silenced by the deracinated manner in which her image has been preserved and reproduced, and her actual interior thoughts and emotions are unavailable to the viewer. It is, therefore, theoretically possible to support such an alternate reading. However, my research into the Cook family archives makes me skeptical of its force. I take my cues from the general social context surrounding the photographer and his subject. What I am interested in recovering is not some pure and transparent version of the young woman's inner life, which would be both impossible and presumptuous, but the character of the historical setting within which her image—stripped of her voice—was circulated.

2

The Greeks had a word, *ekphrasis,* that we don't have, which designated an art that we also don't have—the virtuoso skill of putting words to images. Writing recently in *The New York Times,* John Updike reported his joy on discovering this word, for it named what had long been an insistent but faintly embarrassing passion of his and made it seem legitimate. Similarly Bryan Wolf recently came out in *The Yale Journal of Criticism* as a "closet ekphrastic . . . [hurling] caution and nicety of distinction to the winds . . . and [arguing] both for the rhetoricity of all art and the ideological work performed by all rhetoric."[4] However, ecstatic ekphrastics hardly ever turn to photographs. For instance, not one of the readings legitimated by Greek paternity in Updike's recent book of essays on art, *Just Looking,* is of a photograph, even though Updike devotes the entire lead essay to the Museum of Modern Art (MoMA) in "What MoMA Done Tole Me," and the MoMA he remembers haunting for an unforgettable twenty months between August of 1955 and April of 1957 housed at that time what was arguably one of the most important collections and display spaces of photographs in the country.[5]

Serge Guilbaut and Christopher Phillips have both demonstrated that, through its cooperation with the government and its curatorship of the photography collection at that time, MoMA turned itself into one of the country's most productive bastions of cold war ideological politics.[6] Perhaps it is too much to have expected John Updike in particular to have noticed any of this, even though he was there during the very months that "The Family of Man" exhibition was installed in MoMA and was drawing enormous crowds of visitors. "The Family of Man" was an anthology of images edited to show the universality of daily human life, which purportedly revolves around utterly de-historicized, utterly naturalized experiential categories such as birth, death, work, knowledge, and play. Supported by quotations from "primitive" proverbs or verses from the Bible, the message of this spectacle sent by the American government all over the world was that we are all one family. But Updike's noncoincidental neglect of these photographs and attention to the more prestigious realm of high art painting suggests more than a personal lapse. It represents a decided critical tendency that is not Updike's alone; and it suggests the need of inventing another term, *anekphrasis,* to be coined from its opposite. *Anekphrasis* would describe an active and selective refusal to read photography—its graphic labor, its social spaces—even while, at the same time, one is busy textualizing and contextualizing all other kinds of cultural documents.[7]

Anekphrasia is not innocuous. The comparative neglect of critical attention to the raced, classed, and gendered productions of the photographic image is a form of cultural resistance. It represses the antidemocratic potential of photography. The dynamic meanings of cultural forms produced and marketed since the mid–nineteenth century cannot be fully adduced without concurrent attention to the way that those cultural forms have used photography to naturalize and enforce their message. One might even go so far as to say that anekphrasis itself is an institutionalized form of racism and sexism, insofar as photography has always been deeply involved in constituting the discourse of the same. In the analysis that follows, I address one instance of this refusal. I join an unread photographic moment with the discourse of nineteenth-century sentimentality because by and large, with quite serious results, cultural theory has so far refused to attend to it.

All cultural theory is not guilty of anekphrasis. Indeed, feminism has sustained a major critical engagement with the photographic image. No one has ever attributed more social power to the photographic image than the antipornography movement. Crucial questions about the commodification of representations of women's bodies in advertising; the cultural enforcement of women's positioning as representation, as image; and the reconstruction of a basis for female spectatorship that moves out from under the dominion of the "male gaze" have had their most serious considerations within feminist analysis of photography and film. Yet even within this significant enlargement of the critical gaze, feminist interpretation has often made it seem as if issues of sexuality can be separated analytically from those of race and class.[8] Though the feminist movement has been brilliantly effective in forcing discussion of the domination and objectification of women by men, it has been relatively silent about the internal dynamics of objectification within its own ranks, woman over woman, and about the ways in which women themselves have gained and lost from the racial and class power differentials among men. Second-wave feminism allowed the image of the middle-class white woman to circulate as the signifier of the category "woman." But gender distribution is not the same thing as race distinction. The notion that they are parallel inequalities and that an analysis of the sexism of photographic practice will automatically yield a model for thinking about race as a category of difference is one of feminism's anekphrases. So that, although feminism sees photographs, it has become a question, frankly, of just what is it that feminism sees in those photographs.

Sentimentality was a theory of gender. It held that differences among the domestic lives of peoples were natural rather than historical differences and that a new education in domesticity was necessary both for white males and nondominant peoples. That is in good part why twentieth-century white feminist criticism has been able to retrieve so successfully the sentimental writings of the "Other American Renaissance."[9] Both forms of cultural critique— white domestic ideology in the nineteenth century and white feminist theory in the twentieth—largely bracket questions of race and class in an imperializing, single-minded insistence on the critical specificity of gender. However, sentimentality left another record of these operations, in photographs, through which it is possible to see around the edges of its masquerade as nature. Photography was part of the master narrative that created and cemented cultural and political inequalities of race and class. I hope that seeing sentiment in photographic images encourages our society to see itself.

3

A young woman sits for the camera in a good striped dress with a white collar (see figure 1).[10] A small, simple broach is successfully pinned exactly at the central meeting place of the two starched white points of the collar that rise up slightly from the surface of her dress. Formally, with its quiet precision, its broad simplification of background space, its tonal balance, its graphic playfulness, and its flat, tight framing of the figure, this image has the look of the long tradition of plain style American portraiture that unites the primitive folk art practices of the early itinerant portraitists like Ammi Phillips and Erastus Salisbury Field with the vernacular masterpieces of the J. S. Plumbe and Southworth and Hawes daguerreotypes. And iconographically, this image also relates to a long symbolic tradition, that of the Madonna and Child, a tribute to the highest achievement that Womanhood can attain in Christian culture, and a paean to the actual woman who occupies that mythical role. "Craftsmen of Western art have revealed better than anyone else the artist's debt to the maternal body and/or motherhood's entry into symbolic existence," writes feminist critic Julia Kristeva in "Motherhood According to Bellini":

> Not only is a considerable portion of pictorial art devoted to motherhood, but within this representation itself, from Byzantine iconography to Renaissance humanism and the worship of the body that it initiates, two attitudes toward the maternal body emerge, prefiguring two destinies within the very economy of Western representation. . . . Worship of the figurable . . . or integration of the image accomplished in its truthlikeness within the luminous serenity of the unrepresentable.[11]

Like this photograph, the painted Madonna is often rendered in vivid detail, and like this photograph, the attentive "truthlikeness" to the materiality of

Figure 1

Figure 2

Figure 3

Figure 4

Figure 5

Figure 6

Cook Collection

Figure 7

Figure 8

Figure 9

Figure 10

the figure in the depiction often blends into some other unidentifiable expression that is "unrepresentable" or disengaged. Painted Madonnas usually hold the baby Jesus but look away. In this averted gaze, Kristeva notes,
"the maternal body slips away from the discursive hold" to become an "in-
accessible" refuge of the sacred.[12]

It used to be only artists' models or wealthy, aristocratic women who could
see themselves painted in this role, but the discovery of photography in the
nineteenth century allowed millions of ordinary mothers to have images
made in that virginal and compelling guise. On the strength of its formal
and symbolic characteristics alone, this photograph should take its place in
the procession of American religiously influenced art. And like the Catholic
paintings of the Madonna that the Protestant Harriet Beecher Stowe urged
her readers to hang upon the walls of their homes to signal the sisterhood
of spirit and the communal reservoir of art that nurtured faith no matter of
what denomination, formally considered, this photograph would be an up-
holder of the canons of domestic sentiment.

However, "a nursemaid and her charge," as this photograph is entitled in
We Are Your Sisters, edited by Dorothy Sterling, or "former slave with white
child," as it is captioned in *Labor of Love, Labor of Sorrow,* by Jacqueline Jones,
is not an image of the vaunted female icon of Christian humanism, nor is it
an example of popular folk art; and merely to repeat such a formal or an
iconographic analysis would be deeply misleading. In fact, this image ironizes
both the self-absorption of Kristeva's depiction of Western religious painting and the unexamined populism of the vernacular approach to the photographic image. For this image was made in Virginia, circa 1865, by a skilled
white studio photographer named George Cook of his own family's "nursemaid," for his own family's consumption. Cook was a northerner who settled in the south just before the Civil War. He is widely known for his pictures of military officers on both the Union and the Confederate sides of
the war. But after the war he continued to photograph, maintaining a thriv-
ing studio business in Richmond. According to Norman Yetman, the one
historian who has written even briefly about the conditions under which the
picture was made, the young woman depicted is almost certainly a slave or
only just recently freed. Since the baby on her lap appears white and she is
black, most viewers would assume that it is not her baby at all but another
woman's child. And, in fact, the baby is Heustis Cook, the son of the photographer, who himself grew up to be a photographer like his father but specialized in making pictures of former slaves. "Heustis Cook," notes Yetman,
"was one of the first of the 'field' photographers who packed his buggy with
cameras, glass plates, plate holders, colodion, silver nitrate, plus his tent or
'darkroom' and all his developing supplies and took photography to the back
roads." The father and son's collection of pictures of the former slave population of Virginia, South Carolina, North Carolina, and Washington, D.C.,

is now in the Valentine Museum in Richmond, Virginia. A substantial port-folio of their images was reproduced in *Voices from Slavery,* edited by Norman Yetman, in 1970.[13]

This Madonna is therefore a weirdly skewed rendition of the Christian story. The young woman, like Mary, holds a baby who is the son of her mas-ter. As his more than maternal servant, she, like Mary, tends to a child who, like Christ, will make a living record of the future, a future in and of which she, herself, will not be able to speak. But this baby is not the baby that God the Father gave her to bear. That baby, if it exists, is elsewhere. Despite her youth and beauty, this woman cannot be merely another mother who com-memorates the ecstatic moment of typological juncture, the swelling pride of Womanhood fulfilled, since as a slave or former slave she has been at the same time human chattel and, to adopt Orlando Patterson's pungent fig-ure, a social corpse. Motherhood may be what the genre marks as woman's great accomplishment, but sitting for the camera as the white woman sat, in the pose that the white woman held, holding, in fact, the white woman's baby, within the iconographical space and actual society that claimed for white women an exclusive right to occupancy, the slave or servant brings into ex-istence not her own family's precious keepsake, but a monument of dou-bleness and double entendre. Rather than bonding figure to type, the pho-tograph displays instead the innumerable barriers and memories in the way of that apotheosis. The "unrepresentable," that Kristeva invokes, is not some abstract sacred principle, but the materiality of the figure of a young black woman.

In the earliest years of its existence, photography was laminated to senti-mental functions along with domestic novels, domestic advice manuals, ed-ucational reform propaganda, and abolitionist agitation. As the middle-class home became the port of entry for sentimental fictions of all sorts, the hall table and the parlor accumulated photographs at an impressive rate. Like domestic novels, the resulting accumulation of images helped to make, not merely to mirror, the home. Photography was another mode of domestic self-representation. It worked by staging affect or imaging relation—*seeing senti-ment* as a way of organizing family life. "Our cabin measured 16 x 20 feet in the clear," wrote one white settler in Montana, "The logs were chinked and painted with clay. The floor was of earth, beaten hard and smooth—a box cupboard held our stock of dishes and cooking materials. Beside it stood the churn. The flour barrel was converted into a center-table whereon reposed the family Bible and photograph album with their white lace covers."[14] Or, as Nathaniel Hawthorne observed in his notebooks, when Sophia rearranged the parlor and put a table with books and pictures at its center, the new house in Lennox became a home.

The valorization of the visual image of the middle-class white woman as the signifier of the category "woman" that makes other social relations invisible took shape in the early nineteenth century. Sentimental ideologies of womanhood explicitly turned to images to mark the social divisions advanced by the middle class and to make them seem to be rooted in something actual. Photography, invented in 1839, was an even better technique than drawing or painting for making images of "nature," and photography was therefore conscripted for the sentimental cause.[15] The idea was, if you could take pictures of something, it must exist. To the middle-class nineteenth-century viewer, a photograph was a "mirror" of nature, and not only that but unlike other mirrors it had a "memory" too. Photography inscribed, therefore, a very powerful image of the "real."

But what this idea disguised is the fact that photographs have meaning only as elements of a set. Photographic meaning is a system of relations that are established not in but between images. In the words of Patricia Holland, Jo Spence, and Simon Watney, photography is ideological in that it is a "set of relations established between signs, between images—a way of narrating experience in such a way that specific social interests and inequalities are thought about, discussed and perpetuated."[16] Or, in the formulation of Griselda Pollock, to interpret images of women it is necessary to develop "a notion of woman as a signifier in an ideological discourse in which one can identify the meanings that are attached to woman in different images and how the meanings are constructed in relation to other signifiers in that discourse."[17] Nineteenth-century bourgeois domestic photography, then, became as productive and constitutive a force as it did because it related images of women to one another and to other cultural practices through a hierarchizing narrative of social signs. Photographic sentiment helped to create the hierarchies that, ostensibly, it only recorded.

In the sheer accumulation of these photographic images, in the simple weight of the fact that now there were so many of them when before 1839 there had been none, there is also another significance. Far from exhausting demand, photography in the early years provoked a seemingly limitless further appetite. If, as critics have argued, sentimental fiction fed the hunger for middle-class self-transformation through the institution of a depth psychology of self-monitoring, self-possession, and self-control, sentimental readers were also evidently famished for corresponding views of the visible surface of their lives. Critics have suggested that these images were personal fetishes, bulwarks against nineteenth-century anxieties of separation and early death, and no doubt that is true. But looked at in the aggregate, this cannot have been their only function. As codifications of class and identity, these ubiquitous reflections of private life in private homes must also have demarcated the edges of social visibility and invisibility for a group of people who, not yet secure, repeatedly invoked the materiality of appearances to justify their claim to dominance and their every incursion into the private space of others.[18] Anxious for separation, for a visible difference in display and deportment that could squelch any challenge to the distinctive privileges they claimed, middle-class people must have found in the very numbers of domestic photographs that filled their homes an assurance that real family life was coincident with the kind of families the photographs showed.

I suggest that persons outside the magic circle of nineteenth-century domesticity—slaves, Native Americans, Mexicans, later the Eastern European immigrants, the Filipinos, and the Chinese—pose an interesting problem of exclusion in relation to such uses of photography. I also suggest that it is a problem that can be illuminated by examining the relation of these Others to the regime of sentiment, taken as an aggressive, rather than merely a private, social practice. In this view, the culture of sentiment aimed not only to establish itself as the gatekeeper of social existence, but it aimed at the same time to denigrate all other people whose style or conditions of domesticity did not conform to the sentimental model. Since the sentimental home was the model home, it followed that anyone else's home was in need of reform. And since the sentimental image was the model image, it also followed that any other photograph was an image of lack. The partitioning off of a domestic space for photographic display in the home accompanied a categorization of difference between those who did and those who did not own a "home" to decorate with their own images—a distinction for the making of which photography, even more than the written word, was a state of the art technique.

It was not that other persons were actually unseen. Slaves, servants, the poor, the infirm, the socially dispossessed, were in evidence in virtually every domestic landscape, and in one way or another their presence affected virtually every middle-class household. Not only that but, as Philip Fisher has shown, the gathering force of sentiment as a social ideal was driving home the idea that it was necessary to have a philanthropy that included precisely these people.[19] The problem was managerial, an orchestration of the gaze. If the function of middle-class domestic photographs was to precipitate a seemingly natural mirror image of the sentimental home out of the household, it would follow that the household, although it visibly and palpably sustained the home, as well as heterogeneous images, would need to be rendered functionally invisible. The ideal of "domestic individualism," as Gillian Brown has called it, extended even to the image of the domestic unit itself.[20] Such a unit could not appear in photographs as the heterogeneous and corporate product that it actually was.

In the aggregate, historical photographs indicate that families addressed this editorial problem in a variety of ways. One was obvious and easy. In a family portrait made in the studio of a professional photographer, the household could depict itself as composed only of those members that it wished to portray. Slaves, servants, renegade sons, unsightly or unstable dependents, all were easily excised. They simply needn't be included in the trip to the studio. And, in fact, by far the greatest number of family studio portraits have this appearance. Although there were alternative practices, and there are numerous contradictory collections, the weight of the archive of mid-nineteenth-century middle-class family portraits is not only overwhelmingly white, like the mid-nineteenth-century middle-class family, but also affectively harmonious and physically eugenic.[21] Looking at many of the images of the family in mainstream historical collections, one would hardly know that other people were around. When an itinerant photographer came to a family's residence, however, as sometimes happened in the early years, the act of composing the family's public image needed to be more explicit. For at least some families, it appears to have been more difficult under these circumstances to manage so closely a properly narrow approach to its own social construction. There are numerous photographs that show servants, for instance, on the edges of the family group, on the lawn, or under the trees. They are standing in the background, but they are clearly visible. The servants are not depicted in these photographs as family members, but sentiment is extended towards them as well.

In the Cook family collection, such a photograph exists. The family has arranged itself on the front porch and steps of their country house, expressing their sense of the pleasures of their leisure by holding a set of croquet mallets conspicuously in the front row. At the side of the house, almost out of sight around the corner but nevertheless clearly visible as an "outsider within," is the figure of a black man (see figure 2).[22] Whether the interpersonal as well as the ego boundaries were more or less permeable in such a structure would be a matter for debate, but the existence of such images points to at least a certain level of ambiguity about where and how to draw the line.

Occasionally, however, a family like the Cooks might choose to make or to purchase individual portraits of their slaves or servants, as an item to add to their own accounts or memorabilia. The majority of sentimental domestic images of slaves that I know of come from situations like this. Maybe it was a kind of conspicuous consumption. And in any case, with slaves it was not always necessary to worry about drawing the line, since usually the line would be drawn by color. In this particular instance, George Cook was a photographer and could do as he wished, which made the acquisition of such a picture easy. In point of fact, the Cooks—both father and son—were very interested in making photographs of former slaves, and after the Civil War they made a great many images of black life in and around Virginia. These, too, are framed chiefly as sentimental, humanistic images within the representational codes of the nineteenth-century bourgeois portrait (see figures 3–8).

By and large, the sentimentality in all the Cooks' postslavery images appears on the surface to be well intentioned towards black people and, aside from some egregious counter examples, such as the figure of the banjo player (see figure 9), they are, at least apparently, generous towards the personalities and human worth of their sitters.[23] The majority of the photographs

clearly present themselves as representing the former slaves to be people of
dignity, with few or no visible debilitating marks of slavery. In the Cooks' images, in fact, the former slaves appear as bona fide members of the universal "Family of Man." Such images could easily have had a place in Steichen's
exhibition.

It is not within the scope of the present essay to explore fully the extent
to which this impression of an absence of wounding mystifies the historical
relation between the photographic gaze of the Cooks and the former slave
population upon whom they trained it. However, I can here at least sketch
certain of its ominous associations by quoting briefly from the contemporaneous poetry of Benjamin Batchelder Valentine, a close family friend of
the Cooks, in whose Richmond mansion, now turned into a museum, the
Cook family archive is located. In Valentine's book, *Ole Marster and Other Verses*,
published posthumously in 1921, Valentine makes a sustained apology for
slavery and the social order it supported. Here, for instance, is his poem entitled "The Race Question," which is written, as is most of his poetry, in a
black dialect voice:

> When I wuz young de color'd folks
> Wuz 'low'd ter lay de bricks;
> Dey climbed de scaffolds, toted hods,
> An' made de mortar mix.
>
> Dey'd handle hammers, saws an' planes,
> An' any tools dey'd choose—
> It wan' no folks 'cep' niggers den
> Whar use' ter half-sole shoes.
>
> In dem dyar times 'twas nigger backs
> Whar gave de scythes de swing;
> 'Twuz big, black, shiny nigger arms
> Whar made de anvils ring.
>
> An' settin' on de wooden horse
> Wid staves betwix' dey laigs,
> Wid drawin' knives an' hic'ry poles
> De niggers hooped de kaigs.
>
> You couldn' fin' no barber shop
> Dat we-all folks wan' dyar—
> De little ones er-shinin' shoes,
> The big ones cuttin' hyar.
>
> Wid high up gem-man names print' on
> De mugs er-settin' roun';
> Er heap o' niggers made dey piles
> Frum shaves an' breshin' down.

But 'tain' so now, nor dat it aint,
De white-folks cuts us out;
Dey jumps right in an' gits de wuk
'Fo' we knows what dey's bout.

Dey 'trac's de trade—dem out-land folks—
Dem 'Talians, Dutch, an' Greeks,
Aldo' 'tain' none whar understands
De 'spressions whar dey speaks.

Dey shaves an' shampoos all day long,
Dey never, never stops—
Dey don' pick banjers for dey fr'en's,
An' cake-walk in de shops.

De Orishman is wuss er all—
Jes' time er nigger nod,
He step right up an' shev' him down
An' grab er hol' his hod.

An' den de Unions layin' bricks,
Dey hollers out ter Mike—
"Ef dat dyar nigger gits dat hod,
We-all is gwine ter strike."

Den ev'y body on de job
Er-j'inin' in de fray,
Jes' tells de niggers, up an' down,
Ter go 'long out de way.

De bosses don' cyar nothin' 'tall;
Dey say we's mighty slow;
Dey kinder laugh an' los it's time
De nigger got ter go.

An' ef we turns den ter de farms,
Whar we had ought ter been,
We dyar gwine find some big machines
Fer us ter buck erg'in.

Dey's took an' drove out all de scythes—
I'clar, it is er crime
Ter reap, wid one dem whirlin' things,
De whole crop at er time.

I know we's gittin' mighty larned—
Folks say we's making has'e;
Dyar's heap o'sass an' argyment
'Bout "Progress er de Race."

I 'lows we' settin' up de tree—
De nigger's on er boom—

But I wan' know whar 'bouts is I
Gwine git some elbow room.

Er-stydy'n' bout one question, Suh,
Nigh bu'sts my brain 'jints loose.
"Is niggers now er-cotchin' holt,
Er is day off de roos'?"[24]

In the opinion of Mary Newton Stanard, who wrote the introduction to
Ole Marster and Other Verses, "Southern negroes brought up by 'Ole Marster'
and 'Ole Mistis,' and even descendants of these dear, dark folk who inherited
their character, manners, speech and devotion to 'we all's white folks' are
rapidly becoming mere tradition, and with them is passing from the American scene something vital, something precious."[25] But Valentine, who was one
of the "white people who were associated with them in a relation unique then
and impossible now, whom they loved and served and who loved and served
them," was one of the few who "possessed a supreme gift for interpreting them
so that through his work they will live always." Stanard knew of this "gift" from
her own experience, for Valentine used to give performances in which he impersonated the "faithful colored folk" in dialect verse in his "old and storied
Richmond mansion, whose rooms were filled with books and treasures of artistic and sentimental value." To attend a performance of these poems, remembered Stanard, was "an unforgettable experience":

> Under the quaint humor which bubbled on their surface flowed a deep
> current whose echo could be heard in his mellow, lilting voice, for all its
> contagious chuckles, and which could be glimpsed in his expressive eyes
> for all their merry twinkling—showing that with fine imagination, with
> sympathy amounting to genius, he felt at once the picturesque traits of
> his subjects which shallower interpreters are prone to caricature and their
> mental and spiritual processes. Whether or not the philosophy which was a
> marked characteristic of these simple souls was an original development or
> was imbibed from their "white folks" and passed on in intensified form to
> their "white folks'" children, is impossible to say, but as seen in the work of
> "Ben Valentine" it is as typical of the interpreter as of the interpreted. Each
> portrait in the gallery which his negro verse comprises is sketched with un-
> erring touch from some point of vantage peculiar to itself, and the whole
> thus presents, as nearly complete as could be within the bounds so circum-
> scribed, a visualization of a vanishing race.[26]

Thus, the poems published in *Ole Marster and Other Verses* are evidently the
texts of the performance pieces that Valentine used to present. It is likely
that the Cook family attended Valentine's performances in Richmond. Certainly they would have known of them. And probably, part of the interest
that the father and son sustained in "taking photography to the back roads"
was to present a parallel in photography to the kind of "visualization of a

vanishing race" that their friend Benjamin Valentine was producing in dramatic verse. As Valentine's poem," The Race Question," establishes, the purpose of this effort to visualize was to turn back the clock; to force reconstruction to deconstruct; to argue that slavery was not only harmless but also better for the "simple souls" than the freedom that followed.

This trajectory is why the Cook photographs bear no visible relation to the hardly distant violence of slavery but only allude directly to the dignity of their subjects. Such innocent images are much more useful than images of harm would have been for the white supremacist movement that surged throughout Richmond and all over the South of the Reconstruction era, and after, to establish that slavery *did* no violence. But the photograph that George Cook made of the nursemaid punctures this reverie.[27] It is distinct from the rest of the "portrait gallery" because of the intimate nature of its cross-racial subject. The baby, like the domesticity, is his.

The contradiction that the photograph of "a nursemaid and her charge" poses, for critical consideration of a structure of sentimentality like that of the Cooks, is that such a use of photography within the private zone of the family runs directly afoul of a basic sentimental principle. It was clearly articulated by Stowe, Warner, Gilman, and others that the images of women that are to be accumulated for the domestic circle—women whose physical presence, by being photographed, was in fact to be rendered permanently and intimately familiar to the family—should be images of women of sensibility in its white, middle-class incarnation. The domestic image is a kind of alternative religious testament for the white, middle-class household, and photographs, like paintings, are a way of instructing children. "Pictures . . . and statuary . . . speak constantly to the childish eye, but are out of reach of childish fingers," wrote Harriet Beecher Stowe.

> They are not like china and crystal, liable to be used and abused by servants; they do not wear out; they are not consumed by moths. The beauty once there is always there; though the mother be ill and in her chamber, she has no fears that she shall find it wrecked and shattered. And this style of beauty, inexpensive as it is, is a means of cultivation. No child is ever stimulated to draw or to read by an Axminster carpet or a carved center-table; but a room surrounded with photographs and pictures and fine casts suggests a thousand inquiries, stimulates the little eye and hand.[28]

The people in such photographs do not have to be kin. As the mid-nineteenth-century cult of collecting celebrity images in cabinet photographs demonstrates, they could be strangers, just so long as they were an uplifting influence. Middle-class sensibility was the possession and mark of the moral being of such a person. Images like these, as Stowe put it, were all extensions of the moral function of the middle-class mother.

But a photograph such as this of a servant or a slave could destabilize the comforting economy of this vision, just as it could destabilize the relation of figure to type in the Madonna. Certainly very few of them were made for domestic uses. Photographing the "nursemaid" does not threaten the hegemony of sentiment, but it can "raise a thousand inquiries," questions that one might not want the "little eye and hand" to ask. Unlike the white mother, the black "nursemaid" does not come to possess an inward sensibility by the re-creation of her image in the sentimental vein. In spending the time and money on the photograph, in accumulating her image in the mode of a member of the family, the Cooks were not displaying her as a woman, a mother, a person. It was her job to "enhance by contrast," as Harryette Mullen has put it, the maternal power of her mistress.[29]

In the one instance that I have located of a photographic portrait that Cook made of his wife, the ideological framing and mis-en-scène of the figure contrasts with the portrait of the "nursemaid" (see figure 10). Much about the portrait of Mrs. Cook is similar to that of the "nursemaid." She is dressed in a similar style to that of her slave or servant, with a brooch pinned at the meeting place of the two halves of the white collar of her dress. The two young women seem to be about the same age. But unlike the "nursemaid," Mrs. Cook as an individual is the sole focus of the camera, and she wears as if by simple right a wreath of flowers in her hair, symbols of freshness and natural innocence that have not been provided to the "nursemaid." The "nursemaid," in contrast, wears a uniform. The portrait of Mrs. Cook seems, at least to me, to bear the mark of patriarchal protection that attempts to cast her in an ethereal light. The camera concentrates on the luminosity of her eyes, on the gentle smile that plays about her lips, and on the way that the braid in her hair picks up light like a halo. The figure is different from the family figures on the porch, of whom Mrs. Cook was possibly one, in that its scale and close-up focus magnifies the impression of a delicate individuality and distinction. It is also different from the figure of the "nursemaid," in that the image of the slave or servant does not offer supplementary signifiers that register her as innocent and fragile womanhood, thus placing her within the bounds of southern patriarchal male protection.

In another of Valentine's poems, entitled "Mammy's Charge," the figure of the nursemaid is counterposed to that of the mother in such a way that every considerable virtue the nursemaid evinces is "outshone" by the fact that the mother has died, gone to heaven, and become a star.[30] In this poem, the little girl's mother has died and a grieving "Mammy" has been given the assignment of keeping the child occupied during the day of the funeral. "Mammy" holds her up before the window, and eventually the child falls asleep in her arms:

> My heart is mos' broke, Judy, an' my haid is achin' bad,
> Dis is de sor'ful's evenin', honey, dat I is ever had.

Dey knowed I love dat dear sweet chile, an' now her Mummer's daid
Dey could trus' her ole black mammy fer ter treat her good, dey said.

So dey lef' me in de nu's'ry fer ter keep de chile up dyar,
But I still culd heah de service, an' de preacher read de pra'r;
De chile too kotch de singin', an' de tears I had ter hide,
When, in play she kep' on 'peatin', "O Lord, widme abide."

When de fune'al it wuz over, an' de hearse wuzdriv' away
I try might'ly fer ter 'muse her, an' ter keep herdyar at play,
But she 'sist on askin' questions like, "What is my Farver gone?
I wants ter see my Mummer; will she stay 'way frum me long?"

I cyar' her ter de winder, an' she look' out in de street,
'Tel she got so tired waitin' dat she went right fas' asleep;
But I set dyar in de twilight an' I hel' de little dear,
'Tel de street wuz on'y darkness, an' de stars bein ter 'pear.

Den one star come out, Judy, whar I never sees befo',
An' I look at it so studdy dat de tears wuz 'bleege ter flow;
Den I tu'n an' see my darlin', in her sleep, begin ter smile;
An de new star seem' a-shinin' right down upon de chile."

Despite the tender warmth and sympathy extant in "Mammy's" gaze, it's clear that benediction comes only from the mother, who is, not coincidentally, "up above." If my comparisons of the photographs are apt, this enhancement by contrast should also illuminate the Cook's portrait of "Mammy's Charge." It was evidently her part in the family to represent the best of earthly care, whereas her mistress allegorized eternal love. It is relevant that this is also not an unfamiliar role for white women who, in sentimental structures, show their truest strength when dead.

But photographing the "nursemaid" threatens to alter the balance of power between these "facts" of sentiment and hidden others. It threatens to give her a social currency, as an outsider inside the home, that she should not have. Therefore, it seems apparent that although the Cooks allowed the photograph to pass the outward signs of feminine sensibility over her figure —the baby, the Madonna-like pose, the domestic reference, indeed almost all of the chief technologies of gender—they used them as a caul rather than as signs of human relation. And for the young woman portrayed within this extension of domestic representation, being rendered with visible sentiment makes her social personhood more invisible than ever. The portrait is, in Spiller's words, a "violent jamming, two things enforced together in the same instance, a merciless, unchosen result of the coupling of one into an alien culture that yet withholds its patronym." As a "nursemaid," she might really teach the baby; but as an image, she must have less meaning than a piece of furniture.

This reification is apparent in the subsequent history of the Cook family photograph. Putting her in their photograph seems to have been almost like hiding her in plain sight. The Cook family themselves could not have bothered to read the complicated body language and facial expression of the "nursemaid" in the photograph in their midst; or reading it, they could not have lent it even the remotest capacity to signify. Otherwise the photograph, coded as a sentimental family momento of her faithful devotion, must have acquired a more problematic meaning than its history as a cherished keepsake of the family would allow. Arguably, it is as much an image of the violation of her social personhood as are the more infamous Zealey daguerreotypes of Delia, Renty, and Jack; and it is as eloquent a record of the social relations that grew out of slavery.[31] The photograph of the teenaged, barebreasted Delia was given by a South Carolina slaveholder to Professor Louis Agassiz of Harvard University to help him to "study anatomical details of 'the African race'" in order to "prove" his theory that blacks were a distinct species, separately created. Harryette Mullen writes of Delia,

> History preserves only the picture of her body, photographed as a "scientific" exhibit. Prefiguring the critique of bourgeois power/knowledge monopolized by privileged white males, represented by private tutors who serve the slaveholding elite in Williams' *Dessa Rose*, Morrison's *Beloved*, and Johnson's *Oxherding Tales*, are the historical encounters of slave women with white men of science: Dr. James Norcum ("Dr Flint" in Jacobs's narrative), who instructed his slave that she had been "made for his use"; Dr. Strain, who desired visual proof of Sojourner Truth's sex, viewing the self-empowered black woman as a freak; and Professor Louis Agassiz, who conceived a project in which the illusory immediacy of the subjugated image would provide seemingly irrefutable proof of African inferiority through a photographic display of black bodies, a project in which racial and sexual differences were to be read as perceptible evidence of inferiority.[32]

For Mullen, Agassiz' "coercive recording of her bare-breasted image leaves her silent, underscoring Delia's materiality as "property" and "exhibit," as "scientific evidence," a unit of data within a master discourse controlled by white men, bent on denying her subjectivity. . . . But what is most at stake . . . for me is that something of Delia [in the expression of her eyes] escapes or at least challenges the subjugating gaze that holds her body captive."[33]

Similarly, what is at stake for me in the photograph of the "nursemaid and her charge" is that something in her body language "escapes or at least challenges the subjugating gaze that holds her body captive." The compelling visual pattern of the striped dress is uncannily like a subliminal message to the viewer to "read between the lines." If the white cloth at the bottom of the frame, which a viewer easily could process at first as a single, vague entity, were earlier interpreted entirely as the infant's dress, it will now resolve itself assertively into two distinct shapes—the apron that designates a servant or slave as well as the clothing of the child. The cloth across the young woman's left shoulder, which might have been something any mother or nanny would use in a multitude of ways to protect and shelter and swaddle the baby and herself, comes to appear as much a curtain separating the two as it does the implement of any ritual of care or bonding. As one looks more closely it becomes apparent that the cloth covers unnaturally and entirely her left arm and hand; in fact, that it has been arranged or flung upon her much as if she were a chair or some other piece of upholstery, so as to set off the baby's head against a dark solid surface that corrects for the photographically busy background of the eloquent striped dress. Evidently it was important that the baby's individuality come through sharply in this portrait; and for this purpose, the woman is merely the setting, the not quite perfect background that needs to be improved. But her body language suggests that she comprehends this expediency and that she resents it, for she makes no effort to hold or cradle the baby, but merely suffers him to be balanced upright and exhibited to the camera as he waves his arm in the crook of her exaggeratedly extended elbow.[34]

There is an additional layer of meaning encoded in this image of the "nursemaid and her charge," one that I have not been able to establish on any historical grounds. Nevertheless, it seems appropriate to say that nursemaids nurse babies, that in order to nurse a baby one must have recently borne a baby oneself, and that therefore the visible presence of Heustis Cook in the image may erase the presence of the "nursemaid's" own baby, who remains invisible. What the social relationships were that surrounded *that* baby, if it existed, are impossible to tell.[35]

Not only the Cooks refused to read this photograph. Although the "nursemaid and her charge" has three times recently been reprinted in widely read books on African American history, including two feminist books—in Norman Yetman's *Voices from Slavery;* in Dorothy Sterling's *We Are Your Sisters,* and in Jacqueline Jones' *Labor of Love, Labor of Sorrow*—it has never yet drawn a critical glance beyond Norman Yetman's general assessment that her image, like all the images in the Cook collection, is "sensitive . . . honest . . . [and] forthright" and that "a quality exists in each of them that marks them as an interesting composition and a work of art in their own right."[36] Furthermore, each time it has been reprinted, the photograph has been rendered outside of the particular context of its production. What does this continuing anekphrasis tell us about the allegiances of our critical institutions that have, since slavery, continued to govern the interpretation of the photographic gaze? Does seeing nineteenth-century middle-class "sentiment," that critical turn that has been so vitally important for the establishment of a feminist standpoint in literary criticism, actually function as a mechanism of displacement, ensuring that other sentiments will not be seen?

It is commonly alleged that photography was a democratic medium, one that made portraits available "to the millions." Yet, as Jeanne Moutoussamy-Ashe has pointed out, "if indeed photography was a 'democratic art,' then it was so only to the extent that those who used the process were free to express themselves. If slaves were allowed to be creative, they were only to be creative in their menial labors, such as carpentry and basketry work for their slave owners."[37] The ability to express themselves was severely restricted in the most basic of ways. Although Deborah Willis-Ryan, former curator of photographs and prints for The New York Public Library's Schomburg Center for Research in Black Culture and now at the Smithsonian Institution, has ascertained that several hundred African American photographers were working throughout the United States from 1840 to 1940, most of them were free men and women. Scholars generally agree on prices of an individual studio portrait of top quality that would have placed them beyond the personal resources of almost any mid-century Southern slave. It is fair to say that slaves thus did not generally make their own photographs, nor did they generally have studio photographs made of themselves, unless it was at the behest and with the money of their masters. This meant that a slave's photograph could be used in countless ways to serve the discourse of the masters and that the slave's self expression in photography would be in the mode of subversion, like the self expression of the "nursemaid."

This is not democracy. Against the sheer weight of the accumulated valorization of images of the white family and against the fact that the white family was virtually the only context in which the "nursemaid" would have a portrait made, the requirement that visible subversion be coded inside of sentiment made it functionally invisible. Nor could self-knowledge and self-assurance be gained from the photographic image as it was gained by white people, because considering how it was made, the image could not be trusted. In fact, slaveowners used photographs of the slave family effectively as a means through which to increase their psychological domination. Moutoussamy-Ashe reports the following rare correspondence between Louisa Piquet, born a slave, and her slave mother, Elizabeth Ramsey.[38] The story is told in full by Louisa Piquet herself, in the slave narrative she dictated to the Reverend Mr. Mattison of the A.M.E. Church.[39] Elizabeth Ramsey and her daughter Louisa had been separated since Louisa was fourteen, and in this correspondence they are sending photographic portraits to one another. They communicated with the permission of their masters through letters written for them by others:

March 8, 1859
Whorton, Texas

My Dear Daughter,

I want you to have your ambrotype taken also your children and send them to me I would give the world to see you and my sweet little children; my god bless you my dear child and protect you is my prayer.

Your affectionate Mother
Elizabeth Ramsey

Later, after Louisa answered her mother's letter and also asked for a daguerreotype, Elizabeth Ramsey wrote to her daughter that:

> It is not in our power to comply with your request in regard to the daguerreotypes at this time, we shall move to Matagorde shortly, there I can comply with your request.

And sometime later, the owner of the mother wrote to the daughter that:

> I send you by this mail a daguerreotype likeness of your mother and brother, which I hope you will receive. Your mother received yours in a damaged condition.
>
> Respec'y yours,
> A. C. Horton

A few months after this, the Reverend Mr. Mattison of the A.M.E. Church wrote a letter for Louisa, who was apparently living up north, in which he described the daguerreotypes she received as "both taken on one plate, mother and son, and are set forth in their best possible gear, to impress us in the North with the superior condition of the slave over the free colored people."[40]

Evidently, even these rare photographic tokens of the sentiment of slaves—precisely because they were tokens of sentiment—were made into vehicles for the master's allegations that the family life provided in slavery for Elizabeth Ramsey was superior to the condition of the black people who were free. Therefore, although Louisa Piquet finally obtained photographs of her mother and brother, she could not learn of their true condition from looking at the images. Like wartime propaganda, these images are thoroughly suspect. The pull on the heartstrings, the longing they provoke for mother and home, those sentimental staples, are used here with the calculating malevolence of a man who wishes receipt of the photographs to destroy even the small sense of security that they dangle. Louisa's experience of photography is not separable from the social system in which it was embedded. For her, the camera is no "spirit of fact," no "unimpeachable witness."

4

In 1864, writing in his popular manual *The Camera and the Pencil,* Marcus Aurelius Root observed of photography the usual things, that:

> By heliography, our loved ones, dead or distant; our friends and acquain-

tances, however far removed, are retained within daily and hourly vision. To what extent domestic and social affections and sentiments are conserved and perpetrated by these "shawdow" of the loved and valued originals, every one may judge. The cheapness of these pictures brings them within reach, substantially, of all.

In this competitious and selfish world of ours, whatever tends to vivify and strengthen the social feelings should be hailed as a benediction. With these literal transcriptions of features and forms, once dear to us, ever at hand, we are scarcely more likely to forget, or grow cold to their originals, than we should in their presence. How can we exaggerate the value of an art which produces affects like these?[41]

This was the sentimental axiom.

But Oliver Wendell Holmes was much closer to the mark, although perhaps inadvertently, when, celebrating the discovery of photography, he called photographs "the social currency, the sentimental 'green-backs' of civilization."[42] In a social order that was structured by fundamental racial and sexual inequality and increasingly maintained by the cynical or self-deluded manipulation of affect, the exchange of photographs that helped to cement the regime of sentiment—and with it the triadic system of kinship, conquest, and incorporation that it sponsored—could became the very triage point of human status. Like the currency of money or the currency of freedom, it is the conditions for the circulation of one's image and not the image itself— as we learned again with the televiewing of Anita Hill—that will either cast up individuals onto the shore of social protection through representation or feed them to the void.

Photography has always been a constitutive force not merely reflecting but actively determining the social spaces in which we live our lives. The narratives we make about photography, relating image to image and to other cultural forms, describe the social borders of our thought. Were she writing it now, Gisele Freund's pioneering work on *Photography and Society* would need to be recast: photography *is* society; they are not distinct. As a social institution, American photography commemorates a popular struggle to envision— and the struggle to be visible in—a modus vivendi for American lives. The right to see and be seen, in one's own way and under one's own terms, has been the point of contention.

But impressive as is this capacity to envision lives, American photography has also had a capacity to destroy them. Photography has always been an enforcer, with the power to make certain things invisible just as surely as it has made other things appear. It behooves us now to learn just how this differentiating function of photography has proceeded, so as to loosen its grip on the continuing production of democratic signs and cultures. We must seek out the cognitive appropriation of the Real. The moral positivist's "mirror with a memory" in the nineteenth century must become the historian's "memory with a mirror" in the twentieth.

"Thanks to its code of connotation, the reading of a photograph is always historical," wrote Roland Barthes. "It depends on the reader's 'knowledge,' just as if this were a matter of a real language, intelligible only if one has learned its signs."[43] "To articulate the past historically," wrote Walter Benjamin, "does not mean to recognize it 'the way it really was.' It means to seize hold of a memory as it flashes up at a moment of danger. Every image of the past that is not recognized by the present as one of its concerns threatens to disappear irretrievably."[44] But what do they mean by history?

For Barthes, a historical reading calls upon a fund of knowledge about the past. In looking at a photograph, Barthes is interested in reading signs of the way things were. He is a linguist, a translator. He translates the meaning of the image from knowing of its past. But for Benjamin, all knowledge is in the present, about the present. The only reason that Benjamin wants to remember the way things were is to help in a present emergency. Benjamin's term *articulate* is a pun. To "articulate the past historically" is to speak about history, but it is also to mesh the past and the present into the future, as the wheels of one gear articulate with the next. To "articulate the past historically" is to aid in the birth of the new.

If we have learned in recent years from Barthes and from feminism to do close analysis of photographs, we must learn from Benjamin what for. Surely, it is not the record of the past as it is simply illustrated in photographs, an inert collage of the way things were, a past that accepts the fiction of being over, that is the most important thing about our reading of photographs. Nor is it the past that photography has brought to bear on and in itself, as in the history of the medium.

Instead, the photographic past that ought now to be among our most urgent concerns is the remembrance that photography has helped not only to record but also to shape our current violent predicaments of race, class, and gender. "We would argue," write Patricia Holland, Jo Spence, and Simon Watney, that:

> what is often described as racial difference, as a gulf between black and white similar to that between male and female, is better described as a construction of 'otherness.' Photography has played an important role in identifying people who are not like 'us,' who become the bearers of all those qualities which 'we' find unfamiliar and unacceptable—from the violent and disorderly to the exotic and the quaint. This is the tradition of the representation of 'inferior' groups which has evolved within the history of colonialism and imperialism, and which feeds and sustains contemporary racism. A politics of anti-racism takes on these issues within the social structure and within the realm of representation.[45]

This is to say that since the middle of the nineteenth century, the kind of sentimentality that is the seeing-sentiment has served as one of imperialism's many and least innocent eyes.

NOTES

1. These citations are based on the version of the paper Spillers delivered at the conference on "Psychoanalysis in African American Contexts: Feminist Reconfigurations" at the University of California, Santa Cruz, October 1992. In the significantly revised version of Spillers's paper in this volume, some of these citations have disappeared, and the point of view has shifted to a harsher critique of the status and possibilities of the Real.

2. Roland Barthes, *Camera Lucida* (New York: Hill and Wang, 1981), 26–7.

3. My philosophical position here is informed by Donna Haraway's discussion of partial perspectives in "Situated Knowledges: The Science Question in Feminism and the Privilege of Partial Perspective," *Feminist Studies* 14, no. 3 (1988): 575–99; by the analysis of standpoint theory in Sandra Harding, *The Science Question in Feminism* (Ithaca: Cornell University Press, 1986) and Sandra Harding, *Whose Science? Whose Knowledge?* (Ithaca: Cornell University Press, 1991); by Michel Foucault's discussion of "subjugated knowledge" in *Power/Knowledge: Selected Interviews and Other Writings* (New York: Pantheon Books, 1972); and by Patricia Hill Collins in *Black Feminist Thought: Knowledge, Consciousness, and the Politics of Empowerment* (Boston: Unwin Hyman, 1990).

4. Bryan Wolf, "Confessions of a Closet Ekphrastic," *Yale Journal of Criticism* 3, no. 2 (spring 1990): 185.

5. John Updike, *Just Looking: Essays on Art* (New York: Knopf, 1989).

6. See Serge Guilbaut, *How New York Stole the Idea of Modern Art: Abstract Expressionism, Freedom, and the Cold War* (Chicago: The University of Chicago Press, 1983); and Christopher Phillips, "The Judgment Seat of Photography," in *The Contest of Meaning: Critical Histories of Photography*, ed. Richard Bolton (Cambridge: Massachusetts Institute of Technology, 1989), 14–47. See also Edward Steichen, *The Family of Man* (New York: Museum of Modern Art, 1955); and Roland Barthes's classic deconstruction of it, "The Great Family of Man," in *Mythologies* (Paris: Éditions du Seuil, 1957), 100–102.

7. Alan Trachtenberg has been the chief and most persuasive advocate for the necessity and the difficulty of reading photographs. In his most recent book, *Reading American Photographs: Images as History, Mathew Brady to Walker Evans* (New York: Hill and Wang, 1989), Trachtenberg argues a social constructionist position for photographs as documents of American cultural history: "Just as the meaning of the past is the prerogative of the present to invent and choose, the meaning of an image does not come intact and whole. Indeed, what empowers an image to represent history is not just what it shows but the struggle for meaning we undergo before it, a struggle analogous to the historian's effort to shape an intelligible and usable past" (xvii). The politically nuanced attention that Trachtenberg is advocating as "reading" should not be confused with formalism.

8. An excellent discussion of the pitfalls of a merely additive conceptualization of

oppression may be found in Elizabeth V. Spelman, "Theories of Race and Gender: The Erasure of Black Women," *Quest* 5, no. 4 (1982): 36–62. See also Spelman, *Inessential Woman: Problems of Exclusion in Feminist Thought* (Boston: Beacon, 1988).

9. Jane Tompkins's *Sensational Designs: The Cultural Work of American Fiction, 1790–1860* (New York: Oxford University Press, 1985) is the outstanding example of this critical thrust.

10. The photographs I am analyzing in this essay may be found in the George Cook Collection of the Valentine Museum in Richmond, Virginia. The "nursemaid and her charge" has been often reprinted, but there are hundreds of unpublished images by George and Heustis Cook extant in the archive. I want to take this opportunity to thank the staff of the Valentine Museum for their cooperation, and especially Barbara Batson and Teresa Roane, curators of the photographic collection, for their generous responses to my requests.

11. Julia Kristeva, "Motherhood According to Bellini," in *Desire in Language,* trans. Leon S. Roudiez (New York: Columbia University Press, 1980), 243.

12. Ibid., 241, 247.

13. Norman Yetman, *Voices from Slavery* (New York: Holt, Rinehart and Winston, 1970).

14. From *Covered Wagon Days* (The Arthur Clarke Company, n.d.), quoted in Robert Taft, *Photography and the American Scene* (New York: Dover, 1964), 138.

15. The locus classicus and still one of the best discussions of this process is Roland Barthes, "Myth Today," in *Mythologies,* 109–59.

16. Patricia Holland, Jo Spence, and Simon Watney, *Photography/Politics: Two* (London: Comedia Publishing Group, 1986), 2.

17. Griselda Pollock, "What's Wrong with 'Images of Women'?" *Screen Education* 24 (1977): 25–33.

18. Richard Brodhead's discussion of the function of domestic fiction in the consolidation of the early-nineteenth-century bourgeois family offers an illuminating, and substantially parallel, example of the "cultural work" (Jane Tompkins's term) accomplished by sentimental cultural products. See Richard Brodhead, "Sparing the Rod: Discipline and Fiction in Antebellum America," in *Representations* 21 (winter 1988): 67–96.

19. Philip Fisher, *Hard Facts: Setting and Form in the American Novel* (New York: Oxford University Press, 1985).

20. Gillian Brown, *Domestic Individualism: Imaging Self in Nineteenth-Century America* (Berkeley: University of California Press, 1990).

21. This statement should not be taken to imply that there were no black photographers or photographs of black families. Quite to the contrary. As Angela Davis has written in *Women, Culture, Politics* (New York: Vintage Books, 1990):

> Many will find it astonishing that Black people became involved in photography shortly after the invention of the daguerreotype: Jules Lion, who became acquainted with this process in France, may well have introduced it to the city of New Orleans. But, then, how many prominent scientists, scholars, and artists have been banished from historical records for no other reason than their racial heritage, only to be revealed, shamefully late, as outstanding contributors in their fields? Jules Lion, Robert Duncanson and

J. P. Ball ought not now to evoke new responses of surprise. Rather, they should be celebrated as evidence of what knowledgeable persons should have strongly suspected all along. Yes, Black photographers were active during the very earliest stages of their medium's history. Granted, there were but a few, for slavery imposed a historical prohibition on virtually all forms of open aesthetic creation; only music, misunderstood as it was by the slaveocracy, was permitted to flourish. But what about the untapped artistic potential of those millions of slaves? Do we dare imagine how many pioneering Black photographers there might have been had more favorable socioeconomic circumstances prevailed? (221)

Deborah Willis-Ryan, Valencia Hollins Coar, and Jeanne Moutoussamy-Ashe have published the major works to date on the history of black photography in the nineteenth century, and a great deal more research is currently underway. See Deborah Willis, *Black Photographers, 1840–1940: A Bio-Bibliography* (New York: Garland Publishing, 1985); Deborah Willis, *Early Black Photographers, 1849–1940,* with the Schomburg Center for Research in Black Culture (New York: The New Press, 1992); Valencia Hollins Coar, *A Century of Black Photographers, 1840–1960* (Providence: Rhode Island School of Design, 1983); and Jeanne Moutoussamy-Ashe, *Viewfinders: Black Women Photographers* (New York: Dodd, Mead and Company, 1986).

22. *Outsider-within* is the term Patricia Hill Collins uses to designate the social position of the black woman domestic worker in white families. I have here extended it to apply to the social position of the black man connected with the Cook family as well. See discussion in Collins, *Black Feminist Thought*, 10–13.

23. For an excellent account of the complex implications of the banjo player portrait, see Eric Lott, *Love and Theft: Blackface Minstrelsy and the American Working Class* (New York: Oxford University Press, 1993).

24. Benjamin Batchelder Valentine, *Ole Marster and Other Verses* (Richmond, Va.: Whittet and Shepperson, 1921), 60–63.

25. Mary Newton Stanard, foreword in Valentine, *Ole Marster and Other Verses*.

26. Ibid.

27. I am using the term *puncture* here in accordance with Roland Barthes's account of the *punctum* in *Camera Lucida*. I differ from Barthes, however, in that the *punctum* he seeks is a purely private sensation, whereas my notion of the *punctum* includes as well the registration of ideological rupture, like puncturing a balloon that has kept one from seeing where one really is.

28. Harriet Beecher Stowe, *Household Papers and Stories* (Boston: Houghton Mifflin, 1896), quoted in Lynn Wardley, "Relic, Fetish, Femmage: The Aesthetics of Sentiment in the Work of Stowe," *The Yale Journal of Criticism* 5, no. 3 (fall 1992): 180.

29. See Harryette Mullen, "'Indelicate Subjects': African American Women's Subjugated Subjectivity," in *Sub/versions: Feminist Studies* (Santa Cruz: University of California, 1991).

30. Benjamin Batchelder Valentine, "Mammy's Charge," in *Ole Marster and Other Verses*, 56–57.

31. Alan Trachtenberg published several of these photographs in *Reading American Photographs,* along with an extensive discussion of them. Some are also published in Melissa Banta and Curtis M. Hinsley, *From Site to Sight: Anthropology, Photography,*

and the Power of Imagery (Cambridge: Peabody Museum Press, 1986). They are also discussed in Moutoussamy-Ashe, *Viewfinders*, 5.

32. Harryette Mullen, "Indelicate Subjects."

33. Ibid.

34. This reading accords with the assessment by Barbara Christian of the mammy figure in slave narratives: "unlike the white southern image of mammy, she is cunning, prone to poisoning her master, and not at all content with her lot." Barbara Christian, *Black Feminist Criticism, Perspectives on Black Women Writers* (New York: Pergamon, 1985), 5. See also Trudier Harris, *From Mammies to Militants: Domestics in Black American Literature* (Philadelphia: Temple University Press, 1982), and Patricia Hill Collins, "Mammies, Matriarchs, and Other Controlling Images," in *Black Feminist Thought*, 4–90. But I also want to add a cautionary note to the idea I am suggesting that resistance to the master discourse may be legible in the body language and discursive signs of the photograph. This is what I believe, but I believe it tentatively, or, as Jacques Derrida has put it, "sous *erature*." As both Carla Kaplan and Franny Nudelman have recently argued, the assignation by a would-be "emancipatory reader" of a language of resistance to individuals who are placed in situations of domination and oppression is a complex wish, and such an assignation, when it is merely projection, may be a subtle form of "othering." See Carla Kaplan, "Narrative Contracts and Emancipatory Readers," *Yale Journal of Criticism* 6, no. 1 (spring 1993): 93–119; and Franny Nudelman, "Harriet Jacobs and the Sentimental Politics of Female Suffering", *ELH* 59 (1992): 939–64. Yet, to refuse to read such a language is also to objectify. My exertion, in this essay, has been to contextualize the photograph historically in ways that make it possible to support a disruptive reading of the signs of both the domination and resistance that I see. However, my major "emancipatory" effort here is directed not toward the woman in the photograph, whom I do not know, nor toward the position of persons she represents, which would be presumptuous, but towards a broader discussion of the social role of photography under conditions of social inequality and radical disempowerment, such as slavery, or immediate post-slavery "reconstruction" life. This is a discussion which has been seriously distorted by "sentiment."

35. Gabrielle Foreman first pointed out to me the possible link between a "nurse-maid," nursing, and the invisible presence of a child of her own.

36. Yetman, *Voices from Slavery*, no page.

37. Moutoussamy-Ashe, *Viewfinders*, 7.

38. Ibid., 6–7.

39. Rev. H. Mattison, A.M., *Louisa Piquet, the Octaroon: A Tale of Southern Slave Life* (1861), reprinted in *Collected Black Women's Narratives*, ed. Anthony Barthelemy (New York: Oxford University Press, 1988). For invaluable commentary on the Piquet narrative and an analysis of the response of Louisa to the "male gaze," see Gabrielle Foreman, "Who's Your Mama? Louisa Piquet and White 'Mulatta Genealogies'" (paper presented at the Nineteenth-Century American Women Writers in the Twenty-First Century Conference, Harriet Beecher Stowe Center and Trinity College, Hartford, Connecticut, June 1996).

40. This correspondence is quoted in Moutoussamy-Ashe, *Viewfinders*, 6–7, and in *Louisa Piquet, the Octaroon*, 31, 34, 35.

41. Marcus Aurelius Root, *The Camera and the Pencil* (Pawlet: Helios, 1971), 26–27.

42. Oliver Wendell Holmes, quoted in Taft, *Photography and the American Scene,* 143.

43. Roland Barthes, *Image-Music-Text,* trans. Stephen Heath (New York: Hill and Wang, 1977), 28.

44. Walter Benjamin, "Theses on the Philosophy of History," in *Illuminations,* ed. Hannah Arendt (New York: Schoeken Books, 1973), 255.

45. Patricia Holland, Jo Spence, and Simon Watney, *Photography/Politics: Two* (London: Comedia Publishing Group, 1986), 7.

"Beyond Mortal Vision"

Harriet E. Wilson's *Our Nig* and the American Racial Dream-Text

Katherine Clay Bassard

1. "IN THE BEGINNING . . . "

My project rises from delight, not disappointment. It rises from what I
know about the ways writers transform aspects of their social grounding
into aspects of language, and the ways they tell other stories, fight secret
wars, limn out all sorts of debates blanketed in their text. And rises from
my certainty that writers always know, at some level, that they do this.
TONI MORRISON, *PLAYING IN THE DARK*

[P]eople of color have always theorized—but in forms quite different
from the Western form of abstract logic.
BARBARA CHRISTIAN, "THE RACE FOR THEORY"

Harriet E. Wilson's 1859 novel *Our Nig; or, Sketches from the Life of a Free Black*
stands as a kind of Genesis of the African American, black women's, and
American literary canons. The first novel by an African American woman
writer and the first novel by an African American published within the U. S.,
Our Nig has secured a place within overlapping literary traditions on course
syllabi, as well as attracting—for a pre-Emancipation African American text
at least—a good deal of criticism and analysis.[1] And, as the preceding quotations bear witness, Wilson knew she was making history and understood
the important implications of what she calls in the preface to the novel her
"experiment." As the writer of a northern slave narrative, Wilson was quite
aware of the uniqueness of her writerly positionality.

Our Nig tells the story of Frado, a spirited mulatta who, through the death
of her black father and the abandonment of her white mother, ends up an
indentured servant in the home of a white, middle-class, New England family, the Bellmonts. Wilson's agenda, which she spells out in her preface, is to
portray Mrs. Bellmont as "wholly imbued with *southern principles*," a charac-

terization central to Wilson's overall project of exposing the northern indenture system as a kind of slavery. As Wilson announces on the title page
of the text, her story is set "in a Two-Story White House, North" in order to
show "that slavery's shadows fall even there."

I chose *Playing in the Dark* to open this analysis precisely because it is a critical text written by an African American woman who has recently won the
Nobel Prize for Literature based on her accomplishments in the genre of
the novel.[2] That is, Wilson, at the beginning of the tradition of African American women novelists, and Morrison, at the "end" of this lineage, have much
to say to each other.[3] Before turning to *Our Nig*, I dwell on Morrison's erudite theorizing of a critical project that (she tells us three times) "rises" from
overlapping concerns of subjectivity ("aspects of . . . social grounding"), utterance ("aspects of . . . language"), and epistemology ("what I know"; "my
certainty that *writers always know*"), because these issues are crucial for understanding the complexity of Wilson's engagement with race, gender, and
literary representation in pre-Emancipation America.

The central site for Morrison's analysis in *Playing* is a psychical-discursive
process she refers to as "American Africanism," which figures within the white
American writer's text as "a sometimes allegorical, sometimes metaphorical,
but always choked Africanist presence" (17). Characterized by "significant
and underscored omissions, startling contradictions, heavily nuanced conflicts," American Africanism produces a national literature whose signifying
traits are "in fact responses to a dark, abiding, signing Africanist presence"
(6, 9). Morrison's shift of the terms of "call and response" here is significant.
For if white American subjectivity is refigured as a "response" to a (largely
created) "Africanist call," by what means do Africans in America come to recognize themselves? If the national literature is founded on "responses to . . .
Africanist presence," what could be the African American response to this
response?

It is here within *Playing* that a discourse of "African Americanism" rises
out of the shadows of the racializing ideology.[4] Morrison writes:

> The principal reason these matters loom large for me is that I do not have
> quite the same access to these traditionally useful constructs of blackness.
> Neither blackness nor "people of color" stimulates in me notions of
> excessive, limitless love, anarchy, or routine dread. I cannot rely on these
> metaphorical shortcuts because I am a black writer struggling with and
> through a language that can powerfully evoke and enforce hidden signs
> of racial superiority, cultural hegemony, and dismissive "othering" of people
> and language which are by no means marginal or already and completely
> known and knowable in my work. My vulnerability would lie in romanticiz-
> ing blackness rather than demonizing it; vilifying whiteness rather than
> reifying it. (x–xi)

Indeed, African Americanism derives its discursive power from its self-reflexivity, its self-consciousness about both the possibilities and the risks in written language. This self-reflexivity derives from an African artistic and performing heritage that, as Barbara Christian reminds us in "The Race for Theory," forms the basis of African American interpretive and theorizing practices.[5] It derives, as well, from the ability of the diasporic African American subject to see what is supposed to remain unseen: the subtle but destructive mechanism of American Africanism. As a vantage point—Du Bois called it "double consciousness"—African Americanism derives from a social positionality which sees the construction of whiteness, catches it, if you will, in its reflexive posture vis-à-vis its construction of a discourse of blackness as a discourse of difference. Unlike "African Assimilationism" in which "American means white, and Africanist people struggle to make the term applicable to themselves with ethnicity and hyphen after hyphen after hyphen" (Morrison 47), African Americanism is not an exercise in psychical-discursive application but represents the creative insistence of an African American theorizing heritage. And it is within this culture-specific context that African writers in the Americas come to "tell other stories, fight secret wars, limn out all sorts of debates blanketed in their texts." Morrison's description of the revelatory potential of African Americanist theorizing—a revelation that occurs to her when she begins reading "as a writer"—is illuminating: "It is as if I had been looking at a fishbowl . . . and suddenly I saw the bowl, the structure that transparently (and invisibly) permits the ordered life it contains to exist in the larger world. In other words, I began to rely on my knowledge of how books get written, how language arrives" (17).

The arrival of Harriet Wilson's text to the literary scene—both in terms of its first edition in 1859 and its more recent entrance to the literary critical venue—marks the arrival of a "novelized" African Americanist and female discourse. We could say that *Our Nig* emerges simultaneously out of the "shadows" of the institution of slavery and out of the shadow of American Africanist racial representation. Mae G. Henderson's outline of black women's revisionism in "Speaking in Tongues" charts a process "from intervention to appropriation and revision of the dominant discourse. Henderson writes: "The initial expression of a marginal presence takes the form of a disruption—a departure or a break with conventional semantics and/or phonetics. This rupture is followed by a rewriting or rereading of the dominant story, resulting in a 'delegitimation' or the prior story or a 'displacement' which shifts attention 'to the other side of the story.'"[6] It is in this sense that I refer to *Our Nig* as an African American women's Genesis narrative. Wilson's project in *Our Nig* is the creation of a "myth of origins" out of which nominally free black women's subjectivity can emerge as subject of its own story. In order to accomplish this, she must unwrite—delegitimize and displace—two powerful myths of origin, themselves intertwined in mutually constitutive ideologies of race and gender: the biblical narrative of Genesis, on which much of my analysis dwells, and the law of *partus sequitir ventrem*—the edict that the child shall follow the condition of the mother. That Wilson intends *Our Nig* as a black female Genesis narrative is clear from its structure. The biblical text of Genesis moves from the Creation, through Eden, the Fall, and the emergence of God's covenant with the people of Israel, ending with the Joseph narrative in chapters 37–50. Wilson's novel begins with a story of creation and "fall"—the saga of "lonely Mag Smith," Frado's mother—and ends, in the very last sentence of the novel proper, with a reference to Joseph. First, the end.

2. THE LAW OF THE FATHER-PHARAOH

> But think on me when it shall be well with thee, and show kindness, I pray thee, unto me, and make mention of me unto Pharaoh, and bring me out of this house: for indeed I was stolen away out of the land of the Hebrews: and here also have I done nothing that they should put me into the dungeon.
>
> Genesis 40:14–15 (kjv)

In order to understand the meaning of Wilson's signifying on this "Master['s] Text," I take up Henderson's "hermeneutical task" of interpreting Wilson's "speaking in tongues," the metainterpretive strategies both within and surrounding the text of *Our Nig*. I call Wilson's discourse "metainterpretive" because the issue of interpretation is both method and event within the novel.[7] That is, the text not only provides a hermeneutical ground within its narrativity but also foregrounds the act of interpretation as a performative element of the text. This is accomplished through a complex web of intertextualities both referenced directly and unnamed within the text.

One of the most important intertexts occurs within the last sentence of the novel. To date, however, no reading of *Our Nig* has taken up the implications of the novel's "ending," which includes a reference to Genesis 40. I say "ending" because, after a moment of conventional closure in which the narrator recounts the "destiny" of the Bellmont family, a closure that purports to be, as the last chapter title promises, "the Winding Up of the Matter," the text reopens, as it were, onto an-other and unfamiliar landscape. In a gesture that prefigures Toni Morrison's *Beloved*, Frado becomes disembodied: she appears as a haunt, refiguring the terrain of memory and desire. Wilson writes that "Frado has disappeared from their [the surviving Bellmonts'] memories, as Joseph from the butler's, but she will never cease to track them till beyond mortal vision" (131). The ambiguity of the phrasing here leaves room for multiple readings. Yet I can't help but be drawn to the locution "beyond mortal vision." It suggests for me that there is something beyond the text's visual field of representation, an-other kind of vision for which the revisionism of the tale of Joseph and the butler serves as an important lens. I turn now to the biblical account of Genesis 40 in order to discern Wilson's critical interpretive intervention as she points beyond the biblical narrative to "'the other side of the story'" (Henderson 35).

Sold into slavery by his jealous older brothers (Gen. 37), Joseph is jailed by his master, Potiphar, for allegedly raping Potiphar's wife, who has accused Joseph after he resists her sexual advances (Gen. 39). Chapter 40 opens as two of Pharaoh's servants, the butler and the chief baker, are thrown into jail, Joseph having "offended their Lord the king of Egypt" (Gen. 40:1). Both men dream that night and awake the next morning in agony because "there is no interpreter" to assign meaning to their dream-texts (Gen. 40:8). Claiming that "interpretations belong to God" (Gen. 40:8), Joseph successfully interprets the dreams, and it is at this point that he pleads with the butler to whom Wilson refers, saying, "Think on me when it shall be well with thee . . . and make mention of me unto Pharaoh, and bring me out of this house" (Gen. 40:14). Joseph's plea for "remembrance" is neither sentimental nor gratuitous but material and economic. Having performed his labor (of interpretation), his request is that of one who expects to receive justice and proper payment or reward, in this case, the reward of freedom ("bring me out of this house"). True to Joseph's prophetic interpretation, the butler is restored to favor by Pharaoh, only to break his promise: "Yet did not the chief butler remember Joseph, but forgat him" (Gen. 40:23).

By invoking Joseph at the end of *Our Nig*, Wilson positions herself, the narrator, and the main character Frado, simultaneously and within multiple narratives as betrayed kin, slave, prophet, and, significantly, as interpreter of dream-texts. This multiple self-positioning foregrounds interpretation as a leading figure in the novel's plot as well as important to its structural metadesign. Like Joseph, Wilson's authorial labor demands remembrance and material reward. Writing out of economic bondage, Wilson tells a tale of northern indenture in which the multiple strains of Joseph's saga are bound together in the interlocking complicities of race, gender, and class.

Long before Freud's theorizing of the dream as a realm of condensations and displacements, Wilson, through the appropriation of the biblical narrative of Joseph, signals the sociohistorical efficacy of race as the underside of the American dream or nightmare. Though the butler and baker dream separate dreams with opposite consequences (the butler is restored to favor while the baker is executed), the biblical narrator's reporting of the dream event is strangely ambiguous: "And they dreamed a dream both of them, each man his dream in one night, each man *according to the interpretation of his dream*" (Gen. 40:5; emphasis added). The ambiguity caused by shifts between singular and plural reveals the social grounding of the dream via interpretation as social meaning. The dream(s) signifies both unity and plurality, singularity and relatedness. Inherent to the structure of the dream(s), according to the biblical narrator, is meaning as sign of imminent social relations; that is, each man dreams in relation to the Law of the Father-Pharaoh who determines guilt or innocence, death or life. The prison of the biblical text's linguistic structuration contains the meaning of symbolic processes condensed and displaced within each and all dream-texts: favor or disfavor with Pharaoh or Father leads inevitably to either life or death. Joseph's interpretive ability resides, at least in part, in his understanding of the social text of power; hence, his own plea "remember me unto Pharaoh" (Gen. 40:14).

It is with the emergence of the social ground that "dream," in the characteristic psychoanalytic way of conceiving an individual text of relationality, gives way to "myth" or paves the way for "mythography" to enter. Specifically, in *Our Nig*, the bourgeois family and American race relations are "two dreams" that are "one," born of "a season in[-]ward" (Gen. 40:4) as domestic relations under patriarchy and American slavery come together "in a Two-Story White House, North." Yet Wilson complicates the biblical narrative through the doubling of the American Africanist inscription—"*Our Nig* / by 'Our Nig'"—which simultaneously signals and displaces a racializing and dehumanizing White Gaze. It allows Wilson to tell (at least) two stories at once. Frado, as the Bellmont's Joseph, interprets the relations of power within the Bellmont household even as the narrator interprets Frado's interpretation for the "gentle reader" in light of Wilson's overall authorial purpose.

Like the Joseph narrative in Genesis, *Our Nig* begins with narratives of family betrayal. Frado's poor white mother is first betrayed by a white lover who promises to elevate her station through marriage. Having "surrendered to him a priceless gem," her virtue (6), Mag is abandoned along with the unnamed lover's "other victims." Mag then marries Frado's father Jim, "a kindhearted African" (9), a liaison that lowers her status even further in the eyes of white society. Upon Jim's death, Mag takes up with Seth, another black man, eschewing "the rite of civilization or Christianity" (16), descending even lower on the social scale. At Seth's suggestion, she goes along with a scheme to "give the children [the two mulattos who result from her marriage to Jim] away" (16), perpetuating the cycle of abandonment and family betrayal.

Abandoning Frado to the home of the Bellmonts is tantamount to selling her into slavery, because Mrs. Bellmont is, in Mag's description, "a right she-devil" (17). Mag rationalizes her betrayal by noting that the high-spirited Frado is in need of "severe restraint" (20); she and Seth lead the child by the hand along a "weary march" (20) that configures Frado's entry into the American social Symbolic. As they pass a schoolyard, the shouts of children taunt them: "'Halloo!' screamed one, 'Black, white and yeller!' 'Black, white and yeller,' echoed a dozen voices" (21). Narrated through a chiasmic structure of call-and-response, the voice of "one" and the "echo" of "a dozen voices" structures a reproduction of societal consensus on the meaning of skin color. Moreover, "black, white and yeller" names the family structure of Seth or Jim, Mag, and Frado through their relative positions in the color text of American race relations. The voices from the schoolyard, prefiguring Frado's own initiation into the Symbolic of the Bellmont household and the schoolroom in chapter 3, thus map out two types of relations as color text displaces and mocks the father-mother-child triad. Seth as the "father" who is "not father," and thus rejects fatherhood, is inscribed under the sign "black," which collapses the figures of both Jim ("the kind-hearted African") and Seth in a gesture of effaced paternity.

Significantly, Mag is unresponsive to the taunting. The narrator tells us that "she had passed into an insensibility no childish taunt could penetrate" (21). Mag's psychical paralysis, her "insensibility" to the societal figuration of racial relations, leads to a reinforcement of her decision to break up her "family" as she "extend[s] the separation once so easily annihilated by steadfast integrity" (21). To keep the family together by keeping her children would mean, for Mag, holding onto the knowledge of interracial marriage and her own acts of miscegenation. Mag's alienation from the "sneering world" of white society (7) is figured in the cramped space of the "hovel" that she inhabits after her first "fall" and to which she returns after Jim's death. It is in public venues like the schoolyard that the American racial text derives its power. Yet as we are poised to read Mag's "insensibility" as a liberating posture, a positionality that allows her to pass beyond the social text that would assign moral value (right or wrong) to sexual contact between the races, the familial narrative reminds us that, in order to jettison from her consciousness racial inscriptions that assign "norms" of sexual propriety, Mag must give up her mulatto children because they embody the painful nexus of sexuality and race. The children, then, become "texts" that would condemn her.

In the paragraph immediately following this racial and familial mapping, the (white) bourgeois family structure is portrayed through the chronotope of the Bellmont house, "a large, old fashioned, two-story white house, environed by fruitful acres, and embellished by shrubbery and shade trees" (21). Invoking the power of myth and sacred narrative, Wilson writes:

> Years ago a youthful couple consecrated it as home; and after many little feet had worn paths to favorite fruit trees, and over its green hills, and mingled at last with brother man in the race which belongs neither to the swift or strong, the sire became grey-haired and decripid [*sic*], and went to his last repose. His aged consort soon followed him. The old homestead thus passed into the hands of a son, to whose wife Mag had applied the epithet "she-devil," as may be remembered. John, the son, had not in his family arrangements departed from the example of the father. The pastimes of his boyhood were ever freshly revived by witnessing the games of his own sons as they rallied about the same goal his youthful feet had won; as well

as by the amusements of his daughters in their imitations of maternal duties. (21–22)

This passage inscribes the patriarchal home of the Bellmonts within a sentimental vision that recalls both the American cultural ideal of the bourgeois family (in contrast to the "family" of Mag-Jim or Seth-Frado) and the narrative of Eden and the Fall of Genesis. Like Morrison's repetition of the Sally, Dick, and Jane story at the beginning of *The Bluest Eye,* this passage presents a vision of domesticity as mythic as it is socially "self-evident." In contrast to the family narrative of Mag, Jim or Seth, and Frado that opens the novel, this vision of domesticity admits neither betrayal nor broken kinship bonds. Instead, through the figure of the two-story house, the narrator represents a narrative of family bonding and generational continuity. The two-story house contains, here, two stories, overlapping narratives of two generations of Bellmonts for whom the house signifies entitlement as sacred ("consecrated") space. The material means of economic status and wealth remain outside the frame because the "youthful couple" inhabit this space as innocently as do Adam and Eve the Garden of Eden. The first Bellmonts become a kind of first man and woman of the Bellmont family myth.

Significantly, this passage hints at what will become an ambivalent displacement of the patriarch-pharaoh in chapter 3. We are introduced to the present Bellmonts obliquely through patriarchal generation: "the old homestead passed into the hands of a son." Yet "John, the son" is named only after the narrator recalls the naming of his wife as "she-devil." Mrs. Bellmont becomes the serpent in the garden, reinscribing woman as tempter and threat to patriarchal ownership of sacred space (garden and house). Once named, however, "John, the son" is restored as reproducer of the family myth: he "had not departed from the example of his father." The momentary instability of a family named through woman as disrupter and tempter achieves social equilibrium as John's childhood games "were ever freshly revived by witnessing the games of his sons" who are "about the same goal" (22). Moreover, the social posture of women is reestablished as "*his* daughters" perform "imitations of maternal duties" (22; emphasis added).

Like the taunting games of the disembodied children's voices who call out from the schoolyard, childhood "pastimes" mark the generational efficacy of gender relations. Yet once again we have the "closing" of a narrative whose reopening is foreshadowed and foretold. Informed that "John is wearing the badge of age" and that "most of his children were from home . . . some were already seeking homes of their own," Aunt Abby makes an appearance as "a maiden sister" who "occupie[s] a portion of the house" (22). The house as chronotopic representation of generational patriarchy thus admits into its representational space a "barrenness" that disrupts the mythic promise of replication (through reproduction) and fecundity.

These gestures of disruption through antithetical characters, the "she-devil" Mrs. Bellmont and the maiden (and religious) Aunt Abby, motion toward the Real disrupter of the consecrated bourgeois family myth: the presence of Frado who "entered the house" via Mag's lie. Frado's presence signals "the imposition" (27) of the "black, white and yeller" racial text into the white patriarchal home. Urging the family to "keep her," Jack, one of the Bellmont sons, states that "'she's real handsome and bright, and not very black either'" (25). Jack repeats, in condensed form, the "black, white and yeller" racial mapping referenced earlier. Mary's announcement, "'I don't want a nigger 'round me,'" and Mrs. Bellmont's reply, "'I don't mind the nigger in the child. I should like a dozen better than one'" (26), reverberate with the "one" voice echoed by "a dozen" in the schoolyard. It is within this conversation that Frado is (re)named even as she is (re)positioned within yet another configuration of "family" politics. Responding to Mary's complaint that "'she'll be of no use . . . right under foot all the time,'" Jack retorts, "Poh! Miss Mary; if she should stay, it wouldn't be two days before you would be telling the girls about *our* nig, *our* nig!" (25–26). That this declaration of ownership, of possession of Frado within the confines of the racial text, repositions her is clear by the decision to place her "in the L chamber" to sleep (26). Arguing that "'it's good enough for a nigger'" (26), Mrs. Bellmont remarks that when Frado outgrows the cramped space of the L chamber, "'she'll outgrow the house'" (28). Frado is further described by the narrator as "in some relation to white people she was never favored with before" (28).

3. *PARTUS SEQUITIR VENTREM:* OF BLACK WOMEN BORN

1662. Act XII. Children got by an Englishman upon a Negro woman shall be bond or free according to the condition of the mother, and if any Christian shall commit fornication with a Negro man or woman, he shall pay double the fines of a former act.

VIRGINIA STATE LAW

But the phenomenon is no different which by the mere recoil of a "But" brings to light, comely as the Shulamite, honest as the dew, the negress adorned for the wedding and the poor woman ready for the auction-block.

JACQUES LACAN, "AGENCY OF THE LETTER IN THE UNCONSCIOUS"

Lonely Mag Smith!

HARRIET E. WILSON

I have been calling *Our Nig* a Genesis text of African American women's novelistic discourse. Yet the first character we meet in the novel is a white women who is, we are told in the chapter title, "Mag Smith, My Mother." If, as I argue, Wilson's project is to construct a myth of origins for black female subjectivity, what are we to make of a black womanhood (in the form of Frado's traumatic "coming of age story") that emerges out of a fallen white womanhood? How do we account for our entrance into a black woman's text through white maternity?

In his introduction, Gates disagrees with Nina Baym's idea of the "overplot" of white women's sentimental novels in which the mother is pronounced "'least guilty'" of blame for "the heroine's woes." He claims that "*Our Nig* does not share [this] respect for mothers" (xlvii). Yet Claudia Tate in *Domestic Allegories of Political Desire* argues that Wilson tries to construct a "discourse of maternal desire" based on the construction of Mag as "an inherently good mother": "Frado does not hold her mother personally responsible" (35, 37). In this way, Tate reads the novel as "a complex maternal discourse" that "provides Wilson with a double symbolic recovery of the lost mother" in the form of Mag Smith's portrayal and Frado's own motherhood at the novel's end. Further, Tate concludes that "the text conflates the maternal obligation with authorial desire" (38).

What I focus on here, however, is not whether or not Mag Smith is a "good" or "bad" mother. Such debates center on the conflation of Frado, the narrator, and Wilson, and I find appeals to autobiography—on the assumption that Wilson herself was a mulatto with a white mother and a black father—unsatisfactory. It is true that the threshold of the Bellmont house marks a narrative and textual boundary figured in part by the sudden disappearance, after chapter 3, of first-person pronouns in the chapter headings. But rather than speculate on Wilson's own parentage or her possible "loss of authorial control," I see this threshold as a sign of our entry into a different narrative mode—"life," as it were giving way to "myth." That it is in the context of the Bellmonts' White Gaze that Frado is renamed "Nig" and repositioned as "slave" is significant not because Wilson may have "suddenly" decided to fictionalize her story, but because it marks a progression in narrative strategy (recall Henderson's descriptive of the process of marginal "disruption")— from "intervention" in a "master narrative" to "appropriation and revision" of a prior story—in order to bring about its delegitimation. In other words, on a metalevel, Wilson goes from *pointing to* an "other" story via her interventions into the biblical Genesis narrative to *voicing* the Other story by taking on the origin myth that truly shadows this text—the law of *partus sequitir ventrem:* "Children got by an Englishman upon a Negro woman shall be bond or free according to the condition of the mother."[8]

This seventeenth-century Virginia law of crime and punishment proposes a crime that is not really a crime (the rape of black women by white men), which results in a punishment that is no punishment at all (the offspring of such encounters shall follow "the condition of the mother"). *Partus sequitir ventrem* in its sleight of hand by which black children are depaternalized and the rape of black women decriminalized not only effaces paternity and sanctions (through economic incentive) the rape of enslaved black women by white enslavers, but it also constructs the condition of slavery as the province of enslaved black women. That is, the enslaved black mother becomes the reason for the chattel status of her progeny. The perniciousness of the mandate that the "children . . . shall be bond or free according to the condition of the mother" derives not only from its status as law but also its function as a peculiarly twisted myth of origins.

Researchers have commented that, given the patriarchal structure of English society at this time, this law appears to come "out of the blue." Yet I would argue that the law is an extension of patriarchy as it reenacts a biblical understanding of women as the originators of suffering and affliction. Just as the biblical Eve, "the mother of all living," is scripted as the originator of man's fallen, sinful state, here the black woman becomes the origin of the "fall" of millions of black children (male and female) into perpetual slavery. This feminization of the slave condition assigned blame for the condition of enslavement to black women living under U.S. slavery. Black people are enslaved, according to this legal mythmaking, and regardless of the color or condition of the father, for one reason and one reason alone: because they are of black women born.[9]

The vilification of black women as the originators of both "blackness" and chattel status genders Morrison's understanding of the discourse of American Africanism. And it is this insidious myth that constitutes the "shadows" out of which emerge the first three chapters of *Our Nig*. That is, I suggest we read the figure of Mag Smith both as she is "blackened" by her "fallenness" and contaminated by intercourse with black men and, paradoxically, as her whiteness remains stubbornly visible vis-à-vis the blackness of her mulatto children, particularly Frado. Contrary to readings of the novel that see the figure of Mag Smith as evidence of Wilson's break with the "traditional" miscegenationist coupling of white male and black female, I argue that Mag's character remains tied to and in fact stands in for the black mother.

This type of reversal—of figure and ground, dark and light, contours and shadows, photo and negative, which Morrison encodes in the title *Playing in the Dark: Whiteness and the Literary Imagination*—bears directly on the African Americanist performative strategies of *Our Nig*. It is a part of the "ethic of divine reversal" (Weems, "Reading *Her Way* Through the Struggle") that drives the text through the various biblical intertexts I have been discussing. Indeed, the novel stages many disruptive displacements—from South to North, from Mr. Bellmont's patriarchal power to Mrs. Bellmont's womanly tyranny—as a way of performing its interpretive task. Yet the figure of Mag Smith as a white mother of black children is particularly disturbing. As Patricia Williams writes of Judge Sorkow's opinion in the Baby M custody case, notions of racial and sexual propriety turn on "not-so-subtle images of which mothers should be bearing which children":

> Is there not something unseemly, in our society, about the spectacle of a white woman mothering a black child? A white woman giving totally to a black child; a black child totally and demandingly dependent for everything, sustenance itself, from a white woman. The image of a white woman suckling a black child; the image of a black child sucking for its life from the bosom of a white woman. The utter interdependence of such an image; the merging it implies; the giving up of boundary; the encompassing of other within itself; the unbounded generosity and interconnectedness of such an image. Such a picture says there is no difference; it places the hope of continuous generation, of immortality of the white self, in a little black face.[10]

Yet whereas Williams's description seems to be of a disruptive countertext to the text of racial and sexual "normativity," Wilson's Mag Smith, in abandoning her children, particularly Frado, forecloses the potential counternarrative through a *méconnaissance*. In the moment that Mag speaks the discourse of American Africanism in (mis)naming her own children—"'Who'll take the black devils?'" (16)—her whiteness becomes not an image of blurred racial boundaries but a reinscription of racialized hierarchies. The misrecognition is further reinforced in her rationalization of abandoning Frado because of the child's willfulness. Again I cite Williams's *Alchemy:* "One of the things passed on from slavery, which continues in the oppression of people of color, is a belief structure rooted in a concept of black (or brown or red) antiwill, the antithetical embodiment of pure will" (219).

Wilson's gesture of representing a "fallen" poor white woman as socially "black" yet racially white disrupts the conflation of blackness and servitude—race and condition—as they are represented to converge in the figure of the black mother. In this sense, Wilson signals that the equation of blackness and enslavement is a discursive and legal "marriage," a miscegenation of terms. By tracing the source of Frado's blackness and Africanity through Jim's paternity and originating her subsequent servitude with Mag, Wilson is simultaneously denaturalizing the legal and discursive presumption of blackness with servitude and "rescuing," if you will, the black mother from originary blame.

If, as I'm suggesting, the law of *partus sequitir ventrem* constitutes in large part the "slavery's shadows" of the novel's title page, the law itself is a shadowy (mis)representation of black women's sexual violation. Recalling Lacan's figurations of the "black but comely" Shulamite bride in the biblical Song of Songs and the "poor but honest" prostitute on the auction block, Wilson's rewriting of *partus sequitir ventrem* revolves around a signifier in which "meaning 'insists'" but does not "consist": [11] Wilson ultimately voices a story that remains to be told. In the preface, she writes that she has "purposely omitted what would most provoke shame in our good anti-slavery friends at home." And again at the end of the novel proper, the narrator exhorts the reader with respect to Frado to "refuse not, because some part of her history is unknown, save by the Omniscient God. Enough has been unrolled to demand your sympathy and aid" (130). Through multiple dizzying displacements and disruptions, the text announces its own omissions, utters its own silences. Wilson is perhaps alerting us that the silences, the missing history, is precisely where the Real story begins.

NOTES

A version of this paper was presented at Stanford University as a part of a series entitled "'Race,' Racial Representation and the Nineteenth Century Literary Imagination" on April 22, 1994.

1. The full title is *Our Nig; or, Sketches from the Life of a Free Black, in a Two-Story White House, North. Showing that Slavery's Shadows Fall Even There. By "Our Nig."* Henry Louis Gates Jr. identified the author as Harriet E. Wilson and documented that she was, in fact, a black woman. The details of his scholarly investigation are recounted in the introduction to his edition of the novel (New York: Random House, 1983), vii–lix. All citations from the novel will be taken from this edition. Other important treatments include Hazel V. Carby, *Reconstructing Womanhood: The Emergence of the Afro-American Woman Novelist* (New York: Oxford University Press, 1987); Claudia Tate, *Domestic Allegories of Political Desire: The Black Heroine at the Turn of the Century* (New York: Oxford University Press, 1992); and Ann duCille, *The Coupling Convention: Sex, Text, and Tradition in Black Women's Fiction* (New York: Oxford University Press, 1993).

2. Toni Morrison, *Playing in the Dark: Whiteness and the Literary Imagination* (Cambridge, Mass.: Harvard University Press, 1992), 4.

3. I do not assume a correspondence between the novelist Wilson, the character Frado, and the narrator of Our Nig—not because a relationship does not exist but because it is so complex as to be unproductive for analysis. For me, *Our Nig* is less "a fictional third-person autobiography" as Henry Louis Gates claims in the introduction to his edition, and more what Audre Lorde calls in *Zami* a "biomythography." That is, *Our Nig* posits "life" producing "myth" even as it assumes mythmaking as central to the construction of subjectivity. In this vein, I emphasize the "novelness" of the text as a way of countering a prevailing tendency to see it as rather simplistically "autobiography."

4. I use the term *racializing* rather than *racial* here to signal the ways in which the construction of African peoples into a black "race" involved a process of othering vis-à-vis whiteness. By understanding "race" as a process of othering, I allow for the possibility of a different set of "racial" meanings on the part of African Americans themselves.

5. Barbara Christian, "The Race for Theory," *Cultural Critique* 6 (spring 1987): 52.

6. Mae Gwendolyn Henderson, "Speaking in Tongues: Dialogics, Dialectics, and the Black Woman Writer's Literary Tradition," in *Changing Our Own Words: Essays on Criticism, Theory, and Writing By Black Women,* ed. Cheryl A. Wall (New Brunswick: Rutgers University Press, 1989), 35.

7. For an excellent treatment of black women's interpretive relationship to the

Bible, see Renita J. Weems, "Reading Her Way Through the Struggle: African American Women and the Bible," in *Stony the Road We Trod: African American Biblical Interpretation*, ed. Cain Hope Felder (Minneapolis: Fortress Press, 1991), 57–77.

8. The law is cited in A. Leon Higginbotham Jr., *In the Matter of Color: Race and the American Legal Process, the Colonial Period* (Oxford: Oxford University Press, 1978). For an excellent black feminist psychoanalytic exploration of these issues, see Hortense J. Spillers, "Mama's Baby, Papa's Maybe: An American Grammar Book," *Diacritics* 17 (summer 1987): 65–81.

9. It is important to note here that what has actually taken place is a crude conflation of the biblical misreading of the Noah story (which posited Noah's curse of his third son Ham as the rationale for the enslavement of African peoples) with the Eve myth. On the use of the Noah text in Genesis see Winthrop Jordan, *White over Black: American Attitudes toward the Negro, 1550–1812* (New York: W. W. Norton, 1977). This issue has been of particular interest to African American scholars in religious studies who have treated the subject extensively. See especially Charles B. Copher, "Three Thousand Years of Biblical Interpretation with Reference to Black Peoples," in *African American Religious Studies: An Interdisciplinary Anthology*, ed. Gayraud S. Wilmore (Durham, N.C.: Duke University Press, 1989), 105–28; Riggins R. Earl Jr., *Dark Symbols, Obscure Signs: God, Self, and Community in the Slave Mind* (Marybell, N.Y.: Orbis, 1993); and Theophus H. Smith, *Conjuring Culture: Biblical Formations of Black America* (New York: Oxford University Press, 1994).

10. Patricia J. Williams, *The Alchemy of Race and Rights: Diary of a Law Professor* (Cambridge, Mass.: Harvard University Press, 1991), 226–27.

11. Jacques Lacan, *Ecrits: A Selection*, trans. Alan Sheridan (New York: W. W. Norton, 1977), 153.

Redeeming History
Toni Morrison's *Beloved*

Helene Moglen

Since the twinned birth of bourgeois capitalism and the novel in the eighteenth century, realism and fantasy have represented the Janus-faced Enlightenment through their several genres, constituting each other as fictive modes while appearing to be mutually exclusive.[1] Functioning to illuminate the shadow side of individualism, rationalism, and social progress, early fantastic fictions revealed the price paid for the increasing rigidity of epistemological, social, sexual, and racial boundaries. In gothic fictions written at the end of the eighteenth and in the beginning of the nineteenth centuries, the anxieties and wishes that had been excluded from realistic narratives in the interests of personal and social identity appeared in supernatural form to belie realism's myths of finished bodies, linear histories, distinct differences, and integrated texts.[2] Then, as realistic fictions of the nineteenth century employed social, sexual, and racial "others" thematically in order to mediate external and internal conflict, fantastic fictions became more psychologically focused, and dissolved the distinction between self and other by revealing how the Other serves as an instrument in the construction of the self.[3] It is possible to read, as part of this discourse of differentiation and subjectification, both Freud's theoretical narratives and the revisions of them phrased by Anglo-American and French feminists, as well as by Lacan. Reading the theory and the fiction as expressive of the same tradition helps us to understand the power of the fantastic to map the social and psychological relations of self and other, as well as the genre's tendency to enmesh itself in the obsessional dynamic it explores. Adopting this approach, I wish to show how in *Beloved,* Toni Morrison significantly reconceptualizes the psychological dynamic of differentiation and the social consequences of othering by radically interrogating the fantastic tradition within which she also writes.

At the border of the unconscious and the conscious—or, in Lacanian terms, at an edge between the Imaginary and the Symbolic—the fantastic, through all of its genres, struggles to undo the processes of signification and differentiation that are fundamental to psychological and social experience. Its narratives reflect the encounter between the I and the not-I that takes place in the development and enculturation of the self. For Freud, the process of differentiation is staged at a moment between primary narcissism and object love. Lacan names it the "mirror stage," a phase of the Imaginary that he locates between the chaos of the Real and the formal structures of the Symbolic. It is here that the self comes to know itself as object, as if it were reflected in the gaze of others. Freud's superego is born here, as is Lacan's ego-ideal (*Je-idéal*). For both Lacan and Freud, this is the social self that watches, reproaches, and directs, enforcing the systems of cultural difference that are rooted in psychic differentiation. While realism expresses the boundaried aspirations of that self, the fantastic voices its desire to return to the wholeness that existed before the fall into fragmented subjectivity and cultural difference. While the realistic narrative thematizes a rational cultural order, the fantastic reproduces the contradictory strategies that the subject employs both to heal and to deny its alienation. Anxieties aroused by psychic fragmentation are projected in fantasy onto others who are then distinguished as radically different from the self, at the same time that the differences that threaten the ego's integrity are denied and union with the Other, who represents those differences, is experienced as essential for the self's completion. In the first instance, the Other is the object of intense fear and hatred; in the second, an object of equally intense desire. And although the resolution to the quandary of the self—caught as it is between fear and desire—ostensibly takes place with the entry of the subject into the Symbolic Order, that resolution is necessarily undermined by the deeper psychic functions that determine it but which it knows only in a mediated form. Always resistant, the fantastic narrative may be subsumed under but cannot be merged with its realistic Other, and when it is itself the dominant mode, it ends inevitably with dissolution or in death—the only gestures capable of finally interrupting the repetitive cycle that denies alterity while affirming it.[4]

The process of differentiation through which the subject is constructed finds stark expression in the fears of difference that inform sexual, racial, and socioeconomic stereotypes.[5] These fears not only structure fantastic fictions; they also permeate the theories we deploy to understand psychic anxieties and their fictive representations. So, in psychoanalytic theory, cultural misogyny pervades the developmental story, and woman, as the phobic object, is perceived both as castrated and castrating. Addressing cultural and personal misogyny in their rewritings of that story, American feminists have used object relations theory to give originary force to the mother-child dyad instead of to the oedipal triangle. Tracing different processes of differentiation, and therefore different relational patterns for women than for men, they have explored the implications of such differences for cognitive styles, moral philosophies, and sexual practices.[6] Significant as this work has been, its tendency merely to reverse the marginal and dominant terms of the developmental narrative—substituting male for female, female for male—has strengthened a dynamic that ensures the reproduction of stereotypical thinking. Developmental accounts of the construction of racial identities have been oppositional in similarly problematic ways. For example, Frantz Fanon insists upon the connection between psychic development and cultural psychosis, and grounds the "massive psychoexistential complex" of racism in the "subjective insecurity" of separation anxiety and the radical experience of fragmentation (55). Citing Lacan, he argues that the white man is threatened by the black man with the destructuration of his bodily image, while the black man rejects the black Imaginary for a white ego-ideal and is doomed to seek from his white Other the fundamental recognition that is inevitably withheld (161).[7] While Homi Bhabha changes the site of othering in his extension of Fanon's Lacanian argument, he does not disrupt the mirroring dynamic. Insisting upon the ways in which stereotypical relations are based, for both the colonizer and the colonized, on an alienation within identity, he emphasizes not the relation of self and Other, but the otherness of the self. The native subject whom the colonizer defines at once as harmlessly primitive and terrifyingly savage serves in his judgment as a fetish object similar to the phallic mother in Freud's account. In both cases, the fetish allows the assertion and disavowal of difference that threatens psychic wholeness, and offers a compromise that reinforces while it veils the regressive struggle of alterity. In racial as in sexual terms, therefore, the closed cycle of subjectification that is rooted in the Imaginary comes to seem as unalterable as it is determinant.

The point is that feminist and racially centered psychoanalytic theories have provided readings of the dynamic of othering that, while helpful in accounting for the deep structure of stereotypes, have also tended to reproduce the dyadic thinking which it has been their project to interrogate. Like the gothic fictions from which they have descended, these revisionary narratives rehearse the hallucinatory delusions of the Imaginary and participate in the shared psychosis of the cultural Symbolic. With other fantastic readings of ideology and desire, they reveal the difficulty that we always have in locating a world elsewhere—a place to stand from which to see the social and psychic landscape as not only changing but as available to change. They suggest the extent to which the limits and possibilities of the fantastic conception are in large part established by perspectival positionings *within* the dominant ideologies that are interrogated. Although it is true that fantasy seeks to name the unnameable, that which is named implicitly as real determines what can be imagined as unspoken. Exclusions shape inclusions, as we know, and both are products of the belief systems through which they are conceived. So Rochester's mad wife marks with her voicelessness the limit of a proper woman's speech. Conrad projects the heart of darkness, but leaves it to others to map its specificities. And while Melville may well have set out to interrogate the ideology of whiteness in *Moby-Dick*, he could not, any more than Ahab, move beyond it, as in writing *Benito Cereno* he could not enter Babo's mind but only imagined him enacting as masquerade the white idea of blackness.[8]

In the American and European traditions, the ideologies that have defined realism and its fantastic double have been largely white, heterosexual, male, and middle-class. Though differently conceptualized in terms of gender, female-authored writings in this genre have reflected the same dominant sexual, racial, and socioeconomic relations. Exploring the conflictual dynamic of race from the perspective of the racial Other, Fanon and Homi Bhabha were able to revise significantly the mindscapes of Lacan and Freud. But because they did not interrogate the gender bias that they inherited, their blind spots remained structurally the same. Defining the struggle of racial identity at the level of the male Imaginary, they did not move beyond their oppositional definitions to resist the fetishizing phallicism of psychoanalytic theory. Inevitably, this affected not only their analyses of the relations of race, but also their treatments of the then-secondary othernesses of gender and of class. The subject that they define is universalized in its maleness and embedded in a history that, as psychology's Other, is appropriated and erased.[9]

To achieve a more adequate and more emancipatory understanding of difference, we must refuse theoretical binarisms and insist upon the centrality of history in our analyses. The social relations of a culture are not simply oppositional, as we know, but are multiple and complexly interactive. Desire is performed within history at the intersections of gender, race, sexuality, and class, and although there are no epistemological positions at this level outside of those relations, there are many shifting and even contradictory positions within them. Further, the history of the subject is not limited, in Lacanian terms, to the Imaginary and Symbolic but extends backward to the moment of the Real. To travel back through the mirror of the Imaginary toward that primal space is to claim another dimension of self-formation that underlies and resists the dynamic of othering. In the fundamentally misogynistic mode of the fantastic, that moment has been ambivalently identified with the primal mother: the origin of all difference and the site of ultimate loss, so powerful that her presence can never be directly known but only mediated through the fears and longings of her sons and daughters. The fantastic narrative seems to gesture always toward her at the same time that it veils her in obscurity. Like the whiteness of Moby Dick and the blackness of Conrad's Africa, she is thought to mark all difference that is the absence of differentiation; she holds the promise of all meaning that is also the threat of meaninglessness. She reveals the fetishizing nature of language, the impotence of the symbolic: the unmasking of the ideal of whiteness as illusion. Asocial, she is outside of history. Apolitical, she neither changes nor can she be responsible for change. She is often represented by the death wish that erases resistance, and in this form she overwhelms the subversive impulses of the fantastic in its many genres.

In *Beloved,* Toni Morrison lifts the primal mother out of that prelinguistic space and returns her to history, exploring the complexities of her social construction at the same time that she deepens our understanding of the place within the self from which that mythic figure is believed to come. By centering in her narrative a black woman who is, not incidentally, a mother, Morrison documents the tragic human cost of being "other," and takes us into the dim regions of desubjectification and undifferentiation that were not explored by Freud or by Lacan. As a result, she refuses the conventional oppositions of realism and the fantastic, of the Symbolic and the Imaginary, and of the sociopolitical and the psychological. Moving beyond the Fanonian conception of *The Bluest Eye,* which largely assumed a black subjectivity constructed in relation to a white ego-ideal, Morrison asks more radical questions about the construction, destruction, and reconstruction of a socioeconomic, gendered, and racial subject. In a work that is the product of both romance and realism—neither romantic realism nor realistic romance—a whole tradition is, in effect, revised: Bertha speaks, the heart of darkness is illuminated, and Ahab encounters Moby Dick and lives. By reconceptualizing the relation of the genres that she writes within, Morrison radicalizes both realism and the fantastic, and establishes new structures through which to reproduce and to reeducate desire.

In a "Conversation" with Gloria Naylor, Toni Morrison explains that *Beloved* was inspired by the stories of two quite different women. One was the story of Margaret Garner, a slave who attempted the murder of her four children— successfully killing only her baby daughter—when she was caught as a fugitive: "She had made up her mind that they would not suffer the way that she had and it was better for them to die" (584). The other was the story of an eighteen-year-old girl shot by a jealous lover. The girl ensured his escape with her silence, but deprived of medical care, she paid for her silence with her life. Morrison was interested in the "female form of love" that these two historical figures exemplified, suggesting to her as they did that "the best thing that is in us is also the thing that makes us sabotage ourselves" (585). In considering "what it is that compels a good woman to displace . . . her self," Morrison imagined the psychic selves of her historical subjects not as integral and whole, but rather as internally divided. Projecting the self as other *to* itself—as "a *twin* or a thirst or a friend"—Morrison conceptualized *Beloved* in the fantastic mode while giving it a realistic reference. She followed the tradition of early gothic in conceptualizing the split-off self as a supernatural spirit that lives into the present after death, marking in its own immateriality the materiality of history; and she follows the romantic tradition by projecting it also as a ghostly double that enacts fragmentation and alienation, mirroring "others," who are also projections of the self and are themselves internally divided.

Serving both of these fantastic functions, Beloved is literally the ghost in the machine of Morrison's fiction. She is the haunting spirit of the baby daughter whom Sethe as a captured fugitive kills. She is that part of Sethe that, truncated, cannot be adequately mourned: a profound rupture that cannot be healed. She is the other of the others—of Sethe's daughter, Denver, and of Paul D, Sethe's lover—evoked by their desire from a place beneath blocked memory. But Beloved is also more than this, and it is here that Morrison situates herself at the boundary of fantasy and realism: she is the representative of the "sixty million and more" victims of slavery: of a collective tragedy that, as history, must be remembered and redeemed. Beloved's story is a story of personal and collective loss: the deprivation of home, abandonment by an enslaved mother, the erasure of a disinherited father, the alienation of her body in rape and of her mind in the shattering of the mirror of identity.

If Beloved speaks to the inadequacies of memory in its efforts to retrieve a personal and collective past, she speaks even more powerfully, through her mediations, to the risks and dangers of forgetting.[10] To repress memory, "to keep the past at bay," is to divert it into the dark silences and crippling diversions of hysteria: Denver's two-year muteness after she discovers from a classmate that her mother murdered her baby sister; Sethe's stammer, from the time of her own mother's lynching to the time when she meets and falls in love with Halle; Halle's madness after he witnesses Sethe's violation; Paul D, who "locks away his heart in a tobacco tin buried in his chest" and "shuts down a generous portion of his head" in order to avoid reliving the symbolic castration of his imprisonment; and Baby Suggs, who takes to her bed after the murder of her grandchild, to ponder color: the color that Sethe, after she saws off the head of her baby, is no longer able to see. Paul D can urge Sethe to remember—"Go as far inside as you need to, I'll hold your ankles. Make sure you get back out" (46)—but the truth is that neither of them can confront in themselves that which would make it possible for each to listen to and hear the other. For those who have survived the collective trauma of racism, "the day's serious work is beating back the past" (73).

The hysteria that allows the self to survive, but not to prosper, mirrors the cultural psychosis that is its cause. As hysteria signs itself as an inability to represent, cultural psychosis articulates itself as a disease of representation. The compromises sought by fears of psychic fragmentation are achieved through representational systems that order difference at specific historical moments on behalf of hegemonic interests. Through mutually constitutive discourses of sexuality, race, class, and gender, some subjects are marked collectively as phobic objects. Schoolteacher, the slave-master who inherits Sweet Home along with Sethe, Paul D, and Halle, beats one of his black men "to show him that definitions belong to the definers, not to the defined" (190), but the power relations of representation are revealed as more complex than Schoolteacher's arrogance allows. In fixing the "other," one fixes oneself as the Other of the other. The fetishized object is shaped by fetishistic desire, and the need to objectify reproduces the fear of objectification that produces it. In the terms of *Beloved,* black men and women struggle to throw off the white imago that reflects them to themselves, while white women and men bind themselves inextricably to the grotesque doubles projected by their own irrational anxieties. Morrison's project is to explore the ways in which those who have been systematically deprived of psychic and social identities can in fact sustain and reinvent themselves, while she wishes also to reveal how those positioned as oppressors might not be doomed endlessly to repeat the fearful processes of their own de-subjectification.

Toward the end of *Beloved,* Stamp Paid—a former slave—listens to the "undecipherable language" that emanates from Sethe's house, and he identifies the mumbling voices as those of nameless black and angry dead bemoaning the psychic alienation imposed upon them by whites who had then to suffer it themselves:

> Whitepeople believed that whatever the manners, under every dark skin was a jungle. Swift unnavigable waters, swinging screaming baboons, sleeping snakes, red gums ready for their sweet white blood. In a way, he thought, they were right. The more coloredpeople spent their strength trying to convince them how gentle they were, how clever and loving, how human, the more they used themselves up to persuade whites of something Negroes believed could not be questioned, the deeper and more tangled the jungle grew inside. But it wasn't the jungle blacks brought with them to this place from the other (livable) place. It was the jungle whitefolks planted in them. And it grew. It spread. . . . [U]ntil it invaded the whites who had made it. Touched them every one. Changed and altered them. Made them bloody, silly, worse than even they wanted to be, so scared were they of the jungle they had made. The screaming baboon lived under their own white skin; the red gums were their own. (198–99)

Though Stamp Paid analyzes the causes of psychic fragmentation at the level of the Symbolic, the voices that he hears reveal a deeper level of meaning. Not nameless at all, these voices prove to belong to Sethe and Beloved, who are attempting in their bafflement to heal the deepest wounds of violent separation. In their encounter, which is grounded in the preoedipal rather than in the oedipal moment, the central presence is the mother's, not the father's, and the fetish object that is unveiled as fundamental is not the phallus—as Lacan and Freud would have it—but the lost signifier that is the breast: the milk-filled breast of the black woman. This is made clear in the novel's primal scene, which is staged by Schoolteacher with his nephews as an experiment intended to demonstrate the animality of blacks. Recalled by Sethe, it centers on "two boys with mossy teeth, one sucking on my breast the other holding me down, their book-reading teacher watching and writing it up" (70). It is a scene that haunts Sethe in her flight from Sweet Home, intent on bringing her milk to one infant daughter and bearing the other in freedom. And it is the memory of this scene that motivates her finally to murder. It is a scene that reduces Halle, who watches it, to a figure of childish impotence, "squatting by the churn smearing the butter as well as the clabber all over his face because the milk they took is on his mind" (70). A perversion of the primal scenes that Freud describes as marking the origins of the subject, sexuality, and sexual difference, this scene lays bare the whites' impulse to reject black subjectivity in order to eradicate the black roots of the white Imaginary.[11] A nursing that is also an enforced milking, an appropriation of maternal nurturance as eroticized violence, a parodic rewriting of the family connection: all reveal the knot of power, anger, fear, and desire that bind the white man to the black woman—the white child to the black breast.

We have come increasingly to recognize the significance of the nursemaid in Freud's work and, more broadly, in the late Victorian bourgeois male imagination.[12] Responsible for the child's most intimate functions, the nursemaid, despite her inferior status, had the power to shame, to discipline, and to arouse. Erotic and degrading, she opened the claustral cell of the nuclear family to social difference which, through her, was sexualized.[13] As the impure "other" of the maternal ideal, she was identified with infantile pleasure, anxiety, and dependence. The fascination and desire that she inspired were intensified by prohibition, and made resistant to the societal control by which they were deformed. In similarly deep and pervasive ways, the black slave woman haunted the cultural and personal Imaginary of the antebellum South. Often wet nurse as well as maid, she figured intimacy and was rejected as taboo. The locus of separation and the site of longing, she was the source of goodness, an object of repulsion, the promise of merging, and the mark of differentiation. To claim her, as Sethe is claimed, through a violent sexuality that reproduces while it denies her maternal connection, is to assert masculine and racial autonomy through incestuous transgression. A similar fetishistic act that disavows through degradation occurs when the chained male slaves—Paul D among them—are forced as a group to perform fellatio on their guards. It is a ritual of white male bonding intended to humiliate its victims by feminizing them, parodying while rehearsing the primal act of nurturance.

The material project of slavery, as *Beloved* makes clear, is the commodification of the black body; the psychic result is that body's sexualization. So Paul D, who believed he knew his value "as a laborer who could make profit on a farm," discovers, when he is sold by Schoolteacher from Sweet Home, "the dollar value of his weight, his strength, his heart, his brain, his penis, and his future" (226). Sethe's worth, like the worth of all black women, is greater than a male laborer's because she is also, crucially, a breeder: herself property, she reproduces property in her children. Without legal status or acknowledged familial connection, both male and female slaves are excluded from the world of social subjects. Defined biologically, they are, like animals, granted sexual function but not gender definition. Because they are represented ideologically as only "male" and "female," the roles of men and women are systematically denied them. But to be ideologically identified with nature is also to be identified with nature's otherness. The fears and desires associated with miscegenation and black potency—the white fetishization of the black breast and penis—reflect the power of that identification: the psychological cost of the material project. If the problem for white people, then, is the social and psychological management of negrophobia, the critical act of social and psychological resistance for black people involves a reclamation of sexual and cultural identity in the absence of social rights and privileges.[14] In laying bare the agonies of this process, Morrison extends and interrogates the accounts of subjectification that have been offered by male psychoanalytic theorists and by many psychoanalytic feminists.

As Morrison conceptualizes the process, it begins with the one social function that blacks cannot be denied in the nightmare world of slavery: that of mothering. Whereas males are called upon to act as studs, and as fathers are known generally in absence,[15] the fact of maternity continues to exist when all appurtenances are stripped away. Though the black patronymic is erased, the child inherits its mother's statusless condition. That inheritance paradoxically marks social affiliation and identity: historical continuity that originates in a place before othering. Although slave children are not the material possessions *of* their mother, they are, as Morrison suggests, possessed by her in the intensity of a relationship that resonates in memory. The story that Morrison tells provides a version—with important differences—of psychoanalytic narratives that, in their male and female forms, represent the mother as the irreducible matrix of the child's development: the unachievable object of a desire that cannot know but must forever seek its origins. For Freud, the maternal body grounds the recurrent experience of the uncanny, motivating the matrophobia that motivates the oedipal narrative. It is the home that is most intimately familiar and always strange. It holds the promise of blissful mergence and the threat of fearful obliteration. For Lacan, the mother is a more elusive figure who enables the child's entry into a world of language in which she must herself be always silent. Feminists who have attempted to reclaim that mother in their rereadings of Lacan and Freud have assumed similar postures of infantile dependence in creation myths that both idealize and blame her.[16] It is the same ambivalence that structures fantastic fictions: the male fear and desire before such fantasized omnipotence, as in Ahab's quest for Moby Dick; the female obsession with dead, displaced, and insane mothers whose power they must, at all costs, escape.[17]

Beloved removes this omnipotent and yet powerless mother from the place before desire and brings her into history in the figure of the black woman whose children are born into the alienated relations of slavery. Her story has many variations in the novel, but its shape is constant over time. She is remembered by Sethe as an aching absence: a distant, barely recognizable figure laboring in the fields; a body so disfigured in death that even the brand that marked her cannot be read. From another slave, Sethe learns of the spiritual and psychic violence, physically enacted, that characterized her life. Abduction first and rape; resistance staged in the murder of children born of violation, in thwarted efforts to escape, and in a nameless action that lynching punishes. Sethe seeks her in a series of substitutes: in Nan, the slave woman who nursed her after the white babies had drunk their fill; in Mrs. Garner, her mistress at Sweet Home; and finally in Baby Suggs. In her own life, Sethe attempts to fill her absence by providing as mother what she could not be provided as daughter, but she discovers that she is also implicated in the cycle of violence by which she was herself produced.

Deprived of a social identity and placed outside the law, Sethe conceives of herself as the primal mother has been conceived: not in and for herself but in relation to her children. Nourishing them, she nourishes herself; sustaining them, she sustains a gendered subjectivity that has them as its point of reference. She knows "that anybody white could take your whole self for anything that came to mind. Not just work, kill, or maim you, but dirty you. Dirty you so bad you forgot who you were and couldn't think it up" (251). But she believes that there is one part of herself that is excluded from that violation: "The best thing she was, was her children. Whites might dirty *her* all right, but not her best thing, her beautiful, magical best thing—the part of her that was clean" (251). When Schoolteacher and his nephews appropriate her maternal body, she discovers that there is no aspect of her self that is in fact secure against the violations of that society. Still, because she does not differentiate her children from herself, she believes that she can destroy them *by* herself when the alternative is to have them placed once more in the power of the master. For a moment, she claims the right to *be* the primal mother, giving and taking life without responsibility to another with a subjectivity not her own. It is from that mother that Sethe's two sons, Howard and Bugler, finally flee. It is Denver's fear of her that makes her mute, that gives her nightmares, that imprisons her in the yard, desperately attempting through her despairing love to forestall what happened once from happening again.

But because the primal mother is a mythic projection, she cannot be embodied any more than Sethe can be excluded or can exclude herself from a human community of rights and responsibilities. As Sethe comes to recognize when she thinks of Schoolteacher's book about the inferiority of blacks, "I made the ink, Paul D. He couldn't have done it if I hadn't made the ink" (271). It is through Beloved that Sethe learns the significance of her act because it is to her murdered daughter that she feels the need to justify the past. For Sethe, Beloved is the infant whom she bore into slavery; the child for whose liberty she was willing to sacrifice her life; the slaughtered innocent whose headstone she purchased with her body; the baby ghost whose spiteful presence gave her solace; and the spectral girl who embodies her own desire both as abandoning mother and as abandoned daughter. Though Beloved is all of this for Sethe—and something different for Denver and Paul D—Morrison is at pains to suggest the ways in which she is, like all "others," possessed of her own narrative and immersed in a collective history. In herself, she may be, as Paul D suggests, any "young coloredwoman . . . drifting from ruin" (52); or she may be the specific girl whom Stamp Paid remembers as "locked up in the house with a white man over by Deer Creek. . . . Folks say he had her in there since she was a pup" (235). Beloved tells a version of Stamp Paid's story to Denver, describing herself as "snatched away from a woman who was hers," and violated by the one "whiteman" whom she knew (119). In the transitional voice of the preconscious, speaking what she remembers not as words but as pictures, she tells of the Middle Passage— the journey from freedom to captivity—when the eternality of home and the unity of self were lost. The recurrent theme of all her stories suggests that whoever Beloved is, and whoever she is for others, her longing is the longing and her rage the rage of all children abandoned in untimely separation from their mothers and oppressed as others in an alien culture. Her need and her resentment reflect and answer to Sethe's own.

What Beloved, as daughter, wants from Sethe, and what Sethe, as daughter-mother, wants from Beloved, is the connection shattered in the mirror in which identity is achieved: a return to the place before othering—the place before desire. Beloved remembers the woman who, like Sethe's mother, never smiled at her; the mother who, like Sethe's mother, was collared and who, like Sethe herself, wore shining earrings. She remembers an Edenic moment of wholeness: "I am not separate from her there is no place where I stop her face is my own and I want to be there in the place where her face is and to be looking at it too a hot thing" (210). She remembers the instant when the unity was lost—an instant, for her mother, of suicide and, for herself, of a kind of psychic death: "I see the dark face that is going to smile at me . . . it is my dark face that is going to smile at me . . . she goes in the water with my face" (212). Before her rebirth into Sethe's life, she too dives beneath the water, into the mirror where, Narcissus-like, she sees the fragmented pieces that make up her self: "My face is coming I have to have it I am looking for the join I am loving my face so much my dark face is close to me I want to join . . . I want to be the two of us . . . I want the join" (213). When she emerges from the water, she believes that she has found in Sethe's face the face that she once lost. "She smiles at me and it is my own face smiling. I will not lose her again. She is mine" (214). And it is in Sethe that she submerges once again.

"Mine." It is the only word that Stamp Paid can make out in "the conflagration of hasty voices" that he hears as belonging to the dead. It is the word spoken initially—in a fantastic chorus—by Denver, Sethe, and Beloved. But Denver claims Beloved as "mine," because it is only from Beloved that she derives a sense of her own separateness. When Beloved looks at her, she experiences herself as a subject, "pulled into view by the interested, uncritical eye of the other" (118). Replacing the daddy for whom Denver longs, Beloved triangulates the suffocating dyadic relation that Denver has had with Sethe, and provides her a transitional space from which she can prepare herself to enter a social world in which the horror of her mother's past is known. But it is precisely because she wants to be recognized as integral that she is finally irrelevant to her mother and her sister, each of whom desires the other not in relation but in identity. For Beloved, "[Sethe] is the laugh. I am the laughter" (214). For Sethe, the blood that runs in Beloved's veins, the blood that she in desperation spilled, is also her own nurturing milk. It is a reciprocal desire that at first facilitates the healing retrieval of memory as Sethe, to give Beloved pleasure, tells stories of a past that had been shrouded previously in silence. But as they voice their pain, they speak increasingly to themselves and not to one another. Their feelings are not expressed in words but, as Stamp Paid recognizes, in sounds; their references, as Beloved observes, are imagistic. And as they follow their needs into a darkness before language, they are unable to find a direction back.

Denver realizes that the desire of each to return to a place in which she can merge with and possess the other initiates a life-and-death struggle that neither can survive. Beloved's voraciousness, which makes it seem to Denver that she has "invented desire," is clearly matched by Sethe's insatiable need to sustain at all costs the life that she had taken. "Sethe was trying to make up for the hand-saw; Beloved was making her pay for it. . . . Sethe didn't really want forgiveness given; she wanted it refused" (251, 252). As in many fantastic fictions, the urge to complete the self takes a perversely sadomasochistic turn that maintains both Sethe and Beloved on the border of mutual and self-destruction. Sethe, who gives her substance to Beloved, begins to starve to death. Beloved, pregnant with Paul D's child, swells also with Sethe's life, upon which—in its separateness—her own psychic survival depends.

In the relation between Beloved and Sethe, Morrison takes us to the place toward which the fantastic always gestures and from which realism shrinks.

It is a place similar to the one Kristeva has explored in her discussion of "abjection": a psychic state identified with the archaic experience of differentiation and grounded in the preoedipal moment named by Kristeva as the "semiotic." Existing at the border of language and desire, abjection cannot be grasped by the linear logic of realism, but—affective and heterogeneous—it resonates with the impulses of the fantastic. It is accessible directly through social and psychological processes of de-subjectification and can be reached as well through the mediative power of poetry and religion. A place of horror that is also transformative, the abject unveils the void upon which the signifying process relies. Revealing the primary fetishism of language, it also provides, in the pure signifiers of its own semiotic discourse, evidence of a sign system that is not linguistically based.[18]

In *Powers of Horror,* Kristeva describes the way in which individuals located at the border between neurosis and psychosis return to a state of abjection in order to initiate their projects of psychic reparation. By accepting "the first authentic feeling of a subject in the process of constituting itself," they can begin to experience desire and engage "what will become, but only later, objects" (47). In *Beloved,* at the intersection of realism and fantasy, Morrison maps a similar progress at a specific historical moment. In her exploration of the deconstructive and reconstructive processes of subjectification, she provides a reading of what Fanon called the "massive psychoexistential complex" of racism (55), breaking through the obsessive cycle of the Imaginary and opening out the oppositional relations of desire. She shows how the racial and sexual othernesses of the Symbolic originate in archaic fear and aggression, which, in the preoedipal relation, project as threatening to the self a yet-unlocalizable object. It is the fear that precedes desire (primary narcissism later masked as incest) that Schoolteacher and his nephews seek to contain. By constructing the boundaries of their subjectivities through transgression, they deconstruct—at material and psychic levels—the subjectivities of the defiled others. As the othered others, Sethe and Paul D struggle by evading memory to evade the abjection to which they have been reduced; but like the patients of whom Kristeva writes, they can move out of the abyss only by traveling through it. Beloved serves as the intermediary in their voyages: a split-off fragment of themselves that, as both plenitude and absence, represents the promise and horror of the archaic world in which subjectification begins.

Priced, sold, chained, and collared, Paul D learns that manhood cannot "lie in the naming done by a whiteman who was supposed to know," for Schoolteacher can erase the honorific "man," bestowed by Garner, and "break into children what Garner had raised into men" (220). Everything, Paul D learns, rested on Garner's being alive, for "without his life, each of theirs fell to pieces. Now ain't that slavery, or what is it?" (220). Enduring the loss of his brothers, the lynching of one friend, and the imposed madness of another, Paul D knows the rooster, Mister, to be "freer, better than me. Stronger. Tougher" (72). On the chain gang, he is reduced to a state of abject fear from which he runs as a fugitive, locking his memories "in that tobacco tin buried in his chest where a red heart used to be" (72–73). There is no past to ground him, and he is filled with awe and envy when he hears of other people's families. He comes to believe that he can only find the core of his manhood in paternity, and asks Sethe to bear his child. It would be a way, he thinks, "to hold on to her, document his manhood and break out of the girl's spell—all in one" (128). But Beloved's spell must be endured. Beloved moves him like a "rag doll," out of Sethe's bed and from her house. What he feels for her ("young enough to be his daughter") is some "life hunger," more primal than desire. "She reminds me of something," he thinks. "Something look like I'm supposed to remember" (234). And although he feels that he is lost if he acknowledges his connection to her, it is a loss that he must plumb if he is to find himself. When he responds finally to her plea— "I want you to touch me on the inside part and call me my name" (116)— "he didn't hear the whisper that the flakes of rust made . . . as they fell away from the seams of his tobacco tin. So when the lid gave he didn't know it" (117). What he experiences as an incestuous desire proves to be a profoundly renewing encounter: "Afterward, beached and gobbling air, in the midst of repulsion and personal shame, he was thankful too for having been escorted to some ocean-deep place he once belonged to" (264). In the place before memory and desire—the place of primary narcissism that is only later marked as incest—he affirms the qualities in himself that have always made it possible for him to hear the secrets of women. Empathic still, but purged of fear, Paul D can now feel Sethe's need without judging it by his own. On the other side of the mirror, he can bathe and hold her, knowing that "she is her own best thing," "a friend of his mind," and "the object of his desire" (273). And Sethe can accept Paul D's story "next to" hers because she has not drowned in the "ocean-deep" place of her relation to Beloved: the place of abjection that is both the cause and, for the "others," the result of the cultural psychosis of racism.

Sethe is saved from drowning, and her fantastic story given social shape, through the intervention of another maternal narrative: that of Baby Suggs. This narrative traces a path from the semiotic to the Symbolic that avoids the suffocating solipsism of abjection and pries open the appropriative cycle of the Imaginary. The movement is propelled by a fluid spirituality that refuses the religious codes of prohibition and taboo.[19] Like Sethe, Baby Suggs has beaten back her past, which, "like her present, had been intolerable" (5). But little as she can remember of her children—all but Halle sold away— she knows still less about herself, since "she never had the map to discover what she was like" (140). When her freedom is bought by the loving labor of her son, she is finally able to possess her self, affirming a sense of "mine" that challenges the "mine" of Beloved and Sethe. She recognizes that the hands that have served others belong in fact to her, and she laughs with joy to hear, for the first time, her own heart beating. As an unchurched preacher, she lets that great heart beat in the presence of the community and makes of the Clearing a holy place. Mother-midwife, she restores the despised others to themselves by teaching them how to embrace their bodies, hearts, and minds, understanding that "the only grace they could have was the grace they could imagine" (88). She recognizes them not only in their othernesses but also as a collectivity. The process of discovery that she initiates in them signifies itself not only in the call and response that sounds connection, but also through the pure expressiveness of the body and in the pleasures of the senses: in dance, in music, in laughter, and in tears, all shared in a ritual of inclusion. And although her teachings cannot prevent the jealousy and resentment that lead to Sethe's betrayal, the images of this time persist, hidden in the minds of those to whom they once belonged. When thirty women respond to Denver's need and come to save Sethe from the ghostly past that is destroying her, "the first thing that they saw was not Denver sitting on the steps, but themselves" as the children they had been, "young and happy, playing in Baby Suggs' yard, not feeling the envy that surfaced the next day" (258). For Sethe, who watches them arrive, "it was as though the Clearing had come to her with all its heat and simmering leaves, where the voices of women searched for the right combination, the key, the code, the sound that broke the back of words" (261). The enactment of collective memory rooted in the semiotic transforms a timeless present into a future of possibilities by redeeming the past.

The knowledge which is identified in *Beloved* with this aspect of the maternal body, although primal, is powerfully enacted within history. It is an affective knowledge, more expressive than language and deeper than desire, that sustains Baby Suggs, despite despair, through her appetite for color. It is this same knowledge that invests the words "Oh, baby," spoken to Denver by Lady Jones, with a softness and kindness that "inaugurate[s] her life in the world as a woman" (248). With the others who give Denver food and facilitate, with their stories of Baby Suggs, the making of a past, Lady Jones provides another version of this maternal presence that allows relation in separateness. Hers is a knowledge shared by those who have few stakes in reproducing the power relations of the cultural Imaginary and Symbolic: black women most of all, but also black men like Paul D, Halle, and Stamp Paid, and all those others who, by extending the boundaries of community, refute implicitly the view that relations of otherness are necessarily oppositional. The territory of connection is identified early in the fiction when, at Denver's birth, Amy and Sethe together enact a meaning that breaks the back of words: "There on a summer night surrounded by bluefern they did something together appropriately and well . . . a slave and a barefoot whitewoman with unpinned hair . . . wrapping a ten-minute-old baby in the rags they wore. . . . The water sucked and swallowed itself beneath them. There was nothing to disturb them at their work. So they did it appropriately and well" (84–85).

The image of this scene, recalled repeatedly by Sethe and memorialized in Denver's name, is the only social reference that Denver has until she steps off the edge of the world that is Sethe's yard, to seek help for her mother and Beloved. Its social meaning is reaffirmed across three generations by Mrs. Bodwin, who finally rescripts Schoolteacher's role when she performs her own "experiment," educating Denver for college.

It is, then, the doubled figure of the black mother—for Sethe and Baby Suggs can be read in the tradition of the fantastic as twinned versions of the maternal presence—that Morrison uses to redefine the relation of romance and realism: the psychological and social. Refusing to cede precedence to one, she necessarily redefines the nature of both. By demonstrating how realism brings the translinguistic meanings of the semiotic into the coherent structures of the Symbolic, she also shows how the profound complexity of psychic life is historically formed and historically enacted. While Beloved must be sacrificed if Sethe is to be socially integrated, she continues to exist as do the images of all past events, "not just in rememory, but out there, in the world" (36): the world of the cultural semiotic. Beloved's fantastic story is "not a story to pass on," for it can neither propel nor extend the narrative that it suffuses. At the end, although Beloved is "disremembered and unaccounted for," she must remain always on the edge of evocation. As the novel teaches us so powerfully, the elusive erotics of connectedness necessarily underlies, as it potentially disrupts, the socially structured erotics of desire.

NOTES

I am particularly grateful to Elizabeth Abel, Myra Jehlen, Evelyn Keller, and Seth Moglen for their careful readings of the essay as well as for their warm support of this as other of my projects. I am also grateful for faculty research funds granted by the University of California, Santa Cruz.

"Redeeming History: Toni Morrison's *Beloved*" was originally published in *Cultural Critique* 24 (1993): 17–40. Reprinted by permission of Oxford University Press.

1. In his book *The Fantastic,* Tzvetan Todorov defines the fantastic as a genre and analyzes it in terms of the hesitation experienced by a person who is familiar with the laws of nature when he or she encounters a supernatural event. That feeling of hesitation can be resolved on the level of the uncanny (the supernatural explained) or the marvelous (the supernatural accepted), but in the case of the pure fantastic— *The Turn of the Screw* provides him an example—it is not resolved at all. Texts that induce this form of hesitation are, for Todorov, genuinely subversive in that they offer a sense of the transgression of boundaries, a shocking experience of limits. I follow

Rosemary Jackson, rather than Todorov, in defining the fantastic not as a genre but as a literary mode of writing productive of a range of genres that themselves produce, regulate, and structure desire. With Jackson, I am interested in exploring the psychoanalytic implications of the fantastic, but I diverge from her in my concern for the ways in which the fantastic can help us to extend psychoanalytic readings to illuminate the relation of gender, race, and class to the construction of subjectivity.

2. One would include in a list of significant early gothic novels, for example, Horace Walpole's *The Castle of Otranto,* Charles Brockden Brown's *Wieland; or The Transformation,* Matthew Lewis's *The Monk,* and Anne Radcliffe's *The Italian* and *The Mysteries of Udolpho.* Though the genre of romance dominates the fantastic mode in the nineteenth century, the absurd might be said to represent the other side of modernism—which replaces the real—whereas magical realism represents the dominant, dark side of postmodernism.

3. Some of the relevant English texts in this category are *Frankenstein, Wuthering Heights, Dr. Jekyll and Mr. Hyde,* and *Dracula;* in America, *Moby-Dick, Benito Cereno,* and the tales of Poe and Hawthorne.

4. For example, the stories of the madwoman in *Jane Eyre* and the nun in *Villette,* as well as those of the criminals and sexually rebellious women throughout Dickens's novels, are relevant here.

5. In his book *Difference and Pathology,* Sander Gilman suggests that the deep structure of the stereotype is rooted in the individuation process when the child projects both a good and a bad self in order to reflect its sense of control or lack of control of the external world. These crude mental representations "perpetuate a needed sense of the difference between the 'self' and the 'object,' which becomes the 'other'" (18). The complexity of the stereotype derives from the social context in which it is elaborated.

6. I am referring here to Nancy Chodorow, *The Reproduction of Mothering;* Jessica Benjamin, *The Bonds of Love;* Carol Gilligan, *In a Different Voice;* Evelyn Fox Keller, *Reflections on Gender and Science;* and Sara Ruddick, "Maternal Thinking."

7. Henry Louis Gates Jr. points out in his essay "Critical Fanonism" that Fanon does tend to contradict himself in his discussion of the construction of black and white subjectivity, sometimes taking the Lacanian perspective, sometimes treating black and white as fixed phenomenological points, and indicating at least once that the Antillean looking in the mirror sees himself as "neutral" in color. Gates valuably demonstrates the ways in which various theorists (Homi Bhabha, Abdul JanMohamed, Gayatri Spivak, and Albert Memmi) have elaborated the aspect of Fanon's argument that can be used in support of their own.

8. In her essay "Unspeakable Things Unspoken: The Afro-American Presence in American Literature," Morrison comments on the shaping influence of blackness as a present absence in nineteenth-century romance. She identifies Melville with Ahab in recognizing and struggling heroically with the horrors of the ideology of whiteness. It seems to me that Morrison is clearly writing in this romantic tradition, rather than in the tradition of magical realism, as some have thought. Indeed, Morrison expresses her own suspicion of the use of "magical realism" as a label for her novels in an interview with Christina Davis in *Présence Africaine.*

9. Abdul JanMohamed has argued similarly that Homi Bhabha erases the significant inequities of colonialist practice in his emphasis on the reciprocal oppositions

of the Imaginary. JanMohamed redefines the functioning of the Imaginary and the Symbolic in textual terms, however, without interrogating the psychoanalytic paradigm.

10. Stuart Hall writes: "The past that speaks is not simple and factual. Our relation to it, like the child's relation to the mother, is always already after the break" (226).

11. For Freud, the primal fantasies (primal scene, castration, seduction) are all related to problems of origin, "a representation of and a 'solution' to whatever constitutes a major enigma for the child. Whatever appears to the subject as a reality of such a type as to require an explanation or 'theory,' these phantasies dramatise into the primal moment or original point of departure of a history. In the 'primal scene,' it is the origin of the subject that is represented; in seduction phantasies, it is the origin or emergence of sexuality; in castration phantasies, the origin of the distinction between the sexes" (LaPlanche and Pontalis 332).

12. See Swann; Gallop; and Stallybrass and White.

13. Jane Gallop writes: "Class conflict and revolution are understood as a repetition of parent-child relations. This has always been the pernicious apoliticism of psychoanalysis. It has also been hard to argue against without totally rejecting psychoanalysis. . . . What is necessary to get beyond this dilemma is a recognition that the closed, cellular model of the family used in such psychoanalytic thinking is an idealization, a secondary revision of the family. The family never was, in any of Freud's texts, completely closed off from questions of economic class. And the most insistent locus of the intrusion into the family circle (intrusion of the symbolic into the imaginary) is the maid-governess-nurse. As Cixous says, 'she is the hole in the social cell'" (144).

14. In her important book *Reconstructing Womanhood,* Hazel Carby documents the ways in which African American women intellectuals both used and resisted the ideology of white womanhood that had othered them, in order to define a discourse of black womanhood that allowed them to reclaim a gendered subjectivity.

15. Hortense Spillers has argued in "'The Permanent Obliquity of an In(pha)llibly Straight'" that the representation of incestuous desire in fictions about the black father and daughter speaks to the confusions that surround this relation as a result of the father's absence in slavery and in traditional black culture. In "Mama's Baby, Papa's Maybe," Spillers also interrogates psychoanalytic theory by considering the effect of slavery on African American kinship and gender structures, but the focus of her argument—and her conclusions—are quite different from my own.

16. See Chodorow and Contratto.

17. See Kahane.

18. As Kristeva describes it: "The abject is the violence of mourning for an 'object' that has always already been lost. The abject shatters the wall of repression and its judgments. It takes the ego back to its source on the abominable limits from which, in order to be, the ego has broken away—it assigns it a source in the non-ego, drive and death. Abjection is a resurrection that has gone through death (of the ego). It is an alchemy that transforms death drive into the start of life, of new significance" (15).

Kristeva finds justification for her assertion of the centrality of the discourse of abjection in Freud's theorization of the sign as including acoustic, tactile, and visual images. Whereas heterogeneity is contained in the Symbolic Order by the process of condensation which ensures the relation of word and visual image, Kristeva suggests that one can detect "an attempt at *direct semanticization* of acoustic, tactile, motor, visual, etc. coenesthesia" when condensation collapses, along with the oedipal triangle by which it is supported (53). Semanticization of this sort—present in everyday discourses and crucial in those of poetry and religion—belie Lacan's insistence upon the primacy of condensation in the signifying process and suggest the desirability of revising the oedipal paradigm of subjectification that Lacan affirms as central.

19. Kristeva writes: "It is within that undecidable space, logically coming before the choice of the sexual object, that the religious answer to abjection breaks in: defilement, taboo, or sin" (48).

WORKS CITED

Benjamin, Jessica. *The Bonds of Love: Psychoanalysis, Feminism, and the Problem of Domination.* New York: Pantheon, 1988.

Bhabha, Homi K. "The Other Question: Difference, Discrimination, and the Discourse of Colonialism." *Literature, Politics, and Theory: Papers from the Essex Conference, 1976–1984.* Ed. Francis Barker et al. London: Methuen, 1986. 148–72.

Carby, Hazel. *Reconstructing Womanhood: The Emergence of the Afro-American Woman Novelist.* New York: Oxford UP, 1987.

Chodorow, Nancy. *The Reproduction of Mothering: Psychoanalysis and the Sociology of Gender.* Berkeley: U of California P, 1978.

Chodorow, Nancy, and Susan Contratto. "The Fantasy of the Perfect Mother." *Rethinking the Family: Some Feminist Questions.* Ed. Barrie Thorne with Marilyn Yalom. New York: Longman, 1982. 54–75.

Davis, Christina. "Interview with Toni Morrison." *Présence Africaine* 145 (1988): 141–56.

Fanon, Frantz. *Black Skin, White Masks.* Trans. Charles Lam Markmann. New York: Grove, 1967.

Gallop, Jane. "Keys to Dora." *The Daughter's Seduction: Feminism and Psychoanalysis.* Ithaca: Cornell UP, 1982. 132–50.

Gates, Henry Louis, Jr. "Critical Fanonism." *Critical Inquiry* 17.3 (1991): 457–70.

Gilligan, Carol. *In a Different Voice: Psychological Theory and Women's Development.* Cambridge: Harvard UP, 1982.

Gilman, Sander. *Difference and Pathology: Stereotypes of Sexuality, Race, and Madness.* Ithaca: Cornell UP, 1985.

Hall, Stuart. "Cultural Identity and Diaspora." *Identity: Community, Culture, Difference.* Ed. Jonathan Rutherford. London: Lawrence and Wishart, 1990. 222–35.

Jackson, Rosemary. *Fantasy: The Literature of Subversion.* New York: Methuen, 1981.

JanMohamed, Abdul. "The Economy of Manichean Allegory: The Function of Racial Difference in Colonialist Literature." *Critical Inquiry* 12.4 (1985): 59–87.

Kahane, Claire. "The Gothic Mirror." *The (M)other Tongue: Essays in Feminist Psychoanalytic Interpretation.* Ed. Shirley Nelson Garner, Claire Kahane, and Madelon Sprengnether. Ithaca: Cornell UP, 1985. 334–51.

Keller, Evelyn Fox. *Reflections on Gender and Science.* New Haven: Yale UP, 1985.

Kristeva, Julia. *Powers of Horror: An Essay on Abjection.* Trans. Leon Roudiez. New York: Columbia UP, 1982.

LaPlanche, Jean, and J.-B. Pontalis. *The Language of Psycho-Analysis.* Trans. Donald
  Nicholson-Smith. New York: Norton, 1973.
Morrison, Toni. *Beloved.* New York: Knopf, 1987.
———. "Unspeakable Things Unspoken: The Afro-American Presence in American
  Literature." *Michigan Quarterly Review* 28.1 (1989): 1–34.
Naylor, Gloria, and Toni Morrison. "A Conversation." *Southern Review* 21.3 (1985):
  567–93.
Ruddick, Sara. "Maternal Thinking." *Feminist Studies* (Summer 1980): 342–67.
Spillers, Hortense. "Mama's Baby, Papa's Maybe: An American Grammar Book." *Di-
  acritics* 17.2 (1987): 65–81.
———. "'The Permanent Obliquity of an In(pha)llibly Straight': In the Time of the
  Daughters and the Fathers." *Changing Our Own Words: Essays on Criticism, Theory,
  and Writing by Black Women.* Ed. Cheryl Wall. New Brunswick: Rutgers UP, 1989.
  127–49.
Stallybrass, Peter, and Allon White. "The Maid and the Family Romance." *The Poli-
  tics and Poetics of Transgression.* London: Methuen, 1986.
Swann, Jim. "Mater and Nannie: Freud's Two Mothers and the Discovery of the Oedi-
  pus Complex." *American Imago* 31 (1974): 1–64.
Todorov, Tzvetan. *The Fantastic: A Structural Approach to a Literary Genre.* Trans.
  Richard Howard. Ithaca: Cornell UP, 1975.

III

Race, Psychoanalysis, and Female Desire

Re-Placing Race in (White) Psychoanalytic Discourse

Founding Narratives of Feminism

Jean Walton

1. INTRODUCTION

It has become a commonplace for psychoanalytic feminist scholars to return to the "great debate" of the 1920s and 1930s, when central figures in the movement explored the question of whether an autonomous model of female sexuality should or could be delineated as distinct from the male-based model that had been privileged in Freud's accounts. Indeed, this debate is recapitulated in diverse collections of essays, in which the arguments of the original protagonists in the debate are variously summarized (Freud, Jeanne Lampl-de Groot, Helene Deutsch, Ruth Mack Brunswick, Marie Bonaparte, Karen Horney, Ernest Jones, Joan Riviere, Melanie Klein), and then contemporary analysts or theorists take up the arguments anew, extending or revising conceptualizations of "female sexuality" in both clinical and applied areas of psychoanalysis.[1] Psychoanalysis has, in other words, been from its inception an explicit and obvious terrain for exploring and critiquing sexual and gendered difference. It has been both a tool for and obstacle to political intervention in gender and sexual oppression.

In contrast, until the work of Frantz Fanon in the 1950s, and, more recently, of other theorists in the last decade, psychoanalysis was not seriously considered a likely arena for the exploration and critique of racialized constructions of subjectivity.[2] As it was being institutionalized, psychoanalysis seemed to thrive on the "eternal problem" of how to extend and modify Freud's male-centered theories of sexual development so that they would be equally applicable to women, but it shrank from the charge that it was also focused too narrowly on the subjectivity of the white, European patients who provided the clinical material from which it was elaborated. It is as if the integrity of the psychoanalytic project was threatened by the treatment of perceived and fantasized racial difference as potentially constitutive of psychic development. Perhaps this integrity was, after all, based on psychoanalysis's unacknowledged racial whiteness.

A critic such as Bronislaw Malinowski, who questioned the ethnocentrism of psychoanalysis, was roundly and dismissively attacked by Ernest Jones in his 1928 review of the anthropologist's *Sex and Repression in Savage Society*. Malinowski's criticism of psychoanalysis, except for its evocation of the "savage" and "barbarous," seems just as valid and pressing today:

> The complex exclusively known to the Freudian school, and assumed by
> them to be universal, I mean the Oedipus complex, corresponds essentially
> to our patrilineal Aryan family with the developed *patria potestas,* buttressed
> by Roman law and Christian morals, and accentuated by the modern econo-
> mic conditions of the well-to-do bourgeoisie. Yet this complex is assumed to
> exist in every savage or barbarous society. This certainly cannot be correct.[3]

And elsewhere: "'It is obvious that the infantile conflicts will not be the same in the lavish nursery of the wealthy bourgeois as in the cabin of the peasant, or in the one-room tenement of the poor working man'" ("R" 369). To challenge the universality of the Oedipus conflict was to threaten the psychoanalytic enterprise at its very foundations; Jones had to deflect such an argument by diagnosing Malinowski's critique as a patient's "resistance" to a painful psychological truth: "Dr. Malinowski breaks out into a vigorous repudiation of the psycho-analytical views about the Oedipus complex, denounces them as 'metaphysical,' and commits a number of easily avoidable misunderstandings of my statements which present all the familiar marks of 'unconscious resistance'" ("R" 368); or by caricaturing his argument, then countering it by implying that the sampling of analysands upon which the Oedipus complex was based was much more diverse than Malinowski realized: "It all comes of the wicked psycho-analytic habit of restricting their observations to the upper classes of the large European cities and not taking into account other classes and other races. Whatever makes Dr. Malinowski think that this is so? Has he not even heard of the existence of free psycho-analytical clinics?" ("R" 368–69). Jones is not suggesting, of course, that the "savage" Trobrianders whose sexual life Malinowski constructs could be found seeking treatment in "free psycho-analytic clinics," but he does imply that patients who are to be found in such clinics (presumably the working classes and people of color) provide enough of a diverse sampling of humanity that conclusions based on them are applicable to people in all cultures, whatever their relative status in a given socioeconomic structure. Malinowski, who seemed at first to be an ally in demonstrating "the application of psychoanalytic methods to a savage race" (thereby proving these methods to be universal), had to be disowned by Jones because he "either denies altogether or reduces to the utmost shadowy proportions the three most fundamental tenets of psycho-analysis: the doctrines of infantile incest, of repression, and of the unconscious" ("R" 373). Early challenges to the andro-centrism of Freud's theories led to vigorous and extended engagement in the questions of how subjects become gendered and sexualized; but as Jones's review of Malinowski's book demonstrates, comparable criticisms of psy-choanalytic ethnocentrism had to be relegated to the "outside" of what was coming to be a powerful and influential institution, so that the question of how subjects become racialized could not even become a legitimate one within that institution.[4]

Indeed, with a few notable exceptions, little has been asked throughout the history of psychoanalysis about what kind of knowledge might be pro-duced if articulations of gendered subjectivity were considered in terms of their being dependent upon or imbricated in implicit assumptions about "whiteness" and "blackness," given that perceptions and fantasies of racial difference might form a significant axis of identity formation. In much of the early psychoanalytic literature, "femininity" or "masculinity" was coming to be understood as a "mature" stage, one attained after successfully com-pleting a developmental sequence that culminated in heterosexualized gen-dered adulthood.[5] In the cases I consider here, however, a racial subtext in-forms this developmental model, in which maturity also implies the full assumption of a heterosexualized *raced* adulthood; according to this model, one must be fully "white" (or perhaps fully one's "race," however that might locally be constructed) in order fully to become a subject. Such a subtext could not become explicit, perhaps because early psychoanalysts would have argued that a male-female binary is a much more "universal" one than a black-white binary insofar as all humans are assumed to grow up in a con-text where they are distinguished from one another by gender, and where one is constituted by one's identification within and desire across that bi-nary division. According to this argument, it would make sense to examine the impact of a gender division if one is attempting to elaborate (as the psy-choanalysts were) a "universal" understanding of the human psyche, of hu-man sexuality, of human desire and identification; but it would not make sense to interrogate how one identifies and desires as a racialized subject be-cause not everyone is presumed to grow up affected by a black-white binary.

And yet, psychoanalytic literature itself reveals that racialized binaries were and continue to be a reality in the world inhabited by Freud's patients and the patients of other psychoanalysts for as long as the institution has existed. Certainly this is the case for white Americans in a country with a history of a racialized slavery system, of racialized lynching practices, of racialized di-visions of labor, indeed, of a racialized history of child care, where the tasks of the "mother" so typically described in psychoanalytic accounts of early de-velopment (nursing, cleaning, eroticizing certain zones of the body, assist-ing in the acquisition of language, mediating in the mirror stage) were (and continue to be) undertaken by black women in the white slave-owning or servant-employing household. It could be argued that it is just as much the case for Europeans, whose fantasmatic life is permeated by the Orientalist and Africanist ideologies that underwrite and justify what, by the time psychoanalysis was in its nascent stages, had become a long and vexed history of European colonialist expansion and decline. Yet in most psychoanalytic literature, which was concerned almost exclusively with white subjects, racial difference was only an intermittent and peripheral focus of attention. It only came up when, as in the case of Jones's review of Malinowski, psychoanalysts responded to the way in which their assumptions were borrowed or challenged by anthropologists. Even in these instances, fantasized or perceived racial difference was still not relevant to an understanding of how the white European subject was constructed; "race" functioned rather as an untheorized but characteristic mark of a "primitive" culture that had not as yet been repressed by civilization and its discontents. "Race" was blackness, in other words, and seemed to have nothing to do with the "civilized" white human subject.

One need not even turn to the records of Jones's "free clinics" to find analysands who provided material with which racialized subjectivity could have been more explicitly theorized by psychoanalysis, even in the early years when the institution was being codified and consolidated as a scientific, clinical, and modernist institution. In the examples I consider at length here, the constructions of racial difference provided by these white analysands are so deeply imbricated in their sexual and gender identities that it is curious that the analysts, who are otherwise at pains to make significant contributions to the understanding of female subjectivity, treat the references to race as though they are irrelevant. Subsequent readers of these texts have participated in what has come to be a hegemonic silence on the issue of race; and feminists, whose investment in the "great debate" of the 1920s around gender and sexuality has been perhaps the deepest of all, are unwitting participants in this collusion.

2. (WHITE) FEMININITY AS A MASQUERADE IN JOAN RIVIERE

One of the most frequently cited essays of the great debate of the 1920s is Joan Riviere's 1929 paper "Womanliness as a Masquerade," which has repeatedly been deployed for its potential to deconstruct an essentialized notion of femininity and to characterize it as a "masquerade" in a phallic economy of desire that may or may not hide a repressed but potentially destabilizing female eroticism. As is evident from the work of Claire Johnston, Stephen Heath, Mary Ann Doane, John Fletcher, Teresa de Lauretis, and others, Riviere's essay (and Jacques Lacan's passing mention of masquerade in "The Meaning of the Phallus") has become a prime generative site for theoretical interventions in gendered subjectivity in the realm of feminist film theory. Elsewhere, Luce Irigaray draws upon the masquerade to posit a female desire that exceeds a dominant masculine economy; Judith Butler points up the extent to which the masquerade is indicative of a coercive heterocentric matrix; and Emily Apter critiques it, using it as a foil for her elaboration of a feminist ontology of femininity grounded in theories of female fetishism.[6]

Riviere's case study is indeed tantalizingly rich with implications; it provides a suggestive glimpse of the political and cultural milieu within which she practiced and wrote and could function as a crucial site at which to continue the project of historicizing the way in which psychoanalysis came to be institutionalized as a discursive and clinical instrument of control and resistance. Yet there is an explicit delineation of racial difference in the essay that has not been adequately explored; if feminists have mobilized Riviere's work to reconceptualize female subjectivity, they have not acknowledged how that subjectivity is a specifically white one, how it depends for its coherence on the figuring of black men and the elision of black women. As Mary Ann Doane has pointed out (though not with reference to Riviere), "The force of the category of race in the constitution of Otherness within psychoanalysis should not be underestimated. . . . Psychoanalysis can, from this point of view, be seen as a quite elaborate form of ethnography—as a writing of the ethnicity of the white Western psyche" (*FF* 211).

A brief review of the key features of Riviere's essay serves as a reminder of how striking it is that little has been made of its fantasy of racial difference. After announcing that she will demonstrate how "women who wish for masculinity may put on a mask of womanliness to avert anxiety and the retribution feared from men," Riviere introduces us to a "particular type of intellectual woman" whom she has been treating as a patient.[7] The unnamed subject of this case study is described as "an American woman engaged in work of a propagandist nature, which consisted principally in speaking and writing" ("W" 36). After every public performance, she is obsessed by a need for reassurance, which leads her "compulsively on any such occasion to seek some attention or complimentary notice from a man or men at the close of the proceedings in which she had taken part or been the principal figure; and it soon became evident that the men chosen for the purpose were always unmistakable father-figures" ("W" 36). Riviere goes on to say that this "masquerade" of womanliness (excessive "flirting and coquetting") is to be understood as a means of "propitiating" the potentially retaliatory father figure by offering herself to him sexually ("W" 37).

But when Riviere endeavors to trace this compensatory behavior to the woman's early fantasy life, we find the woman "defending" herself not against white, powerful father figures, but against another figure who might, like her, experience a similar anxiety about speaking from a position of authority: the black man living in the southern United States. Riviere tells us that

[this] phantasy [of offering herself sexually to a potential attacker] had been very common in her childhood and youth, which had been spent in the Southern States of America; if a negro came to attack her, she planned to defend herself by making him kiss her and make love to her (ultimately so that she could then deliver him over to justice). But there was a further determinant of the obsessive behavior. In a dream which had a rather similar content to this childhood phantasy, she was in terror alone in the house; then a negro came in and found her washing clothes, with her sleeves rolled up and arms exposed. She resisted him, with the secret intention of attracting him sexually, and he began to admire her arms and caress them and her breasts. The meaning was that she had killed father and mother and obtained everything for herself (alone in the house), became terrified of their retribution (expected shots through the window), and defended herself by taking on a menial role (washing clothes) and by *washing off* dirt and sweat, guilt and blood, everything she had obtained by the deed, and "disguising herself" as merely a castrated woman. ("W" 37–38)

Riviere interprets the "negro" of these fantasies as another of the power-wielding father figures who must be reassured that she has not stolen their masculinity: "In that guise [as castrated woman] the man [presumably the "negro" of the fantasy] found no stolen property on her which he need attack her to recover and, further, found her attractive as an object of love" ("W" 38). Apparently it makes no difference in Riviere's account that the "man" in question here is black and that culturally sanctioned fantasies in which a white woman is sexually attacked by a black man form a significant component of dominant white racist hegemony in the United States. Only the imagined attacker's gender is significant, not his race.

As we shall see, Riviere's essay is similar to other instances in the 1910s and 1920s when racial difference forms the *content* of the fantasy life of a white female subject, and yet it is *not* apparently a constitutive component of the psychoanalytic interpretation of the analyst. In other words, the explicit discourse on gender and sexuality of the period was informed by implicit assumptions about racial difference. Because of its later importance for feminists, Riviere's essay is a crucial starting point from which to explore the ramifications of this double imbrication.

To facilitate such an exploration, it is useful to note how the question of who does or does not have the penis in Riviere's text can be translated into a question of one's relation to the phallus as it is elaborated in Lacan's later discussion of masquerade in "The Meaning of the Phallus" (1958). By shifting the emphasis from penis to phallus, we may be able to see how Riviere has possibly misread her patient's imagined attacker as a father figure; it may be more pertinent to see him as occupying a position similar to that of the woman, insofar as he, too, might have reason to engage in masquerade to ward off retaliation by those who fear he has usurped their position of privilege. Before exploring the implications of such a rereading, however, I want to address the possibility that Riviere and her patient have subverted at least one aspect of hegemonic racism by imagining black men as equally capable as white men of serving as father figures.[8] To perceive the black man as a father figure might seem to lay the groundwork for restoring to black men the patriarchal power that had been historically denied them, even as it was deemed essential to masculine subjectivity. In this sense, it might be argued that according the black man the status of father figure is (in an antiracist project) a positively weighed fantasy. Such an imaginary "gift" to the black man is cruelly compromised, however, by the way in which the father figure is coded in Riviere's text: that which will punish women who dare to compete and that must therefore be seduced and diffused. If the black man was, indeed, perceived as a father figure by Riviere's patient, he was, at least in one version of the fantasy, soon divested of that status so that it could be restored to white male figures of authority.

It is then more in keeping with the real material conditions faced by black men in the 1920s to consider that, contrary to Riviere's interpretation, her patient may have perceived the "negro" of her fantasy as occupying a position much like her own, that is, that his claim to patriarchal power would, like hers, have been interpreted by white men as a transgression worthy of punishment. In Lacanian terms, both the woman and her "attacker" behave as though they possess the phallus, though only one of them has recourse to feminine masquerade as a defense against retaliation for such behavior. Riviere says of her patient that "the exhibition in public of her intellectual proficiency, which was in itself carried through successfully, signified an exhibition of herself in possession of the father's penis, having castrated him. The display once over, she was seized by horrible dread of the retribution the father would then exact. Obviously it was a step towards propitiating the avenger to endeavor to offer herself to him sexually" ("W" 37). It is at this point that Riviere introduces the childhood fantasy of an attacking "negro," and she takes it for granted that since the black man has a penis that could be "stolen," he can therefore be interpreted as another version of the father figure whose anger must be assuaged. But, though the penis can be attributed to all men (as opposed to women), it must be pointed out that the phallus cannot. By fantasizing a black man, Riviere's patient is calling upon a figure whose relation to the phallus, as signifier of white male privilege in a racialized, patriarchal society, is as tenuous as her own.

Consider what takes place in the Riviere essay in terms of its implied elaboration of a phallic economy. According to Lacan, no one can really "have" the phallus, though men and women of all races may strive to appear to have it, with varying material repercussions.[9] In the standard Freudian account of masculine subjectivity, what is perceived as a "lack" in women (that is, the absence of the penis) is not tolerable from the little boy's (nor apparently the man's) perspective. This "lack" in the woman is threatening because it means that the man may also lose his organ; hence, he feels the necessity on his part to disavow and cover over her "lack" via the fetish.[10] In Lacan's work, the standard binary that forms itself around the phallus is not "having the phallus" on one side and "lacking the phallus" on the other. Rather, lack must, once more, be covered over; thus, in Lacan, the man must appear to "have the phallus" and the woman must appear to "be the phallus" (this way no one is "lacking" the phallus). Indeed, the woman must appear to "be the phallus" precisely so that the man may be assured that he "has" it. Judith Butler clarifies this in the following way: "For women to 'be' the Phallus means, then, to reflect the power of the Phallus, to signify that power, to 'embody' the Phallus, to supply the site to which it penetrates, and to signify the Phallus through 'being' its Other, its absence, its lack, the dialectical confirmation of its identity" (*GT* 44). A masquerading woman in Lacan is one who masquerades in order to be the phallus that he must be reassured he has.

Riviere's patient has placed herself in relation to her so-called lack in conflicting ways. At no point does her "lack" appear as such; when she speaks in a public forum, she appears as "having the phallus," and she rightly suspects that this will not be tolerated by her male audience. Thus, after the performance, through the masquerade, she reappears as "being the phallus," in order to reassure the listening men that they "have" it after all. But the introduction of the cross-racial fantasy signals that we are not dealing with a simple male-female binary at all; rather, a third term enters the picture. The fantasy of the attacking "negro" suggests that this woman's relation to the phallus, and thus to her "womanliness" as a masquerade, is inflected by her imagined relation to the black man's relation to the phallus. Riviere simplifies matters by seeing the black man as another representative of the "father" on the male side of a gender binary. But Riviere's patient is addressing her masquerade to two quite differently constructed male audiences. Consider the specific details of the fantasy again: "If a negro came to attack her, she planned to defend herself by making him kiss her and make love to her (ultimately so that she could then deliver him over to justice)." Since her "defense" is to seduce the attacker, it would appear that she does not regard his aggression to be sexually motivated at first. In other words, she understands him to be attacking her for other reasons. Given the historical realities of postslavery America, it is worth noting that she appears to "have" the phallus (that is, to be in a position of power and authority) both as a woman and as a white woman. As a white woman, her appearing to have the phallus is culturally sanctioned when it is a question of her relation to a black man. Historically, white men and women who had enjoyed the privileges of white supremacy in the South during slavery were, during and after Reconstruction, experiencing loss of power and perceiving it to be usurped by black men. To desire the phallus, then, as a white woman was to desire something both culturally proscribed (insofar as she was a woman) and culturally sanctioned (insofar as she was white) by a white hegemonic racist and patriarchal culture. The question is, how does the white woman negotiate this contradiction, particularly as it is played out in her fantasies about black masculinity?

By playing the masquerade to the black man as audience, she will appear to "be the phallus" in order that he will, in turn, want to have her as the phallus, to have her as the "site to which" he will penetrate. As soon as his imagined aggression has been thus defined as sexual in nature, she will then "deliver him over to justice." That "justice," of course, in the violently racialized context that is the American South, will likely consist in the literal castration and lynching of the offending black man at the hands of the white men whose legal and social prerogative it is to be the proper possessors of the phallus. In masquerading as the phallus for the black man, Riviere's patient will have succeeded in transforming him into the phallus, which she can then hand over to the true father figures in this scenario, the white men who are the administrators of the "justice" that is evoked. Indeed, according to Martha Hodes, though it might have been a black man's "political or economic authority and independence" that led to violent retaliation on the part of whites, that authority and independence were customarily linked to a supposed sexual threat he posed to white women, so that his lynching was understood to be a result of his sexual, as much as his political, aggression: "Whether true or untrue, what comes through consistently in the testimony [of KKK witnesses] is the way in which extreme white anxiety over sexual liaisons between white women and black men was linked to fears of black men's political and economic independence."[11] In Riviere's essay, then, we find evidence about the way in which this "extreme white [male] anxiety" inflects a white woman's attempt to negotiate her own "political and economic independence." Riviere notes that for this woman "womanliness . . . could be assumed and worn as a mask, both to hide the possession of masculinity and to avert the reprisals expected if she was found to possess it—much as a thief will turn out his pockets and ask to be searched to prove that he has not the stolen goods" ("W" 38). Whereas she can turn her pockets out and show that she has no penis after all, the black man she fantasizes about cannot do so, and his horrific punishment will be, after all, his literal castration and death.

There is a second part to the cross-racial fantasy, however, that complicates this picture somewhat. Again, Riviere sees the black man in the patient's dream as analogous to the father whose retribution the patient fears for having usurped his position. Her washing of the clothes is interpreted as her attempt to wash off the "dirt and sweat, guilt and blood, everything she had obtained by the deed" of killing her parents. However, it is just as plausible that this washing is evident of her desire, and her anxiety about this desire, to identify with blackness. As Sander Gilman has pointed out, it would have become a commonplace by the 1920s to associate sexuality, and in particular a sexuality that exceeded or contradicted a clearly heterocentric model (as in the case of the prostitute, the lesbian, or the hysteric), with the image of the "hottentot," the stereotype of black female subjectivity.[12] Interestingly, the patient's dream does not end with the turning over of the black man to "justice"; this time, she is content "'disguising herself' as merely a castrated woman," as Riviere puts it, so that he will caress her arms and breasts. Significantly, the only other erotic dreams she has are "frequent homosexual dreams with intense orgasm" ("W" 39). Up until this point, Riviere's patient has been presented as either superficially heterosexual (gaining satisfaction in sexual relations with her husband only because her anxiety is thus allayed) or as frigid. But, as Butler points out, Riviere's patient could be understood as a kind of "homosexual without homosexuality"; "the donning of femininity as mask may reveal a refusal of a female homosexuality and, at the same time, the hyperbolic incorporation of that female Other who is refused [the patient, through masquerade, becomes the object—that is, a woman—whom she forbids herself to love]" (*GT* 53). Moreover, Butler explains, this predicament is "produced by a matrix that accounts for all desire for women by subjects of whatever sex or gender as originating in a masculine, heterosexual position. The libido-as-masculine is the source from which all possible sexuality is presumed to come" (*GT* 53). If a person feels desire for a woman, in other words, this person must be understood to be desiring from a masculine, heterosexual position, since it is assumed that the libido is, by nature, masculine. But I would add that just as the cultural matrix is "[hetero]sexualized" in a certain way, it is also "racialized" in a certain way, and this must be taken into account in any consideration of how either "femininity" or sexuality is being constructed in psychoanalytic texts of the 1910s and 1920s. For if this matrix is marked by an assumption of the libido-as-masculine, it is also paradoxically marked by an equally coercive assumption of the libido-as-black, a trope that informed the fantasy life of more than one analysand in the early days of psychoanalysis and yet was not seriously interrogated until the work of Frantz Fanon.

3. THE LIBIDO-AS-BLACK AND PHOBOGENIC OBJECTS

In "Contributions to the Masculinity Complex in Women" (1917), Dutch analyst J. H. W. van Ophuijsen recounts his analysis of five women who suffer from a "masculinity complex." He notes with interest that three of the women "informed me of their own accord that they possessed 'Hottentot nymphae'"; this fact, which they had already noticed very early in their lives, led them to the conviction that they were different from other women.[13] By "Hottentot nymphae," van Ophuijsen means the supposedly enlarged female sexual organs that black women in Africa were reputed to possess. As Sander Gilman points out, ethnographic constructions of the "Hottentot" had become by the end of the nineteenth century (and, judging by van Ophuijsen's article, well into the twentieth) the paradigm of black female sexuality, notable less for her black skin than for the supposed abnormal development of her genitalia and buttocks. Anthropological and medical "research" in the nineteenth century served only to confirm the observations of eighteenth-century travelers who had "described the so-called Hottentot apron, a hypertrophy of the labia and nymphae caused by the manipulation of the genitalia" ("BB" 232). Throughout the century, African women were exhibited in Europe as examples of a "primitive" sexuality, dissected upon their death, and their genitalia put on display for scientific (and public) scrutiny. Thus, Gilman describes the fate of Sarah Bartmann, an African woman displayed throughout the early part of the century: "The audience which had paid to see her buttocks and had fantasized about the uniqueness of her genitalia when she was alive could, after her death and dissection, examine both, for Cuvier [a contemporary pathologist] presented to 'the Academy the genital organs of this woman prepared in a way so as to allow one to see the nature of the labia'" ("BB" 232, 235). The European fixation on the "Hottentot nymphae" endured for well over a hundred years according to Gilman: "Sarah Bartmann's genitalia and buttocks summarized her essence for the nineteenth-century observer, or, indeed, for the twentieth-century one, as they are still on display at the Musée de l'homme in Paris" ("BB" 235). Gilman also documents the continuing publication of books into the early twentieth century linking the "pathological" and "atavistic" sexuality of European prostitutes and lesbians to the "primitive" sexuality of the Hottentot.[14]

It is as though van Ophuijsen's patients sought to assert sexual and gender identities that would challenge and contradict the strictly (white) feminine one that had hitherto been culturally prescribed (and was about to become psychoanalytically codified) in terms of passivity, receptivity to the "active" male, and de-emphasis of the pleasures of the clitoris. Since it had become probable by the 1910s that defiance of the feminine role would inevitably be "diagnosed" as a "masculinity complex" (that is, if you do not wish to be "feminine," you must wish to be "masculine"), these women would seem to have sought an alternative means of asserting a gendered identity that both was and was not officially "feminine." Drawing from the kinds of clinical or anthropological depictions of the genitals of African women that would doubtless have been circulating in the early twentieth century, they found images of themselves in a mirror that was striking for its racialized, not its masculine-gendered, depiction of sexual difference. If van Ophuijsen's patients are "claimers" (to use Freud's term, later promulgated by Marie Bonaparte, for women who refuse to renounce the sexual pleasure of the clitoris), it is an imagined black, but nevertheless female sexual identity they are claiming, not a male one. Yet, caught up in the rigid binary of masculine and feminine, in which *black*—as synonymous with *genital* and *libidinal*—is permanently subsumed under *masculine*, van Ophuijsen cannot acknowledge that these white women are enacting a specifically cross-racial, rather than cross-gendered, identification. His ensuing observations reveal that, although he cannot find a "masculine disposition," "appearance," or "expression" in these women, he nevertheless takes their remarks as primarily indicative of their fantasies of possessing male genitalia: "I did not find to any great extent in any of these cases what is called a masculine disposition; nor indeed a masculine appearance and expression, a contempt for men, or a predilection for masculine activities. I would rather define the attitude present as one of rivalry with men in the intellectual and artistic spheres."[15] Doubtless it is their "rivalry with men in the intellectual and artistic spheres" that has marked these white women as somehow deviant in terms of their sexuality or gender in the first place, and that might have prompted in them the same anxiety about white, male retribution felt by Joan Riviere's patient. Once again, a racialized Other is invoked by a woman as a means to distance herself from "femininity" while at the same time not seeming to encroach on "masculinity." But psychoanalysis as an institution was not able to theorize the importance of this, since it was not until Fanon's work that the category of the Other could be conceived of in racialized, as well as sexualized terms.

In "The Negro and Psychopathology," Fanon reconsiders Lacan's theory of the mirror stage in an explicitly racialized context:

> It would indeed be interesting, on the basis of Lacan's theory of the mirror period, to investigate the extent to which the *imago* of his fellow built up in the young white at the usual age would undergo an imaginary aggression with the appearance of the Negro. When one has grasped the mechanism described by Lacan, one can have no further doubt that the real Other for the white man is and will continue to be the black man.[16]

This chapter of *Black Skin, White Masks* is an extended elaboration of the ramifications for psychosexual development in a culture that has fostered the production of the black body as "phobogenic" (that is, the cause of phobia in whites, and, more crucially, in blacks who have been brought up to believe they are white). To follow through on this analysis, Fanon draws upon, though does not explicitly acknowledge, the way in which the female body is also phobogenic (as that thing whose lack is so feared it cannot be perceived as such). Fanon's explanation of the white woman's fantasy "A Negro is raping me" supplies a striking counterpart to Joan Riviere's text. For in his text, too, the white woman who experiences such a fantasy is exemplary of "certain failures or certain fixations" in women who have not successfully acceded to their mature sexual roles as passive partners (*BS* 178). Fanon relies without question on the work of Helene Deutsch and Marie Bonaparte, both of whom shared the general consensus in the debate of the 1920s that, as Fanon puts it, "alternatively clitoral and clitoral-vaginal and finally purely vaginal, a woman—having retained, more or less commingled, her libido in a passive conception and her aggression, having surmounted her double Oedipus complex—proceeds through her biological and psychological growth and arrives at the assumption of her role, which is achieved by neuropsychic integration" (*BS* 178). There remain vestiges in these women of an "active Oedipus complex," corresponding to "the clitoral stage," meaning that the clitoris is "perceived as a diminished penis," and that the girl, like the boy, has "impulses directed at the mother; she too would like to disembowel the mother" (*BS* 178–79).

This fantasy of disemboweling the mother is, by the time Fanon reiterates it, a commonplace in the psychoanalytic literature of male and female analysts alike. It makes up an obligatory component of Riviere's analysis:

> In consequence of disappointment or frustration during sucking or weaning, coupled with experiences during the primal scene which is interpreted in oral terms, extremely intense sadism develops towards both parents. The desire to bite off the nipple shifts, and desires to destroy, penetrate and disembowel the mother and devour her and the contents of her body succeed it. These contents include the father's penis, her faeces and her children. ("W" 40–41)

Riviere is drawing directly from Melanie Klein, whose 1929 discussion of reparation I consider at length in the next section of this article. Klein theorizes that "[the most profound anxiety experienced by girls] is the equivalent of castration-anxiety in boys. The little girl has a sadistic desire, originating in the early stages of the Oedipus conflict, to rob the mother's body of its contents, namely, the father's penis, faeces, children, and to destroy the mother herself."[17] However, for each analyst (Klein, Riviere, Fanon) the way in which the woman will mitigate the anxiety produced by this fantasy is theorized differently; in all three cases, racial difference becomes an element in the analysis, but only in Fanon's text is it explicitly acknowledged. For Riviere, the daughter wards off anxiety by occupying her father's position, from which she can seem to put herself "*at the service*" of her mother:

> In this appalling predicament the girl's only safety lies in placating the mother and atoning for her crime. She must retire from rivalry with the mother and, if she can, endeavour to restore to her what she has stolen. As we know, she identifies herself with the father; and then she uses the masculinity she thus obtains by *putting it at the service of the mother.* She becomes the father and takes his place; so she can "restore" him to the mother. ("W" 41)

But, as we have seen, this strategy is inevitably inflected by fantasies of the attacking "negro" and of her own "blackness," which must be washed off. That it is possible to "steal" an imagined penis from the mother (that is, the father's penis in her) suggests again that the penis, or phallus, that is stolen from the attacking black man is imagined as originally belonging to the white father. Klein ignores the question of either penis or phallus, focusing on how a daughter effects "reparation" to her injured mother via artistic impulses, though, as we shall see, at least one of the paintings this daughter produces depicts a racialized figure that, once again, goes unremarked by the analyst. Fanon, however, brings racial fantasies to the forefront in his account of how a woman, still under the influence of an inadequately displaced clitoral sexuality, negotiates her anxiety about desiring to disembowel her mother.

As a young woman enters what Fanon calls "the folklore and the culture along roads that we know, the Negro becomes the predestined depositary" of her aggression towards the mother. Thus:

> when a woman lives the fantasy of rape by a Negro, it is in some way the fulfillment of a private dream, of an inner wish. Accomplishing the phenomenon of turning against self, it is the woman who rapes herself. We can find clear proof of this in the fact that it is commonplace for women, during the sexual act, to cry to their partners: "Hurt me!" They are merely expressing this idea: Hurt me as I would hurt me if I were in your place. The fantasy of rape by a Negro is a variation of this emotion: "I wish the Negro would rip me open as I would have ripped a woman open." (*BS* 179)

In Fanon, as in Riviere, there is a sense that a woman's racial fantasy occurs almost as a consequence of a "failure" to attain a fully mature femininity; or, rather, the fantasy becomes a means to negotiate her forbidden "masculine" tendencies. Here, the woman identifies with the black man who (via "folklore and the culture") is reputed to have the instrument she would need to disembowel her mother: a mythically larger-than-life penis. But as a woman she also occupies the position of the mother whom she wishes to disembowel, thus giving expression both to her "masculine" aggression and her guilt at this aggression. Though it is valuable for its critique of the libido-as-black, Fanon's analysis of the cross-racial rape fantasy nevertheless becomes a means to reify the myth of femininity as masochism; the fantasy can only be understood as a means for women to express their own self-destructive impulses, and no interrogation is made of the means by which the female (maternal) body must be constructed as a phobogenic object. In Riviere, the fantasy becomes a means to reify the myth of the black man as wielder of a threatening phallus; he can only be conceptualized as a father figure, so that both a significant aspect of his commonality with the white woman, as well as the specificity of his difference from her, are necessarily elided. Fanon is well aware of the specifically racialized matrix that informs the rape fantasy he considers. What he is not able to articulate is the heterocentric matrix that prompts him to posit this fantasy as symptomatic of a somehow failed white femininity, and to admit that he knows nothing about the woman of color

(*BS* 179–80). By the same token, the absence of an awareness of the racialized matrix subtending her patient's fantasy prevents Riviere, as well as most
of the feminist critics who rely upon her, from seeing how womanliness as a
masquerade is simultaneously a masquerade of whiteness.

4. (WHITE) REPARATION WITH A NAKED NEGRESS IN MELANIE KLEIN

In the same year that Riviere published her essay on female masquerade,
friend and colleague Melanie Klein developed her theory of "reparation" in
an essay that is, for our purposes, just as striking for its evocation and then
dismissal of a racialized figuration in the fantasy life of a female subject.
Though Klein was not primarily concerned with elaborating a theory of femininity or female sexuality at the time, she was careful to distinguish between
the genesis of reparation in women as opposed to men; hence, her essay "Infantile Anxiety-Situations Reflected in a Work of Art and in the Creative Impulse" is divided in two parts, one focusing on a male, the other on a female
subject. After discussing the male protagonist in the libretto of a Ravel opera
(*The Magic Word,* written by Colette), Klein analyzes an essay entitled "The
Empty Space" by Karin Michaelis, in which Michaelis gives a biographical
sketch of her friend Ruth Kjär, a wealthy woman who becomes a painter and
who is the case study upon which Klein bases her conclusions about the "earliest danger-situation in a girl's development" ("I" 215).

As we have already seen, Klein was instrumental in emphasizing early infantile aggression toward the mother and in theorizing its succession by a
reparation phase, which becomes the source of creativity later in life.[18] The
story of Kjär, as Klein summarizes it from Michaelis's account, concerns a
"beautiful, rich and independent" woman who, aside from a flair for interior decoration, has "no pronounced creative talent" ("I" 215). Although she
seems to have a full life, is an active theater and concert goer, climbs moun-
tains, and travels extensively, she experiences bouts of severe depression,
which Michaelis describes in these terms: "There was only one dark spot in
her life. In the midst of the happiness which was natural to her, and seemed
so untroubled, she would suddenly be plunged into the deepest melancholy.
A melancholy that was suicidal. If she tried to account for this, she would say
something to this effect: 'There is an empty space in me, which I can never
fill!'" ("I" 215) Kjär seems to experience some happiness after she is married, but the "empty space" returns and continues to haunt her. Klein quotes
from Michaelis thus:

> "Have I already told you that her home was a gallery of modern art? Her
> husband's brother was one of the greatest painters in the country, and his
> best pictures decorated the walls of the room. But before Christmas this

brother-in-law took away one picture, which he had only lent to her.
 The picture was sold. This left an empty space on the wall, which in some
inexplicable way seemed to coincide with the empty space within her."
("I" 215)

Unable to wait for a new painting from the brother-in-law, Kjär declares to
her husband that she will "'try to daub a little on the wall myself'" ("I" 215).
This first effort launches a very successful painting career, which Klein briefly
describes before explaining how this story illustrates her theory about infantile anxiety. "Now what is the meaning of this empty space within Ruth,"
Klein asks, "or rather, to put it more exactly, of the feeling that there was
something lacking in her body?" ("I" 216). We are already familiar with the
answer:

> The little girl has a sadistic desire, originating in the early stages of the
> Oedipus conflict, to rob the mother's body of its contents, namely, the
> father's penis, faeces, children, and to destroy the mother herself. This
> desire gives rise to anxiety lest the mother should in her turn rob the little
> girl herself of the contents of her body (especially of children) and lest her
> body should be destroyed or mutilated. ("I" 217)

The rest of the article is taken up with a description of the content of the
paintings Kjär produced after her first attempt to fill the space. They are almost all portraits of female family members, the most significant ones (for
Klein) depicting Kjär's mother first as an old, then as a young, woman. Klein
remarks:

> It is obvious that the desire to make reparation, to make good the injury
> psychologically done to the mother and also to restore herself was at the
> bottom of the compelling urge to paint these portraits of her relatives.
> That of the old woman, on the threshold of death, seems to be the expres-
> sion of the primary, sadistic desire to destroy. The daughter's wish to destroy
> her mother, to see her old, worn out, marred, is the cause of the need to
> represent her in full possession of her strength and beauty. By so doing
> the daughter can allay her own anxiety and can endeavour to restore her
> mother and make her new through the portrait. In the analyses of children,
> when the representation of destructive wishes is succeeded by an expression
> of reactive tendencies, we constantly find that drawing and painting are used
> as means to restore people. ("I" 218)

As I have already mentioned, however, Klein's analysis is quite astonishing
in its indifference to the content of the first painting Kjär produces to fill
up the "empty space" on the wall and in herself. Kjär's husband is far from
indifferent: "'She drew him with her, saying: "Come, you will see!" And he
saw. He could not take his eyes from the sight; could not take it in, did not
believe it, *could* not believe it'" ("I" 216). Her brother-in-law is equally
alarmed: "'You don't imagine you can persuade me that you painted that!

What a damned lie! This picture was painted by an old and experienced artist. Who the devil is he? I don't know him!'" (quoted in "I" 216). And yet, this same picture has no bearing on Klein's theory of reparation, since this is the only passing reference she makes to it: "In seeking the explanation of these ideas [of infantile anxiety and reparation], it is instructive to consider what sort of pictures Ruth Kjär has painted since her first attempt, when she filled the empty space on the wall with the life-sized figure of a naked negress" ("I" 217). The de-emphasis of the racialized nature of this prelude to a series of portraits of the artist's mother and sister is all the more remarkable given that Michaelis, in the article from which Klein draws, gives special attention to the painting and even goes so far as to imply an identificatory relation between the artist and her subject matter.

In the opening of "The Empty Space," Michaelis notes that her friend is Danish and Irish Canadian, and then inexplicably she attributes to her "a couple dashes of black African blood" ("ein paar schwarze Afrikablut-spritzer").[19] Whether we can attribute this fantasy of mixed race to Michaelis or Kjär herself is uncertain, but Michaelis continues the suggestion in her second reference to Kjär's painting:

> That night Ruth can not sleep much. The picture on the wall is painted, that is certain—it is not a dream. But how has it happened? And what next? Is painting like writing books? One says that every human being could write a book, the book about oneself. Should this picture—which by the way portrays a young negress—should this picture be the first and last at the same time? ("RK" 204–5)

According to Michaelis, then, Ruth here considers the possibility that this first painting is, like one's first and only book, autobiographical. In her narration of the story, Michaelis has withheld the race of the woman in the painting until this moment, as though to strike the reader more emphatically with the notion that Kjär is giving outward expression to a felt identification with racial blackness. In the first reference to the painting, perhaps because she is eager to emphasize Kjär's unexpected artistic expertise, Michaelis leaves out indications of the woman's race, focusing primarily on her gender, on her posture, on composition and lighting: "The empty space is filled with a lifesized woman. She is half sitting, half lying, her skin is like gold, she lowers her face against one shoulder, the light falls through a small window. In front of this window an ebony table with a large stoneware pitcher" ("RK" 204). These are the details meant to convey to the reader what so astounds Kjär's artist brother-in-law; he cannot believe the painting has not been produced by an experienced, *male* artist ("Who the devil is he? I don't know him!"). In her narrow focus on the mother-daughter relation, Klein neglects to reflect on how this painting becomes Kjär's admission ticket to the male-defined and -dominated world of high artistic production. Her home, as we have been told, is a "gallery of modern art"; yet she cannot find herself, as artist, included among her brother-in-law's paintings. That she is yet another of van Ophuijsen's women who seek "rivalry with men in the intellectual and artistic spheres" is suggested by the fact that she feels compelled to fill the empty space left by the male painter with an attempt of her own. Like Riviere's patient, by taking up the paintbrush and thereby endeavoring to usurp her brother-in-law's place as artistic producer, she risks being perceived as having "stolen" his token of masculinity. It is reasonable to suppose that she is as anxious about the father's as about the mother's retribution for her gender transgression.

The content of the first painting is crucial, then, to understand how it is designed to simultaneously effect Kjär's entry into a primarily male domain and placate potentially retaliatory father figures for having "stolen" the phallus. To paint a female nude is, perhaps, in and of itself to seek legitimacy as creator of high art. As Lynda Nead suggests: "More than any other subject, the female nude connotes 'Art.' The framed image of a female body, hung on the wall of an art gallery, is shorthand for art more generally; it is an icon of Western culture, a symbol of civilization and accomplishment."[20] To become an artist is to place oneself in a very specific position vis-à-vis the female body; it is to become the means by which that body is abstracted and contained: "The female nude can thus be understood as a means of containing femininity and female sexuality. If . . . the female body has been regarded as unformed, undifferentiated matter; then the procedures and conventions of high art are one way of controlling this unruly body and placing it within the securing boundaries of aesthetic discourse" (*FN* 2). By attempting to maintain and police the "boundaries of aesthetic discourse," Kjär seeks to escape the body that stands for "unformed, undifferentiated matter," that same body which she has experienced as harboring an "empty space."

And yet Kjär paints not simply a "female nude" but what Michaelis, at the end of her essay, refers to as a "lifesized figure of a naked negress." It is a representation of a woman's body that would seem to be racially differentiated from the artist's own, but Michaelis suspects it might be the painted version of the "book about oneself." It is curious that, given her eagerness to assert Kjär's unexpected artistic talent, Michaelis uses the word *naked* at this point rather than the more high-toned *nude*. Though much art-historical debate has attempted to establish and valorize a distinction between *naked* and *nude*,[21] since *"even at the most basic levels the body is always produced through representation. . . . There can be no naked 'other' to the nude"* (*FN* 16). Another way of putting this is to say that if there *is* a "naked 'other,'" it is not the body outside of representation but, rather, the body within a representation that is recognized, in some way, to be materially specific. Manet's *Olympia* bears what T. J. Clark sees as the "signs" of nakedness precisely because it indexes its subject's social class. And, as Gilman points out in his 1985 reading of

Olympia, the "signs" of nakedness include not only class but racial indicators. According to Gilman, Olympia is sexualized by the presence of her black servant, and, though she is a white prostitute, this whiteness is meant to be suspect.[22] A nude, then, is a depiction of a (female) body whose whiteness is *not* in any way suspect, since it is assumed that to be white is not to be specifically "raced." To paint an unclothed black woman is, it would seem, by definition to paint a "naked," sexualized woman.

Why, then, might Ruth Kjär expect her first painting to accomplish the double task of effecting her entry into the male domain of high art while simultaneously deflecting retaliation from angry father figures whose phallus she has "stolen"? As a wealthy woman who traveled extensively and whose house was a "gallery of modern art," Kjär was no doubt familiar with the tradition of the white female nude and its naked black counterparts in Manet, van Gogh, Gauguin, and Picasso. Michaelis's varying descriptions of Kjär's "naked negress" suggest that its status within the tradition of this naked versus nude dichotomy is ambiguous: the painting is described, at first, as a semireclining woman with "skin like gold," lit by the light falling through a window, her racial identity displaced perhaps onto the "ebony table" nearby; later she is described as "a young negress"; and at the end of the sketch Michaelis reveals that she is unclothed, referring to her as "the lifesized composition of the naked negress" (the term Klein adopts). Thus we are, by turns, invited to consider her status first as a classically arranged figure belonging to the abstract, universal domain of the aestheticized female body, then as a particularized female figure insofar as she is designated by a racial term, then finally as both racialized and "naked" (rather than "nude"), which would seem to contradict the implied classicism of the first description. If Kjär has presumed to fill an "empty space" hitherto reserved for the male paintbrush, it is possible that, by this ambiguous depiction of an unclothed female body that is at once both black and classical, she hopes, like Riviere's patient, to appear to restore the phallus to its "rightful" wielders. The "naked negress," like the "attacking negro," could be interpreted as a kind of sacrifice within the gendered scene of power negotiations between a white woman and the white men whose retaliation she fears. Indeed, just as Riviere's patient imagines she will "deliver to justice" her attacking "negro," so too Michaelis invokes the authority figures by whom Kjär's paintings will be judged: "Now that the first pictures are being brought before the right art criticism, whose duty it is to show mistakes, one will say that Ruth Kjär is supposed to 'learn'" ("RK" 206).

But Michaelis follows this line of thought by proposing that Kjär be exempt from such judgment and therefore exempt from the necessity of "learning" or being officially trained as an artist. "But it is smarter if she didn't ['learn']. Because what she has now she has because of God's grace" ("RK" 206). It is as though an implied double primitivism is being admitted here: Kjär paints "primitively" because she has no prior training, and the first thing she paints is a "primitive" "naked negress." It might be suggested that her masquerade is a masquerade of "primitiveness"; the potentially retaliatory brother-in-law need not punish Kjär for having stolen the paintbrush since she is not an artist in the sense that he is an artist; rather, as her "self-portrait" as "naked negress" will attest, she is an untutored primitive whose nakedness reveals no stolen instrument.

Even within the terms of a theory of reparation, where both Kjär's "empty space" and her reparative painting are understood to have resulted from anxiety about an infantile desire to disembowel her mother, Klein's admission of, then subsequent silence about, the racialized content of that first painting is suspect. That Klein's theory is predicated upon an example containing this unexamined representation suggests that it is, in itself, a theory of a specifically white female subjectivity. Klein closes the essay by noting that, although the "earliest anxiety-situation" for girls arising from fantasies of aggression towards the mother may "be the cause of serious illness and many inhibitions," "the case of Ruth Kjär shows plainly that this anxiety of the little girl is of greatest importance in the ego-development of women, and is one of the incentives to achievement" ("I" 218). Klein's theory has been valorized for its contradiction of Freud's schema, in which the woman's "super-ego is never so inexorable, so impersonal, so independent of its emotional origins as we require it to be in men" because it is only those who can be threatened by castration—that is, those who have penises—who will experience an "incentive" to cultural achievement.[23] Yet Klein insists that both ego and super-ego are possible in women; moreover, they do have "incentives to achievement" by virtue of their fear, if not of castration, then of being disemboweled by a retaliating mother. It turns out, however, that, at least in one representative case, such incentive is announced by a reparative image that tells us the white female imaginary is occupied not only by a fantasized retaliatory white mother but also by a racially differentiated Other. This Other is not male, not white, and apparently crucial in negotiating how attempts at achievement will be received in a world where achievement is traditionally a white man's prerogative. The filling of a psychological empty space with a naked negress was clearly a significant trope for both Kjär and her enthusiastic biographer. But something about the specific obsessions of psychoanalysis prevented Klein, the third white woman in this *mise-en-abîme* of female representations, from exploring that significance in such a way that it might seriously transform the institution she was both entering and creating.

5. CONCLUSION

Psychoanalytic feminist theory participates in what can only be a self-defeating process of disavowal insofar as it deploys psychoanalysis as a means of rewriting female subjectivity yet remains silent about race.[24] Given the urgency, since the 1910s and 1920s, of feminist and lesbian interventions in psychoanalysis and in psychoanalytically informed feminist critique, it has seemed strategically crucial to bracket off, elide, ignore, or trivialize the ways in which race (however that may be constructed in a specific context) manifests itself in the process of theoretical, social scientific, and identity-driven investigations. Though it is not always made explicit, the assumption is that instances of racialized identifications and desires must be separated or siphoned off from case material (such as Riviere and Klein's) that seems particularly promising as a matrix for interrogating how gender and sexuality have been constructed, performed, and policed. By removing or ignoring race, the case material can thus be restored to a more "pure" state in which an exploration of gender can proceed unhindered by "extraneous" considerations.

The Riviere essay is perhaps the most striking case in point. It may be that its enduring fascination for feminist scholars of both gendered and sexual subjectivity inheres only partly in its elaboration of femininity as a masquerade. While masquerade has undergone a richly diverse array of theoretical reinscriptions, revisions, and transformations, Riviere's indifference to the racialized components of her patient's fantasies is reproduced with a striking monotony by her feminist successors. It would seem, thus, that the peculiar readiness of Riviere's essay as a "usable" text lies to a great extent in the permission it gives to invoke, only to ignore, the cultural constructions of race that inform it, the better to focus on the more seemingly universal issues of gender and sexuality. With the exception of Emily Apter's discussion of masquerade in her book *Feminizing the Fetish,* Mary Ann Doane's appropriation of Riviere's work is the only one I know of to have at least mentioned in passing that "Riviere's patient has a number of sexual fantasies linking blacks, sexuality, power, and degradation—fantasies which are rarely, if ever discussed in the critical accounts of Riviere's concept of masquerade" (FF 38). And yet, in her 1991 book *Femmes Fatales,* even Doane restricts her analysis of psychoanalytic constructions of race to a separate chapter on Freud's "dark continent" trope.[25] Though she makes mention of the racial material in Riviere, her two chapters on feminine masquerade proceed as if a discussion of female subjectivity could somehow transcend, or forget, its racialized contexts.

Emily Apter's reference to the racial fantasy of Riviere's patient is, like Doane's, somewhat cursory and functions merely as a supplement to her analysis of why the concept of masquerade is inferior to the concept of the fetish as the grounding for a feminist elaboration of femininity. She points out that "with its language of veils, masks, and sexual travesty, the discourse of the masquerade seems always to participate in the very obfuscation of femininity that it seeks to dispel."[26] But if feminists are not convinced by this argument (Apter seems to imply), then they might want to dissociate themselves from Riviere on the basis that to rely upon her case study would be to participate in racist assumptions. Apter concludes her brief discussion of the racial fantasy in Riviere by suggesting that the "lesson we might draw" from it is that "the chosen prototype of the masquerading woman is a problematic figure—abstracted from history and culture and blind to the psychosexual politics of racism.[27] As I have suggested, however, it is precisely the way in which Riviere, and her masquerading woman, are problematic that makes them especially promising as prototypes for understanding how femininity has been constructed and played out within its particularly racialized contexts.

Teresa de Lauretis provides a striking example of how foregrounding the racially problematic prototype is equally important in the project of elaborating specifically lesbian subjectivities. In discussing van Ophuijsen's article on the "masculinity complex" in her book *The Practice of Love: Lesbian Sexuality and Perverse Desire,* de Lauretis restricts her consideration of the racialized trope of the "Hottentot nymphae" to a "brief digression" (that is, presumably not central to her critical exploration of the construction of female homosexuality in psychoanalytic literature) (*PL* 35). After summarizing Gilman's work on the Hottentot Venus, de Lauretis directs our attention to the work of Carla Scott, whose Ph.D. qualifying essay, "The Hottentot Effect: The Crisis of Black Lesbian Representation," sketches out how black lesbian narratives such as Audre Lorde's *Zami* can function as "sites of resistance to 'the legacy of the Hottentot Venus' and as the creation of a new discursive space for theorizing black lesbian subjectivity" (*PL* 36–37). The project of specifying and reclaiming black lesbian subjectivity is, indeed, a crucial one. Yet, this section of de Lauretis's text gives the impression that white women's fantasies of having "Hottentot nymphae" are more pertinent to an investigation of black than of white female subjectivity. The "sexuality" in de Lauretis's book title is marked only as "lesbian," not as "white," unwittingly making the book pose as establishing a racially unmarked theory of lesbian subjectivity (its whiteness barely acknowledged) to be supplemented by other racially marked "versions" in texts such as Scott's.

This problem is reproduced in "Recasting the Primal Scene," de Lauretis's otherwise brilliant reading of Sheila McLaughlin's film *She Must Be Seeing Things,* which first appeared as "Film and the Visible" in *How Do I Look? Queer Film and Video* (the published version of papers given at a conference by the same name in New York in 1989) and then revised and incorporated into *The Practice of Love.* In the transcription of the discussion that followed de Lauretis's paper at the New York conference, de Lauretis is asked if she can "say something about the critique of *She Must Be Seeing Things* [which depicts a white woman and a black Latina in a lesbian couple] in regard to its treatment of racial difference." In response, de Lauretis notes that a common objection to the film "seems to be that [it] poses the question of racial difference, but then avoids it by collapsing it into questions of cultural or ethnic difference. This observation strikes me as correct, but I don't think the film allows one to deal with it beyond locating it as a problem." Because, as she explains, the film does not explicitly address its own construction of racial difference in a way that would allow her to "rethink and say something interesting about the relations of race, sexuality, and desire," she remains adamant throughout the discussion period (during which she is challenged repeatedly on the issue) that there is little more to be said, in the context of her project, about the film's depiction of race. She contrasts the film to "other lesbian texts that do not elide race, like Audre Lorde's *Zami*" and Cherríe Moraga's play *Giving up the Ghost,* which *have* allowed her to write about "the issue of race in feminist theory and in lesbian representation."[28] Though she makes reference to them in a brief footnote, the conference participants' questions about the racial trope in *She Must Be Seeing Things,* as well as de Lauretis's consideration of them, are dropped from the version of her reading of the film that appears in *The Practice of Love,* the better to foreground the film's primary concern with "sexuality and fantasy" as well as how it is "informed by the critique of representation produced by the work of avant-garde filmmakers as well as feminist film critics and theorists" (*PL* 86). Not surprisingly, given her interest in the work of (white) "feminist film critics and theorists," de Lauretis's reading of McLaughlin evokes once more Riviere's masquerade essay and the feminist uses to which it has been put, without remarking on the racial trope at the center of the essay or elaborating on how it might inform subsequent white women's (indeed, white lesbians') fantasies of racial difference. Having asked how Riviere's white patient engages in culturally produced and reinforced fantasies of racial difference in order to negotiate proscribed intellectual pursuits as well as prohibited sexual desires, we might then ask how a white lesbian filmmaker like McLaughlin either reproduces or departs from Riviere as she mobilizes locally constructed assumptions about racial difference in the 1980s and 1990s, even though, like Riviere, she is not explicitly foregrounding those assumptions in her project. As I hope I have been suggesting, analysis of white-authored works that evoke, even as they elide, race can tell us much about the "issue of race in feminist theory and lesbian representation," in particular, about how to make visible the otherwise unmarked whiteness of such texts and of how they subtend the whiteness of "lesbian sexuality" as it has been constructed thus far. The rich and subtle work of white lesbian-feminist theorists such as de Lauretis can no longer afford to bracket off the question of how white fantasies of racial difference, whether or not they seem to be *about* race, inflect the work they do.

I have brought into view the racialized components in the case studies by Riviere, van Ophuijsen, and Klein not in order to displace the theorizations of gender and sexuality enabled by those texts but to foreground how those theorizations depend upon an untheorized racial domain. So far, white-authored psychoanalytic attempts to make an argument for a specifically "feminine" or "female" subject-position have only succeeded by their persistent refusal to ask questions about the historically determined whiteness of the models they employ. Feminism as an institution has thus reenacted the way in which psychoanalysis as an institution defensively armored itself against charges of ethnocentrism (as illustrated by the Jones-Malinowski debate). Having acknowledged this, I would suggest that the project now is investigating, in very specific and detailed ways, local constructions of racialized identification and desire, especially in those areas where the discourses of psychoanalysis and feminism intersect and enrich each other.[29] The objective of such a project would not be to establish a more comprehensive ontology of femininity, or of female or lesbian sexuality but, rather, to interrogate the ways in which the feminist ontologies hitherto constructed are implicated in a vexed genealogy of racialized discourse. We need to expose and address the way in which whiteness has come to pose as deeply constitutive of female subjectivity, even in the most groundbreaking work of feminists to date.

NOTES

I would like to thank Mae Henderson for having provided a public forum for a short version of this paper by accepting it for the "Proprieties and Improprieties" Panel at the 1993 MLA Convention in Toronto, and Sally Drucker and James E. Morrison for inviting me to read the section on Riviere at the "Journey Proud" conference in Durham, N.C., in June 1994. I am indebted also to Lauren Berlant, Elizabeth Abel, and E. Ann Kaplan for encouraging me to complete the long version. Most important, Mary Cappello is to be credited for her invaluable observations, insights, and editorial advice during every stage of this project, as well as for inspiring me, by the example of her own rich and comprehensive scholarship, to broaden the scope of my critical undertakings.

"Re-Placing Race in (White) Psychoanalytic Discourse: Founding Narratives of Feminism" was originally published in *Critical Inquiry* 21, no. 4 (1995): 775–804. University of Chicago Press. Reprinted by permission of the University of Chicago Press.

1. According to Teresa Brennan, feminist texts of the 1970s and 1980s constitute the second "great debate" after a relative silence following the first debate of the 1920s and 1930s. See Teresa Brennan, *The Interpretation of the Flesh: Freud and Femininity* (New York: Routledge, 1992), 37. Before the second debate, notable publications included Marie Bonaparte, *Female Sexuality*, trans. John Rodker (New York: International Universities Press, 1953), which includes an overview of the early literature; Hendrik M. Ruitenbeek, ed., *Psychoanalysis and Female Sexuality* (New Haven, Conn.: College and University Press, 1966), with essays by Ernest Jones, Jeanne Lampl-de Groot, J. H. W. van Ophuijsen, Karen Horney, Helene Deutsch, Joan Riviere, Sandor Lorand, Bonaparte, Clara Thompson, Phyllis Greenacre, A. H. Maslow, Judd Marmor, and David A. Freedman; and Janine Chasseguet-Smirgel, ed. and trans., *Female Sexuality: New*

Psychoanalytic Views (1964; reprint, Ann Arbor, Mich.: University of Michigan Press, 1970), which includes an overview of the early literature and essays by Chasseguet-Smirgel, Christian David, Béla Grunberger, C.-J. Luquet-Parat, Maria Torok, and Joyce McDougall. The second debate, which is still in progress, got underway with the publication of Juliet Mitchell, *Psychoanalysis and Feminism* (New York: Pantheon Books, 1974), and branched out into two main directions, one drawing from Lacan's work (for example, Jacques Lacan and the *école freudienne, Feminine Sexuality,* trans. Jacqueline Rose, ed. Juliet Mitchell and Jacqueline Rose [New York: W. W. Norton, 1985], with introductory essays by Rose and Mitchell recounting the early debate), the other, directly or indirectly, from Kleinian psychoanalysis (for example, Nancy Chodorow's object-relations oriented *The Reproduction of Mothering: Psychoanalysis and the Sociology of Gender* [Berkeley: University of California Press, 1978]). The participants in feminist psychoanalytic discourse around female sexuality over the past two and a half decades are too numerous to list in detail here.

   2. For a sense of how little attention has been given to race in feminist intersections with psychoanalysis, see the following entries in Elizabeth Wright, ed., *Feminism and Psychoanalysis: A Critical Dictionary* (Cambridge, Mass.: Blackwell, 1992): "black feminist critique of psychoanalysis" by Biodun Iginla, "black feminist psychotherapy" by Beverly Greene, and "race/imperialism" by Rey Chow, who notes that "works devoting equal attention to race, imperialism, feminism and psychoanalysis are rare. This has much to do, historically, with the socially and economically privileged status enjoyed by the practice of psychoanalysis in the West" (363). Following are a few of the recent exceptions to the silence on race in psychoanalysis: Elizabeth Abel, "Race, Class, and Psychoanalysis? Opening Questions," in *Conflicts in Feminism,* ed. Marianne Hirsch and Evelyn Fox Keller (New York: Routledge, 1990), 184–204; in the domain of psychoanalytically informed feminist film theory, see E. Ann Kaplan, "The Couch Affair: Gender and Race in Hollywood Transference," *American Imago* 50 (winter 1993): 481–514, and Mary Ann Doane, "Dark Continents: Epistemologies of Racial and Sexual Difference in Psychoanalysis and the Cinema," in *Femmes Fatales: Feminism, Film Theory, Psychoanalysis* (New York: Routledge, 1991), 209–48, hereafter abbreviated *FF.* Sander L. Gilman's ongoing work has been invaluable for its documentation of the relationship between race and gender in the medical, literary, sexological, and psychoanalytic discourses of the past two or three centuries; see, for example, his *Difference and Pathology: Stereotypes of Sexuality, Race, and Madness* (Ithaca, N.Y.: Cornell University Press, 1985). Of note in the clinical domain are Patrick Colm Hogan, "The Politics of Otherness in Clinical Psychoanalysis: Racism as Pathogen in a Case of D. W. Winnicott," *Literature and Psychology* 38, no. 4 (1992): 36–43, and Dorothy Evans Holmes, "Race and Transference in Psychoanalysis and Psychotherapy," *International Journal of Psycho-Analysis* 73 (spring 1992): 1–11, a continuation of a discussion that has been ongoing for the last decade and a half among clinical practitioners about the extent to which race is a factor in the psychotherapeutic situation.

   3. Bronislaw Malinowski, quoted in Ernest Jones, review of *Sex and Repression in Savage Society* by Bronislaw Malinowski, *International Journal of Psycho-Analysis* 9 (July 1928): 365, hereafter abbreviated "R."

   4. See Henrietta L. Moore's entry "anthropology and cross-cultural analysis" in Wright, *Feminism and Psychoanalysis* for more on the Jones-Malinowski controversy. According to Moore, their disagreement set the terms of debate about "what ana-

lytical weight and status should be given to cross-cultural variation" (3). She notes that the result of their clash was "a split between anthropology and psychoanalysis," though her entry concerns itself more with this split's "profound effect on subsequent developments" in anthropology than on its implications for psychoanalysis (3). For example, she notes evidence in anthropological research that "the concept of the person based on the humanist notion of the SUBJECT is not universal: concepts of the person and the acting, knowing subject vary enormously cross-culturally" (7). She goes on: "It is evidence of this kind that could be used to produce a radical critique of certain psychoanalytic theories and to question assumptions about the universality of developmental processes; but anthropology has yet to produce such a critique" (7). Nor, it could be argued, has psychoanalysis, insofar as it, too, has been marked by its necessary disavowal of anthropology's questions since the Jones-Malinowski debate.

5. For a persuasive account of the heteroteleology in psychoanalytic accounts of gender acquisition, see Judith Butler, "Prohibition, Psychoanalysis, and the Production of the Heterosexual Matrix," in *Gender Trouble: Feminism and the Subversion of Identity* (New York: Routledge, 1990), hereafter abbreviated *GT.*

6. For the most extensive uses of the masquerade in film theory, see *FF;* Claire Johnston, "Femininity and the Masquerade: *Anne of the Indies,"* in *Psychoanalysis and Cinema,* ed. E. Ann Kaplan (New York: Routledge, 1990), 64–72; Stephen Heath, "Joan Riviere and the Masquerade," in *Formations of Fantasy,* ed. Victor Burgin, James Donald, and Cora Kaplan (New York : Methuen, 1986), 45–61; John Fletcher, "Versions of Masquerade," *Screen* 29 (summer 1988): 43–70; and Teresa de Lauretis, "Recasting the Primal Scene: Film and Lesbian Representation," in *The Practice of Love: Lesbian Sexuality and Perverse Desire* (Bloomington, Ind.: Indiana University Press, 1994), hereafter abbreviated *PL.* Luce Irigaray draws on the masquerade in her *This Sex Which Is Not One,* trans. Catherine Porter (Ithaca, N.Y.: Cornell University Press, 1985), 83–85. Butler's incisive analysis of Riviere appears in *GT,* 43–57, and Emily Apter critiques the masquerade in her *Feminizing the Fetish: Psychoanalysis and Narrative Obsession in Turn-of-the-Century France* (Ithaca, N.Y.: Cornell University Press, 1991), 65–98.

7. Joan Riviere, "Womanliness as a Masquerade," Burgin, Donald, and Kaplan, *Formations of Fantasy,* 35, hereafter abbreviated "W."

8. My thanks to a reader at *Critical Inquiry* for prompting me to consider this interpretation of the passage.

9. The "relations between the sexes," Lacan says, "revolve around a being and a having" the phallus, which is in itself a matter of "'appearing'" to have the phallus, "so as to protect it on one side and to mask its lack on the other" (Lacan, "The Meaning of the Phallus," in *Feminine Sexuality,* 83–84).

10. See Sigmund Freud, "Fetishism," in *The Standard Edition of the Complete Psychological Works of Sigmund Freud,* trans. and ed. James Strachey, 24 vols. (London: Hogarth Press, 1953–1974), 21:152–57.

11. Martha Hodes, "The Sexualization of Reconstruction Politics: White Women and Black Men in the South after the Civil War," in *American Sexual Politics: Sex, Gender, and Race since the Civil War,* ed. John C. Fout and Maura Shaw Tantillo (Chicago: University of Chicago Press, 1993), 65, 64.

12. See Sander L. Gilman, "Black Bodies, White Bodies: Toward an Iconography of Female Sexuality in Late Nineteenth-Century Art, Medicine, and Literature," *in*

"Race," Writing, and Difference, ed. Henry Louis Gates Jr. (Chicago: University of Chicago Press, 1985), 223–61, hereafter abbreviated "BB."

13. J. H. W. van Ophuijsen, "Contributions to the Masculinity Complex in Women," in Ruitenbeek, *Psychoanalysis and Female Sexuality,* 63.

14. For example, he notes a study of the "criminal woman," subtitled *The Prostitute and the Normal Woman,* by Cesare Lombroso and Guillaume Ferrero (1893) in which illustrations "deal with the image of the Hottentot female and illustrate the 'Hottentot apron' and the steatopygia"; Lombroso "regards the anomalies of the prostitute's labia as atavistic throwbacks to the Hottentot" ("BB" 245). An 1870 text by Adrien Charpy "begins by commenting on the elongation of the labia majora in prostitutes, comparing this with the apron of the 'disgusting' Hottentots" ("BB" 248). In Theodor Billroth's 1877 handbook of gynecology, "a detailed presentation of the 'Hottentot apron' is part of the discussion of errors in development of the female genitalia" and "the Hottentot's anomalous sexual form" was linked to "the overdevelopment of the clitoris, which [Billroth] sees as leading to those 'excesses' which 'are called "lesbian love."' The concupiscence of the black is thus associated also with the sexuality of the lesbian" ("BB" 237). In 1905, Abele de Blasio "published a series of case studies on steatopygia in prostitutes in which he perceives the prostitute as being, quite literally, the Hottentot" ("BB" 248).

15. Van Ophuijsen, "Contributions to the Masculinity Complex in Women," 63.

16. Frantz Fanon, *Black Skin, White Masks,* trans. Charles Lam Markmann (New York: Grove Weidenfeld, 1967), 161 n. 25, hereafter abbreviated *BS.*

17. Melanie Klein, "Infantile Anxiety-Situations Reflected in a Work of Art and in the Creative Impulse," in *Love, Guilt, and Reparation and Other Works, 1921–1945* (London: Virago, 1975), 217, hereafter abbreviated "I."

18. On the importance of Klein to more recent feminist theory, see Margaret Whitford's entry on Klein in Wright, *Feminism and Psychoanalysis.* Whitford suggests that Klein's influence on feminism has been only indirect (via object-relations theory, for instance), partly "because her work appears to locate FEMININITY and feminine heterosexual desire in innate drives" (192). Recent publications, however, suggest a more direct "return" to Klein among feminists; see Jacqueline Rose, *Why War?— Psychoanalysis, Politics, and the Return to Melanie Klein* (Cambridge, Mass.: Blackwell, 1993), and Janice Doane and Devon Hodges, *From Klein to Kristeva: Psychoanalytic Feminism and the Search for the "Good Enough" Mother* (Ann Arbor, Mich.: University of Michigan Press, 1992).

19. Karin Michaelis, "Ruth Kjär," in *Flammende Tage: Gestalten und Fragen zur Gemeinschaft der Geschlechter* (Dresden: Blackwell 1929), 200, hereafter abbreviated "RK." This is a German translation of the same book written by Michaelis in Danish, published in the same year. It is possible that Klein read the article on Ruth Kjär in an English or German version published in a different forum with the title "The Empty Space." I am indebted to Beverley Driver Eddy, who is writing a biography on Michaelis, for having sent me a copy of the Kjär chapter in *Flammende Tage.* I would also like to thank my colleague Doris Kirschner for her English translation of this text.

20. Lynda Nead, *The Female Nude: Art, Obscenity, and Sexuality* (New York: Routledge, 1992) 1, hereafter abbreviated *FN.*

21. Nead clarifies the implications of this choice of terms in her genealogy of the nude-naked debate in art-historical discourse. Drawing from the work of Kenneth

Clark, John Berger, and T. J. Clark, Nead documents a persistent binary that characterizes these writers' positions, concluding with Clark's praise for the "nakedness" of Manet's *Olympia* because it is a "sign of class (or, more precisely, working-class) identity," thus refusing to function as a classical nude, which would be "'a picture for men to look at, in which Woman is constructed as an object of somebody else's desire'" (*FN* 16). As Nead points out, however, in the work of all three art historians "the discourse on the naked and the nude . . . depends upon the theoretical possibility, if not the actuality, of a physical body that is outside of representation and is then given representation, for better or for worse, through art" (*FN* 16).

22. Indeed, that part of Olympia's specificity in her "blackness" is attested to by Picasso's satiric rendition of the painting in 1901, which Gilman describes thus:

> Olympia is presented as a sexualized black, with broad hips, revealed genitalia, gazing at the nude flâneur bearing her a gift of fruit, much as Laura bears a gift of flowers in Manet's original. . . . Picasso owes part of his reading of the *Olympia* to the polar image of the primitive female as sexual object, as found in the lower-class prostitutes painted by Vincent van Gogh or the Tahitian maidens à la Diderot painted by Paul Gauguin. Picasso saw the sexualized female as the visual analogue of the black. ("BB" 251)

Gilman points out that, in a later painting depicting Zola's Nana, the white prostitute has taken on the characteristics that had been established by medical discourse as typical of the "Hottentot": plumpness, pronounced buttocks, and the atavistic "Darwin's ear." "Thus," writes Gilman, "we know where the black servant is hidden in *Nana*—within Nana. Even Nana's seeming beauty is but a sign of the black hidden within" ("BB" 251). For Gilman, "Manet's *Nana* thus provides a further reading of his *Olympia,* a reading which stresses Manet's debt to the pathological model of sexuality present during the late nineteenth century" ("BB" 251).

23. See Freud, "Some Psychical Consequences of the Anatomical Distinction between the Sexes," in *The Standard Edition,* 19: 248–58.

24. Toni Morrison's book *Playing in the Dark: Whiteness and the Literary Imagination* (Cambridge, Mass.: Harvard University Press, 1992) offers a literary analogue to this disavowal. In the long essay "Black Matters," Morrison notes with fascination the way in which some of the most powerful literary critics, in their "lavish exploration of literature" manage "*not to* see meaning in the thunderous, theatrical presence of black surrogacy—an informing, stabilizing, and disturbing element—in the literature they . . . study" (13). As a critic who is herself a writer, Morrison came to realize that in literature written by whites, "the fabrication of an Africanist persona is reflexive; an extraordinary meditation on the self; a powerful exploration of the fears and desires that reside in the writerly conscious. It is an astonishing revelation of longing, of terror, of perplexity, of shame, of magnanimity" (17). Instead of turning politely away from the racial constructions in the "great" white texts of Western literature, Morrison urges that we interrogate the precise ways in which the compelling richness and complexity of these texts depend upon and are buttressed by those racial constructions.

25. In "Dark Continents" in *FF,* Doane offers a rich exploration of the implications of Freud's trope of the "dark continent" as a metaphor for female sexuality, as well as a critique of the sexual politics in Fanon's texts, and suggestive readings of *The Birth*

of a Nation and Sirk's *Imitation of Life*. And yet, even though the term *masquerade* reappears in "Dark Continents," it has by this time been evacuated of its valence as a concept for (white) female subjectivity and functions rather as a generalized indicator for how "Blackness is a costume which is worn or removed at will by whites [as in blackface], while whiteness in its symbolic dimension (the white robes of the Ku Klux Klan) is also a form of masquerade which conceals an identity" (*FF* 229). What would happen in Doane's reading of *The Birth of a Nation* if the link were made explicit between the woman in Riviere's case study and the Lillian Gish character, Elsie, who must be saved from the lustful desire of Silas Lynch? Or, more to the point, how might our understanding of Riviere be altered if we were to see her as sharing in the same white fantasy of racialized sexuality that informs the Griffith film?

26. Apter, *Feminizing the Fetish* , 90.

27. Ibid., 91–92.

28. Nancy Graham et al., "Discussion," in *How Do I Look? Queer Film and Video,* ed. Bad Object-Choices (Seattle: Bay Press, 1991), 264, 273, 268–69.

29. Elizabeth Abel has undertaken a project analogous to this one in her comprehensive and provocative essay "Black Writing, White Reading: Race and the Politics of Feminist Interpretation," *Critical Inquiry* 19 (spring 1993): 470–98. See also this volume.

The Quicksands of the Self
Nella Larsen and Heinz Kohut

Barbara Johnson

Nella Larsen's first novel, *Quicksand,* was published in 1928, at the height of the period of black migration from the rural South to the urban North that led to the explosion in cultural and artistic creativity known as the Harlem Renaissance. The novel was immediately greeted with enthusiasm: it won second prize in literature from the Harmon Foundation, and W. E. B. Du Bois called it "the best piece of fiction that Negro America has produced since the heyday of Chesnutt."[1] Readers then and now have indeed read the novel as a dramatization of racial double consciousness,[2] in the form of the all-too-familiar topos of the tragic mulatto. Nathan Huggins, in *The Harlem Renaissance,* writes:

> Nella Larsen came as close as any to treating human motivation with complexity and sophistication. But she could not wrestle free of the mulatto condition that the main characters in her two novels had been given. Once she made them mulatto and female the conventions of American thought—conditioned by the tragic mulatto and the light-dark heroine formulas—seemed to take the matter out of the author's hands. (236)

In other words, Larsen's attempt to present the inner life of her main character was subverted by the force of a literary cliché designed to rob the character of any inner life by subjecting her to a tragic "condition."

The mulatto image, a staple of nineteenth-century literature by white "plantation school" writers and black and white abolitionist writers, is less a reflection of a social or sociological reality than it is a literary and mythic device for articulating and concealing the racial history of this country. Critics such as Barbara Christian, Hazel Carby, and Hortense Spillers have analyzed the ways in which the mulatto represents both a taboo and a synthesis, not only the product of a sexual union that miscegenation laws tried to rule out of existence but also an allegory for the racially divided society as a whole, simultaneously un-American and an image of America as such. In an essay entitled "Notes on an Alternative Model—Neither/Nor," Hortense Spillers writes:

> Created to provide a middle ground of latitude between "black" and "white," the customary and permissible binary agencies of the national adventure, mulatto being, as a neither/nor proposition, inscribed no historic locus, or materiality, that was other than evasive and shadowy on the national landscape. To that extent, the mulatto/a embodied an alibi, an excuse for "other/otherness" that the dominant culture could not (cannot now either) appropriate, or wish away. An accretion of signs that embody the "unspeakable" of the Everything that the dominant culture would forget, the mulatto/a, as term, designates a disguise, covers up, in the century of Emancipation and beyond, the social and political reality of the dreaded African presence. Behind the African-become-American stands the shadow, the insubstantial "double" that the culture dreamed *in the place of* that humanity transformed into its profoundest challenge and by the impositions of policy, its deepest "unAmerican" activity. (165–66)

Nella Larsen herself suggests that her novel should be read through the grid of the mulatto figure by choosing as her epigraph a stanza from a Langston Hughes poem entitled "Cross":

> My old man died in a fine big house.
> My ma died in a shack.
> I wonder where I'm gonna die,
> Being neither white nor black?

Where one might expect a both-and , we find, as Spillers and Hughes suggest, a neither-nor. Nella Larsen's project in Quicksand is to tell the story of the neither-nor self from within.

The question of that neither-nor of racial designation is tied, both in the epigraph and in the novel, to the question of *place:* shack or big house, North or South, Europe or America. In the Hughes poem, the father is white, the mother black. This corresponds to the historical realities of the sexual abuse of slave women by white slaveholders. Nella Larsen's protagonist's parentage, however, is reversed: her mother is a Danish immigrant and her father is a black American. This further complicates the question of race and place, both socially and geographically. The first sentence of the novel, "Helga Crane sat alone in her room," echoes not only the "ins" of the epigraph but even its very rhythm. The last clause of the opening paragraph of the novel continues that rhythm: "Helga Crane never opened her door." It is as though the novel originates within the "stanza" (which etymologically means "room") of its epigraph. The question of place thus intersects with a question of space, of personal space, of the inside and outside boundaries of the self. Helga Crane's closed door circumscribes a space filled with small luxuries: a Chi-

nese carpet, a brass bowl, nasturtiums, and oriental silk. Her room symbolizes the issue of the self as a container (of value, positive or negative). And
the title, *Quicksand,* extends the metaphor of space in a nightmarish direction: the self is utterly engulfed by the outside because there is nothing outside the engulfing outside to save it.

What, then, is the nature of the quicksand into which Helga Crane sinks
in Nella Larsen's novel? Critics have offered various answers. Hiroko Sato
writes: "The title, *Quicksand,* signifies the heroine Helga Crane's sexual desire, which was hidden beneath her beautiful and intelligent surface and
came up at an unexpected moment and trapped her" (84). But for Deborah McDowell, Hortense Thornton, and Cheryl Wall, it is not Helga's sexuality that has trapped her but rather her attempts to disavow it—her own
and society's contradictory responses to it. To be respectable as a "lady" is to
have no sexuality; to have sexuality is to be a jungle creature, an exotic primitive, or an oppressed wife and mother. These readings, which focus on the
centrality of black female sexuality, are responses to earlier readings (mostly
by male critics), which focused on the problems of the biracial self. As Deborah McDowell puts it explicitly, "In focusing on the problems of the 'tragic
mulatto,' readers miss the more urgent problem of the female sexual identity which Larsen tried to explore" (xvii). And Cheryl Wall writes:

> Helga's interracial parentage—her father is black and her mother white—
> troubles her too, but it is not the primary cause of her unease. Her real
> struggle is against imposed definitions of blackness and womanhood. Her
> "difference" is ultimately her refusal to accept society's terms even in the
> face of her inability to define alternatives. . . . *Passing,* like *Quicksand,*
> demonstrates Larsen's ability to explore the psychology of her characters.
> She exposes the sham that is middle-class security, especially for women
> whose total dependence is morally debilitating. The absence of meaningful
> work and community condemn them to the "walled prison" of their own
> thoughts. . . . As these characters deviate from the norm, they are defined—
> indeed too often define themselves—as Other. They thereby cede control
> of their lives. But, in truth, the worlds these characters inhabit offer them
> no possibility of autonomy or fulfillment. (109)

As these critics make clear, *Quicksand* is a complex analysis of the intersections of gender, sexuality, race, and class. It seems, therefore, somehow regressive and discordant to ask what use a psychoanalytic perspective might
be in understanding the novel. How can any insight be gained into all these
structures by focusing on intrapsychic processes? Yet the inside-outside opposition on which such scruples are based is one that the novel constantly
forces us to reexamine. It will also, I hope, force us to reexamine that opposition in the assumptions and interpretive frames of psychoanalysis.

As we have seen, critics often praise Larsen for her psychological sophistication but then go on to interpret the novel in social, economic, and political terms. Such readings illuminate many aspects of the novel but leave certain questions untouched. How, for example, can one account for the self-defeating or self-exhausting nature of Helga Crane's choices? At several points, Helga achieves economic autonomy—when teaching in a southern black college or when working for an insurance company in New York—but she seems each time all too ready to flee to dependency. Economic autonomy does not provide something that economic dependency seems to promise. Then, too, Helga repeatedly reaches states of relative contentment—in Harlem, in Denmark, in Alabama—only to fall into depression again for no obvious reason. Chapter breaks often occur where psychological causation is missing. It is the *lack* of precipitating cause that calls for explanation. And it is the difficulty of defining the causes of Helga's suffering that irritates many readers. Mary Helen Washington summarizes a common reaction to the novel, before going on to critique the terms of such a reaction:

> Nella Larsen . . . published two novels, *Quicksand* and *Passing,* which dealt with this same problem: the marginal black woman of the middle class who is both unwilling to conform to a circumscribed existence in the black world and unable to move freely in the white world. We may perhaps think this a strange dilemma for a black woman to experience, or certainly an atypical one, for most black women then, as now, were struggling against much more naked and brutal realities and would be contemptuous of so esoteric a problem as feeling uncomfortable among black people and unable to sort out their racial identity. We might justifiably wonder, is there anything relevant, in the lives of women who arrogantly expected to live in Harlem, in the middle-class enclave of Sugar Hill, to summer at resorts like Idlewild in Michigan, to join exclusive black clubs and sororities? Weren't the interests that preoccupied Larsen in her work just the spoiled tantrums of "little yellow dream children" grown up? (159–60)

The Harlem Renaissance was indeed the literary coming-of-age of the black middle class, but as Hazel Carby and others have pointed out, it was as much a critique of middle-class values as an espousal of them. Nonetheless, the description of Helga Crane's problems as "esoteric," "arrogant," and "spoiled" suggests to me a parallel with the vague, ill-defined complaints of the middle-class patients treated by Heinz Kohut under the category of "narcissistic personality disorders." I will therefore turn to Kohut's theory as a framework for understanding what Larsen understood about the psychological effects of social conflicts, and then I will take Nella Larsen as a framework for questioning the limits of Kohut's description of the phenomenon he calls narcissism. But first, a summary of the novel and of Kohut's theory of narcissism.

The novel opens with Helga Crane's resolution to leave Naxos, the stifling black school where she teaches, because rather than stimulating growth and creativity in its students, it teaches conformity, low horizons of expectation, and imitation of middle-class white values. She goes to the office of the principal, Robert Anderson, to hand in her resignation and is momentarily tempted by his discourse on service into reconsidering, until he inadvertently insults her and she flees to Chicago, where her white uncle—her mother's brother, Peter Nilssen—lives. Hoping to enlist Nilssen's support while she looks for a new job, she encounters his new white wife, who wants nothing to do with her husband's sister's mulatto daughter. Thrown on her own resources, Helga is rejected for a library job because she lacks "references" and for domestic work because she is too refined. Eventually she gets a job as a speech editor for a prominent "race woman," Mrs. Hayes-Rore, through whom she finds work in an insurance company in New York.

In New York, Helga lives with Mrs. Hayes-Rore's elegant niece, Anne Grey, through whom she gets to know Harlem's glittering society life and, for a time, feels quite contented. But her contentment doesn't last, and when a check arrives from the remorseful Uncle Peter, Helga sails to Denmark, where she lives with her mother's relatives, the Dahls. There, she is treated as an exotic treasure, dressed and wined and dined in splendor, and courted by the famous painter Axel Olsen, who paints her portrait, propositions her sexually, and, in the face of her nonresponse, asks her to marry him. Insulted by the way in which the proposal expresses his generosity and her objectification, she refuses. Homesick for Harlem, she returns to New York for the marriage of Anne Grey and Robert Anderson. Later, at a party, Anderson kisses her, and she is overwhelmed with desire. At a later meeting she intends to give herself to him, but he wants only to apologize and reestablish distance. In despair, she walks into a church, has an intense conversion experience, sleeps with the black minister, Rev. Pleasant Green, marries him, and goes south with him to his rural congregation, where she is soon buried in the physical exhaustion of bearing and caring for four children. As the novel ends, she sees nothing in her environment to value and is pregnant with her fifth child.

Heinz Kohut is known for having developed a psychoanalytic theory of what he called "self-psychology." Lacanians have seen this theory as an example of entrapment in the fictions of the autonomous self generated by the mirror stage. Though such a critique may be justified, I prefer to see Kohut's work as a parallel and much richer exploration of structures of mirroring, of which the mirror stage is one example.

What does Kohut mean by a self? The self, he writes, should not be confused with the ego. The self is not a subject. The self is an image, a representation. Indeed, simultaneous contradictory self-representations may exist in a person. "The self, then, quite analogous to the representations of objects, is a *content* of the mental apparatus but is not . . . one of the *agencies* of the mind" (xv). How is the self formed? Kohut answers: through empathic mirroring. The self is the internalization of the gaze of the other, generally the mother in Kohut's account. Instead of Lacan's statuelike visual self-representation in the mirror, for which the mother serves only as a baby stand, Kohut's self-representation derives from the approval-conveying "gleam in the mother's eye." In the early stages of the formation of the self, therefore, other people are not perceived as separate, true objects, but as parts of the self, as "selfobjects." Other people, including sexual partners and, especially for Kohut, psychoanalysts, can continue to function as selfobjects throughout a person's life.

The psychological structures appropriate to the earliest phase in the development of the self, according to Kohut, are the grandiose, exhibitionistic self ("I am perfect") and the idealized, omnipotent selfobject based on the parent ("You are perfect, but I am part of you"). "The need of the budding self for the joyful response of the mirroring selfobject, the need of the budding self for the omnipotent selfobject's pleased acceptance of its merger needs, are primary considerations." If the child is not appropriately mirrored, is not given the message, "What you are is valuable," at this stage, then the grandiose self and the desire to merge with the idealized selfobject do not fade away but become split off and retain their archaic demands. Rather than being progressively reality-tested and integrated, they keep the unfilled hunger for validation intact, like an open wound. This, I think, is what Helga refers to as "a lack somewhere." Like Helga, the patients Kohut analyzes often have considerable talent and strong aesthetic investments. And, like Helga, they have a tendency to "react to sources of narcissistic disturbance by mixtures of wholesale withdrawal and unforgiving rage" (65). Periods of heightened vitality and contentment are followed by a renewed sense of depletion, often brought about either by the anxiety that arises from an uncomfortable degree of excitement or by a rebuff or merely a lack of attention from the environment. Kohut's theory is, among other things, a revaluation of the moral valence of the term *narcissism,* which is based not on self-satisfaction but on hollowness. Helga's apparent selfishness is based not on an excess of self but on a lack of self.

What does the novel tell us about the origins of Helga's narcissistic deficit? What kind of early mirroring did she receive? Her father, a black man she refers to as a gambler and a "gay suave scoundrel," deserted her mother, a Danish immigrant, before Helga could form any definite relation to him. The mother, "sad, cold, and remote," remarried, this time choosing a white man who treated Helga with malicious and jealous hatred. Helga thus has no early relations with black people, except the image of her father as both desirable and unreliable, and she has increasingly negative relations with the white people who are her only family. But instead of becoming enraged at their lack of empathy for her, she actually learns to empathize with their view of her as a problem *for them.* "She saw herself for an obscene sore in all their lives, at all costs to be hidden. She understood, even while she resented. It would have been easier if she had not" (Larsen, *Quicksand* 29). In other words, she learns to identify with the rejecting other, to desire her own disappearance. Intimacy equals rejection; the price of intimacy is to satisfy the other's desire that she disappear. To be is not to be. It is no wonder that Helga's mode is flight and that her first spoken words in the novel are, "No, forever." The culminating scene of orgasmic conversion in the church is a stark acting out of the logic of self-erasure in a merger with the omnipotent other. As the church service begins, a hymn is being sung:

> Oh, the bitter shame and sorrow
> That a time could ever be,
> When I let the Savior's pity
> Plead in vain, and proudly answered:
> All of self and none of Thee,
> All of self and none of Thee.

As the hymn continues, the refrain changes:

> Some of self and some of Thee,
> Some of self and some of Thee.

Then:

> Less of self and more of Thee,
> Less of self and more of Thee.

Then, at the moment Helga surrenders to the conversion, the moment the text says, "She was lost—or saved," the hymn's final refrain is acted out, but not stated:

> None of self and all of Thee,
> None of self and all of Thee.

The religious conversion, the merger with the omnipotent selfobject, momentarily overcomes the self's isolation but at the cost of the self's disappearance. The narcissistic plot here merges with the oedipal plot: Helga's life, like her mother's, is drastically transformed by a moment of blind surrender.

This ecstatic disappearance is the culmination of a series of encounters in the novel that present the narcissistic logic in less drastic terms. Each time, Helga's vulnerable and defensively haughty self approaches a potential mirror and is, or perceives itself to be, mismirrored. I will analyze two of these moments, the opening encounter with Robert Anderson and the encounter with the Danish painter, Axel Olsen.

Robert Anderson is the principal of the black school in which Helga is teaching at the start of the novel. She has become enraged at the school for its low, self-denying expectations of its educational mission; it accepts the image of blacks as hewers of wood and drawers of water, which has just been repeated to the assembled school by a white preacher. Helga has decided to leave the school immediately and must tell Anderson her reasons. As she waits for him to receive her, she thinks about the school's disapproval of her love for bright colors and beautiful clothes. Upon entering his office, she sees "the figure of a man, at first blurred slightly in outline in that dimmer light." She feels confusion, "something very like hysteria," then a mysterious ease. She begins to explain her resignation to Dr. Anderson in an exchange that resembles an initial psychoanalytic session: he remains detached, prompting her to elaborate on her remarks, probing for her thoughts. She explains that she hates hypocrisy and the suppression of individuality and beauty. He then begins a discourse of "wisdom," telling her that lies, hypocrisy, and injustice are part of life that dedicated people put up with when their goals are high. The text describes Helga's reactions:

> Helga Crane was silent, feeling a mystifying yearning which sang and throbbed in her. She felt again that urge for service, not now for her people, but for this man who was talking so earnestly of his work, his plans, his hopes. An insistent need to be a part of them sprang up in her. With compunction tweaking at her heart for ever having entertained the notion of deserting him, she resolved not only to remain until June, but to return next year. (20)

In this scene, Helga enters with a sense of her embattled grandiose self (her esthetic difference, her individuality and creativity) but is drawn toward the appeal of the omnipotent selfobject, the merger with the idealized other. However, that merger can only exist on the basis of perfect empathy. Anderson inadvertently breaks that empathy in the words he uses to solidify it:

> "What we need is more people like you, people with a sense of values, and proportion, an appreciation of the rarer things of life. You have something to give which we badly need here in Naxos. You mustn't desert us, Miss Crane."
>
> She nodded, silent. He had won her. She knew that she would stay. "It's an elusive something," he went on. "Perhaps I can best explain it by the use of that trite phrase, 'You're a lady.' You have dignity and breeding."
>
> At these words turmoil rose again in Helga Crane. The intricate pattern of the rug which she had been studying escaped her. The shamed feeling which had been her penance evaporated. Only a lacerated pride remained. She took firm hold of the chair arms to still the trembling of her fingers.
>
> "If you're speaking of family, Dr. Anderson, why, I haven't any. I was born in a Chicago slum."
>
> The man chose his words, carefully he thought. "That doesn't at all matter, Miss Crane. Financial, economic circumstances can't destroy tendencies inherited from good stock. You yourself prove that!"
>
> Concerned with her own angry thoughts, which scurried here and there like trapped rats, Helga missed the import of his words. Her own words, her answer, fell like drops of hail.

"The joke is on you, Dr. Anderson. My father was a gambler who deserted my mother, a white immigrant. It is even uncertain that they were married. As I said at first, I don't belong here. I shall be leaving at once. This afternoon. Good-morning." (20–21)

In the act of delivering a compliment, Anderson puts his finger on a wound. By juxtaposing the word *lady* (which at Naxos signifies the denial of sexuality) and the word *breeding* (which for Helga is the name both for forbidden sexuality and for lack of family), he shows not only that he is not omnipotent (since he does not really know anything about her) but also that what he wants to value in her is something she thinks she does not and cannot possess. The mirror breaks, the pattern in the rug loses its design, Helga fragments into chaotically scattering pieces, and she departs in a narcissistic rage.

In Denmark, Helga is drawn to the symmetrically opposite kind of narcissistic satisfaction. There, it is her grandiose exhibitionism that is initially mirrored, rather than her desire to merge with the idealized other. Whereas Helga's difference and fine clothes have been met with hostility and disapproval in the United States, the Danes are fascinated. They urge her to become more exhibitionistic, more exotic, more sensuous. Yet they are at the same time cold and detached. Instead of being repressed, Helga's exhibitionism is expropriated, objectified, commodified, and alienated. This process comes to a head in her relation to Axel Olsen, the portrait painter. When she looks at the portrait he has painted of her, she is represented as thinking, "It wasn't herself at all, but some disgusting sensual creature with her features. Bosh! pure artistic bosh and conceit! Nothing else" (89). This has often been read as her refusal to acknowledge her own sexuality. But far from constituting a mirror designed to confirm her sexuality, this mirror gives her only someone else's narcissistic appropriation of it. She refuses the painter's offer of marriage out of a refusal to be owned by a white man. It is in Denmark that she first feels homesick for Negroes and first identifies with, and forgives, her father. She returns to Harlem.

Several times in the novel, the potential mirror is not a person but a race, a "world." When Helga first arrives in Harlem, she feels keenly a "joy at seeming at last to belong somewhere" (44). When she first arrives in Denmark, she also tells herself that "this, then was where she belonged" (67). Yet each time the surrounding mirror is incapable of sustaining the role of selfobject that she asks of it. The promise of belonging flips over into a pressure to conform. Each mirror limits even as it embraces. But instead of seeing that therefore she herself is composite, a mixture, a process rather than a product, that wholeness itself is a fiction—the problem and not the solution—she goes on believing that both she and the environment can be perfected, made whole, non-self-different. For Helga, there is no middle, no compromise, no gray area—satisfaction must be total, pure, and therefore unreal, short-lived.

She seeks to fill her narcissistic deficit with the environment, not for its own properties but in the attempt to substitute for a missing part of the self. The line between remedy and poison is thin: the magical selfobject must inevitably oppress and disappoint.

What is different about Nella Larsen's treatment of these dynamics is that she shows race itself to be a kind of selfobject from which a self can derive both positive and negative mirroring. Kohut occasionally suggests as much, as when, in a footnote, he writes: "It may be helpful to say that the grandiose self . . . has such analogues in adult experience as, e.g., national and racial pride and prejudice (everything good is "inside," everything bad and evil is assigned to the "outsider"), while the relationship to the idealized parent imago may have its parallel in the relationship (including mystical mergers) of the true believer to his God" (27). As an analysis of the narcissistic roots of racism and race pride, this is quite convincing. But it fails to account for the fact that what is a narcissistic structure for the individual is also a social, economic, and political structure in the world. Racial pride and prejudice are not merely interpersonal phenomena but institutionalized structures in history and culture. In dealing with individual patients, Kohut generally neglects or subsumes the *social* mirroring environment in favor of the dynamics of the nuclear family. The following is a fairly striking example:

> Over and over again, throughout his childhood, the patient . . . had felt abruptly and traumatically disappointed in the power and efficacy of his father just when he had (re-)established him as a figure of protective strength and efficiency. . . . After an adventurous flight via South Africa and South America, the family had come to the United States when the patient was nine years old, and the father, who had been a prosperous businessman in Europe, was unable to repeat his earlier success in this country. . . . Most prominent among the patient's relevant recollections of earlier occurrences of the idealization-disappointment sequence concerning his father were those of the family's first years in Eastern Europe. . . . Suddenly the threat that the German armies would overrun the country interrupted their close relationship. At first the father was away a great deal, trying to make arrangements for the transfer of his business to another country. Then, when the patient was six, German armies invaded the country and the family, which was Jewish, fled. (58–60)

The minor role played in the last sentence by the fact that the family was Jewish is an indication of Kohut's overestimation of the nuclear family as the context for psychic development.

What Nella Larsen does is articulate the relation between the mirroring environment of the nuclear family and the social messages from the environment, which *also* affect the construction of the self. It is as though, for Kohut, the child has no independent experience of history, no relation to the world that is not filtered through the parental images. Yet the social world can indeed set up an artificially inflated or deflated narcissistic climate for the child. Racial privilege would offer an unearned archaic narcissistic bonus that, when threatened, would lead to the characteristic narcissistic rages of racism just as surely as the undeserved narcissistic injury resulting from the insertion of a black child into a hostile white environment would lead to the kinds of precarious self-consolidation Larsen documents in the absence of a strong black mirroring environment.

No matter how empathic a mother or father might be, a parent cannot always offset the formative mirroring of the environment. Indeed, in Kohut, the burden of good mirroring falls, again and again, on the mother. His case histories sound like accusations against the mother, whose own context or needs are not analyzed. By contrast, Nella Larsen locates the failures of empathy not in the mother but in the impossible ways in which the mother finds herself inscribed in the social order. Neither for Helga's mother nor for Helga herself as mother at the end of the novel is the social order nourishing, or even viable. And the split between fathers—the absent black father and the rejecting white father—cannot be understood apart from the stereotypical overdeterminations of such a split in American society as a whole.

The therapeutic desire to effect change in the self alone amputates the energies of change from their connections with the larger social and economic world. As Hazel Carby has written of *Quicksand,*

> Alienation is often represented as a state of consciousness, a frame of mind. Implied in this definition is the assumption that alienation can be eliminated or replaced by another state of consciousness, a purely individual transformation unrelated to necessary social or historical change. Helga does question the possibility that her recurrent dissatisfaction with her life could be due to her state of mind and that if she could change her attitudes she could be happy. But against this Larsen has placed an alternative reading of Helga's progress, that her alienation was not just in her head but was produced by existing forms of social relations and therefore subject to elimination only by a change in those social relations. (169)

As this quotation makes clear, Larsen herself does not ask the reader to choose between a psychic and a social model, but rather to see the articulations between them. To see Helga purely from the inside or purely from the outside is to miss the genius of the text. It is the inside-outside opposition itself that needs to be questioned.

In addition to questioning the inside-outside opposition as an adequate model for the relation between the self and society, Larsen's novel also provides material for a critique of the conception of the self as a locus of value. Throughout this essay, I have echoed and extended Kohut's economic vocabulary of narcissistic investments, deficits, and assets, emphasizing the ways in which Helga Crane alternates between surplus value and lack, grandiosity and worthlessness, between an image of herself as a luxury item and an image of herself as garbage. What luxury and garbage have in common is that each is a form of excess with respect to an economy of use or need. Thus, after humiliating rejections by Uncle Peter's new wife and by the library personnel, Helga spends what little money she has on a book and a tapestry purse, "which she wanted but did not need," and resolves to go without dinner, attempting to fulfill a narcissistic hunger in preference to a physical one. As long as need is ignored, however, the narcissistic imbalance cannot be rectified. This emphasis on the isolated self as a locus of value (positive or negative) risks duplicating, in the psychological realm, the structures Marx identified as "the fetishism of the commodity"—the belief that the commodity, abstracted from both labor and use, "contains" value in and of itself. Both Larsen and Kohut analyze a self that is structured like a commodity. This returns us to the perceived middle-classness of both Larsen and Kohut: it may well be that both the concept of the self and the analytical framework through which we have been discussing it can themselves be analyzed as artifacts of class.

To pursue this question indirectly, I turn to a domain that lies in an intermediary position between the psychic and the social and economic. This is the domain of cultural forms. Kohut often mentions the role of aesthetic investments in consolidating a cohesive self, even in the face of early traumatic environments (an incubator baby, children from concentration camps). Larsen has often been criticized for her lack of investment in African American cultural forms, which appear in ambivalent or degraded guises in her novels (the black church, the rural folk, the black educational establishment, the cabaret, the singers Helga sees in Denmark). But these forms also exert a powerful attraction in the novels, which is what gives the forms so much power to disappoint. Hearing the strains of "Swing Low, Sweet Chariot" in Dvorak's *New World* symphony, Helga is overwhelmed with the desire to be carried home.

The final chapter in Larsen's life as a writer is instructive in this context as a bringing together of questions of culture, narcissism, and economics. After her two very successful novels, Larsen wrote a short story entitled "Sanctuary," in which a black woman harbors a fugitive from justice only to find out that the man she is protecting has killed her own son, Obadiah. The last paragraph of the story reads, "It seemed a long time before Obadiah's mother spoke. When she did there were no tears, no reproaches; but there was a raging fury in her voice as she lashed out, 'Git outen mah feather baid, Jim Hammer, an' outen mah house, an' don' nevah stop thankin' yo Jesus he done gib you dat black face'" (18). The character and the plot were an unusual affirmation of black folk speech and racial solidarity for Larsen. But upon its publication she found herself accused of plagiarism: another writer, Sheila Kaye-Smith, had published a strikingly similar story entitled "Mrs. Adis" about white laborers in Sussex eight years earlier. Larsen responded by saying that

she had heard the story from an old black patient in the hospital where she
worked as a nurse, and her publisher produced several of her drafts. She was
more or less exonerated. Mary Dearborn, in *Pocahontas's Daughters*, raises
questions about the nature of ethnic authorship on the basis of this event:

> Whether Larsen plagiarized from "Mrs. Adis," was influenced by or uncon-
> sciously borrowed from it is not the point. . . . Rather it is significant that
> Larsen's choice of material left her open for such a charge in just this way.
> Again ethnic authorship seems to hinge on the ownership of stories. Does
> the woman who sets down a folk tale then own the tale? Are folk tales fit
> matter for fiction? Because Larsen set down a story told her by another
> woman is she then the author of that fiction? If Larsen had set it all down
> as it happened (recounting her meeting with the black patient then the
> story—would "Sanctuary" be fiction? (57)

What becomes clear in this discussion is that the question of the boundaries of the self can arise in ways that transcend the purely psychic domain
while still opening up the possibilities of a devastating narcissistic wound. If
authorship is ownership, how can folk material be one's own? When oral
sources are written down, to whom do they belong? (This question could indeed be asked of the debt psychoanalytic theory owes to the oral histories
of analysands.)[3] What is the property status of a common heritage? In this
case, it is not even clear that the story "belongs" to the black tradition, since
the other version concerns white workers. If Larsen was writing out of a sense
of still precarious loyalty to a tradition and a people about whom her other
works express more ambivalence, then there is an ironic parallel between
the story and its publication. Like the protagonist of the story, Larsen, out
of an act of racial solidarity, has harbored a fugitive who takes away her own
literary offspring. This is not the fault of the sanctuary, or of the fugitive, but
of the laws of ownership and cultural heritage that define the self as property and literature in terms of the authorial proper name. We will never know
what Nella Larsen might have written next, or what other stories her patients
told her. After the exposure and shame of her aborted "Sanctuary," she traveled on a Guggenheim fellowship to Europe and then returned to nursing
for the next thirty years. She never published again.

Nella Larsen has often been conflated with her heroines, whose narcissistic predicaments she is seen to share. In ending my discussion with her silence, I am making the same equation. But although her disappearance from
the publishing world may well be a narcissistic withdrawal, it is important
not to equate her novels with her psyche. As fully realized representations
of intricate social and psychic structures, they are more like analyses than
like symptoms. The Helga Crane of the novel is never in a position to write
the novel *Quicksand*. As is the case for many similar writers—Baudelaire and
Dostoyevsky come immediately to mind—it is, after all, Nella Larsen who

provides the insight that enables readers to feel that they understand more about Nella Larsen than Nella Larsen does. Which does not mean that the insight is the cure. The literature of narcissism does not satisfy the desire for a workable program for social change, but it does offer the warning that any political program that ignores the ways in which the self can refuse to satisfy need or can seek self-cancellation in place of self-validation will not understand where certain resistances are coming from.

NOTES

"The Quicksands of the Self: Nella Larsen and Heinz Kohut" was originally published in Joseph H. Smith and Humphrey Smith, eds., *Telling Facts: History and Narration in Psychoanalysis* (Baltimore: Johns Hopkins University Press, 1992), 184–99. Reprinted by permission of the John Hopkins University Press.

1. Quoted by Deborah McDowell in her introduction to Nella Larsen, *Quicksand; and, Passing* (ix). All references to *Quicksand* are to this edition.
2. Compare Du Bois's famous formulation from *The Souls of Black Folk:* "It is a peculiar sensation, this double-consciousness, this sense of always looking at one's self through the eyes of others, of measuring one's soul by the tape of a world that looks on in amused contempt and pity. One ever feels his twoness,—an American, a Negro; two souls, two thoughts, two unreconciled strivings; two warring ideals in one dark body, whose dogged strength alone keeps it from being torn asunder" (215).
3. I would like to thank Beth Helsinger for suggesting this.

WORKS CITED

Carby, Hazel. *Reconstructing Womanhood.* New York: Oxford UP, 1987.
Dearborn, Mary V. *Pocahontas's Daughters.* New York: Oxford UP, 1986.
Du Bois, W. E. B. *Three Negro Classics: Up from Slavery. The Souls of Black Folk. The Autobiography of an Ex-Colored Man.* New York: Avon, 1965.
Huggins, Nathan. *The Harlem Renaissance.* New York: Oxford UP, 1971.
Kohut, Heinz. *The Analysis of the Self.* New York: International Universities P, 1971.
Larsen, Nella. "Sanctuary." *The Forum* Jan. 1930: 15–18.
———. *Quicksand; and, Passing.* New Brunswick: Rutgers UP, 1986.
McDowell, Deborah. Introduction. *Quicksand.* By Nella Larsen. New Brunswick: Rutgers UP, 1986. ix–xxxv.
Sato, Hiroko. "Under the Harlem Shadow: A Study of Jessie Fauset and Nella Larsen." *The Harlem Renaissance Remembered.* Ed. Arna Bontemps. New York: Dodd, Mead, 1972.
Spillers, Hortense. "Notes on an Alternative Model—Neither/Nor." *The Difference Within.* Ed. Elizabeth Meese and Alice Parker. Philadelphia: John Benjamins, 1989.
Wall, Cheryl. "Passing for What? Aspects of Identity in Nella Larsen's Novels." *Black American Literature Forum* 20.1–2 (1986): 97–111.
Washington, Mary Helen. *Invented Lives.* Garden City, N.Y.: Anchor, 1987.

Passing, Queering
Nella Larsen's Psychoanalytic Challenge

Judith Butler

Can identity be viewed other than as a by-product of a manhandling of
life, one that, in fact, refers no more to a consistent pattern of sameness
than to an inconsequential process of otherness?

TRINH T. MINH-HA

A number of theoretical questions have been raised by the effort to think
the relationship between feminism, psychoanalysis, and race studies. For the
most part, psychoanalysis has been used by feminist theorists to theorize sexual difference as a distinct and fundamental set of linguistic and cultural relations. The philosopher Luce Irigaray has claimed that the question of sexual difference is *the* question for our time.[1] This privileging of sexual
difference implies not only that sexual difference should be understood as
more fundamental than other forms of difference, but that other forms of
difference might be *derived* from sexual difference. This view also presumes
that sexual difference constitutes an autonomous sphere of relations or dis-
junctions, and is not to be understood as articulated through or *as* other vectors of power.

What would it mean to consider the assumption of sexual positions, the
disjunctive ordering of the human as "masculine" or "feminine" as taking
place not only through a heterosexualizing symbolic with its taboo on homosexuality, but through a complex set of racial injunctions that operate in
part through the taboo on miscegenation? Further, how might we understand homosexuality and miscegenation to converge at and as the constitutive outside of a normative heterosexuality that is at once the regulation of
a racially pure reproduction? To coin Marx, then, let us remember that the
reproduction of the species will be articulated as the reproduction *of* relations of reproduction, that is, as the cathected site of a racialized version of
the species in pursuit of hegemony through perpetuity, that requires and
produces a normative heterosexuality in its service.[2] Conversely, the reproduction of heterosexuality will take different forms depending on how race
and the reproduction of race are understood. And though there are clearly

266

good historical reasons for keeping "race" and "sexuality" and "sexual difference" as separate analytic spheres, there are also quite pressing and significant historical reasons for asking how and where we might read not only their convergence, but the sites at which the one cannot be constituted save through the other. This is something other than juxtaposing distinct spheres of power, subordination, agency, historicity, and something other than a list of attributes separated by those proverbial commas (gender, sexuality, race, class) that usually mean that we have not yet figured out how to think the relations we seek to mark. Is there a way, then, to read Nella Larsen's text as engaging psychoanalytic assumptions not to affirm the primacy of sexual difference, but to articulate the convergent modalities of power by which sexual difference is articulated and assumed?

Consider, if you will, the following scene from Nella Larsen's *Passing* in which Irene descends the stairs of her home to find Clare, in her desirable way, standing in the living room.[3] At the moment Irene lights upon Clare, Brian, Irene's husband, appears to have found Clare as well. Irene thus finds Clare, finds her beautiful, but at the same time finds Brian finding Clare beautiful as well. The doubling will prove to be important. The narrative voice is sympathetic to Irene, but exceeds her perspective on those occasions on which Irene finds speaking to be impossible.

> She remembered her own little choked exclamation of admiration, when, on coming downstairs a few minutes later than she had intended, she had rushed into the living room where Brian was waiting and had found Clare there too. Clare, exquisite, golden, fragrant, flaunting, in a stately gown of shining black taffeta, whose long, full skirt lay in graceful folds about her slim golden feet; her glistening hair drawn smoothly back into a small twist at the nape of her neck; her eyes sparkling like dark jewels. (233)

Irene's exclamation of admiration is never voiced, choked back it seems, retained, preserved as a kind of seeing that does not make its way into speech. She would have spoken, but the choking appears to stifle her voice; what she finds is Brian waiting, Brian finding Clare as well, and Clare herself. The grammar of the description fails to settle the question of who desires whom: "she had rushed into the living room where Brian was waiting and had found Clare there too": is it Irene who finds Clare, or Brian, or do they find her together? And what is it that they find in her, such that they no longer find each other, but mirror each other's desire as each turns toward Clare. Irene will stifle the words that would convey her admiration. Indeed, the exclamation is choked, deprived of air; the exclamation fills the throat and thwarts her speaking. The narrator emerges to speak the words Irene might have spoken: "exquisite, golden, fragrant, flaunting." The narrator thus states what remains caught in Irene's throat, which suggests that Larsen's narrator serves the function of exposing more than Irene herself can risk. In most cases where Irene finds herself unable to speak, the narrator supplies the words. But when it comes to explaining exactly how Clare dies at the end of the novel, the narrator proves as speechless as Irene.

The question of what can and cannot be spoken, what can and cannot be publicly exposed, is raised throughout the text, and it is linked with the larger question of the dangers of public exposure of both color and desire. Significantly, it is precisely what Irene describes as Clare's flaunting that Irene admires, even as Irene knows that Clare, who passes as white, not only flaunts but hides—indeed, is always hiding *in* that very flaunting. Clare's disavowal of her color compels Irene to take her distance from Clare, to refuse to respond to her letters, to try to close her out of her life. And though Irene voices a moral objection to Clare's passing as white, it is clear that Irene engages many of the same social conventions of passing as Clare. Indeed, when they meet after a long separation, they are both in a rooftop cafe passing as white. And yet, according to Irene, Clare goes too far, passes as white not merely on occasion, but in her life, and in her marriage. Clare embodies a certain kind of sexual daring that Irene defends herself against, for the marriage cannot hold Clare, and Irene finds herself drawn by Clare, wanting to be her, but also wanting her. It is this risk taking, articulated at once as a racial crossing and sexual infidelity, that alternately entrances Irene and fuels her moral condemnation of Clare with renewed ferocity.

After Irene convinces herself that Brian and Clare are having an affair, Irene watches Clare work her seduction and betrayal on an otherwise unremarkable Dave Freeland at a party. The seduction works through putting into question both the sanctity of marriage and the clarity of racial demarcations:

> Scraps of their conversation, in Clare's husky voice, floated over to her:
> " . . . always admired you . . . so much about you long ago . . . everybody says
> so . . . no one but you. . . ." And more of the same. The man hung rapt on
> her words, though he was the husband of Felise Freeland, and the author of
> novels that revealed a man of perception and a devastating irony. And he fell
> for such pishposh! And all because Clare had a trick of sliding down ivory
> lids over astonishing black eyes and then lifting them suddenly and turning
> on a caressing smile. (254)

Here it is the trick of passing itself that appears to eroticize Clare, the covering over of astonishing black by ivory, the sudden concession of the secret, the magical transformation of a smile into a caress. It is the changeability itself, the dream of a metamorphosis, where that changeableness signifies a certain freedom, a class mobility afforded by whiteness that constitutes the power of that seduction. This time Irene's own vision of Clare is followed not only by a choking of speech, but by a rage that leads to the shattering of her tea cup, and the interruption of chatter. The tea spreads on the carpet like rage, like blood, figured as dark color itself suddenly uncontained by the strictures of whiteness:

> Rage boiled up in her.
>   There was a slight crash. On the floor at her feet lay the shattered cup. Dark stains dotted the bright rug. Spread. The chatter stopped. Went on. Before her. Zulena gathered up the white fragments. (254)

This shattering prefigures the violence that ends the story, in which Clare is discovered by Bellew, her white racist husband, in the company of African Americans, her color "outed," which initiates her swift and quite literal demise: with Irene ambiguously positioned next to Clare with a hand on her arm, Clare falls from the window, and dies on the street below. Whether she jumped or was pushed remains ambiguous: "What happened next, Irene Red-field never afterwards allowed herself to remember. Never clearly. One moment Clare had been there, a vital glowing thing, like a flame of red and gold. The next she was gone" (271).

Prior to this moment, Bellew climbs the stairs to the Harlem apartment where the salon is taking place and discovers Clare there; her being there is sufficient to convince him that she is black. Blackness is not primarily a visual mark in Larsen's story, not only because Irene and Clare are both light-skinned, but because what can be seen, what qualifies as a visible marking, is a matter of being able to read a marked body in relation to unmarked bodies, where unmarked bodies constitute the currency of normative whiteness. Clare passes not only because she is light-skinned, but because she refuses to introduce her blackness into conversation, and so withholds the conversational marker that would counter the hegemonic presumption that she is white. Irene herself appears to "pass" insofar as she enters conversations that presume whiteness as the norm without contesting that assumption. This dissociation from blackness that she performs through silence is reversed at the end of the story in which she is exposed to Bellew's white gaze in clear association with African Americans. It is only on the condition of an association that conditions a naming that her color becomes legible. He cannot "see" her as black before that association, and he claims to her face with unrestrained racism that he would never associate with blacks. If he associates with her, she cannot be black. But if she associates with blacks, she becomes black, where the sign of blackness is contracted, as it were, through proximity, where "race" itself is figured as a contagion transmissable through proximity. The added presumption is that if he were to associate with blacks, the boundaries of his own whiteness, and surely that of his children, would no longer be easily fixed. Paradoxically, his own racist passion *requires* that association; he cannot be white without blacks and without the constant disavowal of his relation to them. It is only through that disavowal that his whiteness is constituted, and through the institutionalization of that disavowal that his whiteness is perpetually—but anxiously—reconstituted.[4]

Bellew's speech is overdetermined by this anxiety over racial boundaries. Before he knows that Clare is black, he regularly calls her "Nig," and it seems that this term of degradation and disavowal is passed between them as a kind of love toy. She allows herself to be eroticized by it, takes it on, acting as if it were the most impossible appellation for her. That he calls her "Nig" suggests that he knows or that there is a kind of knowingness in the language he speaks. And yet, if he can call her that and remain her husband, he cannot know. In this sense, she defines the fetish, an object of desire about which one says, "I know very well that this cannot be, but I desire this all the same," a formulation that implies its equivalence: "Precisely because this cannot be, I desire it all the more." And yet Clare is a fetish that holds in place both the rendering of Clare's blackness as an exotic source of excitation and the denial of her blackness altogether. Here the "naming" is riddled with the knowledge that he claims not to have; he notes that she is becoming darker all the time; the term of degradation permits him to see and not to see at the same time. The term sustains his desire as a kind of disavowal, one that structures not only the ambivalence in his desire for Clare, but also the erotic ambivalence by which he constitutes the fragile boundaries of his own racial identity. To reformulate an earlier claim, then: although he claims that he would never associate with African Americans, he requires the association and its disavowal for an erotic satisfaction that is indistinguishable from his desire to display his own racial purity.

In fact, it appears that the uncertain border between black and white is precisely what he eroticizes, what he needs in order to make Clare into the exotic object to be dominated.[5] His name, Bellew, like bellow, is itself a howl, the long howl of white male anxiety in the face of the racially ambiguous woman whom he idealizes and loathes. She represents the specter of a racial ambiguity that must be conquered. But "Bellew" is also the instrument that fans the flame, the illumination that Clare, literally "light," in some sense *is*. Her luminescence is dependent on the life he breathes into her; her evanescence is equally a function of that power.

> One moment Clare had been there, a vital glowing thing, like a flame of red and gold. The next she was gone.
> There was a gasp of horror, and above it a sound not quite human, like a beast in agony. (271)

"Nig! My God! Nig!" Bellew bellows, and at that moment Clare vanishes from the window. His speech vacillates between degradation and deification, but opens and closes on a note of degradation. The force of that vacillation illuminates, inflames Clare, but also works to extinguish her, to blow her out. Clare exploits Bellew's need to see only what he wants to see, working not so much the appearance of whiteness, but the vacillation between black and white as a kind of erotic lure. His final naming closes down that vacillation, but functions also as a fatal condemnation—or so it seems.

For it is, after all, Irene's hand that is last seen on Clare's arm, and the narrator, who is usually able to say what Irene cannot, appears drawn into Irene's nonnarrativizable trauma, blanking out, withdrawing at the crucial moment when we expect to learn whose agency it was that catapulted Clare from the window and to her death below. That Irene feels guilt over Clare's death is not quite reason enough to believe that Irene pushed her, since one can easily feel guilty about a death one merely wished would happen, even when one knows that one's wish could not be the proximate cause of the death. The gap in the narrative leaves open whether Clare jumped, Irene pushed, or the force of Bellew's words bellowed her out the window. It is, I would suggest, this consequential gap, and the triangulation that surrounds it, that occasions a rethinking of psychoanalysis, in particular, of the social and psychic status of "killing judgments." How are we to explain the chain that leads from judgment to exposure to death, as it operates through the interwoven vectors of sexuality and race?

Clare's fall: is this a joint effort, or is it at least an action whose causes must remain not fully knowable, not fully traceable? This is an action ambiguously executed, in which the agency of Irene and Clare is significantly confused, and this confusion of agency takes place in relation to the violating speech of the white man. We can read this "finale," as Larsen calls it, as rage boiling up, shattering, leaving shards of whiteness, shattering the veneer of whiteness. Even as it appears that Clare's veneer of whiteness is shattered, it is Bellew's as well; indeed, it is the veneer by which the white project of racial purity is sustained. For Bellew thinks that he would never associate with blacks, but he cannot be white without his "Nig," without the lure of an association that he must resist, without the specter of a racial ambiguity that he must subordinate and deny. Indeed, he reproduces that racial line by which he seeks to secure his whiteness through producing black women as the necessary and impossible object of desire, as the fetish in relation to which his own whiteness is anxiously and persistently secured.

There are clearly risks in trying to think in psychoanalytic terms about Larsen's story, which, after all, published in 1929, belongs to the tradition of the Harlem Renaissance and ought properly to be read in the context of that cultural and social world. Whereas many critics have read the text as a tragic story of the social position of the mulatto, others have insisted that the story's brilliance is to be found in its psychological complexity. It seems to me that perhaps one need not choose between the historical and social specificity of the novel, as it has been brought to light by Barbara Christian, Gloria Hull, Hazel Carby, Amritjit Singh, and Mary Helen Washington, and the psychological complexity of cross-identification and jealousy in the text as it has been discussed by Claudia Tate, Cheryl Wall, Mary Mabel Youmans, and Deborah McDowell.[6] Both Tate and McDowell suggest that critics have split over whether this story ought to be read as a story about race and, in particular, as part of the tragic genre of the mulatto, or whether it ought to be read as psychologically complex and, as both McDowell and Carby insist, an allegory of the difficulty of representing black women's sexuality precisely when that sexuality has been exoticized or rendered as an icon of primitivism. Indeed, Larsen herself appears to be caught in that very dilemma, withholding a representation of black women's sexuality precisely in order to avert the consequence of its becoming exoticized. It is this withholding that one might read in *Quicksand,* a novella published the year before *Passing,* where Helga's abstinence is directly related to the fear of being depicted as belonging to "the jungle." McDowell writes, "since the beginning of their 130-year history, black women novelists have treated sexuality with caution and reticence. This is clearly linked to the network of social and literary myths perpetuated throughout history about black women's libidinousness."[7]

The conflict between Irene and Clare, one that spans identification, desire, jealousy, and rage, calls to be contextualized within the historically specific constraints of sexuality and race that produced this text in 1929. And though I can only do that in a very crude way here, I would like briefly to sketch a direction for such an analysis. For I would agree with both McDowell and Carby not only that is it unnecessary to choose whether this novella is "about" race or "about" sexuality and sexual conflict, but that the two domains are inextricably linked, such that the text offers a way to read the racialization of sexual conflict.

Claudia Tate argues that "race . . . is not the novel's foremost concern" and that "the real impetus for the story is Irene's emotional turbulence" (142) and the psychological ambiguity that surrounds Clare's death. Tate distinguishes her own psychological account from those who reduce the novel to a "trite melodrama" (146) of black women passing for white. By underscoring the ambiguity of Clare's death, Tate brings into relief the narrative and psychic complexity of the novella. Following Tate, Cheryl Wall refuses to separate the psychological ambiguity of the story from its racial significance. Agreeing that "Larsen's most striking insights are into psychic dilemmas confronting certain black women," she argues that what appear to be "the tragic mulattoes of literary convention" are also "the means through which the author demonstrates the psychological costs of racism and sexism." For Wall, the figure of Clare never fully exists apart from Irene's own projections of "otherness" (108). Indeed, according to Wall, Irene's erotic relation to Clare participates in a kind of exoticism that is not fully different from Bellew's. Irene sees in Clare's seductive eyes "the unconscious, the unknowable, the erotic, and the passive," where, according to Wall, "[these] symbolize those aspects of the psyche Irene denies within herself" (108–9). Deborah McDowell specifies this account of psychological complexity and pro-jection by underscoring the conflicted homoeroticism between Clare and Irene. McDowell writes, "Though, superficially, Irene's is an account of Clare's passing for white and related issues of racial identity and loyalty, un-derneath the safety of that surface is the more dangerous story—though not named explicitly—of Irene's awakening sexual desire for Clare" (xxvi). Fur-ther, McDowell argues that Irene effectively displaces her own desire for Clare in her "imagination of an affair between Clare and Brian" (xxviii), and that in the final scene "Clare's death represents the death of Irene's sexual feel-ings, for Clare" (xxix).

To understand the muted status of homosexuality within this text—and hence the displacement, jealousy, and murderous wish that follow—it is cru-cial to situate this repression in terms of the specific social constraints on the depiction of black female sexuality mentioned previously. In her essay, "The Quicksands of Representation," Hazel Carby writes,

> Larsen's representation of both race and class are structured through
> the prism of black female sexuality. Larsen recognized that the repression
> of the sensual in Afro-American fiction in response to the long history
> of the exploitation of black sexuality led to the repression of passion
> and the repression or denial of female sexuality and desire. But, of course,
> the representation of black female sexuality meant risking its definition
> as primitive and exotic within a racist society. Racist sexual ideologies pro-
> claimed the black woman to be a rampant sexual being, and in response
> black women writers either focused on defending their morality or displaced
> sexuality onto another terrain. (174)

In contrast, McDowell sees Larsen as resisting the sexual explicitness found in black female blues singers such as Bessie Smith and Ma Rainey (xiii), but nevertheless wrestling with the problem of rendering public a sexuality that thereby became available to an exoticizing exploitation.[8] In a sense, the con-flict of lesbian desire in the story can be read in what is almost spoken, in what is withheld from speech, but which always threatens to stop or disrupt speech. And in this sense the muteness of homosexuality converges in the story with the illegibility of Clare's blackness.

To specify this convergence let me turn first to the periodic use of the term *queering* in the story itself, where queering is linked to the eruption of anger into speech such that speech is stifled and broken, and then to the scene in which Clare and Irene first exchange their glances, a reciprocal see-ing that verges on threatening absorption. Conversations in *Passing* appear to constitute the painful, if not repressive, surface of social relations. It is what Clare withholds in conversation that permits her to "pass"; and when Irene's conversation falters, the narrator refers to the sudden gap in the sur-face of language as "queer" or as "queering." At the time, it seems, *queer* did not yet mean homosexual, but it did encompass an array of meanings associated with the deviation from normalcy that might well include the sexual: of obscure origin, the state of feeling ill or bad, not straight, obscure, perverse, eccentric. As a verb-form *to queer* has a history of meaning: to quiz or ridicule, to puzzle, but also, to swindle and to cheat. In Larsen's text, the aunts who raise Clare as white forbid her to mention her race; they are described as "queer" (189). When Gertrude, another passing black woman, hears a racial slur against blacks, Larsen writes, "From Gertrude's direction came a queer little suppressed sound, a snort or a giggle" (202)—something queer, something short of proper conversation, passable prose. Brian's longing to travel to Brazil is described as an "old, queer, unhappy restlessness" (208), suggesting a longing to be freed of propriety.

That Larsen links queerness with a potentially problematic eruption of sexuality seems clear: Irene worries about her sons picking up ideas about sex at school; Junior, she remarks, "'picked up some queer ideas about things—some things—from the older boys.' 'Queer ideas?' [Brian] repeated. 'D'you mean ideas about sex, Irene?' 'Ye-es. Not quite nice ones, dreadful jokes, and things like that'" (219–20). Sometimes conversation becomes "queer" when anger interrupts the social surface of conversation. Upon becoming convinced that Brian and Clare are having an affair, Irene is described by Larsen this way:

> Irene cried out: "But Brian, I—" and stopped, amazed at the fierce anger that had blazed up in her.
> Brian's head came round with a jerk. His brows lifted in an odd surprise.
> Her voice, she realized *had* gone queer. (249)

As a term for betraying what ought to remain concealed, *queering* works as the exposure within language—an exposure that disrupts the repressive surface of language—of both sexuality and race. After meeting Clare's husband on the street with her black friend Felise, Irene confesses that she has previously "passed" in front of him. Larsen writes, "Felise drawled: 'Aha! Been 'passing' have you? Well, I've queered that'" (259).

In the last instance, queering is what upsets and exposes passing; it is the act by which the racially and sexually repressive surface of conversation is exploded, by rage, by sexuality, by the insistence on color.

Irene and Clare first meet up after years apart in a cafe where they are both passing as white. And the process by which each comes to recognize the other, and recognize her as black is at once the process of their erotic absorption each into the other's eyes. The narrator reports that Irene found Clare to be "an attractive-looking woman . . . with those dark, almost black, eyes and that wide mouth like a scarlet flower against the ivory of her skin . . . a shade too provocative." Irene feels herself stared at by Clare, and clearly stares back, for she notes that Clare "showed [not] the slightest trace of disconcertment at having been detected in her steady scrutiny." Irene then "feel(s) her color heighten under the continued inspection, [and] slid her eyes down. What she wondered could be the reason for such persistent attention? Had she, in her haste in the taxi, put her hat on backwards?" From the start, then, Irene takes Clare's stare to be a kind of inspection, a threat of exposure which she returns first as scrutiny and distrust only then to find herself thoroughly seduced: "She stole another glance. Still looking. What strange languorous eyes she had!" (177). Irene resists being watched, but then falls into the gaze, averts the recognition at the same time that she "surrenders" to the charm of the smile.

The ambivalence wracks the motion of the narrative. Irene subsequently tries to move Clare out of her life, refuses to answer her letters, vows not to invite her anywhere, but finds herself caught up by Clare's seduction. Is it that Irene cannot bear the identification with Clare, or is it that she cannot bear her desire for Clare; is it that she identifies with Clare's passing but needs to disavow it not only because she seeks to uphold the "race" that Clare betrays but because her desire for Clare will betray the family that works as the bulwark for that uplifted race? Indeed, this is a moral version of the family that opposes any sign of passion even within the marriage, even any passionate attachment to the children. Irene comes to hate Clare not only because Clare lies, passes, and betrays her race, but because Clare's lying secures a tentative sexual freedom for Clare and reflects back to Irene the passion that Irene denies herself. She hates Clare not only because Clare has such passion, but because Clare awakens such passion in Irene, indeed, a passion *for* Clare: "In the look Clare gave Irene, there was something groping, and hopeless, and yet so absolutely determined that it was like an image of the futile searching and firm resolution in Irene's own soul, and increased the feeling of doubt and compunction that had been growing within her about Clare Kendry." She distrusts Clare as she distrusts herself, but this groping is also what draws her in. The next line reads: "She gave in" (231).

When Irene can resist Clare, she does it in the name of "race," where "race" is tied to the Du Boisian notion of uplift and denotes an idea of "progress" that not only is masculinist but, in Larsen's story, becomes construed as upward class mobility. This moral notion of "race" which, by the way, is often contested by the celebratory rhetoric of "color" in the text, also requires the idealization of bourgeois family life in which women retain their place in the family. The institution of the family also protects black women from a public exposure of sexuality that would be rendered vulnerable to a racist construction and exploitation. The sexuality that might queer the family becomes a kind of danger: Brian's desire to travel, the boys' jokes, all must be unilaterally subdued, kept out of public speech, not merely in the name of race, but in the name of a notion of racial progress that has become linked with class mobility, masculine uplift, and the bourgeois family. Ironically, Du

Bois himself came to praise Larsen's *Quicksand* precisely for elevating black fiction beyond the kind of sexual exoticization that patrons such as Carl Van Vechten sought to promote.[9] Without recognizing that Larsen was struggling with the conflict produced, on the one hand, by such exotic and racist renderings and, on the other hand, by the moral injunctions typified by Du Bois, Du Bois himself praises her writings as an example of uplift itself.[10] And yet, one might argue that *Passing* exemplifies precisely the cost of uplift for black women as an ambiguous death-suicide whereas *Quicksand* exemplifies that cost as a kind of death in marriage, where both stories resolve on the impossibility of sexual freedom for black women.[11]

What becomes psychically repressed in *Passing* is linked to the specificity of the social constraints on black women's sexuality that inform Larsen's text. If, as Carby insists, the prospect of black women's sexual freedom at the time of Larsen's writing rendered them vulnerable to public violations, including rape, because their bodies continued to be sites of conquest within white racism, then the psychic resistance to homosexuality and to a sexual life outside the parameters of the family must be read in part as a resistance to an endangering public exposure.

To the extent that Irene desires Clare, she desires the trespass that Clare performs, and hates her for the disloyalty that that trespass entails. To the extent that Irene herself eroticizes Clare's racial trespass and Clare's clear lack of loyalty for family and its institutions of monogamy, Irene herself is in a double bind: caught between the prospect of becoming free from an ideology of "race" uncritical in its own masculinism and classism, on the one hand, and the violations of white racism that attend the deprivatization of black women's sexuality, on the other. Irene's psychic ambivalence toward Clare, then, needs to be situated in this historical double bind.[12] At the same time, we can see mapped within Larsen's text the incipient possibility of a solidarity among black women. The identification between Clare and Irene might be read as the unlived political promise of a solidarity yet to come.

McDowell points out that Irene imagines that Brian is with Clare and that this imagining coincides with the intensification of Irene's desire for Clare. Irene passes her desire for Clare through Brian; he becomes the fantasmatic occasion for Irene to consummate her desire for Clare, but also to deflect from the recognition that it is her desire that is being articulated through Brian. Brian carries that repudiated homosexuality, and Irene's jealousy, then, can be understood as not only a rivalry with him for Clare, but the painful consequence of a sacrifice of passion that she repeatedly makes, a sacrifice that entails the displacement or rerouting of her desire through Brian. That Brian appears to act on Irene's desire (although this, importantly, is never confirmed and, so, may be nothing other than an imaginary conviction on Irene's part) suggests that part of that jealousy is anger that he occupies a legitimated sexual position from which he can carry out the de-

sire which she invested in him, that he dares to act the desire which she relegated to him to act on. This is not to discount the possibility that Irene also
desires Brian, but there is very little evidence of a passionate attachment to
him in the text. Indeed, it is against his passion, and in favor of preserv-
ing bourgeois ideals that she clamors to keep him. Her jealousy may well
be routed along a conventional heterosexual narrative, but—as we saw in
Cather—that is not to foreclose the interpretation that a lesbian passion
runs that course.

Freud writes of a certain kind of "jealousy" that appears at first to be the
desire to have the heterosexual partner whose attention has wandered but
is motivated by a desire to occupy the place of that wandering partner in order to consummate a foreclosed homosexuality. He calls this a "delusional
jealousy . . . what is left of a homosexuality that has run its course and it rightly
takes its position among the classical forms of paranoia. As an attempt at
defense against an unduly strong homosexual impulse it may, in a man, be
described in the formula: "*I* do not love him, *she* loves him!"[13] And, in a
woman and in *Passing*, the following formula might apply: "I, Irene, do not
love her, Clare: he, Brian, does!"

It is precisely here, in accounting for the sacrifice, that one reformula-
tion of psychoanalysis in terms of race becomes necessary. In his essay on
narcissism, Freud argues that a boy child begins to love through sacrificing
some portion of his own narcissism, that the idealization of the mother is
nothing other than that narcissism transferred outward, that the mother
stands for that lost narcissism, promises the return of that narcissism, and
never delivers on that promise. For as long as she remains the idealized object of love, she carries his narcissism, she is his displaced narcissism and, insofar as *she carries it,* she is perceived to *withhold it from him.* Idealization, then,
is always at the expense of the ego who idealizes. The ego-ideal is produced
as a consequence of being severed from the ego, where the ego is understood to sacrifice some part of its narcissism in the formation and external-
ization of this ideal.

The love of the ideal will thus always be ambivalent, for the ideal depre-
cates the ego as it compels its love. For the moment, I would like to detach
the logic of this explanation from the drama between boy child and mother
that is Freud's focus (not to discount that focus, but to bring into relief other
possible foci), and underscore the consequence of ambivalence in the
process of idealization. The one I idealize is the one who carries for me the
self-love that I myself have invested in that one. And accordingly, I hate that
one, for he or she has taken my place even as I yielded it, and yet I require
that one, for he or she represents the promise of the return of my own self-
love. Self-love, self-esteem is thus preserved and vanquished at the site of the
ideal.

How can this analysis be related to the questions concerning the racialization of sexuality I have tried to pose? The ego-ideal and its derivative, the superego, are regulatory mechanisms by which social ideals are psychically sustained. In this way, the social regulation of the psyche can be read as the juncture of racial and gendered prohibitions and regulations and their forced psychic appropriations. Freud argues speculatively that this ego-ideal lays the groundwork for the superego and that the superego is lived as the psychic activity of "watching" and, from the perspective that is the ego, the experience of "being watched": "it (the super-ego) constantly watches the real ego and measures it by that (ego-) ideal." Hence, the superego stands for the measure, the law, the norm, one that is embodied by a fabrication, a figure of a being whose sole feature it is to watch, to watch in order to judge, as a kind of persistent scrutiny, detection, effort to expose, that hounds the ego and reminds it of its failures. The ego thus designates the psychic experience of being seen, and the superego that of seeing, watching, exposing the ego. Now, this watching agency is not the same as the idealization that is the ego-ideal; it stands back both from the ego-ideal and the ego, and measures the latter against the former and always, always finds it wanting. The superego is not only the measure of the ego, the interiorized judge, but the activity of prohibition, the psychic agency of regulation that Freud calls *conscience*.[14]

For Freud, this superego represents a norm, a standard, an ideal that is in part socially received; it is the psychic agency by which social regulation proceeds. But it is not just any norm; it is the set of norms by which the sexes are differentiated and installed. The superego thus first arises, says Freud, as a prohibition that regulates sexuality in the service of producing socially ideal "men" and "women." This is the point at which Lacan intervened in order to develop his notion of the symbolic, the set of laws conveyed by language itself that compel conformity to notions of "masculinity" and "femininity." And many psychoanalytic feminists have taken this claim as a point of departure for their own work. They have claimed in various ways that sexual difference is as primary as language, that there is no speaking, no writing, without the presupposition of sexual difference. And this has led to a second claim that I want to contest, namely, that sexual difference is more primary or more fundamental than other kinds of differences, including racial difference. It is this assertion of the priority of sexual difference over racial difference that has marked so much psychoanalytic feminism as white, for the assumption here is not only that sexual difference is more fundamental, but that there is a relationship called "sexual difference" that is itself unmarked by race. That whiteness is not understood by such a perspective as a racial category is clear; it is yet another power that need not speak its name. Hence, to claim that sexual difference is more fundamental than racial difference is effectively to assume that sexual difference is white sexual difference and that whiteness is not a form of racial difference.

Within Lacanian terms, the ideals or norms that are conveyed in language are the ideals or norms that govern sexual difference and that go under the name of the symbolic. But what requires radical rethinking is what social relations compose this domain of the symbolic, what convergent set of historical formations of racialized gender, of gendered race, of the sexualization of racial ideals, or the racialization of gender norms, makes up both the social regulation of sexuality and its psychic articulations. If, as Norma Alarcón has insisted, women of color are "multiply interpellated," called by many names, constituted in and by that multiple calling, then this implies that the symbolic domain, the domain of socially instituted norms, is composed of *racializing norms,* and that they exist not merely alongside gender norms, but are articulated through one another.[15] Hence it is no longer possible to make sexual difference prior to racial difference or, for that matter, to make them into fully separable axes of social regulation and power.

In some ways, this is precisely the challenge to psychoanalysis that Nella Larsen offers in *Passing.* And here is where I would follow Barbara Christian's advice to consider literary narrative as a place where theory takes place,[16] and would simply add that I take Larsen's *Passing* to be in part a theorization of desire, displacement, and jealous rage that has significant implications for rewriting psychoanalytic theory in ways that explicitly come to terms with race. If the watching agency described by Freud is figured as a watching judge, a judge who embodies a set of ideals, and if those ideals are to some large degree socially instituted and maintained, then this watching agency is the means by which social norms sear the psyche and expose it to a condemnation that can lead to suicide. Indeed Freud remarked that the superego, if left fully unrestrained, will fully deprive the ego of its desire, a deprivation that is psychic death and that Freud claims leads to suicide. If we rethink Freud's "super-ego" as the psychic force of social regulation, and we rethink social regulation in terms that include vectors of power such as gender and race, then it should be possible to articulate the psyche politically in ways that have consequences for social survival.

For Clare, it seems, cannot survive, and her death marks the success of a certain symbolic ordering of gender, sexuality, and race, as it marks as well the sites of potential resistance. It may be that as Zulena, Irene's black servant, picks up the shattered whiteness of the broken tea cup, she opens the question of what will be made of such shards. We might read a text such as Toni Morrison's *Sula* as the piecing together of the shattered whiteness that composes the remains of both Clare and Irene in Nella Larsen's text, rewriting Clare as Sula, and Irene as Nel, refiguring that lethal identification between them as the promise of connection in Nel's final call: "girl, girl, girlgirlgirl."[17]

At the close of Larsen's *Passing,* it is Bellew who climbs the stairs and "sees" Clare, takes the measure of her blackness against the ideal of whiteness and finds her wanting. Although Clare has said that she longs for the exposure in order to become free of him, she is also attached to him and his norm for her economic well-being, and it is no accident—even if it is figured as one—that the exposure of her color leads straightway to her death, the literalization of a "social death." Irene, as well, does not want Clare free, not only because Irene might lose Brian, but because she must halt Clare's sexual freedom to halt her own. Claudia Tate argues that the final action is importantly ambiguous, that it constitutes a "psychological death" for Irene just as it literalizes death for Clare. Irene appears to offer a helping hand to Clare, who somehow passes out the window to her death. Here, as Henry Louis Gates Jr. suggests, passing carries the double meaning of crossing the color line and crossing over into death: passing as a kind of passing on.[18]

If Irene turns on Clare to contain Clare's sexuality, as she has turned on and extinguished her own passion, she does this under the eyes of the bellowing white man; his speech, his exposure, his watching divides them against each other. In this sense, Bellew speaks the force of the regulatory norm of whiteness, but Irene identifies with that condemnatory judgment. Clare is the promise of freedom at too high a price, both to Irene and to herself. It is not precisely Clare's race that is "exposed," but blackness itself is produced as marked and marred, a public sign of particularity in the service of the dissimulated universality of whiteness. If Clare betrays Bellew, it is in part because she turns the power of dissimulation against her white husband, and her betrayal of him, at once a sexual betrayal, undermines the reproductive aspirations of white racial purity, exposing the tenuous borders that that purity requires. If Bellew anxiously reproduces white racial purity, he produces the prohibition against miscegenation by which that purity is guaranteed, a prohibition that requires strictures of heterosexuality, sexual fidelity, and monogamy. And if Irene seeks to sustain the black family at the expense of passion and in the name of uplift, she does it in part to avert the position for black women outside the family, that of being sexually degraded and endangered by the very terms of white masculinism that Bellew represents (for instance, she tells Clare not to come to the dance for the Negro Welfare Fund alone, that she'll be taken as a prostitute). Bellew's watching, the power of exposure that he wields, is a historically entrenched social power of the white male gaze, but one whose masculinity is enacted and guaranteed through heterosexuality as a ritual of racial purification. His masculinity cannot be secured except through a consecration of his whiteness. And although Bellew requires the specter of the black woman as an object of desire, he must destroy this specter to avoid the kind of association that might destabilize the territorial boundaries of his own whiteness. This ritualistic expulsion is dramatized quite clearly at the end of *Passing* when Bellew's exposing and endangering gaze and Clare's fall to death are simultaneous with Irene's offer of an apparently helping hand. Fearing the loss of her husband and fearing her own desire, Irene is positioned at the social site of contradiction: both options threaten to jettison her into a public sphere in which she might become subject, as it

were, to the same bad winds. But Irene fails to realize that Clare is as con-
strained as she is, that Clare's freedom could not be acquired at the expense
of Irene, that they do not ultimately enslave each other, but that they are both
caught in the vacillating breath of that symbolic bellowing: "Nig! My God! Nig!"

If Bellew's bellowing can be read as a symbolic racialization, a way in which
both Irene and Clare are interpellated by a set of symbolic norms governing black female sexuality, then the symbolic is not merely organized by "phallic power," but by a "phallicism" that is centrally sustained by racial anxiety
and sexualized rituals of racial purification. Irene's self-sacrifice might be
understood then as an effort to avoid becoming the object of that kind of
sexual violence, as one that makes her cling to an arid family life and destroy
whatever emergence of passion might call that safety into question. Her jealousy must then be read as a psychic event orchestrated within and by this social map of power. Her passion for Clare had to be destroyed only because
she could not find a viable place for her own sexuality to live. Trapped by a
promise of safety through class mobility, Irene accepted the terms of power
that threatened her, becoming its instrument in the end. More troubling than
a scene in which the white man finds and scorns his "Other" in the black
women, this drama displays in all its painfulness the ways in which the interpellation of the white norm is reiterated and executed by those whom it
would—and does—vanquish. This is a performative enactment of "race" that
mobilizes every character in its sweep.

And yet, the story reoccupies symbolic power to expose that symbolic force
in return, and in the course of that exposure began to further a powerful
tradition of words, one that promised to sustain the lives and passions of precisely those who could not survive within the story itself. Tragically, the logic
of "passing" and "exposure" came to afflict and, indeed, to end Nella
Larsen's own authorial career, for when she published a short story, "Sanctuary," in 1930, she was accused of plagiarism, that is, exposed as "passing"
as the true originator of the work.[19] Her response to this condemning exposure was to recede into an anonymity from which she did not emerge. Irene
slipped into such a living death, as did Helga in *Quicksand*. Perhaps the alternative would have meant a turning of that queering rage no longer against
herself or Clare, but against the regulatory norms that force such a turn:
against both the passionless promise of that bourgeois family and the bellowing of racism in its social and psychic reverberations, most especially, in
the deathly rituals it engages.

NOTES

"Passing, Queering: Nella Larsen's Psychoanalytic Challenge" was originally published
in Judith Butler, *Bodies That Matter: On the Discursive Limits of "Sex"* (New York: Routledge, 1993).

1. See Luce Irigaray, *Éthique de la différence sexuelle* (Paris: Editions de Minuit, 1984), 13.

2. Freud's *Totem and Taboo: Resemblances between the Lives of Savages and Neurotics* (New York: Moffat, Yard and Co., 1918) attests to the inseparability of the discourse of species reproduction and the discourse of race. In that text, one might consider the twin uses of "development" as the movement toward an advanced state of culture and the "achievement" of genital sexuality within monogamous heterosexuality.

3. Nella Larsen, *Passing*, in *An Intimation of Things Distant: The Collected Fiction of Nella Larsen*, ed. Charles Larson, foreword by Marita Golden (New York: Anchor Books, 1992), 163–276.

4. This suggests one sense in which "race" might be construed as performative. Bellew produces his whiteness through a ritualized production of its sexual barriers. This anxious repetition accumulates the force of the material effect of a circumscribed whiteness, but its boundary concedes its tenuous status precisely because it requires the "blackness" that it excludes. In this sense, a dominant "race" is constructed (in the sense of *materialized*) through reiteration and exclusion.

5. This is like the colonized subject who must resemble the colonizer to a certain degree, but who is prohibited from resembling the colonizer too well. For a fuller description of this dynamic, see Homi Bhabha, "Of Mimicry and Man: The Ambivalence of Colonial Discourse," *October* 28 (spring 1984): 126.

6. Where references in the text are made to the following authors, they are to the following studies unless otherwise indicated: Houston A. Baker Jr., *Modernism and the Harlem Renaissance* (Chicago: Chicago University Press, 1987); Robert Bone, *The Negro Novel in America* (New Haven: Yale University Press, 1958); Hazel V. Carby, *Reconstructing Womanhood: The Emergence of the Afro-American Woman Novelist* (London: Oxford University Press, 1987); Barbara Christian, *Black Women Novelists: The Development of a Tradition, 1892–1976* (Westport, Ct.: Greenwood Press, 1980) and "Trajectories of Self-Definition: Placing Contemporary Afro-American Women's Fiction," in *Conjuring: Black Women, Fiction, and Literary Tradition,* ed. Marjorie Pryse and Hortense J. Spillers (Bloomington: Indiana University Press, 1985), 233–48; Henry Louis Gates Jr., *Figures in Black: Words, Signs, and the "Racial" Self* (New York: Oxford University Press, 1987); Nathan Huggins, *Harlem Renaissance* (New York: Oxford University Press, 1971); Gloria Hull, *Color, Sex, and Poetry: Three Women Writers of the Harlem Renaissance* (Bloomington: Indiana University Press, 1987); Deborah E. McDowell, introduction to Nella Larsen's *Quicksand; and, Passing* (New Brunswick: Rutgers University Press, 1986); Jacquelyn Y. McLendon, "Self-Representation as Art in the Novels of Nella Larsen," in *Redefining Autobiography in Twentieth-Century Fiction,* ed. Janice Morgan and Colette T. Hall (New York: Garland, 1991); Hiroko Sato, "Under the Harlem Shadow: A Study of Jessie Faucet and Nella Larsen," in *The Harlem Renaissance Remembered,* ed. Arno Bontemps (New York: Dodd, 1972), 63–89; Amritjit Singh, *The Novels of the Harlem Renaissance* (State College: Pennsylvania State University Press, 1976); Claudia Tate, "Nella Larsen's *Passing*: A Problem of Interpretation," *Black American Literature Forum* 14, no. 4 (1980): 142–46; Hortense Thornton, "Sexism as Quagmire: Nella Larsen's *Quicksand*," *CLA Journal* 16 (1973): 285–301; Cheryl Wall, "Passing for What? Aspects of Identity in Nella Larsen's Novels," *Black American Literature Forum* 20, no. 1–2 (1986): 97–111; Mary Helen Washington, *In-*

vented Lives: Narratives of Black Women, 1860–1960 (New York: Anchor-Doubleday, 1987).

7. Deborah E. McDowell, "'That nameless . . . shameful impulse': Sexuality in Nella Larsen's *Quicksand and Passing*," in *Black Feminist Criticism and Critical Theory Studies in Black American Literature,* ed. Joel Weixlmann and Houston A. Baker Jr., vol. 3 (Greenwood, Fla.: Penkevill Publishing Company, 1988), 141. Reprinted in part as introduction to *Quicksand and Passing.* All further citations to McDowell in the text are to this essay.

8. Jewelle Gomez suggests that black lesbian sexuality very often thrived behind the church pew. See Jewelle Gomez, "A Cultural Legacy Denied and Discovered: Black Lesbians in Fiction by Women," in *Home Girls: A Black Feminist Anthology,* ed. Barbara Smith. (Latham, N.Y.: Kitchen Table Press, 1983), 120–21.

9. For an analysis of the racist implications of such patronage, see Bruce Kellner, "'Refined Racism': White Patronage in the Harlem Renaissance," in *The Novels of the Harlem Renaissance,* ed. Amrit Singh (State College: Pennsylvania State University Press, 1976), 93–106.

10. McDowell writes, "Reviewing Claude McKay's *Home to Harlem* and Larsen's *Quicksand* together for *The Crisis,* for example, Du Bois praised Larsen's novel as 'a fine, thoughtful and courageous piece of work,' but criticized McKay's as so 'nauseating' in its emphasis on 'drunkenness, fighting, and sexual promiscuity' that it made him feel . . . like taking a bath." She cites "Rpt. in *Voices of a Black Nation: Political Journalism in the Harlem Renaissance,* ed. Theodore G. Vincent (San Francisco: Ramparts Press, 1973) 359," in McDowell, 164.

11. Indeed, it is the way in which Helga Crane consistently uses the language of the "primitive" and the "jungle" to describe sexual feeling that places her in a tragic alliance with Du Bois.

12. For an effort to reconcile psychoanalytic conflict and the problematic of incest and the specific history of the African American family postslavery, see Hortense J. Spillers, "'The Permanent Obliquity of an In(pha)llibly Straight': In the Time of the Daughters and the Fathers," in *Changing Our Own Words,* ed. Cheryl Wall (New Brunswick: Rutgers, 1989), 127–49.

13. Sigmund Freud, "Some Neurotic Mechanisms in Jealousy, Paranoia, and Homosexuality," in *The Standard Edition of the Complete Psychological Works of Sigmund Freud,* trans. and ed. James Strachey, 24 vols. (London: Hogarth Press, 1953–1974), 18: 225.

14. Significantly, Freud argues that conscience is the sublimation of homosexual libido, that the homosexual desires that are prohibited are not thoroughly destroyed; they are satisfied by the prohibition itself. In this way, the pangs of conscience are nothing other than the displaced satisfactions of homosexual desire. The guilt about such desire is, oddly, the very way in which that desire is preserved.

This consideration of guilt as a way of locking up or safeguarding desire may well have implications for the theme of white guilt. For the question there is whether white guilt is itself the satisfaction of racist passion, whether the reliving of racism that white guilt constantly performs is not itself the very satisfaction of racism that white guilt ostensibly abhors. For white guilt—when it is not lost to self-pity—produces a paralytic moralizing that *requires* racism to sustain its own sanctimonious posturing. Precisely because white moralizing is itself nourished by racist passions, it can never be the basis on which to build and affirm a community across difference; rooted in the desire to be exempted from white racism, to produce oneself as the exemption, this strategy virtually requires that the white community remain mired in racism: hatred is merely transferred outward, and thereby preserved, but it is not overcome.

15. Norma Alarcón, "The Theoretical Subject(s) of *This Bridge Called My Back* and Anglo-American Feminism," in *Making Face, Making Soul: Haciendo Caras*, ed. Gloria Anzaldua (San Francisco: Aunt Lute, 1990), 356–69.

16. Barbara Christian, "The Race for Theory," in *The Nature and Context of Minority Discourse*, ed. A. R. JanMohared and D. Lloyd (New York: Oxford University Press, 1990), 37–49.

17. Toni Morrison, *Sula* (New York: Knopf, 1973), 174.

18. Henry Louis Gates Jr., *Figures*, 202.

19. I am thankful to Barbara Christian for pointing out to me the link between the theme of "passing" and the accusation of plagiarism against Larsen.

The Stories of O(Dessa)

Stories of Complicity and Resistance

Mae G. Henderson

Ms. Collen Stan: I was blindfolded, gagged, had this thing over my head, my—my hands are handcuffed behind my back, and my ankles are tied together.

Rivera: This starts a seven-year captivity.

Ms. Stan: He put these leather restraints or whatever you want to call them on my wrists. He connected them up on these bars. He grabs this whip, and he starts whipping me and tells me to shut up.

Rivera: So you're in this, like, torture chamber now.

Ms. Stan: Yeah. I just hung there and cried. So, at this point, I thought, "This guy is going to kill me."

TRANSCRIPT, "HUMAN BONDAGE:
THE STORY OF A SLAVE AND HER MASTER"

PROLOGUE

The preceding dialogue, excerpted from the transcript of an interview aired on the *Geraldo Rivera Show,* "Human Bondage: The Story of a Slave and Her Master," recounts in lurid detail the abuse and torture of a woman who was kidnapped and held in captivity as a "sex slave." Collen Stan explains in her own words how the perpetrator, Cameron Hooker (since tried and convicted by the State of California) with the assistance of his wife (who turned state's evidence) abducted her when she was twenty, locked her in a basement, bound her wrists with leather restraints, hooked her arms to the ceiling so that she dangled by her feet, removed her clothing, and beat her with a whip. Although blindfolded, she could see her captor and his wife having sex on a table in the corner of the basement. Lying on a small table next to her, she saw a magazine displaying a woman in the same position. This was the beginning of the seven-year captivity from which she finally escaped.

These events occurred in the late 1970s and early 1980s (she escaped in 1985) in Red Bluff, California, and are paradigmatic for understanding the relation between slavery, violence, and sexuality. First, they present the audience with a kaleidoscope of scenes depicting relations based on the absolute power (of life and death) of one individual over another, a power main-

285

tained both by the actual employment as well as the threat of violence. Second, they expose the ritualistic and symbolic aspects of power in the highly personal and "private" domain of sexuality. Third, they locate woman in the position of subordinate subject in a tripartite ritual of power, violence, and domination.

For our purposes, it is critical that these scenarios are drawn together in a metaphor that links the sphere of sexuality in modern society to the practices of power and domination. Here, Rivera's role as show host and interlocutor allows him to frame the terms ("captivity," "torture," "slave," "master") and setting ("torture chamber") for Stan's recitation. Through her testimony, Stan bears witness to Rivera's title, "Human Bondage: The Story of a Slave and Her Master." This spectacle of "woman in captivity" codes the sexual subjugation of women as bondage, an association that is, in fact, borne out by the history of women in slaveholding societies, where they have been vulnerable to sexual violence as a means of social control.

Transcoding the metaphor of slavery to the sphere of sexuality requires the formulation of a critical feminist discourse that addresses this intersection. Even without the accomplished (although largely uncritical) lead of Rivera, Stan's scene of captivity unavoidably reproduces the relation between pornography and the abuse of women, explicitly fashioned in the magazine photo that models her own bound and captive position. What the excerpt suggests only in part, but the complete transcript makes evident, is the complicity of women who participate in the eroticization of dominance and submission. Clearly, compliance on the part of the wife—and later, the victim—reflect the extent to which the sexual fantasies and practices of women have been conditioned by an ideology of female submission, thereby perpetuating patriarchal violence and domination.

Such a testimony on network television poses unsettling questions implicating victim and perpetrator (both of whom spoke on national network television, the latter from the state penitentiary) as well as spectators and producers in the complicity of reproduction. Despite the fact that Rivera and Stan are engaged in an exposé of sexual atrocity, the media's role in staging desire as production and exploiting it as entertainment point to the "problematic of representation"—even when it is in the service of exposé and critique. Rivera coaxes a willing (for the sake of exposé) Stan into replicating the language and visuals of the pornographic scenarios that are subject to critique. Here, however, the dilemma posed by Stan and Rivera can be instructive to the critic. Like them, the critic must necessarily reproduce elements of the text in the process of analyzing the representation of erotica or pornography, thereby risking the subjection of the spectator-reader to the seductions of desire.

Because Sherley Anne Williams's *Dessa Rose* embodies a paradigm of race and gender conjoined with slavery and sexuality at precisely the moment when the critical issues of complicity and resistance converge, Rivera's "Of Human Bondage" provides an appropriate introduction to the following discussion of Shirley Anne Williams's text. The staging of desire that underscores his production points to the necessity of a critical analysis of slavery that uncovers its repressed subtext: the pornographic. Of course, the "ob-scene" that confronts the contemporary reader has always existed as part of the story of slavery. Most frequently, this aspect is registered by allusions to the physical abuses of black women's bodies (stories "too terrible to tell") recounted by former slaves and abolitionists. This discursive legacy of slavery (and its persistence in the American sexual imaginary) challenges Williams to produce a literary exposé that does not reproduce the structures of desire already encoded in the pornographic scenario. The critic's challenge is to discover a critical method analogous to Williams's literary method—one that illuminates the relationship between slavery and pornography but resists manipulating desire.

1

Williams characteristically invokes an antimodel that clarifies, by contrast, her own narrative investment. My earlier work on Williams predisposes me to take with much seriousness the range of implicit and explicit intertextual references in her work.[1] Her novel *Dessa Rose* provides a unique example of intertextuality, for it dialogically engages not only Williams's own previous work but also two texts outside the African American literary tradition: William Styron's *Confessions of Nat Turner* (based, in part, on Thomas Gray's work of the same title, published in 1832) and Pauline Réage's *Story of O.* Common to all of these works are recurring scenes of political and/or sexual captivity that eroticize(s) relations under the sign of lordship and bondage: white master and slave woman; white interviewer and slave interviewee; writing subject and written object; critic and text. Williams, however, reconceptualizes prior representations of women and blacks at the scene of writing captivity, particularly when the condition of black and/or female subjectivity is their subordination to the writing subject (or interlocutor). Through my reading of *Dessa Rose,* I examine how Williams exposes both Styron's racial masquerade, which appropriates black to white (male) subjectivity, and the racial specificity of Réage's performance of femininity. Through this second, more extended inquiry, I argue that narratives of female masochism must be reconceptualized racially, as Williams rewrites the erotics of white feminine surrender as the politics of black feminist resistance.

2

Dessa Rose appeared in 1987 as an elaboration of Williams's earlier short story, "Meditations on History."[2] Why did Williams, an accomplished poet and short story writer, choose, in her first novel, to revisit and revise this earlier work? What issues does the longer narrative engage that distinguish it from the shorter one? How do the problems introduced by Williams in "Meditations" get worked out in *Dessa Rose*? In addressing these questions, we must look not only to the texts but also at the historical contexts of their production. In a preliminary examination of the historical referents and perspectives of these two works, I demonstrate how Williams weaves into the short story and the novel strands of competing and complementary historical and contemporaneous discourses.

"Meditations" roughly coincides with the first of three sections in the novel *Dessa Rose*. Set in Alabama in 1829, the action revolves around the encounter between an unnamed interviewer-narrator and a pregnant "rebellious slave girl." Dessa, who has been imprisoned in a root cellar, awaits a hanging that is to be postponed until the birth of her child. We learn that Dessa has attacked her master, who has killed the father of her child. As a result, she is sold to a slave trader but manages to escape from a slave coffle, along with several companions, after a fracas in which she kills one of the traders. It is not until after Dessa's recapture, while awaiting her baby's birth before her scheduled execution, that she is introduced to the reader. The unnamed white male who functions as narrator in the story attempts to interview her, recording her story in his journal. His project is to gain information in support of a forthcoming book on how to eradicate slave rebellions. The novella and part 1 of *Dessa Rose* conclude with Dessa's second escape, this time from both the social system and the system of literary representation.

As indicated by the narrator-interviewer's project, the era of the 1820s was a period of slave unrest, marked by memories of the massive conspiracies led by Gabriel Prosser in 1800 and Denmark Vesey in 1822 and fearfully anticipating events such as those leading to Nat Turner's insurrection in 1831. In documenting and elaborating the story of a nineteenth-century female slave rebel, Williams intervenes into a male story of resistance and locates her work within a historical and contemporary dialogue of race struggle.[3] By dedicating her story to black woman scholar and activist, Angela Davis, and prefacing it with a quote from Davis's article, "Reflections on the Black Woman's Role in the Community of Slaves," Williams links her heroine to a tradition of violent resistance to oppression extending from the nineteenth into the twentieth century.[4]

Beyond this, Williams critiques a discourse of race as it informs both historiographical and literary writing. As I have demonstrated elsewhere, Williams's intention to engage William Styron's *Confessions of Nat Turner*, published in 1965, is initially signaled by the title of her short story, "Meditations on History."[5] In his "Author's Note," Styron tells the reader that his intention has been to "re-create a man and his era, and to produce a work that is less an 'historical novel' in conventional terms than a *meditation on history*"[6] (emphasis added).

When Williams published her novel in 1987, she changed the setting from 1829 to 1847, thus advancing the temporal frame of the action by eighteen years. The 1840s, with its increased abolitionist activity and militant resistance to slavery, provides a more dramatic backdrop for the events in the novel, as well as the impetus for much of the character motivation. Significantly both the mid-1840s (the historical period of the novel's enactment) and the mid-1980s (the contemporary period of the novel's production) represent eras of retrenchment on the racial question. Just as the abolitionist movement of the 1840s was undermined by the internal divisions of political pragmatism versus moral suasion, so the civil rights and Black Power movements were undermined by internal strife in the 1970s and 1980s. Moreover, just as the issue of women's participation in abolition provided the background for the subsequent emergence of the women's rights movement in the 1840s, civil rights and Black Power movements set the stage for feminism's challenge to the priority of race as a privileged locus of dissent. Further, just as the abolitionist movement generated a counterresponse from the proslavery faction of southern ideologues, so the politics of civil rights generated a counterresponse from an empowered religious right, a reconstituted conservative Supreme Court, and a polarizing presidential politics of Reaganomics in the 1980s.[7] Finally, the decade of the 1980s also saw emergence of a new academic discourse—the feminist critique, as a counterpart and counterpoint to the racial critique. Like the 1980s, then, the 1840s had been a period of racial turbulence as well as progressive agitation for women's rights.

Accordingly, we can see that Williams's novella and novel draw upon both their fictional and historical settings as well as their contemporary and political settings. "Meditations," written during the 1970s, foregrounds a discourse of race in the wake of the civil rights movement, and *Dessa Rose*, published in the mid-1980s, foregrounds a discourse of race and gender during the period that has since become known as the second wave of American feminism.

In her "Author's Note" (paralleling Styron's), Williams explains that the novel is based on two historical incidents: "A pregnant black woman helped to lead an uprising on a coffle . . . in 1829. Caught and convicted, she was sentenced to death; her hanging however, was delayed until after the birth of her baby. In North Carolina in 1830, a white woman living on an isolated farm was reported to have given sanctuary to runaway slaves. . . . How sad, I thought then, that these two women never met."[8] *Dessa Rose* provides the occasion for such a meeting, an encounter that enables Williams to stage a dialogue between the discourse of slavery and the discourse of nineteenth-century womanhood, reading both through a contemporary dialectic of race and gender. Moreover, in its intervention into the racial critique of the 1960s and 1970s and the feminist critique of the 1970s and 1980s, Williams's novel positions itself at the discursive juncture of two oppositional discourses. In some respects, *Dessa Rose* marks Williams's entry as a woman into the racial critique and as a black into the feminist critique, making her work as a black feminist writer a site of struggle and affirmation in two historically emancipatory but often competing discourses.

Directly engaging Styron in her own "Author's Note," Williams "admits to being outraged by a certain critically acclaimed novel . . . that travestied the as-told-to-memoir of slave revolt leader Nat Turner" (5). In *Dessa Rose*, the white male interviewer-narrator, Adam Nehemiah, like the lawyer in Styron's *Confessions*, functions as an amanuensis for the slave. However, as author-to-be of *The Roots of Rebellion in the Slave Population and Some Means of Eradicating Them* (or more simply, *Roots*), his role also corresponds to Styron's. What is, for Williams, problematic in Styron's text is the mimetic relationship between author and subject. Styron's representation of Nat's voice as formal, poetic, religious-inflected prose links the slave rebel not with the vernacular of the other slaves but with the highly literate author. Thus, although Styron's racial masquerade establishes a homosocial identification with his subject, Nat, it would also appear to cover an oppositional relation between the black male revolutionary and the white liberal writer. Not only is Nat constructed as weak and irresolute, but his liberational impulses are disassociated from the realm of power and resistance and linked to sexual repression in the form of latent homosexuality and pent-up passion for white women. Thus, Styron maintains the distinction between the public and private, dispossessing Turner of his political motivation and constructing him as a subject-object of erotic desire rather than political interest. What is at issue here is not only the emasculation of the black male revolutionary, but also the ends served by such constructions and the degree to which they articulate the author's subjectivity.

3

If Williams's "Meditations," figured in part 1 of *Dessa Rose*, rewrites Styron's controversial *Confessions*, the remainder of the novel rewrites Pauline Réage's equally controversial *Story of O* (originally published in 1954 but translated into English in 1965, one year after the appearance of Styron's *Confessions*). André Pieyre de Mandiargues, who writes an introduction to the original edition of *Story of O*, sees the novel as a mystical allegory of the "Western 'soul,'" whereas Susan Sontag argues that it is a story of erotic desire expressed through religious metaphor. Similarly, Leo Bersani sees it as a universal allegory of human desire in which the coherent unitary subject is "dismembered" through a loss of self. In contrast, Jessica Benjamin sees the narrative as a "fantasy of erotic domination" deriving from a female position

of passivity resulting from her "tendency 'to experience her continuity'" by
"'merging with the mother.'"[9] My own reading of this novel is through what
I take to be Williams's rewriting. Like previous readings, mine is allegorical
in that it "reaches outside of the terms of the text in order to explain textual activity."[10] For the black feminist writer and reader, such a text must be
read as an allegory of white female complicity with the patriarchy, an allegory underscored by the recent discovery of the female authorship of this
text. The relationship between O and her victimizer constitutes a hazardous
alliance in which the patriarchy is further institutionalized by the integration of the white woman into its fundamental structures—structures rang-
ing from psychoanalytic to literary to political practice.

In the United States (as opposed to France), Réage's novel was hailed by
some as a "transgressive erotic classic" and literary manifesto of woman's sexual liberation and by others as a pornographic representation of woman's
degradation. Notably, feminist critic Susan Gubar defines pornography as
"a gender-specific genre produced primarily by and for men but focused ob-
sessively on the female figure."[11] Réage's text, however, represents an example of a genre produced not *by* a man, but *for* a man. Female authorship here
raises the problematic of women assuming authority in controlling their own
images, even—or especially—when those images reproduce "male" images
of women. Although some critics may argue that the author's intent was exposure rather than fantasy fulfillment, the author's own testimony that she
wrote the *Story of O* to rekindle the romantic interest of her lover, Jean Paulhan, would suggest that the text was less "diagnostic" than "symptomatic."[12]

Publication of the *Story of O,* along with that of another French text, the
Portuguese Letters (originally published in 1669), became the occasion for an
extended debate in the early 1970s between American feminist critics Nancy
Miller and Peggy Kamuf. Responding to Kamuf, Miller insisted on a patriarchal signature and line of descent for a text that glamorizes "female suffering around a man." Miller writes, "Kamuf doesn't care whether the *Portuguese* letters were written by a woman or by a man, and I do. Much as I care
if the *Story of O* was written by Pauline Réage or Jean Paulhan . . . I *prefer* to
think that this *positioning* of woman is the writing of a masculine desire attached to a male body." Miller concludes, however, that "this preference is
not without its vulnerabilities. . . . It could," she speculates, "one day be
proved definitively that the heroines of the Portuguese letters and the *Story
of O* were female creations after all. I would then have to start all over again."[13]

It has now been established that the author of the *Story of O* is indeed a
woman, Dominique Aury. Although this was not known to be the case when
I began this essay, my assumptions and argument (unlike Miller's) remain
substantially unchanged. The text now allows us to consider the consequence
when women, occupying the male subject-position, produce male fantasies
of feminine identity. Réage is, in effect, legitimized in her appropriation of

the language, perspective, and vision of woman that is identified as "male."
Nevertheless, whether the *Story of O* is articulated directly by Jean Paulhan
or, as we now believe, ventriloquized by his companion writing under the
nom de plume of Pauline Réage, my task is to address the politics of representation, as well as to show how meaning is produced when the reader or
critic brings a black and feminist perspective to such a text.[14] Assuming, then,
that Simone de Beauvoir is correct when she writes that some women "still
dream through the dreams of men," I read the *Story of O* not as a female story
in which subordination encodes masochism as woman's transgressive erotic
desire; nor do I read it as a subversion of male sadistic desire achieved by
the heroine's spiritual transcendence over physical degradation. Through
Williams's rewriting, I deconstruct a surface "female" narrative of submission, exposing it as a cover story displacing a deeper "male" narrative of manipulation of female fantasy and desire.

   The *Story of O* is preceded by Jean Paulhan's prologue citing a specific historical incident relating to slavery (analogous to similar prologues in *Confessions* and *Dessa Rose*). As in the slave narratives, these prologues or "pre-
texts" serve to guarantee the authenticity or reliability of the tale that
follows. Thus, just as Styron used Gray's document to authenticate his own
tale, so the introduction by Jean Paulhan, identified as a member of l'A-
cadémie Française, is meant to authenticate Réage's narrative. Yet Paulhan's
prefatory remarks inadvertently serve to establish an identification between
guarantor and narrator. (Notably, Williams's own prologue, inscribing Dessa's
personal reveries, functions to subvert rather than authenticate Nehemiah's
construction of the latter in his journal—a literary move that implicitly subverts both Styron's and Réage-Paulhan-Aury's constructions of black and female subjectivity.)

   Paulhan's prologue, "Happiness in Slavery," introduces *Story of O* by way
of an analogy comparing O's response to her "master" with that of a group
of black slaves in Barbados who massacre their master for refusing "to take
them back into bondage":

   In the course of the year 1838, the peaceful island of Barbados was rocked
   by a strange and bloody revolt. About two hundred Negroes of both sexes,
   all of whom had recently been emancipated by the Proclamations of March,
   came one morning to beg their former master . . . to take them back into
   bondage. An Anabaptist minister, acting as spokesman for the group, read
   out a list of grievances which he had compiled and recorded in a notebook. . . . [E]ither from timidity or because he was scrupulous or simply
   afraid of the law, [the master] refused to be swayed. At which point he
   was . . . set upon and massacred . . . by the Negroes.[15]

Thus, not only does Paulhan's allegory compare the slaves' response to their
(former) master with O's relation to her master, it also suggests that Réage's

Story of O may itself be modeled on the genre of the slave narrative. Further, Paulhan refers to a notebook (that is, a journal) in which was compiled a list of grievances recorded by an Anabaptist minister, suggesting yet another parodic aspect of Williams's own journalistic format. The unrecovered notebook, Paulhan speculates, "would seem even more heretical today than it did some hundred and thirty years ago; today," he concludes, "it would be considered a dangerous book" (*Story* xxii–iii). Thus, as the story of slavery is reconfigured as the story of desire in the guarantor's reading, Réage's narrative of desire is rewritten by Williams as a narrative of slavery. By transposing the element of servitude in the narrative of eroticism into a narrative of slavery that reveals the element of the erotic, Williams—in a narrative of slavery where eros is inseparable from domination—reminds the reader of the material rather than metaphorical aspects of slavery.

The association between the story of slavery and the story of desire rests on an affiliation between slavery as an institutionalized system of power—and pornography as a visual and discursive representation of power: both inevitably raise issues of violence and violation. Moreover, in an economy of production and consumption, both slavery and pornography raise questions of control and profit from the commodification of others. Finally, slavery and pornography pose the question of whether what I call "The Stories of O(Dessa)" are narratives of desire or narratives of slavery.[16]

It is useful here to bridge these two narratives—the story of slavery and the story of desire—by recalling a poignant moment in Frederick Douglass's 1845 *Narrative*. He recalls awakening to the horrors of slavery when he witnessed the whipping of his aunt by his master (reputed to be his father) and describes the scene as "a most terrible spectacle"—namely, his master's "great pleasure in whipping a slave":

> I have often been awakened at the dawn of day by the most heart rending shrieking of an aunt of mine whom he used to tie up [to a joist] and whip upon her naked back until she was literally covered with blood. The louder she screamed the harder he whipped. And where the blood ran fastest there he whipped longest. He would whip her to make her scream, and whip her to make her hush; and not until overcome by fatigue, would he cease to swing the blood-clotted cowskin. [17]

This passage, a typical one in the slave narratives, suggests what critic George Cunningham describes as a "world of sadism where the violent and sexual are conflated."[18] Not only an object of exchange in a slave economy, the aunt is also an object of desire within a system unbound by legal or cultural restraints. The sexual imagery encoded in this passage speaks as much to the master's desire for violence as it does to the violence of the master's desire. Such a passage underscores the symbolic and ritual function of slavery as an institution based on power and violence.

The image of the female slave subjugated by the lash (a classic porno-graphic female stance) conveys not only the power of male over female but also the power of master over slave and the power of white over black. It is a race- and gender-inflected image that combines images of unchecked power and sexual pleasure. If blacks are frequently portrayed as women in the verbal and visual iconography of nineteenth-century slavery, it may not be surprising to learn that the historical origins of slavery are traced by schol-ars to the enslavement of women.[19] In language that conflates the discourses of dominance and eroticism with the act of reading, Paulhan warns the reader that "the very act of referring to [such texts] would seem *bound* to make us want to read them and *expose* ourselves to danger" (*Story* xxiii; emphasis added). Thus the reader is placed in a masochistic posture in relation to the text. The "somewhat risky business" to which Paulhan alerts the reader again encodes the dangers of these stories: "From every indication," he writes," the *Story of O* is one of those books which *marks* the reader, which leaves *him* not quite, or not all, the same as *he* was before *he* read it," an interpellation that would seem to figure the reader as masculine (*Story* xxiii; emphasis added). It is in this context that Paulhan informs us that "in her own way O expresses a virile ideal, Virile, or at least masculine" (*Story* xxv). Yet, de-spite the masculine pronominal referents, the position interpellated is feminized—to the extent that it locates the reader (bound and marked) in a passively masochistic position.

In a curious and telling "slip," Paulhan suggests in the introduction that the role of "dangerous" (erotic) books is to "inform and instruct," "to reas-sure us on the subject, the way a father confessor does" (*Story* xxvii). We note that Paulhan's Anabaptist minister, authoring a "lost" text containing an apologia for slavery, is clearly inverted in Williams's Adam Nehemiah, whose projected book on the eradication of the roots of slave revolts remains sim-ilarly incomplete. Nehemiah's journal, refiguring the notebooks of the An-abaptist minister and Thomas Gray, is projected as a book designed not only to relieve the fears of slaveholders but also to be instructive to the preser-vation of slavery.[20]

Like Styron, Réage structures her work around "confessions" or "revela-tions": the *Story of O* is described as a "love-letter" representing the narrator's desire to reveal the innermost sexual secrets of her being. The seductiveness of the text, figured as a "love letter" to the reader and recipient, is replicated in its illocutionary frame: "But to whom is the letter addressed? Who is the speech trying to convince? Who can we ask?" queries Paulhan. Although Paul-han sees O's story as "more of a speech than a mere effusion; of a letter rather than a secret diary" (*Story* xxiv), he nonetheless describes it as a confession, a mode that confirms the value and authority attached to the Other. The fe-male confession, then, becomes an articulation of male mastery through its manipulation and representation of desire. Like a father confessor, Paulhan declares,

> At last a woman who admits it! . . . Something that men have always reproached them with: that they never cease obeying their nature, the call of their blood, that everything in them, even their minds, is sex. That they have constantly to be nourished, constantly washed and made up, constantly beaten. That all they need is a good master, one who is not too lax or kind. . . . [One who] must, when [he goes] to see them, take a whip along. (*Story* xxv)

This construction of O as willingly and willfully subordinate to male super-ordination is meant to gratify male desires for power and male powers of desire. Réage-Paulhan thus conceals what is fundamentally a story of sadistic mastery beneath a story of masochistic submission. Legal scholar Catharine A. MacKinnon would call this the "eroticization of dominance"—and, one might add, "the sexualization of submission."[21]

As a Sadean narrative, the plot of *Story of O,* can be summarized briefly as follows. To please her lover, O, a successful fashion photographer, willingly accompanies him to the chateau at Roissy where she is confined to a small, solitary, cell-like room, released only to satisfy the sexual demands of the male guests.[22] The men at Roissy represent the principle of male dominance in physical and psychological relations. As they explain to O, "If the costume we wear in the evening . . . leaves our sex exposed, it is . . . for the sake of insolence . . . so that you may learn that there resides your master." O is also informed, "Your hands are not your own, nor are your breasts, nor, most especially, any of your bodily orifices, which we may explore or penetrate at will." Further, her masters explain that "in principle [O] would be whipped only on the thighs and buttocks, in other words between her waist and knees . . . but that in all likelihood one of the four men present would want to mark her thighs with the riding crop" (*Story* 15). Not only is O chained, tortured, and whipped, but she is branded as well. If the whip marks signify traces of white and patriarchal authority, the branding suggests a more personal and precise inscription of sexual ownership and authority. Moreover, like the slave woman who becomes an object of economic exchange, O is circulated in an economy of male desire—not only among the male patrons at Roissy, but also between her lover and his half brother, whose name is branded into her flesh and whose iron rings bound her labia.

Yet in *Story of O,* these rituals of debasement have the effect of enhancing rather than diminishing the victim. The protagonist sees her self-abnegation as an act of spiritual asceticism: The more she is physically tortured, the more her experience is represented as mystical. Surprised that the whippings leave her in an "untroubled" and "calm" state (*Story* 23), O can only hope that her

endurance is equal to that of other martyrs, "prisoners she had seen in engravings and in history books, who had been chained and whipped . . .
centuries ago (*Story* 26). She perceives that her lover has prostituted her only
to enhance her value to him: "The more he surrendered her, the more he
would hold her dear. . . . Thus he would possess her as a god possesses his
creatures." Her lover "gave her only to reclaim her immediately, to reclaim
her enriched in his eyes, like some common object which had been used for
some divine purpose and has thus been consecrated" (*Story* 32). For this reason, O discovers that "the chains and the silence, which should have smothered her, strangled her, on the contrary freed her from herself." Her ritual
defilement becomes the means of her purification: "She felt herself literally
to be the repository of impurity, the stink mentioned in the Scriptures . . .
And yet those parts of her body most constantly offended, having become
less sensitive, at the same time seem to her to have become more beautiful
and, as it were, ennobled" (*Story* 44). O discovers in her degradation a dignity and illumination that affirm her spiritual transcendence. Rather than
a site of captivity, the chateau at Roissy becomes the liberating "sacrificial
site" of her priestly initiation.

4

If Réage and Styron construct in their respective works the subjectivity and
sexuality of white women and black men, Williams's project demonstrates
how these fictive discourses are deployed to perpetuate hierarchial differences based on gender and race. If the *Story of O* recuperates the myth of female passivity, *Confessions of Nat Turner* reinforces the myth of black emasculation. In Réage's novel, psychosexual subordination is the condition of
(white) woman's subjectivity; in Styron's novel, psychosexual repression is
the condition of black (male) subjectivity. *Dessa Rose* seeks to deconstruct
these antecedent constructions and, at the same time, open up a space for
the black female, marginalized in Styron's text and subsumed under the categories of "slave" and "woman" in Réage's text.

Williams opens her narrative by deconstructing Paulhan's dialectic of accommodating masters and passive slaves (as well as Styron's dialectic of sexual repression and political revolution.) She rewrites Paulhan's "happiness
in slavery" thematic not only to demonstrate the coercive power relations
inherent in black slavery, but also to represent, more particularly, the coercive relations involved in female sexuality under slavery. *Dessa Rose* deconstitutes Réage's attempt to spiritualize a relationship of sexual slavery and
submission and reconstitutes this relationship through a historical narrative
of enforced physical slavery and resistance. Despite Paulhan's repeated allusions to the "ruthless decency" of this very "decent" book, Réage's narrative is a story of descent "from freedom to slavery," whereas Williams's is a

story of ascent "from slavery to freedom." Further, Williams's strategy—to move the politics of sexual domination from the private into the public sphere—locates sexual desire and fantasy within a larger system of social domination and gender hierarchy.

Williams's intent to enter into dialogue with the *Story of O* is suggested onomastically in her protagonist's ritual of self-naming. In two dramatic acts of self-entitlement, Dessa reaffirms her ability to name herself and her own experience. In the first instance, she says of her would-be captor, Adam Nehemiah, "Why he didn't even know how to call my name—talking about *O*dessa" (*DR* 225; emphasis added). And in the second, she tells Ruth, the white woman who provides sanctuary to runaway slaves in exchange for labor, "My name Dessa, Dessa Rose. Ain't no O to it" (*DR* 232). She is, of course, distinguishing between *Odessa,* an ascription by the white, male slave-master that evokes her problematic literary ancestress, and *Dessa,* her self-entitlement. Her rejection of the *O*—a signifier of "lack"—also signals her rejection of the Other's objectification of her body. Lest there remain any doubt of Williams's intention, a fellow slave from New Orleans explains to Dessa that in French the term *blanc* (creolized as *blank*) means "white," an allusion surely to the encipherment of O as both "white" and "absence."

Williams, however, signals to the reader another kind of intertextual reference, one aptly defined by Gerard Genette's notion of *architextualité.*[23] By interposing into her own text a series of cameos that signify on the conventions of pornography, Williams invokes the genre rather than a specific text. The first scene depicts Ruth nursing Dessa's infant son, thereby juxtaposing the conventions of the pornographic with the racial obscene. The image of the white nursemaid and the black infant dismantles a long tradition in American sentimentality naturalizing the ur-image of the black mammy and the white child. Williams signifies on the stereotypic "mammy-child" image by representing its inversion as the eroticized object of the white woman's self-directed gaze, one that proceeds from an initial response of compulsion and mortification:

> And only when his cries were stilled and she looked down upon the sleek black head, the nut-brown face flattened against the pearly paleness of her breast, had she become conscious of what she was doing. A wave of embarrassment had swept over her and she had looked guiltily around the parlor . . . she had felt some mortification at becoming wet nurse for a darky. . . . [But] she herself liked to watch the baby as he nursed, the way he screwed up his face and clenched his fist with the effort, the contrast between his mulberry-colored mouth and the pink areola surrounding her nipple, between his caramel-colored fist and the rosy cream of her breast. (*DR* 106)

Such a reversal has the subtle effect of transcoding a traditionally sacred iconographic representation of Madonna and child into an obscene image by reinscribing it into the context of a suggestively pornographic scenario.

In two subsequent scenes, Williams provides a counterpoint to Réage and Styron by figuring the white woman in an aggressive posture and the black man in a posture of sexual potency (a combination that could have existed for neither of these earlier writers). This scene provides a series of graphic descriptions of fellatio and cunnilingus between the boy Nathan (a sexually potent refiguration of Styron's emasculated Nat) and Miz Lorraine, his former mistress who had made a habit of taking younger slave lovers:

> She knelt before him and took his penis in her mouth. Terrified, he at first tried fumblingly to pry her head away, but already her mouth and tongue were sending such intense waves of pleasure through him that all he could do was hold her head and moan—and try to control the muscle that threatened to leap from his control. . . . He could hold it no longer. The power of his climax rocked him back onto the bed and he lay there, uncaring. She squirmed onto his still erect penis. Her lips still wet with his come, she sought his mouth. Faintly repelled but already excited by the pull of her vaginal muscles on his penis, he turned his lips towards hers . . . the knowledge that he lay in danger [if exposed], not only of his member but of his life, sent him plunging up a peak of *unspeakable desire*." (*DR* 168–69; emphasis added)

This scene speaks not only to the psychic and physical charge of tabooed desire ("If climax, as some men said, was like death, then a nigger died a double death in a white woman's arms" [*DR* 174]), but also to the passion and aggressiveness of the white woman: Miz Lorraine is a woman who wanted "to be in control" and in whom "nature was strong." Nevertheless, she refuses to allow Nathan to copulate orally with her. And on the single occasion when he attempted to do so, "she had writhed and kicked" (although "he held on until he felt the thick come against his tongue"). When she "threatened to yell rape that night, to sell, to have him flayed. . . . He never took the lead in sex with her again" (168–71). Clearly Miz Lorraine's control here contradicts Réage's script of passive and submissive white femininity, while the representation of the dangers and pleasure of miscegenation (overlaid with undertones of adult-child sexuality) invoke two stock conventions of pornographic representation.

Yet another scene parodies the conventions of pornographic representation by invoking the polychromatic thematics of interracial sexuality—represented here as object of the black woman's gaze. It is Dessa's "startled gasp" that surprises Nathan and Ruth as they are making love: "Nathan was the color of eggplant, a rich, velvety blueblack; beside him, [Ruth's] skin took on a pearly glow. They sweated and rested, his face buried in her bosom, one leg caught between hers. She stroked his back; his fingers played purposefully in matted pubic hair, teasing the slick lips of her vagina. Supine, she waited for him to enter her again" (*DR* 171). In Dessa's eyes ("I never *seed* such a thing!"), the scene before her reprises the earlier scene: "It was like seeing her [Ruth] nurse Money [Dessa's son] for the first time all over again" (*DR* 175). The character of Nathan (after his namesake "Nat") allows Williams to refigure the black man's control of his sexuality, thus subverting Styron's representation of black male emasculation.

But perhaps Williams's most subtle strategy is to signify upon the relation between O and her lover (a story of white male desire and white female submission) in her representation of the relation between Adam Nehemiah and Dessa (a story of white male desire and black female resistance). Dessa's confinement in a root cellar during the period of her "lying in" parallels O's confinement in a solitary cell. It is during this period that Nehemiah attempts to interview Dessa in preparation for his book on slave rebellions. (The relationship between the two clearly parodies a familiar scene—one which we recognize as the writing scene for that category of slave narratives commonly referred to as "as told to" narratives.) In *Dessa Rose,* it soon becomes apparent that Nehemiah cannot configure a reliable or cohesive story in his journal—a manuscript that would be analogous to that of the Anabaptist minister in Paulhan's text ("Happiness in Slavery"). Nehemiah is mistakenly convinced that Dessa has been "used" by her master for his own purposes, thus imagining (falsely) a prior scene of sexuality between Dessa and a white master. Tellingly, the interaction between Nehemiah and Dessa takes on sexual overtones. As the story progresses, the narrator discovers himself increasingly haunted by Dessa. At one point he comments, "It is curious . . . how the negress . . . looks in the sun. For a moment today as I watched her I could almost imagine how [her previous owner] allowed her to get close enough to stick a knife between his ribs" (*DR* 229). Indeed, Nehemiah regrets that he had not the responsibility of "Odessa's *breaking*" (*DR* 68; emphasis added). According to this reading, Dessa (like the slaves in Paulhan's allegory) lacked a "good" master: "What a waste," he rues, "that she should have fallen into hands such as those." While in vain pursuit of a group of slaves who ultimately rescue Dessa, Nehemiah looks forward to "a bed [which would be] most welcome—and, perhaps . . . something to warm it when we get back" (*DR* 69). In the earlier "Meditations" version, the narrator notes that the sheriff "charge[s] that [he] acted like one possessed" (248). It is this hidden narrative of repressed erotic desire, signaled in the sexual coding of the language, that provides the basis for the internal dialogue in Williams's novel, linking it to Styron's and Réage's narratives.

Dessa fears that exposure of her scars and branding will confirm her slave status. Resisting inspection by a white sheriff under the instigation of Nehemiah, she thinks to herself, "I could feel everyone of them scars, the one roped partway to my navel that the waist of my draws itched, the corduroyed welts across my hips, and R on my thighs" (*DR* 223). The literal inscription of Dessa's body, signified by the whip marks and branding around the waist, hips, and thighs, refigure O's markings. The location of the scarring in the area of the genitalia inscribes the sign *slave* in an area that marks her as *woman* ("Scar tissue plowed through her public hair region so no hair would ever grow there again"). The effect is to attempt to deprive the slave woman of her femininity and render the surface of her skin a parchment upon which meaning is etched by the whip (pen) of white patriarchal authority and sealed by the firebrand. Together, these inscriptions produce the meaning of black female subjectivity and sexuality within the discursive domain of slavery.

Just as O must expose her buttocks so that her inscription can be "deciphered" by her master or his surrogates, Dessa is ordered by the sheriff to lift her skirt so that her inscriptions can be "read" by her captors. But unlike Dessa, O internalizes the values and desires that are predicated upon her subordination to a system of male patriarchal privilege. Although both O and Dessa are physically tortured, their responses are radically different: O is passive and submissive; Dessa is disruptive and defiant. O voluntarily surrenders to a system designed to subjugate her; Dessa rebels. O's bondage seems to be self-imposed and a consequence of her masochistic psychic needs; Dessa's enslavement is imposed by those who control the socioeconomic system. O is in emotional and psychological bondage; Dessa is in social and physical bondage. O willingly exposes her scars for all to read and "penetrate"; Dessa refuses to reveal hers, and her successful concealment guarantees her freedom. If exposure and self-revelation structure O's story, concealment and escape provide the structure and motif of Dessa's. It is O's collusion in the subordination of women that makes possible patriarchal dominance, whereas Dessa's resistance functions to subvert both racial and sexual domination.

It is significant, then, that Dessa purposefully drops the *O* from her appellation, for unlike her literary predecessor, Dessa refuses compliance in her own exploitation. The rejection of the *O* (signaling cipher, an emblem of nonbeing) sets Dessa in radical opposition to Réage's heroine. In her insurgency against the expropriation of her text, Dessa interdicts her physical and cultural inscription, whereas O subscribes to the male cultural script, making her, in effect, an encipherment of male desire.

Together, the works of Styron and Réage secure the subject as white and male. In the case of Styron, manhood and sexuality are constituted as attributes exclusive to white males; in the case of Paulhan-Réage-Aury, aggressiveness and self-mastery are constituted as attributes exclusive to white males. In the latter instance, the construction of the feminine as passive, masochistic, and exhibitionistic obscures the construction of the construction masculine as aggressive, sadistic, and voyeuristic. Williams's text, however, displaces notions of feminine passivity and black emasculation by interrogating the ideological structures intrinsic to these works which instate the subject as white and male.

If historically and psychologically the passive feminine represents a cover for the sexually aggressive female, the emasculated black male represents a covering image generated by fear of the "Nigger Rapist." Williams challenges these constructions of black and female identities, along with the supporting ideologies that reinscribe cultural myths and underwrite public policy decisions. Styron's work reinforced popular myths of black male emasculation promoted by the Moynihan Report, a document influential in determining public policy during the 1960s. Réage's novel perpetuates an ideology of submission that reinforces widespread essentialist assumptions regarding women's nature as inherently passive and subordinate. Such eroticization of domination, as Susan Gubar points out in another context, "teaches us to see women as the willing, desirous, and even deserving slaves of punitive masters."[24] Both these works become part of what Michel Foucault describes as the technologies of subjection and subjugation.

EPILOGUE

Styron, Réage, and Williams all, in their own way, produce and reproduce a struggle for meaning and power. Their texts figure scenes of writing captivity; I want to suggest here that they also figure scenes of reading submission and conquest: Styron derives pleasure from the text through an act of mastery of the Other as black, and Réage derives pleasure through an act of submission to the Other as male. But there also exists a power relationship between text and critic, one that Ross Chambers describes as a "vertical power relationship" that entails "a question of 'mastery.'"[25] Playing on the "sexual connotations of textual intercourse," Chambers claims that the power and seductiveness of fiction (much like the seductiveness of a television talk show) resides precisely in its ability to inscribe the desires of the Other. As reader-critics, we must ask ourselves how this process of sexual and textual mastery positions us: what happens when we yield to the mastery of the text? If, as some critics have argued, our pleasure is derived from a position of subjection to the text, the problem becomes how to avoid the passive position and yet preserve our readerly pleasure. How can we avoid being constructed as victims? How can we make reading a "liberatory" rather than a "captive" experience?

If, however, we should construct ourselves oppositionally as "resisting readers"—must we experience our textual pleasure from a position of dominance, thereby reproducing the author's relationship to the text's subject? Must we become voyeurs who experience our pleasure in the Other's victimization? How can we avoid redoubling the positions of submission and conquest in the reading process? In some respects Williams's work models a mode of reading that addresses these questions. *Dessa Rose* instructs us how to read literary as well as social and cultural texts. If Nehemiah suggests that misconstruction is the consequence of (mis)reading from a position of mastery, then Dessa suggests that deconstruction is a consequence of a reading of mastery from the position of victim. It is, in fact, the act of resisting subjugating readings by the master that enables her to achieve self-mastery.

The issue for the politically conscious and morally conscientious reader is how to deconstruct mastery and empower the victim without assuming a position of victimization. Once again, to invoke Chambers, our responsibility as readers is to "free the text from its own limitations," and that is done by identifying the "ideological and cultural constraints that have limited the text's self-conception." Our incumbency as reader-critics is not only the liberation of ourselves from the text but also the liberation of the text—a task that is accomplished by "identifying both the limitations [the text] puts on itself and the means whereby it does this, so that they can be relativized in the act of reading."[26]

There is, however, another kind of textual power that my own critical reflexivity invites the reader to consider: the power (and seduction) of the critical text—in its desire to "master" both the master text and the critical audience. Chambers distinguishes between the vertical power relationship between critic and text and what he describes as the "horizontal" power relationship between critic and critic (or reader). Both relations carry the potential of liberation and constraint, conquest and submission. By engaging such texts—critical and creative—in our own projects, we will necessarily occupy competing positions—competing both with one another and with the text for critical authority, since the act of textual criticism both binds us to and liberates us from constraints of the text. As both literary and critical readers, our projects must be to deconstruct literary fictions and social relations of authority and subjugation. To the degree that her novel deconstitutes positions of dominance and submission, Williams's *Dessa Rose* provides a model for our work.

NOTES

1. See Mae Henderson, "(W)Riting *The Work* and Working the Rites," in *Feminism and Institutions: Dialogues on Feminist Theory,* ed. Linda Kauffman (Oxford: Basil Blackwell, 1989); and "Speaking in Tongues: Dialogics, Dialectics, and the Black Woman Writer's Literary Tradition," in *Changing Our Own Words: Essays on Criticism, Theory, and Writing by Black Women,* ed. Cheryl A. Wall (New Brunswick: Rutgers, 1989), 16–37.

2. Sherley Anne Williams, "Meditations on History," in *Midnight Buds,* ed. Mary Helen Washington (New York: Doubleday, 1980), 200–248.

3. See Elizabeth Fox-Genovese, *Within the Plantation Household* (Chapel Hill: University of North Carolina Press, 1988). Fox-Genovese writes, "Within the slave community tendencies to differentiate between men and women resulted in a view of violent organized revolt as a specialized political and insurrectionary male. None of the most visible revolts took a woman's name. None of these were attributed to a woman's leadership. Nor did slave women organize any of those 'women's' revolts which were common in Europe or Africa" (307).

4. Angela Davis, "Reflections on the Black Woman's Role in the Community of Slaves," *The Black Scholar* (December 1971): 15.

5. See Henderson, "(W)Riting *The Work.*" The present essay draws heavily on my own earlier work on Williams and Styron but extends the implications of that reading into a new direction.

6. William Styron, *The Confessions of Nat Turner* (New York: Random House, 1967).

7. See Melissa Walker, *Down from the Mountaintop* (New Haven: Yale University Press, 1991) for her discussion of the political climate surrounding the setting and production of Williams's short story and novel, although her work does not situate these texts in the context of nineteenth- and twentieth-century women's rights politics. See Walker, however, for another treatment of racial politics somewhat different from my own.

8. Sherley Anne Williams, *Dessa Rose* (New York: Williams Morrow, 1986), 5.

9. See Leo Bersani, *A Future for Astyanax: Character and Desire in Literature* (Boston: Little, Brown, 1976); Susan Sontag, "The Pornographic Imagination," in *Styles of Radical Will* (New York: Farrar/Strauss/Girous, 1969); Jessica Benjamin's *The Bonds of Love: Psychoanalysis, Feminism, and the Problem of Domination* (New York: Pantheon Books, 1988).

10. This is Angus Fletcher's definition of *allegory,* paraphrased by Linda Zwinger in "What She Gets for Saying Yes: O," in *Daughters, Fathers, and the Novel: The Sentimental Romance of Heterosexuality* (Madison: University of Wisconsin Press, 1991), 97–98.

11. Susan Gubar, "Representing Pornography: Feminism, Criticism, and Depictions of Female Violation," *Critical Inquiry* 13 (summer 1987): 713.

12. I am indebted to Susan Gubar for these terms. See ibid., 730.

13. In "Replacing Feminist Criticism," Kamuf rejects the reduction of a "literary work to its signature" as well as what she regards as the tautological assumption that "women's writing is writing signed by women." Her project is to "take an anonymous work which (in the absence of a signature) must be read blind" as an opportunity to interrogate what she describes as "the masks of truth with which phallocentrism hides its fictions." See Peggy Kamuf, "Replacing Feminist Criticism," *diacritics* 12 (1982): 42–47; and Nancy K. Miller, "The Text's Heroine: A Feminist Critic and Her Fictions," *diacritics* 12 (1982) 48–53.

14. From the date of its publication in France in 1954, and in the United States in 1965, the *Story of O* has been steeped in controversy over its content and authorship. A recent *New Yorker* article (August 1, 1994) establishes conclusively that the author was Dominique Aury, lover of the writer Jean Paulhan, who provided the introduction to the novel. Aury explained in an interview that she wrote the novel to reawaken Paulhan's romantic interest. The politics of this authorial collaboration corroborate Hélène Cixous's caveat about equating the sex of the author with that of the text:

Most women are like this: they do someone else's—man's—writing, and in their innocence sustain it and give it voice, and end up producing writing that's in effect masculine. Great care must be taken working on feminine writing not to get trapped by names: to be signed with a woman's name doesn't necessarily make a piece of writing feminine. It could quite well be masculine writing, and conversely, the fact that a piece of writing is signed with a man's name does not, in itself, exclude femininity. It's rare, but you can sometimes find femininity in writings signed by men: it does happen. ("Castration," quoted in Toril Moi, *Sexual/Textual Politics: Feminist Literary Theory* [London: Methuen, 1985], 108.)

15. Jean Paulhan, preface to *Story of O,* by Pauline Réage, trans. Sabine d'Estrée (New York: Grove Press, 1965).

16. To this end, I read the *Story of O,* perhaps oxymoronically, as a "pornographic classic" rather than an "erotic classic." I suggest that a distinction between pornography and female eroticism might well be based on where or with whom the power resides. In my working definition, I further suggest that in pornography, as conventionally represented, the power resides with the male, whereas in what some would claim as "female eroticism," the power resides with the female.

17. Frederick Douglass, *Narrative of the Life of Frederick Douglass* (New York: New American Library, 1968), 24–25.

18. See George Cunningham, "Called into Existence: Desire, Gender, and Voice in Frederick Douglass's *Narrative of 1845*," *differences* 1, no. 3 (fall 1989): 108–36. See also Deborah McDowell, "In the First Place: Making Frederick Douglass and the Afro-American Narrative Tradition," in *Critical Essays on Frederick Douglass,* ed. William Andrews (Boston: G. K. Hull, 1991); and Jenny Franchot, "The Punishment of Esther: Frederick Douglass and the Construction of the Feminine," in *Frederick Douglass: New Literary and Historical Essays,* ed. Eric Sundquist (Cambridge: Cambridge University Press, 1990).

19. See, for example, Gerda Lerner, *The Creation of Patriarchy* (New York: Oxford University Press, 1986) and Orlando Patterson, *Slavery and Social Death: A Comparative Study* (Cambridge: Harvard University Press, 1982).

20. The name of Williams's character, Adam Nehemiah, reverses the name of Nehemiah Adams, a Boston minister who wrote a proslavery account of his experiences in the South, *A South-side View of Slavery* [1854], and who, in an earlier tract, warned women not to speak out in public against slavery—a stance that set him in opposition to both women's rights and abolition.

21. See Catharine A. MacKinnon, "Feminism, Marxism, Method, and the State: An Agenda for Theory," *Signs: Journal of Women in Culture and Society* 7, no. 3 (spring 1982): 515–44.

22. I am indebted to Kaja Silverman's reading, *"Histoire D'O:* The Story of a Disciplined and Punished Body," *Enclitic* 7, no. 2 (fall 1983): 63–81.

23. See Gerard Genette, *Introduction à l'architexte* (Paris: Editions du Seuil, 1979).

24. Gubar, "Representing Pornography," 726.

25. Ross Chambers, *Story and Situation: Narrative Seduction and the Power of Fiction* (Minneapolis: University of Minnesota Press, 1984), 158.

26. Chambers elaborates here, "And that is the role that can be performed by a reading of the situational self reflexivity—the devices of readability—of so-called 'readerly' texts" (*Story and Situation* 27).

IV

Healing Narratives

Pauline Hopkins and William James
The New Psychology and the Politics of Race

Cynthia D. Schrager

In her diary entry of October 26, 1890, Alice James, the invalid sister of Henry and William, wrote of her noted psychologist brother: "William uses an excellent expression when he says in his paper on the 'Hidden Self' that the nervous victim 'abandons' certain portions of his consciousness. . . . It is just the right [word] . . . altho' I have never unfortunately been able to abandon my consciousness and get five minutes' rest" (148–49). As a "nervous victim" herself, Alice undoubtedly felt well qualified to make this characteristically ironic comment on William's article "The Hidden Self," a discussion of French research into multiple personalities in hysterical subjects, which he published in *Scribner's Magazine* earlier the same year. Reviewing pioneering new discoveries about the unconscious then emerging from Jean-Martin Charcot's work at the Salpêtrière Hospital in Paris, James discusses the work of two Charcot disciples, Pierre Janet and Alfred Binet, Janet's *L'Automatisme Psychologique* (1889) the primary focus of his comments. James reports with considerable interest and admiration on a number of case studies of hysterical women in whom traumatic shock resulted in a splitting off of some parts of the personality from the main personality, and on the use of hypnosis or trance-states to resurface these "submerged selves." He concludes: "This simultaneous coexistence of the different personages into which one human being may be split is the *great* thesis of M. Janet's book" (368).

The "new psychology," as it was dubbed, generated considerable interest at the turn of the century not only in academic circles but also among literate middle-class Americans of the sort who composed Scribner's audience.[1] Boston was a geographical center both for academic psychology (of which James, in his position on the Harvard faculty, was one of the early American pioneers) and for the various popular psychologies (from mesmerism and spiritualism to mind-cure and New Thought) that were faddish in nineteenth-century middle- and upper-class culture. In another diary entry, Alice James recounts with delight an unsuccessful encounter with a mind-curist, who found her "too much barricaded" by her "intellectual friends" to receive the cure (153). Whereas Alice was suspicious of any kind of "self-abandonment" of her rational faculty and was reportedly pleased when her lifelong illness was discovered to have an organic rather than a psychological cause (Yeazell 2), William embraced increasingly radical notions about the nature of the unconscious, beginning with his article "The Hidden Self."

Intrigued by passive experiences of consciousness such as spiritistic possession (the turn-of-the-century analog to "channeling"), James maintained a receptivity to the irrational and nonmaterial that set him apart from many of his most famous contemporaries.[2] As a founding member of the American branch of the Society for Psychical Research, he entertained a belief in the possibility of a supernatural realm open to scientific investigation and sought to overcome what he saw as the unfortunate antipathy between the "scientific-academic mind" and the "feminine-mystical mind" (362). Although "The Hidden Self" is full of admiration for the work of Janet, James criticizes the French psychologist for not going far enough in his characterization of the unconscious. Janet's more conservative view was that the subpersonalities he uncovered were limited by the boundaries of the individual ego; in contrast, James was receptive to the possibility that the unconscious might open onto the transpersonal realm and provide an avenue of communication with the spirit world. In "The Hidden Self," James states his less conventional belief "well aware," as he puts it, "of all the liabilities to which this statement exposes me" (373).

Such views would eventually marginalize James from the mainstream of his profession. In search of "scientific-academic" recognition, the discipline dissociated itself from the "feminine-mystical" realm of faith healers and spiritistic mediums and rejected James's blend of science and religion. The future belonged to Freud and his work, as James himself reportedly remarked at the famous 1909 psychological congress at Clark University in Worcester, just one year before his death.[3] In the two decades before the conference, however, James's views, along with those of even more radical proponents of psychical research such as Richard Hodgson and Frederic W. H. Myers, were still within the mainstream of scientific debate. In his concluding remarks in "The Hidden Self," James optimistically calls for a "*comparative study of trances and sub-conscious states,*" including psychical or supernatural phenomena: "Anyone who may be induced by this article to follow the path of study in which [Janet's book] is so brilliant a pioneer will reap a rich reward" (373).

This call by the Anglo American psychologist William James found a sympathetic response in a work by a fellow Bostonian, the African American novelist and *Colored American Magazine* editor Pauline Elizabeth Hopkins. In her

last novel, *Of One Blood; or, The Hidden Self,* Hopkins turned to the new discoveries in psychology for thematic material and, more specifically, used
James's essay "The Hidden Self" as an intertext, although she deliberately
disguised her source.[4] Unlike Alice James, who maintained a lifelong skepticism toward the various psychological discourses that vied to explain, heal,
or otherwise administer to her subjectivity, Hopkins embraced notions
about the unconscious emerging from work with hysterical women as a means
to explore a subject closer to her own heart—the political situation and subjectivity of African Americans in the post-Reconstruction period. Like
W. E. B. Du Bois, whose notion of "double-consciousness" was also profoundly influenced by both James and the new psychology, Hopkins was
deeply engaged by the new discourses about the self emerging at the turn
of the century. Her ideas about this subject appear in her first short story,
"The Mystery within Us," and receive their most sustained treatment in her
last complete novel, in which she fictionally reworks James's essay in order
to represent the complexity of racial subjectivity in post-Reconstruction
America.[5]

   In contradictory movements, her novel both exploits the new psychology
to theorize about the indeterminacy of racial subjectivity and figures racial
identity in terms of a more deterministic discourse of blood. Authorized both
by James's theory of the self and by traditional occult practices that are associated with the figure of the African mother, Hopkins explores the transpersonal dimensions of consciousness in the context of a transnational "black
Atlantic" geography that is linked, in the novel's ultimate vision, to a pan-
Africanist political agenda.[6]

"The Mystery within Us" appeared in May 1900 in the premiere issue of the
Colored American Magazine (*CAM*), a journal dedicated to serving the interests of American citizens of color and promoting African American art and
literature (Carby 122–27). Interestingly, Hopkins's first contribution to the
magazine and first published work of short fiction does not explicitly the-
matize or address issues of race. The short story's narrator relates a story told
by his friend Tom Underwood, a successful and wealthy physician who, five
years earlier, had been driven to the brink of suicide by desperate financial
circumstances. Declaring his belief in "spiritualistic phenomena and the existence of guardian angels" (21), Underwood relates to his friend the following "psychological experience" (24). Late one night, just as he is about
to drink a bottle of poison, Underwood is visited by the spirit of a deceased
physician, Dr. Thorn, whose work he greatly admired. The spiritistic "presence" of Dr. Thorn uses his mesmeric power to prevent the suicide, condemning Underwood's rash act and informing him that God's will is that he
continue the deceased physician's life work. The next morning Underwood
finds on his bedside table the manuscript for the book that makes him rich

and famous. Disclaiming any rational explanation for his experience, Underwood concludes his narration of this strange tale by citing a well-known quotation from *Hamlet* that appears frequently in turn-of-the-century discourses on spiritualism and psychical research: "There are more things in heaven and earth than are dreamt of in our philosophy" (26).

Hopkins's depiction of the problem of suicidal despair and its solutions reflects the widespread interest in this subject among turn-of-the-century Americans. Neurasthenia—that peculiarly American "nervousness" that George M. Beard made famous in 1881—was epidemic among middle- and upper-class "brain-workers." Linked to the "over-civilization" of modern life, it affected, to greater or lesser extent, almost all of the period's notable cultural producers—including William James (Lutz, esp. chap. 2; Feinstein, chap. 12). James's 1895 address to the Young Men's Christian Association of Harvard University, entitled "Is Life Worth Living?" reflects both his own neurasthenic inclinations as well as those of his social class. His opening remarks included this melancholy sentiment, echoed strikingly in the title of Hopkins's supernatural tale: "In the deepest heart of all of us there is a corner in which the ultimate mystery of things works sadly" (1). Following conventional turn-of-the-century wisdom on the relationship between the life of the mind and neurasthenic illness, James attributed suicidal despair to the pessimism "which reflection breeds" and proposed "religious faith" as the answer (6).

In its use of neurasthenic discourse, "The Mystery within Us" intriguingly combines the secular rags-to-riches narrative with a version of its religious antecedent—the spiritual autobiography of sin and redemption. Softening the Calvinist emphasis on sin typical of Puritan conversion narratives to produce a more ecumenical representation of spiritual despair, Hopkins addresses contemporary anxieties about the loss of faith in a post-Darwinian world. Underwood's material success—the rags-to-riches story—is presented as the result of a passive religious experience that leads him to spiritual redemption, rather than as the result of the more familiar Franklinesque narrative of autonomous self-making. In representing the protagonist as an instrument of the divine will whose life is devoted to the service of the larger community, "The Mystery within Us" presents material success as a dividend in the more important business of spiritual uplift. Moreover, it substitutes a spiritual and collectivist ethos for the values of materialism and individualism typically associated with dominant American culture.

The opening chapter of *Of One Blood; or, The Hidden Self* incorporates a number of the thematic elements Hopkins had already treated in "The Mystery within Us": the poor struggling physician protagonist, the depiction of suicidal despair, and the spiritistic visitation that will lead, in the course of the novel, to the redemption of the protagonist and his dedication to a larger, altruistic endeavor.[7] The novel's opening scene finds the protagonist Reuel

Briggs, a poor Harvard medical student of ambiguous ethnic ancestry, deep in morbid thoughts of suicide. Hamlet-like, Reuel wonders whether to "rend the veil" separating this life from the next and thus obtain a solution not only to his poverty and loneliness but also to the questions of the nature of consciousness and immortality that haunt him (442).

A student of mysticism and psychology as well as medicine, Hopkins's protagonist spends his days and nights pouring over esoteric scientific treatises. When the reader first meets Reuel, he is obsessed by certain passages of a book he has been reading entitled "The Unclassified Residuum" by "M. Binet." In fact, all of the quoted passages attributed to Binet are taken verbatim from William James's essay "The Hidden Self," whose opening line provides Hopkins with her invented title: "'The great field for new discoveries,' said a scientific friend to me the other day, 'is always the Unclassified Residuum' . . . a sort of dust-cloud of exceptional occurrences . . . which it always proves less easy to attend to than to ignore" (361). The passages that obsess Reuel and that Hopkins quotes at some length are those that particularly concern James's ideas about the supernatural aspects of the unconscious. Like James, Reuel believes that the "unclassified residuum" of mystical and supernatural phenomena, generally dismissed by the scientific community as "the effects of the imagination," should be included within the realm of respected scientific pursuit (442). As Reuel contemplates these various thoughts, his beliefs are confirmed by a vision of a lovely woman whose appearance temporarily diverts him from his morbid despair.

As in "The Mystery within Us," *Of One Blood*'s thematization of psychology and mysticism initially appears to be disengaged from the sociological and political treatment of the race question that characterizes the majority of Hopkins's fictional and nonfictional work. Reuel's ambiguous desire to "go farther than M. Binet in unveiling the vast scheme of compensation and retribution carried about in . . . the human soul" (448) seems but a faint echo of the question of "compensation and retribution" for the wrongs perpetrated against African Americans under slavery that Hopkins explored in the more realistic mode of her first novel *Contending Forces*.[8]

Indeed, as the opening chapter concludes, Reuel's friend Aubrey Livingston calls attention to precisely this disjunction between Reuel's esoteric preoccupations and the burning political questions of the day when he interrupts Reuel's ruminations with an invitation to attend a concert of the Fisk University Jubilee Singers: "Coming down to the practical, Reuel, what do you think of the Negro problem? . . . I believe it is the only burning question in the whole category of live issues and ologies about which you are silent." Reuel enigmatically replies: "I have a horror of discussing the woes of unfortunates, tramps, stray dogs and cats and Negroes—probably because I am an unfortunate myself" (449).[9] As this brief conversation makes clear, far from representing another thematic departure for Hopkins, *Of One Blood* grafts the political issue of post-Reconstruction racial justice onto the supernatural and psychological themes that had fascinated her in "The Mystery within Us." The question of race—made overt in this first chapter's exchange between Reuel and Aubrey—has in fact been a subtext throughout the opening scene. Reuel's "horror" at the so-called "Negro problem" and his characterization of himself as an "unfortunate" link his morbid psychological state to his social condition as a black man passing as white.

As in the case of Tom Underwood, Reuel's nervous despair might initially be read within a conventional discourse of neurasthenia. His "morbid self-consciousness" marks him as a "brain-worker" and member of the new professional classes; it marks him, at first glance, as white. In keeping with the scientific racism of the period, neurasthenia was thought to affect only individuals of the so-called "advanced" races and religious persuasions, that is white Anglo-Saxon Protestants. As such, the class and race associations of the disease reflected and reinforced the prejudices of the dominant Anglo American culture (Lutz 6–7).[10] By rewriting neurasthenic discourse along the axis of race, Hopkins complicates and revises the racial meanings of the disease. Reuel's neurasthenic despair can be read as both the sign of his professional status, however marginal, and the price of the sacrifice of his black identity that even such a tentative status exacts. If the blues was a name for neurasthenia before it was a name for the African American musical form (Lutz 273), then Reuel's "blues" must here be understood as race-specific.

Reuel's fascination with "the hidden self lying quiescent in every human soul" (448) can be seen, then, as a trope for the situation of the African American who is "passing." Both his morbid self-consciousness and interest in esoteric psychology are embedded in a particular historical experience of African American subjectivity. Hopkins's skillful synthesis of new psychological discourses about the nature of the unconscious with the turn-of-the-century intellectual debate over the race question was not, of course, entirely idiosyncratic. In an essay called "Strivings of the Negro People" published in the *Atlantic Monthly* in 1897 and best known in slightly altered form as the opening chapter of *The Souls of Black Folk* (1903), W. E. B. Du Bois describes African American subjectivity as an experience of "double-consciousness": "One ever feels his twoness,—an American, a Negro; two souls, two thoughts, two unreconciled strivings; two warring ideals in one dark body, whose dogged strength alone keeps it from being torn asunder" (194).[11]

Several critics have noted Du Bois's intellectual debt both to William James, with whom he studied at Harvard University, and to the new psychology. In formulating the notion of "double-consciousness," Du Bois borrowed a term that already had wide currency in the late nineteenth century as a name for the phenomenon of multiple personality.[12] Du Bois's powerful rhetorical image of two souls in one body simultaneously evoked a traditional religious discourse of spiritual possession (with both African and

Calvinist resonances) as well as the emerging secular-scientific discourse on multiple personality that was rapidly supplanting it.[13] This use of spiritistic discourse also extended to Du Bois's figurative use of the "veil"—identified by Arnold Rampersad as the central organizing metaphor of *Souls*—to describe the barrier dividing African Americans and Anglo Americans. The veil metaphor figures the physical separation that divided nineteenth-century Americans along the color line; at the same time, it suggests the "other-world-liness" of the African American who is "born with a veil, and gifted with second-sight in this American world" (45). Du Bois's trope places African American culture closer to the spirit world, contrasting it powerfully with the materialism of Anglo American culture.[14]

The degree to which Hopkins was influenced by Du Bois's rhetorical use of psychological and spiritistic discourses is difficult to know; it is certainly possible, even likely, that she read his 1897 essay "Strivings of the Negro People."[15] In any event, given the evidence of her knowledge and use of James's "The Hidden Self," she was unquestionably influenced directly by accounts of the new psychology through public lectures and in the popular press. The distance between academic and popular psychologies in American culture has always been relatively small, and the new psychology was reported widely in the popular press at the turn of the century. One survey of popular magazines of the period reveals widespread interest in mental healing, hypnosis, and multiple personality, beginning in 1890 and remaining strong into the first decade of the twentieth century (Hale 229–30). James's 1896 Lowell Lectures on Exceptional Mental States, covering such subjects as dreams, hypnotism, multiple personality, and demoniacal possession, were delivered to a general audience and reported widely in such newspapers as the *Boston Transcript* and *Boston Globe* (Taylor).

The strikingly similar confluence of the discourses on the "new psychology" and the "race problem" in the writings of Du Bois and Hopkins is not entirely surprising. For both writers, the various scientific and lay discourses in circulation on psychological and psychical phenomena offered a ready language with which to attempt a representation of African American subjectivity. Both writers borrowed new psychological and psychical research discourses to represent the doubleness of African American consciousness, the experience of being psychically split. Further, both drew on spiritistic discourse to contrast the spirituality of African American culture to the materialism and exploitation of Anglo American culture.

Hopkins and Du Bois thus bring together a remarkably similar network of discourses on race and psyche in their work. Yet Hopkins's use of a surface-depth model of selfhood, which represents a surface consciousness in hierarchical relation to a hidden or submerged (un)consciousness, is quite distinct from Du Bois's notion of "doubleness." Critics have praised Du Bois's model, suggesting that it allows for a "sense of distinctiveness that [does] not imply inferiority" (Bruce, "W. E. B. Du Bois" 305) and contrasting it favorably to the "popular hierarchical doubleness of moral surfaces and depths" (Lutz 246). In using the more hierarchical model, Hopkins is able to achieve both more and less than Du Bois. Whereas Du Bois's model of "double-consciousness" represents the distinctiveness of African American subjectivity, Hopkins, as we shall see, extends the "hidden self" to explore more generally the nature of racial identity for whites as well as blacks in the post-Reconstruction period. At the same time, however, the surface-depth model of the self all too easily lends itself to appropriation within a hierarchical racist discourse of white superiority and black inferiority. It may be precisely this danger that leads Hopkins away from the notion of the "hidden self" toward a more deterministic notion of racial identity by the end of the novel.

Before turning to these dangers and to Hopkins's more deterministic deployment of a discourse of blood, I want to detail her multiple representations of the hidden self, which depend upon an understanding of the history of slavery inscribed into the family history of her main characters. In the course of the novel, Reuel is revealed to be the son of a slave named Mira and her master Aubrey Livingston Sr. Significantly, Hopkins also implies that Reuel is the product of an incestuous relationship, since his grandmother Aunt Hannah, Mira's mother, reveals that she too was kept as the mistress of Aubrey Sr.'s father, referred to simply as "old massa": "As soon as I was growed up, my mistress changed in her treatment of me, for she soon knowed of my relations with massa. . . . Mira was de onlies' child of ten that my massa lef' me for my comfort; all de res' were sold away" (604–5). By implying that Reuel's mother and father are half siblings, Hopkins suggests that the pattern of white patriarchal abuse of slave women is multigenerational and incestuous, resulting in widespread miscegenation. Incest is recognized as a condition of the slave institution. As Aunt Hannah puts it: "Dese things jes' got to happen in slavery" (605). The incestuous relationships among the characters are further intensified in the next generation. Reuel falls in love with and unknowingly marries his sister, Dianthe Lusk, a Fisk Jubilee singer who, in the opening chapter, first appears to him in a vision, and whom Reuel later brings back to life using his mesmeric powers. Dianthe has lost all memory of her past life, and Reuel gives her a white identity in order to take her "out of the sphere where she was born" and make her his wife (479). Aubrey Jr., the apparent half brother of both Reuel and Dianthe, also falls in love with Dianthe. Unaware of the incestuousness of his love, Aubrey uses his knowledge of Reuel's race to sabotage Reuel's attempts to find work in the United States; he then arranges for Reuel to obtain a medical position as part of an archaeological expedition to Ethiopia. With Reuel safely out of the way, Aubrey kills his own fiancée, Molly Vance, and uses his mesmeric influence to force Dianthe to marry him.

Within this complex plot, the metaphor of the hidden self functions in relation to all three of the major characters—Reuel, Dianthe, and Aubrey. Most obviously, the hidden self refers to Reuel's situation as a black man deliberately passing as white and to his complex relationship to his suppressed black identity. Dianthe, too, has a hidden self, but, unlike Reuel, Dianthe's relation to it is passive rather than active, volitionless rather than willed. The narrative elements of Dianthe's story—her employment by a traveling magnetic physician, her seeming death and subsequent reanimation by Reuel, her loss of memory, as well as the creation of her double identity—follow conventions that borrow from two quite different but nevertheless related genres: the medical case study and the literary romance.[16]

Reuel reads Dianthe as an exceptional case study, an unusual instance of "dual mesmeric trance": "Binet speaks at length of this possibility in his treatise. We have stumbled upon an extraordinary case." Indeed, the narrator tells us, "The scientific journals of the next month contained wonderful and *wondering* [?] accounts of the now celebrated case,—re-animation after seeming death. Reuel's lucky star was in the ascendant; fame and fortune awaited him; he had but to grasp them" (472). Molly Vance (Aubrey's fiancée), in contrast, sees Dianthe's story not as a brilliant scientific advancement but as an incredible piece of fiction: "Who would believe . . . that at this stage of the world's progress one's identity could be so easily lost and one still be living. It is like a page from an exciting novel" (489). But whether marvel of science or marvelous fiction, as these two passages would variously have it, the narrative of dual personality clearly offered Hopkins a discourse for representing the complexities of racial identity.[17]

Dianthe's suppressed African American identity survives, despite her loss of memory and the creation of her new white identity as "Felice Adams," and dramatically resurfaces at a social gathering among Boston white society. Possessed by a "weird contralto, veiled as it were," Dianthe is moved unconsciously to sing "Go Down, Moses"—the same spiritual that she had performed as a soloist for the Fisk Jubilee Singers. The other guests are horrified, and the host of the party whispers to his daughter Molly: "Do you not hear another voice beside Mrs. Briggs'?" (502). In this striking image of Dianthe's double-voicedness and the reemergence of her African American identity from "behind the veil," Hopkins powerfully matches Du Bois's more famous conceptualization of African American consciousness and gives it a female form.

Dianthe's susceptibility to mesmeric trance-states and her dual consciousness link her to her mother, Mira, and to the history of black women in slavery. Similarly, Reuel and Aubrey are linked by profession to their father, Aubrey Sr., a noted physician who had authored some books on the subject of mesmeric phenomena "referred to even at this advanced stage of discovery, as marvelous in some of their data" (486). Aubrey recalls his father's habit of hypnotizing Mira for the entertainment of his houseguests:

"My father made the necessary passes and from a serious, rather sad Negress, very mild with everyone, Mira changed to a gay, noisy, restless woman, full of irony and sharp jesting. In this case this peculiar metamorphosis always occurred" (486–87).[18] On one level, the mesmeric bond represented here can be read as figuring the slave institution itself, in which the slaveowner exercises complete control over the will of the slave; at the same time, however, under the neutralizing guise of "entertainment," Mira's subversive secondary personality gives vent to those qualities that are unacceptable within her conventional role as the subservient slave, allowing her to exercise powers of clairvoyance that go well beyond her master's control. When Mira foretells the defeat of the South in the Civil War and her master's death as a Yankee prisoner of war, she is sold away from the plantation; her prophecy is borne out, nevertheless, suggesting that her subversive spiritual gifts cannot be fully controlled by the economic arrangements of slavery.

Whereas Mira is allowed a degree of subversive subjectivity, Hopkins's treatment of Dianthe's mesmeric trances conforms to a more conventional representation of passive femininity.[19] When the unconscious Dianthe is first hospitalized, Reuel administers to her lifeless, prone body while an assembly of doctors looks on. In its juxtaposition of passive femininity with active male spectatorship, the scene recalls the well-known tableau of Charcot demonstrating a case of hysteria to a lecture hall of male doctors as his assistant holds the patient's fainting body (Ellenberger, between 330–31; Auerbach 129). Later, when Dianthe has recovered consciousness, she trusts Reuel implicitly "like a child" (470). In the weeks that follow, Reuel continues his treatment of her by hypnosis, and she in turn asks him to "give me the benefit of your powerful will" to bring about her healing (475).

But Hopkins's introduction of race into conventional representations of mesmerized women (both medical and fictional) complicates contemporary feminist debates that focus on the question of the patient-heroine's agency solely in relation to gendered power relations (see Auerbach). Hopkins deliberately disrupts conventional gender representations of the seductive bond between mesmerist and trance-maiden; Dianthe's "poor, violated mind" was destroyed by the "heartless usage" (489) of a *female* mesmeric physician whose services Dianthe entered "for a large salary" (473–74). Although Dianthe is well compensated for her services, Hopkins's choice of language—"violated mind," "heartless usage"—distinctly implies sexual exploitation that is more typically associated with male mesmerist-seducer figures. Hopkins does not specify the race of the female magnetic physician, but given the fact that the novel is set entirely within white society, the omission of racial indicators suggests strongly that she is white. The double meaning of the phrase "heartless usage," implying exploitation of Dianthe's labor as well as her sexuality, reinforces the unmistakable analogies between the mesmeric bond, which entails the subjugation of one individual's will to another, and the institution of slavery. For black women in slavery, "heartless usage" often meant exploitation of both sexual and nonsexual labor. In this case, Hopkins's choice of gender might be read as an indictment of white women's collusion with the abuses of the slave institution and, by analogy, with the widespread, interlocking practices of lynching and rape of African American men and women in the post-Reconstruction era as an equally heinous form of social control.

In contrast, Hopkins carefully distinguishes Reuel from conventional representations of the physician-mesmerist as seducer: "Absolutely free from the vices which beset most young men of his age and profession, his daily life was a white, unsullied page" (473). The telepathic and mesmeric connection between Reuel and Dianthe is represented in a register that is benign, almost utopian. Reuel's spiritual connection to Dianthe enables him to exercise his will over her, but his mesmeric powers are presented as life-giving and genuinely loving. Moreover, Reuel's departure for Africa directly after the wedding ceremony prevents their spiritual connection from being physically embodied, thus keeping the threat of actual incest from occurring. Finally, Reuel is equally as susceptible as Dianthe to states of passive consciousness. Reuel is visited spiritistically on several occasions both by Dianthe and by his deceased mother. Dianthe's visitation first rouses Reuel from his initial neurasthenic despair, and her supernatural connection to him results in his professional success, leading Elizabeth Ammons to characterize their relationship as one of "mutual revitalization" (82).[20] Reuel himself credits his success with the case to a supernatural source, rejecting the classic American success narrative of autonomous self-making: "I am an instrument— how I know not—a child of circumstances" (471). Like his fictional prototype, Tom Underwood in "The Mystery within Us," Reuel often occupies the "feminine" position in the classic opposition between an active male mesmerist and a passive female trance-maiden, subverting the traditional gendering of these positions .

Hopkins sharply contrasts Aubrey's prurient interest in Dianthe's case to Reuel's exceptionally pure motivations: "Enthused by its scientific aspect, he vied with Reuel in close attention to the medical side of the case, and being more worldly did not neglect the material side" (473). Aubrey's interest in the "material side" of the case exploits the familiar convention of the evil mesmerist who uses his powers to compromise sexually the female heroine. The relationship between Dianthe and Aubrey is conveyed in the highly charged language of the seduction novel: "In vain the girl sought to throw off the numbing influence of the man's presence. In desperation she tried to defy him, but she knew that she had lost her will-power and was but a puppet in the hands of this false friend" (504). Hopkins appropriates the conventions of the seduction narrative to represent black women's sexual exploitation in a white patriarchal culture. Aubrey's coercive control over

Dianthe continues uninterrupted the multigenerational pattern of sexual appropriation of black women by white men that had been exercised under slavery in the previous two generations of their family history. Whereas Reuel's marriage to Dianthe is never consummated, Dianthe is sexually compromised, exploited, and coerced into taking her own life by Aubrey.

The text's characteristically gothic doubling of the male protagonist creates two contrasting heterosexual bonds—one between a black man and woman, the other between a white man and black woman—each of which plays out alternative gendered power configurations that are differentiated along the axis of race. Aubrey's mesmeric influence over Dianthe represents white patriarchal power and its exploitative result; in contrast, the telepathic-mesmeric connection between Reuel and Dianthe suggests the utopian possibility of a mutual heterosexual relationship between black men and women.[21] As a social allegory, at this point in the narrative, the novel might read like this: the betrayal of the black brother Reuel by the white brother Aubrey takes place via the "theft" of the black woman Dianthe.[22] Although this interpretation may seem troubling in its emphasis on the black woman as a passive site of contestation in a struggle between black and white men, it is clearly one level on which the text asks to be read.

Yet this allegorical narrative of black-white relations as the betrayal of black brother by white brother via the figure of the black woman is destabilized in two ways. Most obviously, any attempt to represent a utopian black heterosexual union between Reuel and Dianthe is undercut by Reuel's betrayal, not only of his own black identity, but also of Dianthe's. By withholding from Dianthe the knowledge of her black ancestry and colluding with Aubrey in assigning her a fictitious white identity, Reuel directly enables Aubrey to exploit and blackmail her. But Hopkins also destabilizes the allegorical narrative of black-white relations that she has constructed in another, more fundamental way, revealing in the process yet a third instance of the existence of a "hidden self." In the novel's denouement, Aunt Hannah reveals Aubrey's actual identity and the true Livingston family history: when Aubrey Sr.'s legitimate heir died at birth, Aunt Hannah switched Mira's illegitimate baby for the legitimate Livingston heir. Aubrey, Reuel, and Dianthe share not only the same father but also the same mother; they are "of one blood."

Through the manipulation of Aubrey's racial identity, the category of *whiteness* is destabilized, as is the possibility of conclusively fixing racial identity. At a time of increased legal and scientific attempts to police the color line, Hopkins's representation of the interchangeability of "black" and "white" babies exposes the absurdity of such attempts.[23] In her representation of the complex history of miscegenation in the Livingston family tree and, moreover, in her final revelation of Aubrey's status as a mulatto, Hopkins insists on the presence of intermixed blood in the southern white aristocracy as a historical fact of oppressive social relations under slavery. As Hazel Carby has argued persuasively, Hopkins's "use of mulatto figures engaged with the discourse of social Darwinism, undermining the tenets of 'pure blood' and 'pure race' as mythological, and implicitly exposed the absurdity of theories of the total separation of the races" (140). In mobilizing the trope of the hidden self in relation to Reuel and Dianthe, Hopkins uses the figure of the mulatto to dramatically represent the split consciousness of the African American subject; in the figure of Aubrey, she goes further, exposing the hidden self at the foundation of Anglo American subjectivity and the suppression of the truth of miscegenation upon which the color line depends.

Despite the authority granted Aunt Hannah to reveal the characters' true family histories, the extraordinarily implausible lack of knowledge that Hopkins's characters exhibit with regard to both their own identities and family relationships is never entirely accounted for. Even this implausibility takes on a kind of narrative logic, however, when we recall the "singular forgetfulness" of the hysterical subjects in "The Hidden Self," whose situations captured Hopkins's imagination (364). Describing this amnesia, James wrote: "In certain persons . . . the total possible consciousness may be split into parts which coexist, but mutually ignore each other" (369). Like these hysterical subjects whose multiple personalities are mutually ignorant of one another, Hopkins's characters are divided by the color line and mutually estranged, although they are "of one blood"—part of a single family rather than a single self. Hopkins's remarkable imaginative achievement is her translation of the notion of a hidden self from the intrapsychic field that Janet and Binet investigated to the social field.

The hidden self becomes a metaphor for the suppressed history of oppressive social and familial relations under the institution of slavery, the collective legacy of abusive power relations, rather than merely the residue of repressed individual trauma. The African self is the "submerged self" that must be reclaimed not only by the black man Reuel, who is "passing," but also by the "white" man Aubrey, whose African blood has been suppressed and denied. Hopkins's use of the surface-depth model of selfhood enables her to counter a racist determinist notion of racial identity with a more indeterminate and destabilizing model. By embedding her multiple representations of the hidden self within the larger collective history of black-white social relations, Hopkins exploits the political possibilities of the surface-depth model of selfhood—its usefulness as a way of talking about racial identity as a socially constructed phenomenon.

Yet this achievement, although considerable, is not the sole endpoint of *Of One Blood.* Whereas in *Contending Forces,* the revelation of the characters' true family histories and identities results in restitution and compensation for the wrongs perpetrated against African Americans under slavery, in *Of One Blood,* the revelation of the characters' hidden selves does not result in social justice. Rather, the sequence of events set in the United States ends in a vision of social chaos marked by incest, bigamy, murder, and suicide, suggesting Hopkins's pessimism about the possibility of transformative political change on American ground. The politicization of the figure of the hidden self (described above) offers a powerful allegorical representation of the tragedy of American race relations but not a political solution.

Reuel's participation in a British archaeological expedition to Ethiopia both shifts the plot from an American to a "black Atlantic" geography and translates the metaphor of the hidden self to that of the "hidden city of Telassar," the legendary royal seat of the ancient Ethiopian civilization, which the expedition hopes to discover and excavate. The excavation of the hidden city will enable the expedition's British leader, Professor Stone, to prove his theory that Ethiopia antedated Egypt as the source of Western civilization. Stone's theory of "the Ethiopian as the primal race" (521) challenges racist Darwinian narratives of the period, which posited the inferiority of the African race, with a positive Afrocentric narrative of origins that celebrates Africans as "the most ancient source of all that [Anglo-Saxons] value in modern life" (520).

The deliberateness of this shift from psychology to archaeology, from hidden self to hidden city, is reinforced in the pivotal scene where Reuel's descent down a ruined staircase that will lead him to the hidden city is accompanied by a simultaneous descent into unconsciousness. In its metaphorical association of the uncovering of the mysteries of the unconscious with the work of archaeological excavation, this scene anticipates Freud's often cited analogy between his psychological insights into the preoedipal phase in girls and the archaeological discovery of the Minoan-Mycenean civilization behind the civilization of Greece (40). Reuel's descent into unconsciousness and the hidden city leads to the revelation of his hidden self, his true African identity, and to the discovery of the submerged but still vibrant city of Telassar. The lotus lily birthmark on his breast, the biological mark of race that apparently cannot disappear through miscegenation, identifies Reuel to the inhabitants of Telassar as King Ergamenes, their long-awaited royal heir, "who shall restore to the Ethiopian race its ancient glory" (547). United in marriage to Queen Candace, a dark-skinned incarnation of Dianthe, he will "give to the world a dynasty of dark-skinned rulers, whose destiny should be to restore the prestige of an ancient people" (570).[24]

In this crowning disclosure of Reuel's hidden self, Hopkins metaphorically associates the work of what we might call "self-recovery" with the work of cultural and political reconstruction. By linking Reuel's discovery of his hidden African identity to the recovery of a long-buried Ethiopian civilization, Hopkins represents the African origins of Western civilization and establishes the basis for a contemporary reconstructed Pan-African political community. But if the African portion of the narrative symbolically joins the therapeutic project of self-recovery to the political project of cultural reconstruction, it does so by substituting a model of racial identity rooted in a discourse of blood for the indeterminate model that is suggested by the figure of the hidden self. This deployment of an "identity politics" that is in tension with a notion of race as socially constructed has political and strategic motivations. Although, as I have argued, the surface-depth model afforded by the figure of the hidden self enables inroads against the determinism of turn-of-the-century racial constructions of self, such a model also presents dangers: it risks reinscribing African Americans in the position of the "repressed unconscious" or "secret self" of Anglo America, a construction of selfhood that invokes racist connotations of Africans as "inferior," "primitive," "irrational," or "uncivilized."

Hopkins's allegorical narrative symbolically refutes racist polygenesist views that blacks and whites were separate species, not "of one blood." By the late nineteenth century, however, Darwinian theory had already discredited polygenesists by asserting a common origin for all the races. Instead, social Darwinists had appropriated racist polygenesist arguments about black inferiority into a racist monogenesist argument: blacks and whites had a shared origin, but blacks had over time evolved into an inferior species.[25] The surface-depth model of selfhood lends itself in troubling ways to appropriation by the inferior-superior paradigm of social Darwinism. Although positioning blackness as the suppressed figure in this binary surface-depth opposition offers a powerful representation of American racism in the post-Reconstruction period, Hopkins may have been increasingly dissatisfied with the possibilities the hidden self model afforded for envisioning a more empowering political future for African Americans. Whereas *Contending Forces* and *Hagar's Daughter* both foreground mulatto characters and the reconstitution of families arbitrarily sundered by the color line, *Of One Blood* turns increasingly away from representations of mulatto characters and their deployment as figures of racial indeterminacy and increasingly toward a discourse of blood that reconstructs family and community based on an essential notion of race. In shifting her narrative from America to Africa, Hopkins abandons the gothic figure of the hidden self and the narrative of familial incest, miscegenation, and degeneration as a political allegory for failed race policies in the United States. Instead, she embraces a symbolics of blood that seeks to reconstruct an African bloodline that will form the basis of a reconstructed Pan-African political community.[26]

These two contrasting models of racial identity coexist in her novel, much like two contradictory or "split" personalities might inhabit a single body, a "double-consciousness" that is present in the duality of the very title, *Of One Blood; or, The Hidden Self.* In Hopkins's earlier novels, *Contending Forces: A Romance Illustrative of Negro Life North and South, Hagar's Daughter: A Story of Southern Caste Prejudice,* and *Winona: A Tale of Negro Life in the South and Southwest,* the subtitle glosses the main title. In *Of One Blood; or, The Hidden Self,* the main and subtitles compete with rather than complement one another. Joined by the conjunction that both yokes them together and signifies their oppositional relationship, they name the very doubleness of the text's representation of racial identity, a split that is never satisfactorily reconciled, so that the critic is continually forced to confront its contradictions. On the one hand, the novel's secondary title, *The Hidden Self,* suggests a model of racial identity that is fluid, indeterminate, and socially constructed; on the other hand, the novel's primary title, *Of One Blood,* invokes an essentialist notion of racial identity.

The novel's resolution—which includes not only Reuel's repatriation but also that of his grandmother, the former slave Aunt Hannah—introduces a notion of "home" that is secured through a discourse of blood. Both models of racial identity, albeit contradictory, have important strategic uses for Hopkins. By showing "whiteness" to be a fiction, Hopkins can launch a crucial challenge to the legal separation of the races upon which Jim Crow depends. By reintroducing a notion of "home" and "blood," she can reestablish a network of kinship ties to family and ancestors that at least potentially may enable the formation of a Pan-African community capable of collective resistance and change.

Hopkins's increasing reliance on a politically enabling discourse of blood places fundamental limits on the notion of a hidden self as a figure of racial indeterminacy. But Hopkins also recuperates one important aspect of James's notion of the hidden self within her deployment of the discourse of blood. In attributing his mystical powers to his mother, Mira, Reuel demonstrates his belief in a transpersonal or psychical dimension of the unconscious and links it to his African blood: "He remembered his mother well. From her he had inherited his mysticism and his occult powers. The nature of the mystic within him was, then, but a dreamlike devotion to the spirit that had swayed his ancestors; it was the shadow of Ethiopia's power" (558). This passage establishes a genealogy that links Reuel's psychical power not to his Anglo-Saxon father, with his scientific medical training and the authority he still derives posthumously for the publication of mesmeric studies, but to his African mother's "second sight" and the magical power of what Toni Morrison calls black people's "discredited knowledge" (342). Unlike Aubrey, who has inherited only his white father's exploitative "scientific-academic" mind, Reuel is connected to his maternal African heritage: to his clairvoyant mother, his conjure woman grandmother, and the "feminine-mystical" whose denigration James decried in "The Hidden Self."

Recasting James's "unclassified residuum" as the legitimate epistemological domain of Western science's racial and sexual Other, *Of One Blood* reclaims this discredited knowledge—of Africa, of the maternal—as an antidote to the psychic and spiritual alienation of dominant American culture. It is not surprising, then, that in this novel, as in "The Mystery within Us," Hopkins gives her protagonist the occupation of a healer. In the earlier short story, she presents a neurasthenic physician, who is both healed through a spiritistic experience and rededicated to the service of healing a larger community; in *Of One Blood,* Hopkins adds an explicitly racial dimension to this narrative. Depicting Reuel's spiritual reclamation from the devastating isolation and neurasthenic despair of "passing" to a reconnection with a Pan-African community and collective purpose, she refigures the healer as a political leader whose own spiritual recovery prefigures the possibility of political reconstruction. In her representations of passive experiences of selfhood, Hopkins's critique of the dominant American model of autonomous individualism is both successful and profound.

Spiritistically joining the self to ancestor and community, Hopkins both affirms and politicizes the supernatural realm in ways that anticipate the work of many contemporary African American women writers, including Toni Morrison's desire to "blend acceptance of the supernatural and a profound rootedness in the real world" (342) and Toni Cade Bambara's attempts to fuse the "split between the spiritual, psychic, and political forces in my community" (165).[27] Whereas twentieth-century American culture has largely preserved the division between the material and the spiritual that James tried unsuccessfully to bridge at the turn of the century, many contemporary African American women writers have questioned this opposition, politicizing the split itself. Deliberately traversing the boundaries between science and "pseudo-science," the natural and supernatural, realism and the fantastic, the sociopolitical and the psychological, *Of One Blood* is Hopkins's considerable contribution to that project.

NOTES

Shorter versions of this essay were presented at the American Women Writers of Color Conference in Ocean City, Maryland, May 1992, and at the MELUS Conference at the University of California, Berkeley, May 1993. I am grateful to everyone who has read and commented on this essay. I especially wish to thank John Gruesser and Helene Moglen for their generous suggestions.

"Pauline Hopkins and William James: The New Psychology and the Politics of Race" was originally published in *The Unruly Voice: Rediscovering Pauline Elizabeth Hopkins,* ed. John Cullen Gruesser (Champaign: U of Illinois P: 1996).

1. John Dewey and G. Stanley Hall each published articles entitled "The New Psychology" in 1884 and 1885, respectively (Cotkin 32–35). For a discussion of popular interest in the new psychology, see Hale's chapter 9, "Mind Cures and the Mystical Wave: Popular Preparation for Psychoanalysis, 1904–1910." Ellenberger provides the

most exhaustive general history of the field of psychology. On the emergence of the new psychology in an American context, see Fuller *Americans and the Unconscious* and *Mesmerism;* and Kenny.

2. James's writings on psychical phenomena have been collected in a volume of *The Works of William James* entitled *Essays in Psychical Research.* See also Eugene Taylor's reconstruction of James's Lowell lectures on this subject; and Barzun 227–261. For a general history of spiritualism and psychical research in the United States, see Moore.

3. Ernest Jones recounts this anecdote about James's reception of Freud's American lectures: "William James, who knew German well, followed the lectures with great interest. He was very friendly to us, and I shall never forget his parting words, said with his arm around my shoulder: 'The future belongs to your work'" (57). Michael G. Kenny cites the Worcester Conference as the moment when "psychoanalysis effectively displaced the older psychical research tradition and made the study of psychopathology and the unconscious a thing of this world only" (93).

4. This essay was completed before Thomas J. Otten's essay on the intertextuality of Hopkins and James came to my attention. Otten's article shares my concern with Hopkins's appropriations of new psychological discourse to explore questions of racial identity, and my argument bears a coincidental resemblance to his on several points. My approach differs significantly, however, in its attention to the crucial intersection of race and gender. For another recent discussion of Hopkins's use of James's essay in the larger context of turn-of-the-century Pan-Africanist discourse, see Sundquist *To Wake the Nations* (569–73). Claudia Tate also discusses a James connection, without specifically identifying Hopkins's use of "The Hidden Self" (204–8).

5. Hopkins's interest in the new psychology also manifests itself in the two installments of her last work of serial fiction, "Topsy Templeton." The uncompleted work appeared in the *New Era Magazine,* which Hopkins edited for its two issues (Feb. 1916, 11–20, 48; Mar. 1916, 75–84). I am grateful to John Gruesser for calling these fictional pieces to my attention.

6. I take the phrase "black Atlantic" from Paul Gilroy's brilliant reading of the transatlantic cultural exchanges shaping African American cultural production. In its representation of a transpersonal theory of consciousness that is intimately linked to a transnational subject, Hopkins's novel figures a psychical version of transatlantic travel, one that is extremely suggestive in relationship to contemporary postcolonial critical debates. In an essay published in *Cultures of United States Imperialism,* Kevin Gaines has emphasized the conservatism underlying Hopkins's attempts to "refute racism by adopting a 'scientific' Western ethnological persona," condemning the failure of this strategy to counter effectively racist imperialism at the turn of the century (434). In what follows, I argue that her appropriations of scientific psychological discourse have a far more radical potential as a location of cultural critique.

7. Hazel Carby has observed Hopkins's reworking of the spiritistic and supernatural themes of "The Mystery within Us" in Of *One Blood,* but she focuses primarily on the novel's Pan-African political perspective and establishment of an African genealogy (155–62). This essay extends Carby's reading by exploring the interrelationship between Hopkins's use of psychological and spiritistic themes and her Pan-Africanist politics.

8. In Hopkins's *Contending Forces,* members of the black middle-class Smith fam-

ily are financially restituted for the estate that was wrongfully stolen from their ancestors because of their imputed black blood; the descendant of the man responsible for the initial wrong is punished.

9. Reuel's equation of "stray dogs and cats and Negroes" links him to the Harvard-educated white northerner Cuthbert Sumner in *Hagar's Daughter* who "gave large sums to Negro colleges and on the same princpal [sic] gave liberally to the Society for the Prevention of Cruelty to Animals, and endowed a refuge for homeless cats. Horses, dogs, cats, and Negroes were classed together in his mind as of the brute creation whose sufferings it was his duty to help alleviate" (265–66). By linking Reuel rhetorically to the hypocritical racism of the New England liberal philanthropic tradition, Hopkins immediately establishes the moral bankruptcy of his conscious choice to "pass."

10. Although the racial and class associations of neurasthenia are clear, the gender coding is more ambiguous. George M. Beard found neurasthenia to be more prevalent in men than in women; S. Weir Mitchell, however, preferred the diagnosis of "neurasthenia" to the more common "hysteria" for his mostly female clientele (Drinka 184–209). For a related discussion of the gendering of the disease, see Lutz (31–37).

11. The identical passage appears in *The Souls of Black Folk* (45). For the publication history of the essays collected in *Souls,* see Rampersad 303–4*n*9.

12. Dickson D. Bruce Jr. links Du Bois's use of the term "double-consciousness" both to medical accounts of split personality and to Emersonian transcendentalism ("W. E. B. Du Bois"). On Du Bois's relation to the new psychology, see also Lutz (244–46, 261–75) and Rampersad (74). In his autobiography, Du Bois refers to James as "my friend and guide to clear thinking" (143).

13. For a fascinating account of the transition from a religious to a psychological explanatory framework for multiple personality, see Kenny. Kenny's discussion of the case of Mary Reynolds, the first recorded case of "double consciousness" (1816), also suggests an intriguing line of inquiry. In her letters and diary, Reynolds consistently associated her two personalities with the imagery of darkness and light that reflected the Calvinist dualism of her upbringing. Though Kenny does not pursue this imagery, it suggests strongly how thoroughly the discourse on race may already have been embedded into the discourse on multiple personality well before 1900. Similarly, in one of the more famous case studies of multiple personality in our own century, popularized as *The Three Faces of Eve,* Corbett H. Thigpen and Hervey Cleckley gave their patient the pseudonym "Eve White" and referred to her alter-personality as "Eve Black."

14. The "veil" was also used in white middle-class psychical research circles at the turn of the century to designate the separation between this world and the world beyond the grave. For an example of that discourse, see Anne Banning Robbins's 1909 memoir, *Both Sides of the Veil.* William Dean Howells, another dabbler in psychical research, offers a more skeptical representation of the turn-of-the-century white middle-class interest in the occult in his 1903 short story collection, *Questionable Shapes.* In the larger project from which this essay is taken, I explore more fully the relationship between Du Bois's rhetorical use of the "veil" and the discourses mentioned above, an inquiry that also complicates the simple racialized opposition between the spiritual and the material.

15. In *Contending Forces*, Hopkins presents fictional characters modeled after both Du Bois and Booker T. Washington, using the novel in part as a forum to debate the various positions of the leading black intellectuals of her day. Hopkins's own attitudes on the race issue were much more closely aligned ideologically with those of Du Bois than of Booker T. Washington.

16. In designating a train accident as the cause of Dianthe's loss of memory, Hopkins associated her heroine with a traumatic condition known as "railway spine" or "railway brain" that was a widespread and medically recognized diagnosis in the late nineteenth century (Drinka 108–22). At the same time, she places Dianthe in a literary tradition of mesmerized heroines that includes Hawthorne's Priscilla, James's Verena Tarrant, and du Maurier's Trilby.

17. A number of critics and historians have noted the twin beginnings of psychology and romanticism in the late eighteenth century and the close association between scientific and literary representations of dual personality, particularly in the last two decades of the nineteenth century. See for example, Miller (49–51, 209–44, 329–48). For a compelling feminist reading of the "rich, covert collaboration between documents of romance and the romance of science" in the 1890s, see Auerbach (111). As Claudia Tate observes, Hopkins's choice of the gothic romance genre (Tate refers specifically to the "psychological ghost story") complements her fascination with the new psychology and discursively links *Of One Blood* not only to the psychological writings of William James but also to his brother Henry's fiction as well (205). The relationship between Hopkins's participation in and revisions of the gothic tradition and the kinds of appropriations of scientific-psychological discourses I explore in this essay is beyond the scope of my inquiry. I want to emphasize, however, the mutual interconnectedness of the discourses of scientific psychology and literary romance, conventional disciplinary boundaries notwithstanding, as well as the ways in which these two discourses of "hidden selves" are deeply implicated in a discourse of race (see also note 21).

18. Hopkins apparently borrowed this description of Mira's dual personality from Janet's case study of "Leonie," which is quoted extensively in James's "The Hidden Self." In her "normal state," Leonie was "a serious and rather sad person . . . very mild with everyone." Under hypnosis, she became "gay, noisy, restless" with a "tendency to irony and sharp jesting" (James 366). This type of contrast is typical of medical accounts of white female multiple personalities from Mary Reynolds to "Eve White."

19. Claudia Tate convincingly observes that "Hopkins's serial novels decenter the heroine's prominence," arguing that she "silenced the discourse of female agency, which was a very important feature of [black women's] 1890s domestic novels." My conclusions differ significantly from Tate's characterization of the novel's vision as one of "chronic racial despair" (208).

20. For a more sinister representation of a telepathic heterosexual bond in a white middle-class marriage, see Howells's short story "Though One Rose from the Dead," in *Questionable Shapes*.

21. Taylor Stoehr's discussion, apropos of Hawthorne, of the close generic relationship between the gothic novel, featuring an evil mesmerist or pseudoscientist, and the utopian novel, featuring an idealistic social scientist or reformer, seems to me especially germane to an analysis of Hopkins's revisions of the gothic mode. Taking *The House of the Seven Gables* as an instance of the culmination of the high gothic

novel and *The Blithedale Romance* as an example of the reemergence of the utopian novel, Stoehr reads Hawthorne's work as a case study of the former genre bleeding into the latter (251–75). I would argue that *Of One Blood* can be usefully read as a hybrid of the two genres, combining an American gothic plot that features an evil (white) mesmerist with an African utopian plot that features an idealistic (black) social scientist. Through her explicit engagement with a discourse of race, Hopkins crucially revises the genre, reversing and critiquing the racism implicit in the traditional figure of the gothic double.

22. Elizabeth Ammons similarly reads the novel as an allegory about racism, focusing primarily on Dianthe as an allegorical figure for the plight of the black woman artist (81–85).

23. For an excellent collection of essays on another text of the period that uses the narrative device of black and white babies switched at birth to explore the nature of racial identity, see Gillman and Robinson. On the period's legal and scientific policing of the color line, see Sundquist, "Mark Twain," and Rogin.

24. The "Ethiopian prophecy," which predicted the rise of Africa and the decline of the West, is thematized in the work of many black intellectuals at the turn of the century, including W. E. B. Du Bois, Frances E. W. Harper, and Paul Laurence Dunbar (Moses). For a discussion of Ethiopianism that situates Hopkins's novel in relationship to a larger discourse on Pan-Africanism, especially in the work of Du Bois, see Sundquist, *To Wake the Nations* (551–81). For a discussion of the representation of Egypt and Ethiopia in the work of turn-of-the-century African American historians, see Bruce, "Ancient Africa."

25. On the pre-Darwinian debate over monogenesis versus polygenesis, see Frederickson (71–76), and Gould (chap. 2). On the marriage of polygenesist ethnology and Darwinism, see Frederickson (chap. 8).

26. On the discourse of "blood," see Foucault (124–25). Foucault notes a shift in the late eighteenth century from an aristocratic concern with genealogy to the emerging bourgeois preoccupation with heredity. Whereas the aristocracy had asserted itself through a symbolics of blood and a concern with ancestry, the middle class looked to the health of its progeny. One might turn to a text like Kate Chopin's short story "Desiree's Baby" (1892) for one (tragic) inscription of the bourgeois preoccupation with racially pure offspring. In contrast, *Of One Blood* might be read as a return to an older discourse of aristocratic legitimation to counter emergent white racist discourse on "pure blood."

27. Despite his gender, Reuel arguably prefigures such female healers as Baby Suggs in Morrison's *Beloved* and Minnie Ransom in Bambara's *Salt Eaters*. His positioning within a feminine African lineage partially destabilizes the undeniably patriarchal bias of Hopkins's Pan-Africanist political vision.

WORKS CITED

Ammons, Elizabeth. *Conflicting Stories: American Women Writers at the Turn into the Twentieth Century.* New York: Oxford UP, 1991.

Auerbach, Nina. "Magi and Maidens: The Romance of the Victorian Freud." *Writing and Sexual Difference.* Ed. Elizabeth Abel. Chicago: U of Chicago P, 1982. 111–30.

Bambara, Toni Cade. "What It Is I Think I'm Doing Anyhow." *The Writer on Her Work.* Ed. Janet Sternberg. New York: Norton, 1980. 153–68.

Barzun, Jacques. *A Stroll with William James.* New York: Harper, 1983.

Bruce, Dickson D., Jr. "Ancient Africa and the Early Black American Historians, 1883–1915." *American Quarterly* 36 (1984): 684–99.

———. "W. E. B. Du Bois and the Idea of Double Consciousness." *American Literature* 64 (1992): 299–309.

Carby, Hazel. *Reconstructing Womanhood: The Emergence of the Afro-American Woman Novelist.* New York: Oxford UP, 1987.

Cotkin, George. *Reluctant Modernism: American Thought and Culture, 1880–1900.* New York: Twayne, 1992.

Drinka, George Frederick. *The Birth of Neurosis: Myth, Malady, and the Victorians.* New York: Simon and Schuster, 1984.

Du Bois, W. E. B. *The Autobiography of W. E. B. Du Bois: A Soliloquy on Viewing My Life from the Last Decade of Its First Century.* Ed. Herbert Aptheker. New York: International, 1968.

———. *The Souls of Black Folk.* 1903. New York: New American Library, 1969.

———. "Strivings of the Negro People." *Atlantic Monthly* August 1897: 194–98.

Ellenberger, Henri F. *The Discovery of the Unconscious: The History and Evolution of Dynamic Psychiatry.* New York: Basic, 1970.

Feinstein, Howard M. *Becoming William James.* Ithaca: Cornell UP, 1984.

Foucault, Michel. *An Introduction.* 1976. Trans. Robert Hurley. New York: Vintage, 1980. Vol. 1 of *The History of Sexuality.*

Frederickson, George M. *The Black Image in the White Mind: The Debate on Afro-American Character and Destiny, 1817–1914.* New York: Harper and Row, 1971.

Freud, Sigmund. "Female Sexuality." 1931. *Women and Analysis: Dialogues on Psychoanalytic Views of Femininity.* 1974. Ed. Jean Strouse. Boston: G. K. Hall, 1985. 39–56.

Fuller, Robert C. *Americans and the Unconscious.* New York: Oxford UP, 1986.

———. *Mesmerism and the American Cure of Souls.* Philadelphia: U of Pennsylvania P, 1982.

Gaines, Kevin. "Black Americans' Racial Uplift Ideology as 'Civilizing Mission': Pauline E. Hopkins on Race and Imperialism." *Cultures of United States Imperialism.* Ed. Amy Kaplan and Donald Pease. Durham, N.C.: Duke UP, 1993. 433–55.

Gillman, Susan, and Forrest G. Robinson, eds. *Mark Twain's Pudd'nhead Wilson: Race, Conflict, and Culture.* Durham: Duke UP, 1990.

Gilroy, Paul. *The Black Atlantic: Modernity and Double Consciousness.* Cambridge: Harvard UP, 1993.

Gould, Stephen Jay. *The Mismeasure of Man.* New York: Norton, 1981.

Hale, Nathan G., Jr. *Freud and the Americans: The Beginnings of Psychoanalysis in the United States, 1876–1917.* New York: Oxford UP, 1971.

Hopkins, Pauline. *Contending Forces: A Romance Illustrative of Negro Life North and South.* 1900. New York: Oxford UP, 1988.

———. "The Mystery within Us." *Colored American Magazine* May 1900: 14–18. Reprinted in *Short Fiction by Black Women, 1900–1920.* Ed. Elizabeth Ammons. New York: Oxford UP, 1991. 21–26.

———. *Of One Blood; or, The Hidden Self.* 1902–1903. *The Magazine Novels of Pauline Hopkins.* New York: Oxford UP, 1988. 441–621.

Howells, William Dean. *Questionable Shapes.* New York: Harper, 1903.

James, Alice. *The Diary of Alice James.* 1894. Ed. Leon Edel. New York: Penguin, 1987.

James, William. "The Hidden Self." *Scribner's Magazine* 7 (1890): 361–73.

———. "Is Life Worth Living?" *International Journal of Ethics* 6 (1895): 1–24

———. *The Works of William James.* Ed. Robert E. McDermott. Cambridge: Harvard UP, 1986. Vol. 16 of *Essays in Psychical Research.*

Jones, Ernest. *The Life and Work of Sigmund Freud.* Vol. 2. New York: Basic, 1955.

Kenny, Michael G. *The Passion of Ansel Bourne: Multiple Personality in American Culture.* Washington, D.C.: Smithsonian Institution P, 1986.

Lutz, Tom. *American Nervousness, 1903: An Anecdotal History.* Ithaca: Cornell UP, 1991.

Miller, Karl. *Doubles: Studies in Literary History.* New York: Oxford UP, 1985.

Moore, R. Laurence. *In Search of White Crows: Spiritualism, Parapsychology, and American Culture.* New York: Oxford UP, 1977.

Morrison, Toni. "Rootedness: The Ancestor as Foundation." *Black Women Writers (1950–1980): A Critical Evaluation.* Ed. Mari Evans. Garden City, N.Y.: Anchor-Doubleday, 1984. 339–45.

Moses, Wilson J. "The Poetics of Ethiopianism: W. E. B. Du Bois and Literary Black Nationalism." *American Literature* 47 (1975): 411–26.

Otten, Thomas J. "Pauline Hopkins and the Hidden Self of Race." *ELH* 59 (1992): 227–56.

Rampersad, Arnold. *The Art and Imagination of W. E. B. Du Bois.* Cambridge: Harvard UP, 1976.

Robbins, Anne Banning. *Both Sides of the Veil: A Personal Experience.* Boston: Sherman, 1909.

Rogin, Michael. "Francis Galton and Mark Twain: The Natal Autograph in Pudd'nhead Wilson." Gillman and Robinson 73–85.

Stoehr, Taylor. *Hawthorne's Mad Scientists: Pseudoscience and Social Science in Nineteenth-Century Life and Letters.* Hamden, Conn.: Archon Books-Shoe String P, 1978.

Sundquist, Eric J. "Mark Twain and Homer Plessy." Gillman and Robinson 46–72.

———. *To Wake the Nations: Race in the Making of American Literature.* Cambridge: Harvard UP, 1993.

Tate, Claudia. *Domestic Allegories of Political Desire: The Black Heroine's Text at the Turn of the Century.* New York: Oxford UP, 1992.

Taylor, Eugene. *William James on Exceptional Mental States: The 1896 Lowell Lectures.* New York: Scribner's, 1983.

Thigpen, Corbett H., and Hervey Cleckley. "A Case of Multiple Personality." *Journal of Abnormal and Social Psychology* 49.1 (1954): 135–51.

Yeazell, Ruth Bernard, ed. *The Death and Letters of Alice James.* Berkeley: U of California P, 1981.

Channeling the Ancestral Muse
Lucille Clifton and Dolores Kendrick

Akasha (Gloria) Hull

NARRATIVE #1

One afternoon in 1975, Lucille Clifton and her two eldest daughters—then sixteen and fourteen years old—were sitting idly at home while the four younger children napped. After rejecting an outing to the movies, they pulled down the Ouija board from the closet where they stored the family games. It was a casual item that they had played with before and gotten only "foolishness." Rica said that she would record the message; Lucille and Sidney put their hands on the board. When it began moving—faster than it ever had before—Lucille said, "Sidney!" Sidney answered, "Ma, I'm not doing that, you're doing it." Lucille said she wasn't and asked the board emphatically, "Who is it?" It responded "T . . . H," at which point the two of them removed their hands. When they tried again—this time with their eyes closed—it spelled out "THELMA." Absolutely skeptical, Clifton put the board away. A few days later, they took it down again, with Lucille challenging, "Now, this is not funny. What is happening here?" It answered, "It's me, baby. Don't worry about it. Get some rest," and then dashed off the board.

Both Clifton and her daughters recognized "THELMA" as Lucille's mother, Thelma Moore Sayles, who had died one month before Clifton's first child was born. This unsought, unexpected supernatural contact with her inaugurated Clifton's conscious recognition of the spiritual realm. Her next volume of poetry, *two-headed woman* (1980),[1] charts the turbulence of this awareness, but ends with a calm acceptance of the truth that she has come to know:

> in populated air
> our ancestors continue.
> i have seen them.

i have heard
their shimmering voices
singing. (221)

NARRATIVE #2

One night, Dolores Kendrick, who is usually a good sleeper, could not fall asleep. Getting up at three A.M., she made a cup of tea and began reading the slave narratives in Gerda Lerner's documentary history, *Black Women in White America*. She became totally immersed and was particularly ensnared by the story of Margaret Garner, a woman who in 1856 had slit the throat of one daughter and attempted to kill herself and three other children rather than be reenslaved after an unsuccessful escape for freedom (the same harrowing story from which Toni Morrison's *Beloved* germinated). Kendrick awoke the next morning with an insistent urge to write a poem based on the Garner incident. Beyond this, the voice of the woman was coming to her "loud and clear," even though she had no previous experience with that mode of writing. The voice spoke in a dialect and used words with which Kendrick was not familiar:

> Cain't cry, 'cause I be dead,
> this old tarp 'round me,
> my flesh rottin', my bones
> dryin' out, my eyes movin'
> through some kind of cheesecloth,
> like a fog.

Kendrick did not know that *tarp* was *tarpaulin* until she found it in the dictionary. So, she wrote down *tarpaulin* but then realized that, no, this was a slave woman talking and she should simply listen to what she said. She decided "not to fight it," to "just go and follow what I heard." Thus began a process whereby Kendrick sat down with a stack of black female slave narratives on her lap, read them with intense emotional involvement, and "let the voices work" within her. What eventuated was her 1989 volume, *The Women of Plums: Poems in the Voices of Slave Women*.[2]

Aside from their intrinsic interest, these narratives are remarkable for several reasons. At the most rudimentary level, they reveal how the overt spiritual connection of the two poets, Lucille Clifton and Dolores Kendrick, to black female ancestors provides both the content and creative modality of their work. In this, they are joined by an unprecedented array of contemporary African American women writers who likewise foreground the spiritual in their themes and inspiration: Toni Morrison, Alice Walker, Toni Cade Bambara, Audre Lorde, Paule Marshall, Gloria Naylor, Octavia Butler, and

Sonia Sanchez, to name some of the most prominent. Writing thus, all of these authors are producing literature from historical-cultural specificities of black women's lives in the United States and, more particularly, from African American spiritual traditions (revering the dead, acknowledging the reality of ghosts and spirit possession, honoring "superstition" and the unseen world, giving credence to second sight and other suprasensory perception, paying homage to African deities, practicing voodoo or hoodoo, rootworking, and so on). Other cultures of color and strong ethnicity embrace similar world views, and wherever it is found, this sensibility contradicts dominant Eurocentric ontologies, although nonrational, non-Western modes of apprehending reality are increasingly legitimated by mainstream, mass culture as it moves into "New Age" awareness of our human-planetary connections with larger metaphysical forces and with all beings.

These two narratives about Clifton and Kendrick enhance our understanding of creativity and creative processes. Writers have always talked about their muses or the inexplicable origins of their best and most original work. However, a higher level of clarity and confession is reached when Kendrick and Alice Walker thank their characters for coming to them and Clifton quotes sentences from her automatic writing in her poems. Where in the current theorizing about poetic form and politics is there space to explicitly situate such matters? Studying Kendrick and Clifton through their supernatural consciousness spotlights their achievement in unique and appropriate ways. In addition to the great value of their poetry as art and cultural expression, their willingness to frankly share their spiritual selves and experiences—knowing that this is usually regarded with skepticism—is laudable. Looking first at Dolores Kendrick and then Lucille Clifton, I discuss the transmission of female ancestral energy as a vital force in their lives and poetry.

Dolores Kendrick was born September 7, 1927, in Washington, D.C., where she received her B.S. in 1949 from Miner Teachers College and, after years of teaching English and poetry, her M.A.T. from Georgetown University in 1970.[3] She designed the curriculum for The School Without Walls and served as its humanities coordinator for several years. Since 1972, she has been an English instructor at Phillips Exeter Academy in New Hampshire. Her poems began appearing in small magazines and literary quarterlies during the 1950s, with frequent contributions to Percy Johnston's *Dasein* throughout the 1960s. Her first book, *Through the Ceiling*, was published in the London Paul Breman Heritage series in 1975, followed by *Now Is the Thing to Praise* (1984).

Although Kendrick long conceived of poetry as "a living force capable of working in everybody's life," she had not produced anything as extraordinary as *The Women of Plums* (1989). Nor had she channeled voices from the spirit world. She believes that it may take years of "preparation" of one's spiritual self to be ready for that sort of experience to happen and that she herself would not have been prepared any sooner. Years of contemplative living rendered her open to receive the voices when they came:

> I started that kind of life when I was quite young. I was a great one for going off on retreats and being alone. In fact, I have a whole book of spiritual writings, journals I have done in search of the soul, dealing with one's connection to God and the universe. I've been doing this for a long, long, long, long time. And my mother was very much that way. She raised us to believe in it and not to be afraid of that sort of thing. I just accepted it as a way of life and was extremely comfortable with it. I remember girls in college talking about parties and how strange I was because I liked to be by myself. They would say, "How can you stand being by yourself?" And I'd think, "How can you stand *not* being by yourself!"

Now, as a mature adult, she has "no problems with whatever inner voices are in [her]" and is growing even stronger in "contemplative prayer, in which you just sit and listen." She spends a part of every summer writing at a Benedictine monastery in Boulder, Colorado.

Not a practicing spiritualist of any type, Kendrick only recalls three pre-*Plums* experiences that "may have been introductions to opening parts of me that I didn't know were there." The first occurred some years ago in an old courtyard in Aix-en-Provence, France. Though it seemed pleasant enough, she and a friend felt "funny," "weird," sensed a strange presence that prompted them to want to leave—only to discover bullet holes and a plaque that informed them that the Germans had executed French men in the courtyard during World War II. This same sensing of unseen presences reoccurred one Sunday when Kendrick attended mass at the Catholic church where segregation had forced her to sit in the balcony as a child. Running up to tell a choir soloist how much she had enjoyed her "Met"-quality singing, Kendrick felt all of the black people who had sat there, "all of our grandfathers and aunts and uncles. It was a very strange, wonderful feeling, sustaining." Her prose-poem, "Now is the Thing to Praise," concludes with a rendering of this experience:

> And I: the choirloft holding me too suddenly, opening tired wounds because I remembered my childhood in that loft. . . . And I: in mid-air, stunned, wanting to cry, wanting to lift myself away from all that pain and all that Past. And I: finding their ghosts stilled in the pausing pews, knowing they were surely the true elite, smiling, gracious, leaning upon their fine endurances, the wealth of their witness, their celebrations of longer matters. . . . And I: dazed, restored, brought to my beginnings, in joy. (27)

A third, more uncommon, incident relates to her mother, who died in February 1976. After her mother's funeral, Kendrick returned to the apartment that she had occupied with her. In the apartment, Kendrick kept a small calendar with "wonderful little sayings usually attending to our spiritual natures," which was opened to the week her mother died and the injunction, "Remember the lilies of the field." One morning she rose to discover the same phrase scrawled on the calendar in her mother's print. (Her mother had been a beautiful cursive writer, but exhibited "lousy penmanship" when she tried to print.) Kendrick reports:

> I thought how did that get there? She wasn't even here when that calendar was on my desk. And I never knew or understood how it got there. I ran looking for her occasional print in her own papers and I found it and compared them and surely it was her print. I have that framed and in my room right now. That for me was scary. I just don't know how that happened. But I don't question these things.

Because of these experiences, Kendrick came to the writing of *Plums* having discovered her ability to sense spirit beings, to mystically connect with her own ancestral past, and to accept these phenomena without questioning. After her first Margaret Garner–inspired hearing, she decided "not to go entirely on instincts" but to conduct focused historical research. At the beginning of *Plums,* she acknowledges these references—George Rawick's Federal Writers' Project interviews, *The American Slave: A Composite Autobiography;* John Bayliss's *Black Slave Narratives;* Guy Johnson's *Folk Culture on St. Helena Island, South Carolina;* and the Gerda Lerner history. However, her writing process remained the same: "Basically, I would sit down with this package of narratives and some of my research notes and I'd read them. Some of them became very painful. I began either to get angry or to come out of it crying, so I had to decide just what I was going to do." Not wanting to write "history" or "angry poetry," she fixed on the slave women's strength, thinking about how they and the women in her own family belied the shallow and demeaning media images of African American women.

Kendrick has decided that she "summoned" "The Women of Plums" through the historical texts:

> I would read them and some I would deal with and some I wouldn't. I got the historical outline of the character, who the person was, or the narrative and then I would put it aside and sit down and begin to write. Now what is she saying? What is she really saying? What is the voice here? Once I got the idea of the woman in my head, I began to sit down and write the narrative in her voice, in what I was hearing from her, not in terms of who I was.

Kendrick sees her role as giving voice to women who had not been able to speak for a hundred years but admits that she cannot totally explain the "mechanics":

> We know very little about the creative process. This experience has taught me that. I've always believed that I as an artist am a vehicle through which

the creative energy flows, and that that links me with God. I thoroughly believe that. I don't believe I originate anything. I think God originates it and He in His wisdom has given tons of people on this planet certain talents through which they can bring their art to the surface. I think I saw that manifested very, very strongly in this particular work, and I don't understand it. And I'm not going to try to understand it. I'm just going to try to accept it because I think that there is a level of creativity that people hit that we know very little about.

She encapsulates these sentiments at the beginning of the book:

I thank these women
for coming, and I thank
the good God who sent them.
The Women of Plums

Notable here is an intertwined but still double identification of creative cause: the women themselves who "came," a word suggesting actual physical movement and travel, and God, who might be visualized as standing behind them, "sending" them forward.

Explanations notwithstanding, one fact is certain. The level of creative accomplishment that Kendrick reaches in *The Women of Plums* surpasses her prior achievements. The poems are remarkable productions that evidence their spirit-driven origins and, at their best, deeply affect many readers. Almost all of them chronicle strenuous moments: running away from slavery, having a picnic with a dead best friend, being in love, being prostituted to white men by the master when he needs extra money, praying on the auction block to be bought with daughter and not separately, nursing the Civil War soldiers on both sides of the conflict, sleeping with the master, being beaten, being abandoned, singing lullabies to a downcast child, and so on. The names of the women themselves sound like a litany or a conjuring: Ndzeli, Leah, Peggy, Sophie, Bethany Veney, Prunella, Jenny, Hattie, Rya, Juba, Lula, Lucy, Polly, Aunt Mary, Liza Lily, Jo, Sidney, Lottie, Anne, Julia, Gravity, Harriet, Miss Maggie, Cora Sue, Tildy, Althea, Emma, Aunt Sarah, Vera, and Sadie. As the book jacket aptly states: "Kendrick gives each poem a distinct voice that expresses how these women used their imagination and spirituality to rise above the confines of slavery. Taken together, these poems provide a vivid indictment of the oppression of slavery and the beauty of souls that, no matter their outward bonds, refused to succumb to it."

One of the earliest authentic voices is the Margaret Garner-inspired "Peggy in Killing." With a section labeled "Traveling," the poem begins: "They done found me, / Lord! They done found me again!" The next section, "Visions," powerfully details her reasons for refusing even at the cost of her own and her children's lives to remain unfree:

I tried to escape
from they dark breaths,
they glories, hallelujahs!
they fine houses and sweet fields,
they murders murders murders!
they coffins stenchin' in they smiles,
they *come heah Peggy,*
dress my little one,
then fix her somethin' to eat,
maybe some cake and milk,
and mine sittin' on the stairs
in the cold, in the dark,
waitin' to do some waitin' on
waitin' for the milk to sour
and the cake to crumble,
hearin' all this
without a word, a whimper,
eyes freezin' in they dreams,
hungers freezin' in they dark,
takin' they dreams to supper
like candles meltin',
after 'while no more light,
they walkin' softly
makin' sure they seen and not heard
and they dreams screamin'
in they bright, soft eyes. (29–30)

After she drowns the children, she pronounces herself "dead" and prepares
to sing to the ghosts that watch her, "like a star."

Voice *is* the dominant feature here—as in the other poems. The sound
of engaged, impassioned human expression drives each successive thought
and line, imparting emotional and rhetorical urgency. The dialectal use of
the easier-to-say "they" for *their,* dropping of *g* from *ing* word endings, and
locutions such as "heah" for *here* couple with the common but resonant ad-
jectives like "fine," "sweet," "soft" and everyday concrete nouns such as
"houses," "cake," "stairs," "milk," "supper" to swiftly and strongly communicate, convince, and overwhelm. Even the sarcasm is tellingly nonabstract.
Juxtapositions of archetypal pairs—dark and light, food and hunger, cold
and candles, silence and speech—extend the depth of meaning. The
metaphoric formulations of coffins stenching in the slaveowners' smiles, the
black children's eyes freezing with dreams screaming within them, are plausible as folk inventiveness and, at the same time, poetically effective. These
linguistic qualities combine with the situations described to impart docu-
mentable or intuitively felt historical accuracy: even if no one ever recorded

it, we know that slave children waited on cold, dark stairs to spring into service on command.

It is less easy to talk about another, otherworldly quality that inheres in most of these poems. In "Peggy in Killing," that sense of a different temporal geography, of an unfamiliar reality plane, comes partially from the intensity of her extreme or deranged state. However, it also results from our having been put in direct contact with what amounts to another world through the supernatural agency of the poem's spirit-originator, and from the totally original imaginings from this dimension, imaginings that are partially caught in lines such as:

> I burn and burn
> all inside
> turn to dust
> blow away out over
> they heads when they
> finds me cryin' in a sack. (28)

or:

> I'm travelin' in my bones
> and the Spirit swooshes out
> before I gets a chance to say
> *Amen.* (28)

or her description of the three children's drowning as:

> 'jes takin' them under
> puttin' them there
> for the water to purify
> for they own bloomin'
> under the sea. (32–33)

These predominant qualities of historic truth, voice, and otherworldliness are evident throughout the volume. Sophie, wanting to "know the baptism of words," counts and spells her way up to literacy as she climbs the stairs, reminding herself, too, of "the period and the commas, the stops and the shorts": "Say my prayers with a period. / Listen to Missus with a comma." Aunt Mary, at ten, saw her nine-month-old sister "whupped" to death by their mistress for crying. She begins her long-cadenced recital with: "Ah wants de wind in mah sorrow de las' breathin' of mah / lil' sister holy on mah tongue" (71). In a poem replete with Biblical allusions, she makes up her own individuated origins story, dating from her receipt of free papers from her master:

> Dat be mah
> birthin' mah genesis first day be earth an'

star den wind an' sea
den bird an' lamb den man and woman den
freedom den Me! (71)

The symbolic beauty of Julia carrying life-giving water perfectly under any and all conditions comes through in the simple pride of her saying:

I walks straight into
the mouth of a [dark] doorway,
say, Good evenin' all,
water's here, and I never spill

a drop. (95–96)

There are passages where inspiration and achievement lapse, where the voice loses its hard-to-define but palpable authenticity and sounds like Dolores Kendrick, poet, perhaps too consciously shaping the material. Some of the poems were, in her words, "made up without the benefit of research," although it may not be at all true that these are the weaker works or that they were not enriched by the same general fund of supracreativity. "Jo Abandoned," for example, is a poem where Kendrick operated from more rational control. She uses her real mother's pet name, some of her autobiography, and was "seeing her a lot in doing" the poem. Consequently, Kendrick admits: "I don't know where the voice came in and I interfered or what. I just don't know how that balanced out." The overall impression is a mixed one, of both stellar and pedestrian passages.

The lapses usually occur in poems that also contain brilliant lines. In "Polly and Platt," Polly is stretched beyond endurance by the lust and cruelty of her master. A voice asks, parenthetically and, to my mind, quite inappropriately:

(Was it that? Was something out there
punishing Polly for her big spirit
that let her sleep with a crippled
monster, and she, with impunity?) (69)

Even the diction and grammar of these lines are studied and contrived. They are followed by effective description, which leads ultimately to a moving glimpse of the shell Polly becomes after her too-much-maligned spirit deserts her:

she's moving like ash, floating about
in pieces, her head hung like a scarecrow,

and her smile don't jump into your throat
and make you happy,

the way it used to
when she was herself, walking through daisies
giving God His chores. (70)

Most of Kendrick's commentary on the poems documents the degree to which she was not in complete control of their composition. Jokingly saying that she sometimes felt the women were standing in line crying, "My turn, my turn," Kendrick mentions Jenny as an example. Jenny brought only short pieces (three of them are in *Plums*) but would show up when she wanted to and not when Kendrick called on her for a small poem. With "Prunella's Picnic," Kendrick did not realize until she had finished writing the poem that Prunella's friend was no longer alive: "[Prunella] was in this kitchen talking to her friend, surviving through talking to her—and she's talking about having a picnic. And I thought, 'How can she be having a picnic in the kitchen?' But then it went and it developed. At the end of the poem I looked and I said, 'My God, she's dead. Tula is dead.'" One poem, "Miss Maggie's Little Room," Kendrick thought she could write "all by myself" because, like Miss Maggie, she was a teacher. She completed it in less than an hour and felt very pleased with herself—only to return to it the next day and discover that it was "sheer garbage." Obviously, she had been "writing about Dolores" and had not allowed Miss Maggie to speak. So, after waiting two or three days, she sat down and started again with just the title at the top of the page: "And before long the whole thing began to come to me as though it was being dictated, a totally different poem than the one I had written in the first place."

Looking back on the process of *Plums,* Kendrick has decided that she would not want to write another such book—even though she would accept it if it happened again: "I'm just saying that I'm not going out looking for it. I would not sit in a room at night and conjure these people up and say, 'Now, I need some more of you to speak to me.' I would never do that." Her reason is that the experience was too painful, even though she knew that the women were saying "that they triumphed in the end." The ordeal of not being "yourself," of being "something else" in the service of mediumship was exhausting enough for her to finally stop the process: "I know that whenever you move into this realm, you are using psychic energy that you didn't even know you had. I didn't know if I had any more left and I didn't want to find out. So I just let it go."

Her current endeavor is a volume of poetry hinged on the theme of abandonment. It revolves around the Biblical Samaritan woman at the well and a 1930s Washington, D.C., woman who tragically falls down on her luck, with the two women being projected as one and the same. This work is a "totally Dolores book," written without any perceptible extra-authorial assistance. Kendrick's response to my probing about the two kinds of creative processes yielded the following exchange:

DK: *The Women of Plums* hit a level of psychic intuition, or psychic revelation that is not in this work at all. That does not make this work any less, or *Plums* any more. I think this one is simply dealing with a character the same way a novel deals with a character, and that's a different level of creativity. It may be coming from the same wellspring, but the energies involved are different.

AH: It's very interesting to me that you put it that way because I have to admit that my automatic predilection would be to want to hierarchize them and say that the psychic, spiritual, revelatory work was somehow "superior" to other kinds of work.

DK: I wouldn't do that. I don't believe that. I think that at this stage, as a friend of mine says, comparisons are odious. Do you like Paris better than you do Rome? I think you know what I mean, Gloria.

AH: Yes, I guess I do.

DK: They are different art forms to begin with—if you want to talk about the craft. But I think that what inspires them or creates them (let me use that term) are different types of energy. And that's all it is—just different. I don't think the one is any higher or better than the other.

After the episode with her mother and the Ouija board, Lucille Clifton began "feeling itchy" in her hand. She started doing what she called "listening-hearing," and the idea came to her that she should try writing. When she did, she received automatic messages faster. On one occasion, her pen wrote: "Stop this. You're having conversations with me as if I'm alive. I am not alive. Go. Conversation is for live people." Because of the feel of the spirit, Clifton knew definitely that it was her mother. She says: "You can distinguish. . . . You know if you're in a room with someone. There's a different feeling with different people." Once she asked, "What are you? Have you crossed the void? Are you in the great beyond?" using every high-flown euphemism she could think of—and her mother said, "I'm dead." "Dead!" Lucille replied. "That's cold." She began reading about spiritual phenomena, seeking information and precedents, and realized that "it wasn't a thing that was calling me to come and do it. It was telling me not to do it."

Over a period of time, Clifton came to believe that this was, in fact, her mother, whose presence was also being felt by the rest of the family. All six of her children saw and had experiences of some sort with her. Ultimately, they came to know this dead grandmother better than they knew their father's mother, who was living in Wilmington, North Carolina. Over a period of years, the family, in Clifton's words, "incorporated the nonvisible into our scheme for what is real. It worked for us."

Thus, from the beginning of her initiation into this spiritual world, when she thought that she was "cracking up and taking my children with me," Clifton was led to acknowledge that "perhaps these were who they say they are." At this point, she had been in contact with other beings than her mother through the medium of automatic writing. Her hands always seemed to her to have something "interesting," "powerful," "mysterious" about them. When she started to pay attention (which she had not always done), she noticed that if "something, someone in spirit that was not alive wished to catch my attention, I would feel it in my arm, like an electric current going down my arm." Then she would know to take notice, get a pen or whatever, because something wanted her attention. And she would give it, since experience had taught her that a product of value would result, even if it were small. Clifton notes that there was a progression for her from the slow Ouija board, to automatic writing, to not particularly having to write because she could hear— "but writing and hearing were almost like the same thing." The ability to hear was clearly not imagined: "People can say you're hallucinating, but if you've heard, then you know." She adds that this is similar to the difference between dreams and visions: If you have had a vision, you know the difference; if you have not, then you don't.

Everyone in the Clifton household—Lucille, her husband Fred (a brilliant philosopher and linguist who founded a Baltimore ashram), and their six children—was somehow attuned to suprarational reality. As Clifton declares in her brief autobiographical statement for Mari Evans's critical anthology, *Black Women Writers:* "My family tends to be a spiritual and even perhaps mystical one. That certainly influences my life and my work" (138).

She renders her supernatural experience of her mother in a striking sequence of poems that concludes her 1980 volume, *two-headed woman.* Yet, the differences between her two tellings of the story are vast. Most notably, the poetic text reveals a turmoil and tonal depth that the factuality and humor of her external narrative do not even begin to touch. In addition, they provide an unusual opportunity to see how this personal experience is transformed through creativity into magnificent—and magical—art. The condensation, unerring essence, and richness of resonance of the poems effect the leap from "here" to the "beyond" that characterizes spiritual vision.

Both versions recount the story of a time in life when "a shift of knowing" makes possible the breakthrough to higher levels of awareness and personal power. In a series of possibilities introduced with "perhaps," which grope to explain what is happening, Clifton hits upon the right one at the end of the poem:

> or perhaps
> in the palace of time
> our lives are a circular stair
> and i am turning (216)

The word *turning*—with all of its connotations of cycles, change, karma, and universal flow—appears at significant places in her work. A relevant comparison is her poem by that title in *An Ordinary Woman* (1974), where she sees herself turning out of "white" and "lady" cages into her "own self / at last," "like a black fruit / in my own season" (143). Now, the turning, the metamorphosis she is about to effect, is even more momentous because it supersedes what the Rastafarians call "earth runnings" for a more divine and cosmic dimension. This process (and process it is) involves an experiential crisis of ontology and belief, but it leads "at last" to new and certain knowledge.

Clifton heralds the change in a poem, "the light that came to lucille clifton." The use of her own, real name is startling. She incorporated fanciful references to "lucy girl" in earlier poems but never instated herself with this degree of fullness, formality, and solemnity. In a dramatic move that upsets modesty and convention, the reader is invited to see the person behind the persona, the lady behind the mask. Alicia Ostriker gives a helpful warning to readers who were trained—as she, myself, and many others were—"not to mistake the 'I' in a poem for a real person": "The training has its uses, but also its limitations. For most [contemporary women poets], academic distinctions between the self and what we in the classroom call [used to call] the 'persona' move to vanishing point. When a woman poet today says 'I,' she is likely to mean herself, as intensely as her imagination and her verbal skills permit" (12). In this prefatory poem using her own name, Clifton talks about her shifting summer, "when even her fondest sureties / faded away" and she "could see the peril of an / unexamined life." However, she closed her eyes, "afraid to look for her / authenticity," but "a voice from the nondead past started talking." The poem ends with what can now be recognized as a direct reference to an automatic writing experience:

> she closed her ears and it spelled out in her hand
> "you might as well answer the door, my child,
> the truth is furiously knocking." (209)

In the sequence proper, Clifton begins her story as a deponent in a civil and ecclesiastical court, using religious and legal language (and, again, her full, legal name) to "hereby testify" that in a room alone, she saw a light and heard the sigh of a voice that contained another world. Asking in the next poem, "who are these strangers / peopleing this light?" she is told, "lucille / we are / the Light." Not surprisingly, the following poem begins, "mother, i am mad":

> someone calling itself Light
> has opened my inside. . . .
> someone of it is answering to
> your name. (215)

Then ensue "perhaps" and possible "explanations," and "friends come" and try to convince her that she is losing her mind. But she is able to say to them:

> friends
> the ones who talk to me
> their words thin as wire
> their chorus fine as crystal

their truth direct as stone,
they are present as air.
they are there. (218)

She eschews arguing with these friends in favor of an interrogative conversation with Joan of Arc, another woman—she calls her "sister sister"—who had voices and visions. Clearly, even if no one else does, the two of them know what it is like.

In what is the most tortured of all these poems, "confession," Clifton kneels on the knees of her soul, admitting to an equivocal "father," whose name pleadingly begins each stanza, that she is not "equal to the faith required":

i doubt
i have a woman's certainties;
bodies pulled from me,
pushed into me.
bone flesh is what i know. (220)

She has heard the angels and discerned how to see them. She has seen his, the father's, mother standing "shoulderless and shoeless" by his side, whispering truths she could not know. She wants to know:

father
what are the actual certainties?
your mother speaks of love. (220)

Ending in a repetitious, almost stately babel of words, she tries to run from the "surprising presence" with which she has been confronted, but "the angels stream" before her, "like a torch." There is no escaping this truth. Thus, the final, quiet poem of this section sounds like a reprise or a coda:

in populated air
our ancestors continue.
i have seen them.
i have heard
their shimmering voices
singing. (221)

Thus, Clifton documents her connection with ancestral spirit (conceived as both racial and species antecedents) and arrives at the same place in her poetry as in her actual life: "incorporating the nonvisible" into her scheme of things.

As a girl (born in Depew, New York, in 1937), Clifton evidenced psychometric skills (she could, in her words, "feel what things were feeling" and retrieve lost objects of people she knew), but until 1975 she was not particularly conscious about the extrasensory realm. Since then, her psychic awareness and abilities have increasingly manifested in a range of ways. As a result of being what her dead mother called "a natural channel" (using the term in the mid-1970s before it came into popular parlance), she touch-reads people and their palms, speaks truth about matters from her mouth if she asks to do so and keeps herself from interfering with the message, casts horoscopes, bestows blessings when requested, and continues to negotiate the world as a two-headed woman, that is, one who possesses magical power, who can see what is here and visible as well as that which is beyond ordinary vision.

She is singularly matter-of-fact about her gifts. "Being special," she avers, "has absolutely nothing to do with anything" and is, in fact, "defeating." As her mother put it when she asked her, a bit pompously perhaps, "What shall I do with this Power?": "Think about it this way. You have a teapot, a lot of people have a teapot. Don't abuse yours and you won't break it." At particularly magnetic readings of hers, when the audience was moved to radical action, she has sometimes thought that she could be "dangerous." But it takes her only five minutes, she says, to remember that she is the person who still cannot program her VCR: "So, how important and interesting could I be?"

Speaking more soberly, Clifton reveals that she feels "lucky" and, paradoxically, that "it's a mixed blessing—because sometimes I might get a feeling that I don't want to have." She maintains that whatever abilities she holds "might be gone tomorrow. I don't know." In her accepting, down-to-earth fashion, she sees herself as a multiply constituted, various person: "I'm lots of stuff. And so this [spiritual] thing coming in is just a natural, for me, part of what my life is. There are those I see, those I do not see. Fine." Not surprisingly, she believes that everyone could somehow express "that ineffable thing if they tried, thought about it, and listened." She continues: "I think that people tend to not listen. It's educated out of you. My luck is that I wasn't that educated." She admits that this kind of knowing—what Toni Morrison terms "discredited knowledge"—is almost totally invalidated. Yet she declares with quiet conviction, "If you allow room in your life for mystery, mystery will come" (Evans 342).

Even though spiritual-mystical themes and materials were always present in Lucille Clifton's work, after *two-headed woman* (1980) they become an even more prominent feature, reflected in poems that do the following:

(1)   present mystical experiences (transcendent meditative states, past life glimpses, seeing auras

(2)   deconstruct the current, corrupt hegemonic order as the "other" of a more real and humane, though "invisible" alternative

(3)   racialize, feminize, and mysticize traditional patriarchal Christianity

(4)   project her feeling connectedness with all life—things and beings

(5)   affirm hope, higher values, and joy in the midst of destruction and despair

(6)   show her sense of herself as part of a large, ongoing process of time and change, to which we all bear responsibility.

Most relevant to our present topic is a final group of poems that reveal Clifton's vivid connection with her spiritual genealogy, including her African past and its geography, and also her soulful attunement to other "sisters." An early instance is this untitled tribute to heroines Harriet Tubman, Sojourner Truth, and her grandmother:

> harriet
> if i be you
> let me not forget
> to be the pistol
> pointed
> to be the madwoman
> at the rivers edge
> warning
> be free or die
> and isabell
> if i be you
> let me in my
> sojourning
> not forget
> to ask my brothers
> ain't i a woman too
> and grandmother
> if i be you
> let me not forget to
> work hard
> trust the Gods
> love my children
> and wait. (119)

Another of these poems is written "to merle," "skinny manysided tall on the ball / brown downtown woman" whom she last saw "on the corner of / pyramid and sphinx" ten thousand years ago (171). In her seventh volume of poetry, *The Book of Light,* Clifton imagines into being a maternal great-grandmother, about whom no historical data exists. She is, as she admits, "trying to reclaim and maybe fix a mythology for that part of my family." The poem begins with an apostrophe:

> woman who shines at the head
> of my grandmother's bed,
> brilliant woman

then proceeds to Clifton's musings:

> i like to think . . .
> you are the arrow that pierced our plain skin
> and made us fancy women;
> my wild witch gran, my magic mama
> and even these gaudy girls.
> i like to think you gave us
> extraordinary power and to
> protect us, you became the name
> we were cautioned to forget.

and ends with her instatement of self and lineage:

> woman i am
>
> lucille, which stands for light,
> daughter of thelma, daughter
> of georgia, daughter of
> dazzling you. (13)

This particular project of reclaiming (for self and blood or spiritual family) a mythology (in a space where history and myth are entangled, often indistinguishable categories) is one way to understand what both Clifton and Dolores Kendrick are doing in their work.

Clifton's communications with her mother have slackened in recent years, and the number of poems about her (never that large, considering her general impact on Clifton's life) has likewise decreased. However, a pivotal poem is "the message of thelma sayles," published in 1987. This seems the only one that could easily be read as a direct transcription of her mother's words. Thelma Sayles recalls the factual details of her not particularly happy existence—a husband who "turned away" and recurring fits—and concludes with succinct summary and a passionate injunction to Lucille:

> i thrashed and rolled from fit to death.
> you are my only daughter.
> when you lie awake in the evenings
> counting your birthdays
> turn the blood that clots on your tongue
> into poems. (*next* 53)

Thus, the links are drawn between generations of painful female experience and the writing of salvific poetry, a connection that can be seen with Clifton herself and with Kendrick.

Except for this poem, Clifton—unlike Kendrick—does not seem to have channeled the specific words and language of her work, but—like Kendrick—she analytically isolates distinct strands and modes of her creative process. Her words show that her creativity is inseparable from her spirituality: "Years of experience have allowed me to trust more and more what comes to me, what I can pick up in the world and to incorporate that into my reality structure. And I think some of that is where poems come from." Even though she believes that no one—poet or critic—can really explain the origins of poetry, she jokes, "I wish I did know where poems come from so I could go get some poems. I would like that." One of her pieces in *quilting* (1991) nicely states her case. "When i stand around among poets," it begins, "i am embarrassed mostly" by their "long white heads, the great bulge in their pants, / their certainties." She, in contrast, only pretends to deserve her poetic inspiration:

> but i don't know how to do it,
> only sometimes when
> something is singing
> i listen and so far
> i hear. (quilting 49)

As she explains her process, it is a spirituality-based attentiveness. She recognizes when something catches her poetic awareness: "I still feel in my arms if I am to pay attention to something. And I do." If she is in a car (she does not drive) and feels something, she will look up and around to see what should be noticed and noted. My more pointed questioning produced the following exchange:

AH: Is all of your poetry about channeling?
LC: No.
AH: Does it all result from your having felt the tingle of "pay attention"?
LC: No, no. But it all results from paying attention. I think that always I've
      had a mind that connected things, that could see connections. Why that
      is, I have no idea. I think that it all comes from all of it, Gloria. I think I
      use intellect governed by intuition, and I think I use intuition governed
      by intellect. It's not all consciously done. No poetry is all consciously
      done. It comes out of all of what we are.

At the beginning of the interview, Clifton talked about how central the concept of "light" is to her and how, in all of the poems in *The Book of Light* (then in progress), "there is going to be something that is at least clear." Light (with a capital *L*) is her way of designating Spirit, God, the Universe because, she says, "It is like that. It is like the making clear what has not been clear, being able to see what has not been seen." At the conclusion of the interview, she returned again to her mind's habit of discerning the connections between apparently unlike things. With the two of us working in an apotheosis of harmony that pulled all the pieces together, I remarked that that was the essence of poetic metaphor, the result being light, to which she replied, "And then, you see, the connecting of the nonphysical to the physical is just another step."

NOTES

This essay could not have been written without the gracious cooperation of Lucille Clifton and Dolores Kendrick, both of whom I heartily thank for talking with me. I conducted a telephone interview with Kendrick on December 29, 1991, and conversed with Clifton in Santa Cruz, California, in spring 1991. All information about them that is not otherwise ascribed comes from these exchanges. I also wish to thank the American Association of University Women for the 1991 postdoctoral fellowship that supported this research.

"Channeling the Ancestral Muse: Lucille Clifton and Dolores Kendrick" was originally published in *Feminist Measures: Soundings in Poetry and Theory*, ed. Lynn Keller and Cristanne Miller (Ann Arbor: The University of Michigan Press, 1994).

1. Lucille Clifton's first four volumes of poetry—*good times* (1969), *good news about the earth* (1972), *an ordinary woman* (1974), and *two-headed woman* (1980)—are collected in *good woman: poems and a memoir, 1969–1980*. I will cite page numbers from this source in textual parentheses.

2. Kendrick, *The Women of Plums*. Page numbers for all of her poems will be given parenthetically in the text.

3. The factual data of this paragraph is taken from the back cover of *Through the Ceiling*.

WORKS CITED

Clifton, Lucille. *The Book of Light*. Port Townsend, Wash.: Copper Canyon P, 1993.
———. *good woman: poems and a memoir, 1969–1980*. Brockport, N.Y.: BOA Editions, 1987.
———. *next: new poems*. Brockport, N.Y.: BOA Editions, 1987.
———. *quilting*. Brockport, N.Y.: BOA Editions, 1991.
Evans, Mari, ed. *Black Women Writers (1950–1980): A Critical Evaluation*. Garden City, N.Y.: Anchor Books, 1983. Kendrick, Dolores. *Now Is the Thing to Praise*. Detroit: Lotus P, 1984.
———. *Through the Ceiling*. London: Paul Brennan, 1975.
———. *The Women of Plums: Poems in the Voices of Slave Women*. New York: William Morrow, 1989.
Ostriker, Alicia. *Stealing the Language: The Emergence of Women's Poetry in America*. Boston: Beacon P, 1986.

The Poetics of Identity
Questioning Spiritualism in African American Contexts

Carolyn Martin Shaw

For some African American feminists, spirituality promises connections with the ancestors and the race. Yet I argue that, instead of uniting the race, the prominence of spiritual beliefs and practices in the late twentieth century joins African Americans with others who identify differently, especially New Age religionists. Moreover, the belief that any racial ancestor can speak to and through unrelated members of the race separates the African American practice from many such beliefs and practices in Africa. African American spiritualism can be marked as an origin story that reinforces the identity of this oppressed group within the racist United States. African American feminists' understandings of the sources of inspiration of the creative self through spiritualism is not perceived as a conscious choice, but it is an implicit option for the group affirmation of spiritualism over the individual psychodynamics of Freudian psychoanalysis.

Whereas some African American feminists choose spiritualism over Freudian psychoanalysis as a way of understanding how factors beyond conscious awareness are manifested in individual behavior, both are problematic as systems of explanations or ways of knowing. I am dismayed by the prominence of psychoanalysis and spiritualism in feminist thought in the late twentieth century. Freudian psychoanalysis, because of its rigid gender distinctions, the narrowness of its cultural frame, and its closed, self-referential analytical system, traps the reader in passages leading one to another in an endless maze. Spiritualism certainly opens out to the world, but its otherworldliness and antirationality are implausible and disheartening. I can appreciate spiritualism and psychoanalysis only as art forms, as poetry. Poetry requires that one look to the style and substance of a text, event, or experience, decipher obvious and obscure codes, imagine oneself within contexts constructed by others, and understand that the poem, theory, or belief does not speak from one's own experience but allows one to empathize. A poetic reading of spirituality or psychoanalysis legitimates different levels of knowing, acknowledges situated knowledge, reflexively includes the reader, and presses for compassion for others.

Both psychoanalysis and spiritualism are part of discourses generated by and engendering particular social and cultural conditions. In this paper, I examine claims of African American feminists in regard to spiritualism, in particular, the belief that spirits of the dead survive after death and communicate with the living through mediums. Sparked by Akasha Hull's study (in this volume) of the spiritual beliefs and practices of African American poets in her work on channeling the ancestral muse, I became interested in understanding the prominence of spiritualism in this postmodern era. I am concerned about the relationship between the belief and practice of spirit mediumship observed among the poets and continental African beliefs and practices. Certainly there is continuity with the African past in diasporic cultures, but claiming tradition has never been a sufficient explanation for the persistence of any practice or belief. Cultural traditions take on new or renewed meanings in practice. My reading of the differences between African patterns and African American ones underscores the innovation in the spiritual practices and beliefs featured in Hull's work.

Of the various meanings of psyche—soul, mind, and spirit—some African American feminists have settled on spirit. Of the various interpretations of spirit—consciousness, feelings, sentiment, and religion—they choose to emphasize three views: spirit as an incorporeal animating force, spirit as a vigorous sense of membership or connection with others, and spirit as an everlasting, transcendent quality of individual human beings. Hull writes of a knowingness beyond consciousness, of channeling the ancestral muse, of contact with nonancestors, and of feeling in her body the devastations of unknown others. These experiences highlight community and heritage and the transcendence of ego. I explore the possibility that the emphasis on spiritualism and the concern with what I call africanity, practices and beliefs emanating from African cultural roots, are both responses to the alienation and pathology of the postmodern condition and contributions to the syncretic optimism that also characterizes this moment.

The common ground for psychoanalysis and spiritualism is the unconscious, the recognition that forces beyond those conscious to the individual influence behavior or, to put the same thing another way, that messages from the past shape the present and the future. Psychoanalysis provides theories to identify unconscious forces in social and psychological processes and therapies to disclose destructive unconscious mechanisms, in an effort to achieve ego-control for a more integrated personality or self. In contrast, spiritualism begs the question of the self—in spirit mediumship, two selves may occupy the same body without any obvious harm to the personality. In representing behavior that is beyond conscious awareness as ancestral spirits, spiritualism deproblematizes the unconscious and represents the individual as passive in relation to her own unconscious. The benevolent spirits of deceased kin and kindred spirits may flow through those who open themselves up, without ego-defenses and ego-control.

A major advantage of psychoanalysis in explaining human behavior is its systematization, its clear statement of the elements (dynamic unconscious, sexual and death instincts) and processes (association, repression, conversion, transference) that make up its system, and the vast critical literature and competing schools it has spawned. From the point of view of African American feminists who prefer psychoanalytic interpretations, psychoanalysis allows the impolitic to be spoken and encourages and explains the formation of the individual self with and against others. Freudian psychoanalysis offers pragmatic solutions to dealing with an imperfect world, a nonperfectible world—nonperfectible because, according to psychoanalytic theories, individual desires will always be thwarted by the social contract.

Why would African American feminists prefer spiritualism over Freudian psychoanalysis to deal with the ambiguities and paradoxes of the human condition? Both are concerned with an understanding of the self, with how the actions and effects of the self are manifested in the world, but psychoanalysis builds or reconstructs the ego, whereas spiritualism minimizes ego and emphasizes healing and membership. In psychoanalysis the ego experiences and reacts to the outside world and mediates the experiences between the id (primitive drives and instincts) and the superego (the traditions and constraints of society). In a sense, culture and the ancestors are represented in psychoanalysis by the superego. Building or strengthening the ego allows the person to more consciously assess and negotiate the demands of desire and culture. In spiritualism, the ancestors of the culture are a sacred power to which the individual must lay herself open, not build up her ego in order to assess the demands of the culture but rather put aside ego so as to receive messages from the dead.

The primary advantage of spiritualism over psychoanalysis for African American feminists is the grounding of spiritual connection in the African American community through the stories of connection that can be created through spiritualism. Some psychoanalysts argue that Freud believed that psychoanalysis must be grounded in particular cultural contexts, but others assert that the universals of psychodynamics transcend language and culture (Panas). Spiritualism as practiced by African American feminists can give positive connection to family and the past in ways that psychoanalysis finds problematic, such as transgressed boundaries between mother and child. Spiritualism can be culture-specific, giving connection to Africa and the African diaspora and building social and cultural identity in ways that Freudian psychoanalysis does not. Spiritualism is not necessarily antithetical to psychoanalysis as a system of explanation: you can believe that a spirit speaks through you and that you are still trying to resolve your Oedipus complex. Freudian psychoanalysis is exclusive: it does not allow for the understanding of human behavior by reference to spirit possession or mediumship.

SPIRITUALITY AND POSTMODERNISM

Postmodernism has brought the demise of grand theory and a distrust of Enlightenment tools of progress—rationality, technology, and objective knowledge—leading many to embrace local knowledge and increase their confidence in intuition and reverence and respect for mysteries. Couple the postmodern anti-Enlightenment stance with the identity politics of new social movements that have assaulted the centers of power, claiming legitimacy for the margins, and the African American feminist convergence on the ground of spiritualism and africanity seems almost overdetermined. The failure of the grandest theory, the metanarrative of progress—namely, the supposition that through human control over nature and the rational development of human faculties would come equality, liberty, and "fraternity"—leaves a philosophical hole in the center of Western thought. The relationship between Enlightenment theories and Freudian psychoanalysis is ambivalent, at best, given the salience of sexuality and the unconscious in psychoanalytic theory. But the totalizing theoretical ambition of psychoanalysis has suffered a similar assault on its center from the multiplicities of race, class, gender, and sexuality. The center of Western thought, even before the postmodern crisis, did not fix and contain the thinking and activity of people on the margins—women, the poor, colonized people, and minority populations—who often held (and hold) counterhegemonic ideas. Increasingly, the center has lost its sway, and marginal people and ideas have gained prominence.

The success of social movements in the United States, especially the civil rights movement and the women's movement, in promoting the interests of particular groups of people encouraged the development of more interest groups and a politics of identity. Within this environment, African American feminists moved against the center with a celebration of local knowledge, a redemption of the past, and a rejoicing in intuition, all of which paved the way for an increased popularity of spirituality. The language of recovery and healing pronounces this moment as a time and space of reclamation of cultural heritage and of suppressed women's knowledge.

Spirituality is not new, and I am not trying to explain the existence of spiritual beliefs worldwide and throughout time. I am curious about the social circumstances under which spirituality achieved prominence in postmodern America among educated African American creative writers. In comparison it is worth pondering the popularity of spirituality in late Victorian and early Edwardian England, a time when the scientific investigation of parapsycho-

logical phenomena probably had its peak. A revival of the scientific ratio-
nalizations of spirituality is growing today in spiritualists' embrace of quantum physics' uncertainty principles: whether a "thing" exists as matter or energy, particle or wave, depends on the position of the observer and the tools
of observation. I suggest that the rise of spirituality in the late twentieth century is explained not just in terms of the reclamation or continuity of African
American cultural traditions, but that the popularity of spirituality is strongly
influenced by popular reactions to science, postmodern ideology and the
postmodern condition.

When I speak of the increased popularity of spirituality in the late twentieth century, I refer not only to spiritualism but also to a host of beliefs and
practices associated with New Age religions: belief in past lives (that a contemporary human lived in times past and can tap into that past experience
through various mechanisms), belief in astral projections and out of body
experiences (that a person's consciousness can travel and communicate un-
aided by technology), and belief in the healing powers of crystals. Here, I
focus on spiritualism, "the belief or doctrine that the spirits of the dead, surviving after the mortal life, can and do communicate with the living, esp.
through a person (a medium) particularly susceptible to their influence"
(*Webster's Unabridged*).

The belief in god upon which most churches and religions in the United
States is built and the belief in the goddess that animates individual and group
ritual in nonestablishment religions are both aspects of spirituality. In this
paper, I do not take up the issue of organized religion, but the potency of
conservative fundamentalist Christianity in late-twentieth-century America
is related to the mobilization of hatred and intolerance to define group
boundaries within a politics of identity. Fundamentalism is also a response
to the decentered self and a redemption of the past, both of which characterize the postmodern condition.

Postmodernism, as a theory and a state of mind, encompasses the oppositions of nihilism and vision quests and of malaise and activism. Skeptical
postmodernists such as Baudrillard offer "a pessimistic, negative, gloomy assessment, argu[ing] that the post-modern age is one of fragmentation, disintegration, malaise, meaninglessness, a vagueness or even absence of moral
parameters and societal chaos" (Rosenau 15). Affirmative postmodernists
such as Spivak are "either open to positive political action (struggle and resistance) or content with the recognition of visionary, celebratory personal
nondogmatic projects that range from New Age religion to New Wave life-
styles and include a whole spectrum of post-modern social movements"
(Rosenau 16). The turn to spirituality as well as the call to African cultural
roots evident in African American feminist critics are, in part, effects of the
postmodernist political and social climate, especially as interpreted by postmodern affirmatives. Without denying the timelessness of spirituality, I

point to the forces in the world today that work together to make spiritual-ity appealing: the postmodern anti-Enlightenment turn away from the in-dividual, reason, science, and progress and towards emotion, intuition, ar-cane knowledge, and local truths. New Age spirituality is a reaction to a postmodern condition, aptly depicted by skeptical postmodernists as plagued by fragmentation, disintegration, malaise, vagueness of moral parameters, and societal chaos. The social situation was created by the rise and fall of colonialist and imperialist regimes that have transformed both the dominant and the subjugated, by the expansion of information at such a rate that no individual has control over it, and by the advance of technologies that threaten the health and well-being of the planet. The net result of these com-peting social energies is fragmentation and plurality, disintegration and in-novation, and multiple and conflicting moral parameters.

Postmodernism, in opposition to "Enlightenment *Man*'s" human progress, is typified by the individual's sense of powerlessness, and the responses to it involve a range of possibilities, including pessimistic nihilism, progressivist humanism, activist social movements, primitivism, and affirmative spiritual-ity. The civil rights movement and the women's movement contributed to the destabilizing of the centers of power that characterizes the postmodern condition. They also were avenues for open affirmation of counterhege-monic ideologies, local truths, and spiritual beliefs and practices. African American spiritualism in the late twentieth century is a cultural retrieval and redemption—it cannot be divorced from the surrounding social context.

The social context in which spiritualism is growing in the late twentieth century includes the technological environment of electronic communica-tion media. In the electronic age, physical presence is becoming irrelevant and selves are refracting in time and space (Stone). From telephone com-munication to video and audio representations, from computer networks to virtual reality, people living in the late twentieth century increasingly feel the power of individuals and things not present. An individual can be in more than one place at a time through computer networks, interacting with oth-ers through words on a screen. The identities people create for use in in-teractive computer networks sometimes take on lives of their own, ques-tioning the assumption of one self per body (Stone). The social situation, postmodern sensibility, and technological developments conjoin to create a psychological environment in which the integrity of the person cannot be assumed.

The feeling of personal powerlessness of the fragmented self is also im-plicated in another phenomena on a par with the ascendancy of spiritual-ism in the late twentieth century: the pervasiveness of conspiracy theories. I see a fit between spiritualism and conspiracy theories, insofar as both believe that unseen forces control our lives. The belief that unknown others, whether corporeal or spiritual, are running the world spring from the sense of powerlessness beneath the colossus of national and international economic and political forces. From a skeptical postmodernist point of view, the fragmentation of life and meaninglessness of everyday existence is the bed from which grows the belief that elsewhere others, with no overriding moral commitment to the progress of humanity, conspire to manipulate and destroy democratic leaders and civil society. The affirmative postmodernists turn this ground over, believing in unseen beings who individually and collectively bring insight to the world. (Is "Insight" the opposite of "Enlightenment"?)

The postmodernist fragmentation of society and the self combined with contemporary decontextualized appropriations of the past and of other cultures lead identity groups to create a phantom history as a basis of their cultural redemption. In regards to African American spiritualism, cultural redemption through African roots is ironic. To be rooted in a culture is to be embedded in the group's society, politics, economics, and consciousness. Uprooted traditions and customs do not travel well, but cuttings and clippings do. As identity groups, whether they are based on race, ethnicity, religion, sexual preference, or gender, compete in new social movements, the past is pruned for suitable stories, images, and practices to give coherence and meaning to present configurations. These origin stories, imposing images, and disciplining practices redeemed from the past are more often shadowy reproductions of historic actualities, like the images from the movie or television screen or the ethnographies that present-day Nigerians read to find out how their kinship system is supposed to work. The redeemed images, stories, and practices in any imagined community result from cultural streamlining, mixture, substitution, and recontextualization.

Akasha Hull's work does not make general claims about an imagined African American community or African American spiritual practice. Instead she insists on the primacy of spiritualism in the work of particular black women poets. Yet Hull opens up the possibility that spiritual connections with unseen and sometimes unrelated others not only inspire but also dictate the work of more African American women authors than have been willing to admit to it. I see Hull's affirmation of decentered states and egolessness in the creative process of channeling the ancestral muse as congruent with the postmodernist declaration of the end of the Enlightenment. In concluding her meditation on the ancestral muse, Hull advises in the version of the paper given at the conference that we begin valuing "spiritual contexts where such 'mediumship'/service is honor and power and where individual agency is known to be a petty ego illusion."

AFRICANITY AND SPIRITUALISM

Some may say that the explanation for the persistence (rather than the rise) of spiritualism is much closer at hand than the airy environment of postmodernism: particular beliefs in spirituality emanate from African beliefs and practices transplanted and transformed in the United States. However, saying that spiritualism is African or African American does not explain the reliance on spiritual practices and beliefs among contemporary black feminist writers and critics. The African American "return to roots" is influenced by identity politics in the postmodern world and by the increasing legitimacy of arcane knowledge widespread in the postmodern twentieth century—African American writers and literary critics are as influenced by post-modernity as they are by African cultural continuity.

What does a look at African tradition reveal? Anthropologists have noted the persistence of various African spiritual beliefs and practices in black communities in the New World. In "African Gods in the Americas: The Black Religious Continuum," Sheila Walker discusses the social and political conditions under which the practice of spirit possession introduced to the Americas during the slavery period survived and developed; these conditions included slave policies, the nature and duration of the slave trade, Catholicism and belief in saints, ethnic group cohesion, and self-consciousness. Spirit possession is most prevalent in the New World in the Brazilian Candomble but is also present in Haiti, Cuba, and Trinidad as well as in black Christian churches in New York, Chicago, Oakland, and especially the southern United States (Walker 26). Though anthropologists and psychologists have studied spirit possession as a form of religious sacrament, there has been little attention given to the kind of spirit mediumship that Hull observed in African American women poets.

Anthropologists distinguish spirit possession from spirit mediumship. Iris Berger in a study of East African women spirit mediums characterizes the spirit medium as an agent between the supernatural world and a particular social group (161–62). In spirit possession, the person's trancelike behavior is believed to show evidence that the person is under the influence of a supernatural force, but the interpretation of that behavior may not be accessible or understandable to anyone other than the person in the trance. In other words, the behavior is not necessarily translatable to a concerned social group. Spirit mediumship is different from spirit possession in that in spirit mediumship the associated trancelike behavior is interpreted as a communication from the supernatural world to a particular social group.

Many women serve as spirit mediums in patriarchal social systems in East Africa, organized in cults through which they receive goods in the names of the spirits and for themselves. In some of these situations women are treated as men only during possession, but in other situations a more general elevation of the women is achieved: "Despite the temporary nature of possession, mediums were highly respected members of their societies" (Berger 170–72). Berger concludes that where women's spirit mediumship grew into cults or religious movements, they "were relatively independent of lineage organization. This independence stemmed from the fact that in some areas the new cults eclipsed those of lineage ghosts, whereas in others they took the form of autonomously organized groups not based on kinship" (179). Women are at a serious disadvantage in calling on lineage ancestors or ghosts in these patrilineal systems, in which women are incorporated either as daughter and sister or mother and wife, with neither set of relations equal to men. If the spirit speaking through a medium is not a god or nature spirit but an ancestor, then the group that the medium is an agent for is usually a lineage or kin group. To generalize from the patterns Hull describes, African American ancestors speak to the race rather than to the family. In the racist United States, does race equal family?

My observation of spirit mediumship in contemporary Zimbabwe helps me to distinguish the separate paths that African and African American spirituality have taken. I lived in Africa for two extended periods: in 1971, when I lived upcountry in Kenya with a Kikuyu family on their small plot of land, and in 1983, when I taught at the University of Zimbabwe. In Kenya the family that I lived with were Catholics who went to church on important holidays, and whose belief in the power of Western medicine fruitlessly took them to the local hospital for penicillin injections for colds. In my only visit to a traditional Kikuyu medicine man, I asked for advice about my own problems, and he divined his answer from stones collected from the primary rivers in the territory. When people fell ill he gave them medicines to make them vomit the sickness, and when the ancestors had to be contacted he offered a prayer and sacrifice of roasted meat. In Zimbabwe, I lived in the capital city with university professors for neighbors; there my conversations turned often to computers and spirits—computers because people were just beginning to use them for their everyday work, and spirits because the image of the restless spirits of deceased soldiers, combatants in the recent war to end white domination who had not been buried in their own land, had become a metaphor for political tension as black Zimbabweans struggled to create a nation-state.

Beyond the nationalist discourse, spirits and spirit mediumship were a focus of family life. At the intersection of the nation and the family, a story circulated that never failed to amuse the storytellers: the President of Zimbabwe, Robert Mugabe, had little power in his own extended family because the ancestral spirit who guided the family spoke through a little girl, to whom he had to listen when it came to family decisions. The men who told his story seemed to relish the limits placed on the power of the president, but an outsider should not believe that this little girl had power in her own right. When she was not serving as a medium for the ancestral spirit, she received no special treatment. This is not unusual; being the medium through which an ancestor speaks does not necessarily protect one. One spirit medium in the country of Rwanda who changed her name from "she who lacks support" to "she who cannot be stopped on her way"—in other words, "the invincible"—was beheaded after a conflict with the Rwandan king (Berger 177). On the whole, however, Berger's study of women spirit mediums in East Africa shows that the women's power to effect their will and improve their material well-being were enhanced by their roles as spirit mediums, though women spirit mediums never tried to use their position to change the overall status of women.

While I was in Zimbabwe I worked with the Women's Action Group (WAG) to improve the status of women, and that political organization brought me once again to the issue of spirits and spirit mediums. By bringing rural and urban women together to talk about their problems, WAG found that women who as a result of Zimbabwean independence in 1980 had just been declared legal adults—capable at the age of eighteen to vote, marry without parental permission, enter legal contracts, own property, and have custody of their own children—did not know the full meaning of their rights. Through conferences, literacy pamphlets, nongovernmental agencies, and government ministries, women were informed of these rights. But WAG was surprised to find that some women who wanted custody of their children after the death of their husbands (under customary law, children "belonged" to their father's lineage) refused to exercise their rights of custody because the rights were nothing without the blessing of the children's ancestors. Mothers who took their children away from the children's father's family risked the anger of the patrilineage and the removal of children from the protection of the patrilineal ancestors. The children's well-being, health, even their success at school was in the hands of these patrilineal ancestors, who communicated with the family through the mediumship of one of its members.

Unless women found a way of countering the hegemony of the patrilineal ancestors, they were doomed to live under the rule of their husband's family. An answer to the women's dilemma came in the power of the avenging spirit of the deceased husband, who, if he had agreed before his demise that the wife could have the children after his death (something most men would not be inclined to do), might wreak havoc on his relatives as a whirlwind or other natural disaster. The grandmother's curse and blessing, traced through the maternal line, might also offer help. But usually women stayed with their deceased husband's family and obeyed his ancestral spirit.

The grandmother's spirit in the patrilineal line was concerned with the maintenance of the patrilineage and had the power to pull errant men into line, as I found out at a beer party in the capital city of Zimbabwe. One of my neighbors, a young scientist in the pharmacology department at the University of Zimbabwe, told me that there was increasing tension in his family, especially between his brother and himself, and that his sisters wanted to contact the ancestral spirit of his father's mother for guidance.

I was aware of two major problems in the family, one of which came from the particular political (and economic) moment, and the other from tensions built into the traditional system that were exacerbated with the changing political economy. Newly liberated Zimbabwe enjoyed the return of many of its native sons, men who had been out of the country for ten to twenty years, gaining advanced degrees abroad and missing the worst of the repressive regime of Ian Smith. Men and women who remained in the country had engaged in war against the regime, sacrificing their lives, their careers, and their educations. To some extent women emerged from the war with a vigorous desire to fight sexism as they had colonialism. Educated exiles who returned to Zimbabwe scrambled into higher positions with better pay and more power than many of their brothers (and almost all of their sisters) who stayed to fight the war. This was the case in my neighbor's family: his ex-combatant brother resented the scientist's secure position at the university. The tensions between them ruined family gatherings and left the brothers barely on speaking terms.

The sisters in this family suffered because of the enmity between the brothers. They wanted more help and support from both brothers, but another built-in tension also bothered them. Their ex-combatant brother's wife did not give them the respect and attention they felt they deserved, and the brother did not reprimand his wife for this behavior. The sisters told me that according to their Shona customs, some of a sister's bridewealth—the money and goods her new husband gives to her parents—is traditionally parceled to a brother to use when he marries. Because of this system, women say that they married their brother's wife, and they feel that she should respect, obey, and wait on them. In this family, the sisters felt slighted by their sister-in-law (their brother's wife) as well as by their brother.

The grandmother's spirit was called on to help bring the family back together. When I was invited to come to my neighbor's house to witness the spirit trance, I was prepared for a solemn occasion. To my surprise, when I arrived late, a beer party was going full force, with loud popular music and people dancing, talking, and flirting. In the middle of this room filled with revelers, the sister stood, went into a fixed stare, and started talking in a high, screechy voice. Most people sat down to listen and observe, but some kept on talking as the music played, now softly, in the background. She spoke in Shona, the mother tongue of most Zimbabweans, a language I cannot understand well. Her brother, my colleague at the university, translated for me. Through the medium of her granddaughter, the grandmother spoke several proverbs and sayings that praised family togetherness; then she went into a prolonged diatribe against the errant brother and his wife, mentioning particular offending events and behaviors. After about twenty minutes of this, I became so embarrassed about this public airing and about my receiving translations in the midst of this family event that I just watched the rest of the evening, without knowing what the words meant but feeling the tone and power of the message, especially as the errant brother held his head down and folded into himself.

It is always dangerous, and seldom worthwhile, to make generalizations about Africa, but I will venture the following conclusions as issues to ponder in thinking about the African component of African American channeling of the ancestral spirit. The ancestor comes from a specific family group or lineage, and the invocation of the ancestral spirit is itself an act that contributes to the construction of the group for whom it has power. The message of the ancestor is not always salubrious for women; much depends on the social system in which the descendants live and the particular values they want to reinforce. Many Zimbabwean widows are very much at the mercy of exacting brothers- and sisters-in-law who feel that not only the real and moveable property of deceased brothers, but also their children and the widows themselves, belong to the family who gave bridewealth for them. The family in Africa, as in the United States, is a mixed blessing for women. Women who channel or serve as mediums for spirits are not necessarily accorded honor in their everyday lives, though the power of the spirit they channel is recognized. The distinction between the spiritual power of the medium and the ego and desires of the medium is blurred in practice, where the spirits women channel demand goods and services and the women themselves expect food and material reward for contacting the spirits. In African societies, spirit mediumship may be a form of social control, means of self-aggrandizement, or an affirmation of group solidarity.

SPIRIT OF THE RACE

Toni Morrison in *Beloved* and Julie Dash in the film *Daughters of the Dust,* as interpreted by Barbara Christian (in this volume) and Harryette Mullen, outline the creation of an African American tradition that joins black people together across bloodlines, across lines of tribe, region, and family. In *Beloved,* names that the slaves accepted hid individual identity and built a sense of shared identity, and the believers who communed with Sethe in the clearing are literary representations of the new kinship relations and traditions of community in the United States. As she fills the screen with African American beauty and rituals and the ear with the rich distinctiveness of the Gullah language, Julie Dash, writer and director of *Daughters of the Dust,* creates a community defined as much by African roots as by the experience of slavery in the United States. These works both capture and create African American culture.

Hull's presentation of the wide range of "ancestral" muses for herself, Kendrick, and Clifton participates in the creation of African American culture by indicating a new kinship developed within racist America that opens channels of communication between slave ancestors and their generalized descendants, and between oppressed and exploited people the world over. Only Clifton was in contact with a known direct ancestor; the others received messages from our generalized slave ancestors. They are ancestors, fore-mothers, in that they went before us, endured the trauma of slavery whose aftershocks we still feel today. Kendricks's openness to the message of the oppressed led her to feel the pain of black people who had sat in segregated pews in Catholic church and to experience a "funny" discomfort when on a visit to France she happened upon a courtyard where French men had been executed by Nazis during World War II. Most often in Africa, the spirits of the dead are believed to speak to and influence their direct descendants, members of their family, lineage, or tribe. This too is changing in Africa. Re-cently, African nationalist movements have venerated a particular ancestor spirit, who in sending a message through a medium sends a message to the nation. The spirit of Ambuya Nehanda, the old woman said to have led the first uprising against Rhodesian colonialists at the end of the nineteenth cen-tury, speaking through a medium in exile in a neighboring country, is revered by the Shona people in general as their inspiration and deliverer in the 1972–1980 war against Ian Smith's white regime. The image of this old bare-foot woman wearing a cloak and holding a staff has become a symbol of Zim-babwean nationalism for all tribes and ethnic groups.

In the United States, race sometimes functions like lineage. As an African lineage looks back to its apical ancestors, African Americans may look back to the experiences of founding parents and sense the experience of slave forebears and the oppression of others. The trauma of the race, that which connects all of us as African Americans, is symbolically summoned in the message of spiritualism, creating a kinship of blood but not in blood.

NOTES

I have also published under the name Carolyn M. Clark. I am grateful to several of my colleagues, students, and friends for their comments: Roger Bunch, Kamari Clarke, Abigail Hemstreet, Dan Linger, Christine Mergozzi, Katia Panas, and Bill Shaw. Akasha Hull was most generous in listening to my exploration of this subject.

WORKS CITED

Baudrillard, Jean. *Simulations.* New York: Semiotext(e), 1983
Berger, Iris. "Rebels or Status-Seekers? Women as Spirit Mediums in East Africa." *Women in Africa: Studies in Social and Economic Change.* Ed. Nancy J. Hafkin and Edna G. Bay. Stanford, Calif.: Stanford UP, 1976.
Daughters of the Dust. Dir. Julie Dash. Kino International Film, American Playhouse Theatrical Films in Association with WMG, 1991.
Morrison, Toni. *Beloved.* New York: Knopf, 1987.

Mullen, Harryette. "Dreaming a World for the Unborn Child: The Matter and Spirit in Toni Morrison's *Beloved* and Julie Dash's *Daughters of the Dust*." Conference on Psychoanalysis in African American Contexts, U.C. Santa Cruz. October 1992.

Panas, Katia. "Therapist Perceptions of Cultural Factors in Therapeutic Relationships: The Mexican American." Diss. California School of Professional Psychology, 1982.

Rosenau, Pauline Marie. *Post-Modernism and the Social Sciences: Insights, Inroads, and Intrusions*. Princeton, N.J.: Princeton UP, 1992.

Spivak, Gayatri "The Revolutions That As Yet Have No Model." *Diacritics* 10.4 (1980): 47–48.

Stone, Allucquère Rosanne. "Presence: The War of Desire and Technology at the Close of the Mechanical Age." Diss. U of California, Santa Cruz, 1993.

Walker, Sheila. "African Gods in the Americas: The Black Religious Continuum." *Black Scholar: Journal of Black Studies and Research*. 11.8 (1980): 25–36.

Webster's Encyclopedic Unabridged Dictionary of the English Language. s.v. "spiritualism." New York: Gramercy Books, 1989.

Fixing Methodologies
Beloved

Barbara Christian

Since its publication in 1987, Toni Morrison's *Beloved* has received much acclaim from academic critics as well as more commercially inclined commentators. Reviewers almost unanimously proclaimed it a masterpiece. In just six years the number of critical essays published on this novel rivals those written on only a few other contemporary African American novels: Ralph Ellison's *Invisible Man* (1952), a favorite of American English departments, and Alice Walker's *Color Purple* (1982), a favorite of women's studies departments. Like these two novels, *Beloved* has passed into the mainstream curriculum of our universities, at least for the time being. That passing could be seen as a measure of an increasing awareness of "multiculturalism" and "feminism" in the academy, an awareness for which many people of color and women writers and scholars have struggled.

Yet I am perturbed by the attention, by the *kind* of critical attention *Beloved* has tended to receive, or to put it in our current literary critical language, by the critical discourses that are beginning to appropriate this complex novel. I am not worried that *Beloved* will be destroyed by these discourses, for given the novel's text, it is often illuminated by them. Rather, I am concerned that another critical approach, which I assumed would have resulted in significant analyses, has not often been applied to *Beloved*. As a result of this lack, precisely at this contemporary moment, a desperate moment for African Americans as a group, the power of this novel as a specifically African American text is being blunted.

Unfortunately, the critical reception of *Beloved* indicates that very little has changed in the academic and intellectual community as to who writes and who publishes. True, one would think that, given the supposed craze about African Americans and peoples of color in the widely publicized "Political Correctness Takeover," it would be impossible to claim that little has changed in the academy. Yes, increasingly, nuanced sophisticated criticism is being written on *Beloved*. Many sessions at recent MLA conferences have included presentations on the novel. Feminists are exploring the paradoxical mother-daughter relationship at the center of the novel, especially from a psychoanalytic perspective. African Americanists are examining *Beloved* from the perspective of its revisioning of the history of American slavery, the way Morrison is able to probe those terrible spaces that nineteenth-century slave narrators could not write about. I myself have written about this aspect of the novel in an essay, "Somebody Forgot to Tell Somebody Something." Marxist critics are explaining Morrison's conscious linking of the relationship between production and reproduction as central to the American slavery system. Formalist critics are examining the theme of memory and the role of myth in the novel and are celebrating its innovative techniques.

Even as I have drawn on these various perspectives in my thinking, teaching, and writing about *Beloved,* I am still struck by Morrison's virtually unique accomplishment in this, her fifth novel—that is, her use of the African traditional religious belief that Westerners call ancestor worship. When I peruse the critical commentary that has been written on the novel, I find few analyses that emphasize the point that this is a novel about that unspeakable event, the only event in the brutal history of African Americans about which Morrison has stated there is barely a whisper—that is, the Middle Passage (Morrison, "Interview"). That event is the dividing line between being African and being African American. It is the four-hundred-year holocaust that wrenched tens of millions of Africans from their Mother, their biological mothers as well as their Motherland, in a disorganized and unimaginably monstrous fashion. Yet for reasons having as much to do with the inability on the part of America to acknowledge that it is capable of having generated such a holocaust, as well as with the horror that such a memory calls up for African Americans themselves, the Middle Passage has practically disappeared from American cultural memory. What did, what does that wrenching mean, not only then, but now? That is the question quivering throughout this novel. Have African Americans, How could African Americans, How are African Americans recovering from this monumental collective psychic rupture?

Let me be clear, lest I be misunderstood. I have no argument with psychoanalytic, Marxist, or formalist interpretations of *Beloved.* Although at times I can be testy about any one of these approaches to particular texts, because of its richness of texture, *Beloved* does and should generate many and various, even contending, interpretations. Let me also be clear about another point. The perspective on this novel that has been sadly lacking critical discourse is not what some are currently calling Afrocentrism. In effect the use of the term *centricism* betrays the fact that Afrocentrism is generated from narrow nationalist Western thinking, that it is akin to Eurocentrism, which it apparently opposes but also mimics. Thus many contemporary forms of Afrocentricism undercut the very concept they intend to propose—that there are different interpretations of history and different narratives, depending on where one is positioned, in terms of power relations as well as distinctive cultures and that there are, given the various cultures of our world, multiple philosophical approaches to understanding life. The perspective I am proposing is one that acknowledges the existence of an African cosmology, examines how that cosmology has been consistently denigrated in the West, and explores its appropriateness for texts that are clearly derived from it. Since *Beloved,* as a sign of a continually developing African cosmology,[1] is as much about the period when Africans were forcibly displaced from their Motherland as it is about slavery in North America, it would seem logical for critics to consider how African belief systems might illuminate this text.

As is evident from the many critical pieces written on this subject, memory is a central theme in *Beloved.* Yet memory, as such, is not unique to ex-slaves. One issue that came to mind as I first read *Beloved* was the particular form of this novel's process of remembering and what memory specifically means for its characters. Certainly, one could discuss the meaning of memory in the novel in terms of the preoedipal relationship between mother and daughter that Freud theorized about, or even in general terms about how any group of human beings who suffered a holocaust might repress that horrible memory and experience the consequences of the refusal to remember. Morrison, however, not only points to this general phenomenon of collective amnesia but also, specifically, to why the Middle Passage was, for Africans, a most extreme violation of one of the basic tenets of West African cosmology.

For the past three years, I have been giving a talk called "*Beloved* as Ancestral Worship" to point to that extreme violation and to the process that Morrison uses to expose and dramatize that psychic rupture perhaps for the first time in American literature in such a complex and haunting way. And I have been startled, when I have given that talk, that few teachers or students even know what the Middle Passage is, or that African philosophical traditions exist. As a result, the idea of an African cosmological approach to this literary masterpiece could not occur to them. In contrast to this response, I experienced a distinctly different and dramatic reaction to my talk at a workshop I did with "emotionally disturbed" black patients at a hospital near my university. Unlike so many others who found the novel difficult to follow, these patients felt it to be a healing experience, one that mirrored their sense of their own personal and communal history and returned them to a point, sometimes only short-lived, where they were willing to remember what they had decided they did not want to remember. For many of them, that remembrance had to do with their parents, grandparents, the glimpses of ancestors that they had pushed away. Why did *Beloved* have such an effect on them? Somehow the novel recalled for these patients African American communal beliefs that they thought they had abandoned but had still retained.

I suppose, since my awareness of an African ancestral system did not emanate from my training as a graduate student, nor from my study of literary and critical theory, I should not be surprised that teachers and students do not usually know about it. That this concept reverberates for me throughout *Beloved* has much to do with the fact that practices derived from African religions, specifically in relation to ancestor worship, still persist in the culture from which I come. Why these practices are not often known about by those outside the culture, or even used as a basis of analysis by those from within the culture, might have to do with a pervasive belief within American cultural institutions that Africa does not have a philosophical tradition. It might also have to do with Western academics' denigration of African ancestor worship as superstition. Reading this novel and the studies generated by it has led me to wonder about the types of methodologies that we are exposed to in the American university and how they might be related to culturally dominant patterns in our society.

I certainly did not understand very much about what African ancestral worship was, or what it could mean, when I first read *Beloved*. But I did recognize something from my own Caribbean culture. I was struck by Morrison's representation of the character Beloved as an embodied spirit, a spirit that presents itself as a body. In the Caribbean, spirits are everywhere, are naturally in the world, and are not ghosts in the horror-genre sense of that term. The spirits, the ancestors, to quote a song by the black women's singing group Sweet Honey in the Rock, "are in the wind, in the trees, in the waters, in the rocks." In an interview, Morrison herself reiterated that point: for African Americans, at least until the recent past, the experience of spirits communicating with the living was a natural one rather than a weird, unnatural event. Hence her representation of the spirit character as a body.

Moreover, in my tradition, ancestral spirits must be nurtured and fed, or they will be angry or, at the least, sad. Even today, as they did when I was growing up, many of my folk, before an important event, pour what we call "libations." If one does not, the ancestors are not being given the respect they deserve. If ancestors are consistently not fed or have not resolved a major conflict, especially the manner of their death, they are tormented and may return to the realm we characterize as that of the living, sometimes in the form of an apparently newborn baby. So often I have heard someone in the Caribbean say, "This one is an old one and has come back because she needs to clear up something big." Although Beloved is not a newborn baby in terms of her apparent age, she acts as she would have if she were the age when she was killed by her mother. And there are many references in the text of the novel to her skin and eyes, which appear to be those of a newborn baby. What, I wondered, was Morrison doing? As if fixed at the age of her death, Beloved comes back looking for the face of the mother which is still her face, just as babies when they are around two, the age of the already-crawling baby, cannot yet see themselves as separate from their mother and thus see her face as their face. Morrison seemed to be fusing age-old beliefs from African-derived cultures in the New World with the observations of mothers throughout the world, observations that have been validated by Western scientific psychological perspectives.

I was also struck by the way the character Beloved needs constantly to be fed, especially sweet things, the food that ancestors, even voduns like Erzulie, the Haitian vodun of love, relish. Like bodies, the ancestral spirits in my Caribbean context who come back to visit us eat and drink and are carnal. Yet they differ from the living in that while they do appear as bodies, their eyes and skin, like Beloved's, are those of newborn babes.

Stimulated by these memories from my African-Caribbean culture as well as by Morrison's own remarks in her interviews about the novel, I began to try to articulate whether and how African belief systems might be crucial to an understanding of the novel. In contemplating Morrison's epigraph to *Beloved*, "To the sixty million and more," I was reminded of a recurrent childhood event. I used to wonder aloud who my ancestors were, not only the elders we knew about in my family but also those who had come from Africa. How had they gotten to the Caribbean? How had they managed to survive? I was curious about why no one in my family, as "chauvinistic" a clan as you could find, ever talked about that transition from Africa to the New World. Some elders even tried to deny that we came from Africa and had been slaves, despite the presence of the Market Square where the inscription read that slaves had been auctioned there. Why, I wondered, did we pour libations? To whom were we pouring libations? What were their names? West Africans I knew also poured libations. Reading *Beloved* revived these questions. And listening to Morrison speak about her novel as a prayer, a memorial, a fixing ceremony for those who did not survive the Middle Passage and whose names we did not know, reinforced my desire to approach *Beloved* from an African perspective.

That desire led me to several studies and especially to John Mbiti's *African Religions and Philosophies*, which I had read years before. My exploration in this essay based on Mbiti's book is not meant as a definitive statement as to how *Beloved* might be approached from an African cosmological perspective, but rather as an indication that such an approach might be appropriate for this novel and might yield interpretations in keeping with contemporary African American concerns.

Even now I hesitate to use the term *African ancestor worship;* I worry that I might be denigrating African religions, for the practice I am about to describe has been so maligned in the West that even African scholars apologize when they use the term. The Christian African theologian John Mbiti warns us that in traditional West African societies, Africans do not worship their ancestors. Rather, they believe that when people pass (and this phrase is important, as it is still consistently used by African Americans), that is, "die," in the Western sense, they do not disappear as long as someone remembers them, their names, their characters. Mbiti states: "So long as the living dead is thus remembered, he is in the state of personal immortality" (32). The acts of feeding the dead and pouring libations are meant as symbols, active symbols of communion, fellowship, and renewal. Thus continuity, not only of genes but also of active remembering, is critical to a West African's sense of her or his own personal being and, beyond that, of the beingness of the group.

Mbiti also points out that the ancestors are associated with their land, the piece of nature that they inhabit. The people are the land, the land is the people. He tells us: "The land provides them with the roots of existence as well as binding them mystically to their departed. People walk on the graves of their forefathers, and it is feared that anything separating them from these ties will bring disaster to family and community life. To remove Africans by force from their land is an act of such great injustice that no foreigner can fathom it" (35). For West Africans, a particular tree, rock, or grove embodies that relationship between themselves as human beings in nature, and other aspects of nature that are often seen as separate from human beings. Thus, nature is seen as a part of the human and the divine and is considered sacred in much the same way that churches in the Christian religion are considered sacred. In *Beloved,* Morrison uses this aspect of traditional African religions in her representation of the Clearing, that space from which Baby Suggs preached and the place to which Sethe, her daughter-in-law, comes to communicate with her elder when she has passed on.

In fact, Morrison's entire opus explores that connection between the folk and the land. I will not dwell here too much on her theme of place and displacement in African American life, the sense of homelessness and the intense emphasis on home, because much has been written on this subject. I will only note that she has, from her first novel, *The Bluest Eye,* moved increasingly further back in time to the point in her third novel, *Song of Solomon,* where Milkman, her protagonist, discovers his oldest ancestor, Solomon, in the land of Shalimar; in this novel, the land is as much a character as its human protagonists. However, although Morrison focused on Solomon's flying back to Africa in *Song of Solomon,* she was stopped in her tracks. For in order to get back to Africa, she had to confront the Middle Passage. Not until *Beloved,* her fifth novel, does she try to imagine that terrible space and what it must mean for the Solomons of her third novel.

What does it mean when not only Morrison's protagonists in her first four novels but millions of African Americans in the New World are cut off from their "living dead" and cannot know their names and thus cannot remember them? In not being able to remember, name, and feed those who passed on in the Middle Passage, those who survived had to abandon their living dead to the worst possible fate that could befall a West African: complete annihilation. Mbiti tells us that "to 'die' immediately is a tragedy that must be avoided at all costs" (208). What a tragedy, then, when millions "die" immediately. In a sense, Morrison anticipates that psychic horror by using the wit and irony of the African American tradition in *Song of Solomon,* when she names the descendants of Solomon "the Deads," their name being the result of an error in a white man's records. In *Beloved,* however, wit gives way to a facing of the tragic wrenching of that disnaming, not only for those who did not survive but also for those who did. She evokes that terrible space of being and nonbeing in one of the last passages of *Beloved.*

> Everybody knows what she was called, but nobody anywhere knew her name. Disremembered and un-accounted for, she cannot be lost because no one is looking for her, and even if they were, how can they call her if they don't know her name. Although she has claim, she is not claimed. In the place where long grass opens, the girl who waits to be loved and cry shame erupts into her separate parts to make it easy for the chewing laughter to swallow her all away.

> It was not a story to pass on. (274)

Mbiti tells us that African time is not linear. Rather, the future, in the Western sense, is absent because the present is always an unfolding of the past (21–22). Thus every "future" is already contained in what Westerners call the "past." When one views the novel from this African cosmological perspective it is especially significant that the embodied past is represented by a girl-child who is simultaneously a woman, the character Beloved. It is not surprising, then, that the spirit who is the most wrathful and most in pain is that of a child who dies in a violent, unnatural way, for the child represents the sustenance of both the past and the present as it becomes the future, not only for an individual family but also for the group as a whole. Moreover, in many traditional African societies women, as potential mothers, are the bulwark against immediate "death." For in giving birth to children, mothers produce those who are more likely to know and remember their ancestors. If one has no children, who will pour libations to you (Mbiti 144)? That valuable status that West African women have as mothers is, of course, a double-edged sword, not only for those who are "barren" but also for those who have children whom they cannot mother, which includes passing on the memory of their ancestors.

In *Beloved,* Morrison not only explores the psychic horror of those who can no longer call their ancestors' names but also the dilemma of the mother who knows her children will be born into and live in the realm of those who cannot call their ancestors' names. Sethe's killing of her already-crawling baby is not only the killing of that individual baby but also the collective anguish African women must have experienced when they realized their children were cut off forever from their "living dead," who would never be called upon, remembered, or fed.

In reenacting that plane of in-betweenness; in evoking the desire to forget the pain of wrenching from those whom one can no longer name; in dramatizing the dilemma of not remembering those who have betrayed you and sent you into the arms of the abusers; in insisting on recalling those who have loved you in spite of pain and the need to forget, whether in Africa, the slave ships, or American slave farms; in not being able to forget those who are the ground of one's being, the source of one's origins—Morrison has, in *Beloved*, not just written a powerful novel, she has designed a fixing ceremony. Like African art, her novel works in the world. In a process that is central to African spirituality, her fixing ceremony is not merely that of remembrance for the sake of remembrance, but remembrance as the only way to begin the process of healing that psychic wound, which continues to have grave effects on the present. Those whose names we can no longer specifically call know that we have not forgotten them, that they are our "Beloveds," and that unless they release us from the wrath of the past, the future will be tormented and fractured.

By exploring the novel from the point of view of African cosmology, one sees it for what it could be in the world: a prayer, a ritual grounded in active remembering that might result, first of all, in our understanding why it is that so many of us are wounded, fragmented, and in a state of longing. Then, perhaps, we might move beyond that fracturing to those actions that might result in communal healing and in a redesigning of the contemporary world called the "New World." In acknowledging and naming our holocaust, we feed, remember, and respect those forgotten, raging spirits whom we call the past, whose bodies and blood fed, and continue to feed, the ground on which we walk.

NOTES

"Fixing Methodologies: *Beloved*" was originally published in *Cultural Critique* 24 (1993): 56–59. Reprinted by permission of the Oxford University Press.

1. I owe this insight to Alberto Perez, a student in the Ethnic Studies Graduate Program at the University of California, Berkeley.

WORKS CITED

Mbiti, John. *African Religions and Philosophies.* New York: Doubleday Anchor, 1970.
Morrison, Toni. *Beloved.* New York: Knopf, 1987.
———. Interview. *All Things Considered.* National Public Radio. WNYC, New York. 16 Feb. 1986.
———. "Somebody Forgot to Tell Somebody Something." *Wild Women in the Whirlwind: Afro-American Culture and the Contemporary Literary Renaissance.* Ed. Joanne M. Braxton and Andree Nicola McLaughlin. New Brunswick: Rutgers UP, 1990. 342–62.
Sweet Honey in the Rock. *The Ancestors.* Flying Fish, 1978.

NOTES ON CONTRIBUTORS

Elizabeth Abel is Associate Professor of English at the University of California, Berkeley. She has authored *Virginia Woolf and the Fictions of Psychoanalysis*, edited *Writing and Sexual Difference,* and coedited *The Signs Reader* and *The Voyage In: Fictions of Female Development.* She is currently writing a book on race, gender, and visual politics.

Katherine Clay Bassard is Assistant Professor of English at the University of California, Berkeley. Her interests include religious studies and African American literature and culture before 1900. She has recently completed her first book, *Spiritual Interrogations: Culture, Gender, and Community in Early African American Women's Writings.*

Judith Butler is Professor of Rhetoric and Comparative Literature at the University of California, Berkeley. She is the author of *Gender Trouble* and *Bodies That Matter,* as well as of a forthcoming book entitled *Excitable Speech,* and the coeditor of *Feminists Theorize the Political* and *Erotic Welfare.*

Barbara Christian is Professor of African American Studies at the University of California, Berkeley. She is the author of *Black Women Novelists: The Development of a Tradition, 1892–1976,* and *Black Feminist Criticism: Perspectives on Black Women Writers.* She has also edited a casebook, *Alice Walker's "Everyday Use,"* and is the contemporary editor for the first Norton Anthology of African American Literature.

Ann duCille is Professor of American and African American literature at the University of California, San Diego. She has published *The Coupling Convention: Sex, Text, and Tradition in Black Women's Fiction* and *Skin Trade.* A Guggenheim Fellow in 1994–1995, she is currently working on two other book projects: *Inconspicuous Consumption,* a study of the development of the black middle class in literature, and *The Black Feminist Reader*, an edited volume of black feminist criticism.

Mae G. Henderson is Professor of English at the University of North Carolina, Chapel Hill. She is the editor of *Borders, Boundaries, and Frames: Essays in Cultural Criticism and Cultural Studies*. Her forthcoming book is *Speaking in Tongues: Reading Black Women Writing*.

Margaret Homans teaches English and chairs the Women's Studies Program at Yale University. She is the author of books and essays on nineteenth-century British literature, including *Bearing the Word: Language and Female Experience in Nineteenth-Century Women's Writing* and the forthcoming *Queen Victoria: Royal Representations*.

Akasha (Gloria) Hull is Professor of Women's Studies and Literature at the University of California, Santa Cruz. She is the author of *Color, Sex, and Poetry: Three Women Writers of the Harlem Renaissance* and *Healing Heart: Poems* and is currently completing a book on the spirituality of African American women.

Barbara Johnson is Fredric Wartham Professor in the departments of English and Comparative Literature at Harvard University. She is the author of *The Critical Difference, A World of Difference*, and, most recently, *The Wake of Deconstruction*.

Tania Modleski teaches in the English Department at the University of Southern California and is the author of *Loving with a Vengeance: Mass-Produced Fantasies for Women, Feminism Without Women: Culture and Criticism in a Postfeminist Age*, and *The Women Who Knew Too Much: Hitchcock and Feminist Theory*. She is currently writing a book on women filmmakers working in popular genres.

Helene Moglen is Professor of English Literature at the University of California, Santa Cruz. She has published books on Laurence Sterne and Charlotte Brontë and has recently completed a study of male-authored eighteenth-century fiction entitled *The Anxieties of Indeterminacy: Subjectivity, Sexuality, and the Emergence of the English Novel*.

Cynthia D. Schrager received her Ph.D. in English from the University of California, Berkeley, in 1995 and has taught American literature at the University of California, Santa Cruz. She has published articles in *American Quarterly* and *Feminist Studies* and is currently working on a book-length study on race, realism, and the occult in American culture.

Carolyn Martin Shaw is Professor of Anthropology at the University of California, Santa Cruz. She completed ethnographic fieldwork among the

Kikuyu in central Kenya and was awarded a Fulbright Fellowship at the University of Zimbabwe. In 1995, she published *Colonial Inscriptions: Race, Sex, and Class in Kenya.*

Hortense J. Spillers is Professor of English at Cornell University. During the academic year 1996–1997, she will hold a fellowship at the Center for the Advanced Study of the Behavorial Sciences at Stanford University, where she plans to complete work on a book concerning women and slavery, *In the Flesh: A Situation for Feminist Inquiry,* as well as a collection of her essays.

Jean Walton is Assistant Professor of English and Women's Studies at the University of Rhode Island. She has published articles on Samuel Beckett, Vladimir Nabokov, performer Sandra Bernhard, and the 1930 experimental film *Borderline.* The essay reprinted here is part of a book-length study of white women's racial fantasies in modernism, psychoanalysis, and anthropology.

Laura Wexler teaches Women's Studies and American Studies at Yale University. The author of a forthcoming book, *Tender Violence: Domestic Visions in an Age of U.S. Imperialism,* she has coauthored with Sandra Matthews another forthcoming volume, *Pregnant Pictures: Women in the Age of Mechanical Reproduction.*

Compositor: Integrated Composition Systems
Text: 10/12 Baskerville
Display: Baskerville
Printer: Maple-Vail Book Group
Binder: Maple-Vail Book Group